CAREER OPPORTUNITIES IN THE MUSIC INDUSTRY

FIFTH EDITION

Shelly Field

Ferguson
An imprint of ☑® Facts On File

This book is dedicated to my parents,
Ed and the late Selma Field,
who gave me every opportunity,
supported all my decisions,
and always let me be me.

CAREER OPPORTUNITIES IN THE MUSIC INDUSTRY, FIFTH EDITION

Copyright © 2004, 2000, 1995, 1990, 1986 by Shelly Field

Ferguson
An imprint of Facts On File, Inc.
132 West 31st Street
New York NY 10001

Library of Congress Cataloging-in-Publication Data

Field, Shelly.
    Career opportunities in the music industry / Shelly Field—5th ed.
        p. cm.
    Includes bibliographical references and index.
    ISBN 0-8160-5614-5 (alk. paper)
    1. Music—Vocational guidance. 2. Music—Economic aspects. I. Title.

ML3795.F497 2004
780′.23′73—dc22   20003062234

Ferguson books are available at special discounts when purchased in bulk quantities for businesses, associations, institutions, or sales promotions. Please call our Special Sales Department in New York at (212) 967-8800 or (800) 322-8755.

You can find Ferguson on the World Wide Web at http://www.fergpubco.com

Cover design by Nora Wertz

Printed in the United States of America

VB Hermitage 10 9 8 7 6 5 4 3 2 1

This book is printed on acid-free paper.

CONTENTS

HOW TO USE THIS BOOK

Purpose

When the first edition of *Career Opportunities in the Music Industry* was published, in 1986, there was no single source describing the major job opportunities in music in a clear and simple fashion. Today, five editions later, *Career Opportunities in the Music Industry* is still helping people who aspire to work in the music business to develop a game plan. The book has emerged as one of the leading volumes for helping individuals in their quest for success in this field.

Since the book was first written, the music industry has exploded. Thousands of people are currently working in the music business, and there are literally thousands upon thousands of people who want to get in.

Most people have no idea how to enter the industry. Many dream of becoming recording stars. Others yearn to write songs that will remain with people through the years. Some want to work in the business end of the industry, helping others to climb the ladder of success.

This book helps you discover what it takes to prepare yourself, enter, and succeed in the industry no matter what path you select.

Advances in technology and the music industry have made it easier than ever to launch a satisfying and successful career in the music business. A greater number of smaller, independent record labels are in existence than ever before, and new labels are springing up around the country. VH1, Country Music Television, and a host of other music video television and cable programs make it possible to create hit records almost instantly.

Affordable electronic musical instruments such as keyboards, guitars, and drums, along with computer hardware and software and new computer technology, allow people to play, write, and record music with unprecedented ease. Affordable audio and video equipment makes it easy to create both demos and videos at relatively low cost.

This newly revised edition includes salaries, job profiles, and other career information. It also has updated appendixes with valuable names, addresses, and phone numbers. In many instances, fax numbers, websites, and e-mail addresses have been included as well.

Career Opportunities in the Music Industry was written for everyone who dreams of working in the music industry but doesn't know how to make that dream a reality. The 88 jobs discussed in this book encompass all aspects of careers in the music industry. Almost every category of work can be found in the music business The industry needs secretaries, receptionists, publishers, tour managers, teachers, therapists, librarians, attorneys, accountants, executives, writers, publicists, salespeople, and more.

Sometimes you will have to be creative to find your niche. The trick is to identify your skills and use them to get you in the music business door. Once in, you have a good chance of moving into other positions as you climb the career ladder.

Read through this book and find out what you are qualified to do, or how you can obtain training in your field of interest. You can then work toward one of the most rewarding and exciting careers in the world—a career in music!

Sources of Information

Information for this book was obtained through interviews, questionnaires, and a wide variety of books, magazines, newsletters, and other written material. Some information was gleaned from personal experience working in the industry. Other data were obtained from friends and business associates in various branches of the music business.

Among the people interviewed were individuals involved in all aspects of the music industry. These include record company executives, radio station personnel, tour managers, personal managers, booking agents, accountants, attorneys, church musicians, songwriters, performing artists, and recording acts. Employment agencies were contacted, as well as schools, personnel offices, unions, trade associations, orchestras, operas, and other relevant organizations.

Organization of Material

Career Opportunities in the Music Industry is divided into 12 general employment sections. These sections are Recording and the Record Business; Radio and Television; On the Road; Music Retailing and Wholesaling; the Business End of the Industry; Instrument Repair, Restoration, and Design; Publicity; Symphonies, Orchestras, Operas, Etc.; Arenas, Facilities, Halls, and Clubs; Education; Talent and Writing; and Church Music. Within each of these sections are descriptions of individual careers.

There are two parts to each job classification. The first part offers job information in chart form. The second part presents information in a narrative text. In addition to the basic career description, you will find information on unions and/or associations and tips for entry.

Nine appendixes are offered to help locate information you might want or need to get started in the music business. You can use these reference sections to find colleges, schools, workshops, and training seminars. There are lists of names and addresses for music-oriented unions, trade associations, record companies, booking agencies, music publishers, rights societies, public relations and publicity firms, record distributors, and entertainment industry attorneys. There are suggestions for books and periodicals to read and a glossary to help you learn the lingo.

The music industry holds widespread appeal. Nearly everyone dreams of reaching a star. For some, that star might be a successful career as a popular recording artist, while for others the goal may be recognition as a songwriter. Still others who love music, whatever its genre, might be delighted to work in the recording business or in music education.

With talent, connections, training, the right opportunities, and a little bit of luck, or a combination of these, you can find your star in the music business.

Persevere! I know if you do, you will make it.

— Shelly Field
www.shellyfield.com

ACKNOWLEDGMENTS

I would like to thank every individual, company, union, and association that provided information, assistance, and encouragement for this book.

I acknowledge with appreciation my editor, James Chambers, for his continuous help and encouragement. I also must thank Kate Kelly, who, as my initial editor, provided the original impetus for this book. I gratefully acknowledge the assistance of Ed Field for his ongoing support in this project.

Others whose help was invaluable include the Academy of Country Music; Ellen Ackerman; Julie Allen; Alverno College; American Federation of Musicians; American Guild of Musical Artists; American Guild of Variety Artists; American Society of Composers and Publishers; American Society of Music Copyists; American Symphony Orchestra League; Arista Records; Association of Theatrical Press Agents and Managers; John Balme; Allan Barrish; Warren Bergstrom; Eugene Blabey; Steve Blackman; Joyce Blackman; Broadcast Music, Inc.; B'nai B'rith Vocational Service; Linda Bonsante; Theresa Bull; Al Bumanis, American Music Therapy Association; Earl "Speedo" Carroll; Cantors Assembly; Catskill Development; Anthony Cellini, town of Thompson supervisor; Brandi Cesario, Patricia Claghorn; Janice Cohen; Dr. Jessica L. Cohen; Norman Cohen; Robert Cohen, Esq.; Fred Coopersmith; Jan Cornelius; Robert Crothers; Crawford Memorial Library staff; Margaret Crossley; Meike Cryan; Daniel Dayton; W. Lynne Dayton; Carrie Dean; Scott Edwards; Michelle Edwards; Cliff Ehrlich, Catskill Development; Ernest Evans; Julie Evans; Sara Feldberg; Deborah K. Field, Esq.; Greg Field; Lillian (Cookie) Field; Mike Field; Robert Field; Finkelstein Memorial Library staff; Jack Furlong; Richard Gabriel; David Garthe, CEO, Graveyware.com; John Gatto; Sheila Gatto; Morris Gerber; Larry Goldsmith; Sam Goldych; Hermann Memorial Library staff; Joan Howard; Hudson Valley Philharmonic; Jo Hunt, DeLyon-Hunt & Associates; International Alliance of Theatrical Stage Employees; International Association of Auditorium Managers; International Brotherhood of Electrical Workers; International Alliance of Theatrical Stage Employees; International Association of Auditorium Managers; International Brotherhood of Electrical Workers; Julia Jacobs; Jimmy "Handyman" Jones; K-LITE Radio; Dave Kleinman; Janice Kleinman; Dr. John C. Koch; Las Vegas Review Journal; Bob Leone; Liberty Central School; Liberty Public Library staff; Ernie Martinelli; Robert Masters, Esq; June E. McDonald; Phillip Mestman; Rima Mestman; Metropolitan Opera; Beverly Michaels, Esq.; Martin Michaels, Esq.; Monticello Central School High School Library staff; Monticello Central School Middle School Library staff; Jennifer Morganti; Music Business Institute; Music Educators National Conference; Florence Naistadt; National Association for Music Therapy; National Association of Broadcast Employees and Technicians; National Association of Broadcasters; National Association of Music Merchants; National Association of Schools of Music; National Association of Recording Merchandisers; National Music Publishers Association; Earl Nesmith; Jim Newton; New York State Employment Service; Nikkodo U.S.A., Inc.; Ellis Norman, UNLV; Heather Dawn O'Keefe; Ivy Pass; Ed Pearson, Nikkodo USA; Piano Technicians Guild; Anita Portas, IATSE; Practising Law Institute; Public Relations Society of America; Doug Puppel; Ruth Qualich; Harvey Rachlin; Ramapo Catskill Library system; John Riegler; Reverend Bruce Rentz; Doug Richards; Susan G. Riley, ASOL; Sheldon Rosenberg; Gary F. Roth, BMI; Diane Ruud, Nevada Society of Certified Public Accountants; Joy Shaffer; Raun Smith; Smith Employment Agency; Songwriters Guild; Aileen Spertell, Smith Employment Agency; Laura Solomon; Debbie Springfield; Matthew E. Strong; Sullivan County Community College; Sullivan Country Performing Arts Council; The Teenagers; Thrall Library staff; Marie Tremper; David D. Turner, Music Business Institute of Atlanta; United States Department of Labor; Brian Vargas; Pat Varriale; Kaytee Warren; Dr. Ray Williams, director of education and marketing, NAMM; Carol Williams; John Williams; John Wolfe, General Manager, WTZA-Television; WSUL Radio; WTZA; WVOS Radio; Dr. Diana Worby; Rachel Worby; Henry J. White; Johnny Worlds; and George Wurzbach.

In addition, because there is such a great mystique surrounding the music business, much of the material was provided by sources who wish to remain anonymous. My thanks to them all the same.

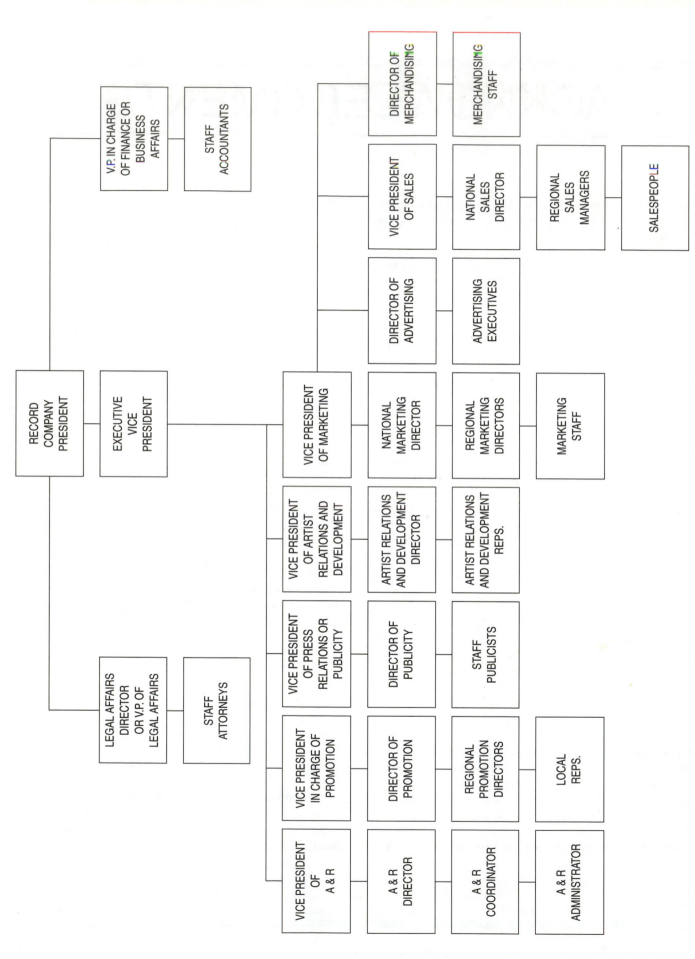

TABLE OF ORGANIZATION—TYPICAL RECORD COMPANY

INTRODUCTION

Music means different things to different people. To some, music is healing; to others, it's pure entertainment. Music often brings back memories. Hearing an old song on the radio, for example, often makes us remember what we were doing at the time the song first was popular.

Music is often referred to as the universal language. As far as anyone can remember, it has existed. It may not always have taken the sophisticated forms that we know today, but it was music just the same.

Throughout history people made music for different reasons. Primitive people used drums to send messages. Drums also accompanied dance in ceremonies and celebration. People sang for joy and in sadness. Some people sang to make time go by more quickly or to take their minds off the drudgery of hard, tedious work.

Whatever else music is, today it is a multibillion-dollar business. Thousands work in the music business, and many more reap the benefits and pleasures of music.

As you read over the various sections in this book, searching to find the "perfect job," keep in mind that there is no one way to get into the music business. There are many methods. I have given you the guidelines. You have to do the rest.

Within each section of this book is the information necessary to acquaint you with most of the important jobs in the industry. A key to the organization of each entry follows.

Alternate Titles

Many jobs in the music business, as in all industries, are known by alternate titles. The duties of these jobs are the same; only the name is different. Titles vary from company to company.

Career Ladder

The career ladder illustrates a normal job progression. Remember that in the music business there are no hard-and-fast rules. Job progression may not necessarily follow a precise order.

Position Description

Every effort has been made to give well-rounded job descriptions. Keep in mind that no two companies are structured exactly the same. Therefore, no two jobs will be exactly the same. For example, note figure 1. This illustrates a table of organization of a typical record company. However, another company might have a different table of organization. That company might have people reporting to other executives, or eliminate some positions on the chart or add others.

Salary Ranges

Salary ranges for the 89 job titles in this book are as accurate as possible. Salaries will depend on how big a company is, where it is located, and the applicant's experience.

Employment Prospects

If you choose a job that has an EXCELLENT, GOOD, or FAIR rating, you are lucky. You will have an easier time finding work. If, however, you're interested in a job that has a POOR rating, don't despair. The rating only means that it is difficult to obtain a job—not impossible.

Advancement Prospects

Plan to be as cooperative and helpful as possible in the workplace. Don't try to get away with doing as little work as possible. Be enthusiastic, energetic, and outgoing. Do that little extra that no one asked you to do. When a job advancement possibility opens up, make sure that you're prepared for it.

Education and Training

Although the book only covers the minimum training and educational requirements, it pays to get the best training and education possible. A college degree does not guarantee a job in the music business, but it might help prepare a person for life in the workplace. Education and training also encompass courses, seminars, programs, on-the-job training, and learning from others.

Experience, Skills, and Personality Traits

These will differ from job to job, but getting started along any career path you choose will probably take a lot of perseverance. Being an outgoing individual helps. Contacts are important in all facets of the music business. Make as many as you can. These people will be helpful in advancing your career.

Best Geographical Location

You will note that most jobs in record companies and the business end of the industry are located in the major music capitals, such as New York City, Los Angeles, and Nashville. Jobs in talent and performing can also be found in other culturally active areas. Opportunities in teaching, retailing, wholesaling, and related fields may be found almost anywhere in the country.

Unions and Associations

Unions and trade associations offer valuable help in getting into the business, obtaining jobs, and making contacts. They may also offer scholarships, fellowships, seminars, and other programs.

Tips for Entry

Use this section for ideas on how to get a job and gain entry into the area of the business in which you are interested. When applying for any job, always be as professional as possible. Dress neatly. Don't wear sneakers. Don't chew gum. Don't smoke. Always have available a few copies of your résumé with you, neatly typed and well presented.

Use *every* contact you have. Don't become fixated on the idea that you want to get a job by yourself. If you are lucky enough to know someone who can help you obtain the job you want, take him or her up on it. You'll still have to prove yourself at the interview and on the job. Nobody can do that for you.

Once you get your foot in the door, learn as much as you can. Do that little extra bit of work that is not expected. Be cooperative. Be a team player. Don't burn bridges; it will hurt your career. Ask for help. Network. Find a mentor.

The last piece of advice in this section is to *be on time* for everything. This includes job interviews, phone calls, work, and meetings. People will remember when you're habitually late, and it will work against you in advancing your career.

Have faith and confidence in yourself. You *will* make it in music eventually, but you must persevere. In many instances the individual who didn't make it in the music business is the one who gave up too soon and didn't wait that extra day.

Have fun reading this book. Use it. It will help you find a career you will truly love. When you do get the job of your dreams, do someone else a favor and give him or her the benefit of your knowledge. Help others learn about the business.

We love to hear success stories. If this book helped you in your quest for a job in the music industry and you would like to share your story, go to www.shellyfield.com and let us know.

Good luck!

RECORDING AND
THE RECORD BUSINESS

A & R COORDINATOR

<table>
<tr><td style="text-align:center">CAREER PROFILE</td><td style="text-align:center">CAREER LADDER</td></tr>
</table>

CAREER PROFILE

Duties: Find talent for a record company to sign; locate tunes to match with specific artists on the label's roster

Alternate Title(s): A & R Representative; Artist and Repertoire Coordinator, A & R Staffer; Talent Acquisition Rep

Salary Range: $27,000 to $85,000+

Employment Prospects: Poor

Advancement Prospects: Fair

Best Geographical Location(s) for Position: New York City, Los Angeles, and Nashville are music capitals

Prerequisites:

Education or Training—High school diploma is a minimum requirement; college degree may be required or preferred by major labels

Experience—Experience in music or record business helpful

Special Skills and Personality Traits—Foresight; ability to see past "raw" talent; self-confidence; enjoyment of music; ability to deal well with people

CAREER LADDER

```
┌─────────────────────────────┐
│       A & R Director        │
└─────────────────────────────┘

┌─────────────────────────────┐
│      A & R Coordinator      │
└─────────────────────────────┘

┌─────────────────────────────┐
│     A & R Administrator;    │
│  A & R Assistant or Trainee │
└─────────────────────────────┘
```

Position Description

An A & R (Artist and Repertoire) Coordinator or rep performs a variety of functions depending on the record company he or she works with and its size.

The main duty of the A & R Coordinator is to find talent for the company to sign up. He or she may do this in a number of ways. The A & R Coordinator may visit clubs and/or showcases checking out new talent. The individual may listen to tapes and demo records and/or watch videocassettes of acts performing. The A & R Coordinator may also try to sign up existing talent, such as individuals currently signed with another record label. In cases such as this, the A & R Coordinator might either wait for the act's contract to expire, or, in rare cases, try to buy out an existing contract. When A & R Coordinators are vying for an established act to sign with their company, they do everything in their power to make their contract more attractive than competing companies' contracts.

The A & R Coordinator has another important duty. He or she is often responsible for finding (or helping to find) songs for the artists signed to the record label. These can be located in a number of ways. One is by going through the masses of tapes and demos of new tunes that are mailed or brought to the record company by would-be song writers. Another method is to listen to old hit records or classics that might be arranged in a new or current fashion. The A & R Coordinator might put a staff writer of the record company together with the artist in an effort to come up with that all-important hit tune. The new artist might also be a writer and have a healthy supply of his or her own material from which a potential tune might be selected.

Once a tune is picked, the A & R Coordinator locates a producer who will work well with the act. The A & R Coordinator might also help an unmanaged or poorly managed act find a management team, lawyers, business managers, accountants, etc.

The A & R Coordinator works very closely with the act from the moment they are signed with the label. He or she takes the act under his or her wing and tries to build it into a total artistic, creative, and commercial success.

If an act is unhappy about anything, whether it be a CD not selling well or difficulties with an assigned producer, the act would talk to their A & R Coordinator.

The A & R Coordinator works closely not only with the act, but also with the various other departments in the company to assure the act the best possible chance of attaining success.

The A & R Coordinator is usually responsible to the vice-president in charge of A & R, the vice-president in charge of talent acquisition, or the A & R Director. It depends on how the particular record company is structured.

The hours for the A & R Coordinator are often irregular and long as a result of late nights at clubs seeking out talent and the nature of the job.

Salaries

Depending on the size of the record company, salaries can be quite high for this position. Salaries can range from $27,000 to $85,000 plus annually. Salaries at the lower end of the scale are paid to individuals working in smaller, independent labels. In addition, A & R Coordinators are often given bonuses for signing existing "superstar" talent or an artist who makes it big.

Employment Prospects

There are many people who want to work as A & R Coordinators. As a matter of fact, there are more people than there are positions.

If a record company requires an A & R Coordinator, they will usually try to find a qualified individual within the ranks of the company. Exceptions are made, however, when an A & R Coordinator has worked at another company and proved him or herself by finding artists who consistently hit the top.

Employment prospects are increasing with the growing success of smaller, independent labels.

Advancement Prospects

Once an individual gets into a record company, he or she has the opportunity to move up the career ladder. As an A & R Coordinator, the individual may move into the position of A & R Director. The person may also be hired by a bigger, more prestigious company for the same position. To move ahead, the individual must prove him or herself by signing acts that hit the top of the charts.

Education and Training

An A & R Coordinator must usually have at least a high school diploma. Major labels generally prefer that their staff members hold a college degree.

Degrees or courses in music merchandising, the music business, communications, marketing, advertising, etc. are useful. In addition, there are a number of seminars, workshops, and programs put together by associations and organizations that are helpful both for their educational value and for the opportunity they provide for developing contacts.

Experience, Skills, and Personality Traits

A & R Coordinators usually have worked in the music business, the record business, and/or radio prior to accepting their positions.

The A & R Coordinator must have a unique type of foresight that comes into play when watching a new act or listening to a new tune. He or she must have that special ability to see past the raw talent to the potential talent an act or record could have. The individual must have the self-confidence to stand by his or her decision and not be swayed.

Unions and Associations

A & R Coordinators may belong to the National Academy of Recording Arts and Sciences (NARAS) as associate members. They might also be members of the Country Music Association (CMA) or the Gospel Music Association (GMA).

Tips for Entry

1. If you are interested in getting into an A & R position, try to get a job in a record company performing any task possible. Many companies promote from within. An energetic, talented, bright individual can move up.

2. You might want to begin your career by checking out local talent. If you can recognize talent, you might very well find it in a local act. You might want to work with this act as a manager or agent. You will be gaining valuable experience.

3. Read the trades and books or magazines on trends in the music and record business. Trends often repeat themselves over a period of years. This information may be useful to your career.

4. Look for a position as an intern with a record company. This will help you gain needed experience and make contacts in the industry.

A & R ADMINISTRATOR

CAREER PROFILE

Duties: Plan budgets for artists signed to the record label; deal with clerical functions and administration of the A & R department

Alternate Title(s): A & R Administration Representative

Salary Range: $25,000 to $55,000+

Employment Prospects: Poor

Advancement Prospects: Fair

Best Geographical Location(s) for Position: New York City, Los Angeles, and Nashville are music capitals

Prerequisites:

Education or Training—High school diploma; college degree may be required or preferred by some companies

Experience—Experience in record company is useful; bookkeeping positions are helpful

Special Skills and Personality Traits—Ability to budget; ability to work with numbers; enjoyment of music; ability to communicate both verbally and on paper

CAREER LADDER

```
┌─────────────────────────────┐
│      A & R Coordinator      │
└─────────────────────────────┘

┌─────────────────────────────┐
│     A & R Administrator     │
└─────────────────────────────┘

┌─────────────────────────────┐
│  A & R Assistant or Trainee │
└─────────────────────────────┘
```

Position Description

An A & R Administrator works in the A & R department along with the A & R coordinators. If the record company is a small one, he or she might assume the duties of both A & R administration and coordination. In a large record company, however, the A & R Administrator is responsible for much of the clerical functions of the department.

The individual is responsible for planning budgets for the artists who are signed to the label. Working on the annual or semiannual budget for the coming year is one of the more important functions of the A & R Administrator. He or she must analyze previous budgets, current acts, and projected estimates of costs. The A & R Administrator must then come up with a working budget for the recording of the acts.

As the year progresses, the individual working in A & R administration keeps an eye on the budget in relation to the expenses. Staying within a budget means that the A & R Administrator is doing his or her job. The individual might work exclusively with one or two studios in order to build up a great volume of studio time. With this volume, the A & R Administrator can often receive discounts on time.

The A & R Administrator keeps track of all monies spent for recording studio time, session musicians, talent, and miscellaneous expenses. These costs are all logged. It is through this log that expenses for each recording act can be tracked.

The A & R Administrator also submits bills and purchase orders to the proper individuals in the accounting department. He or she must make sure that these bills are submitted and paid on time. Union regulations stipulate certain time limits for musicians' payment schedules. A late bill could result in a union dispute.

The A & R Administrator works with the A & R coordinator in monitoring the progress of a label's recording acts in order to determine how much of a project has been recorded, when the record will be ready for release, the amount the recording has cost to date, whether the act is within budget, etc. This information is compiled into reports that are given to various department heads in the recording company.

If the act is receiving tour support from the record company, the A & R Administrator must keep records of all monies laid out on behalf of the group. This is often recouped later from record sale monies.

The A & R Administrator is additionally responsible for obtaining all pertinent information that will be on the completed record packaging. This information includes the name of the group, the members of the group, other musicians who played on the record, producers, tunes, lengths of songs, how the songs will be sequenced on the recording, and any other additional material the act, its management, and the producer want on the packaging.

The A & R Administrator might have to apply for copyright materials and applications for any songs, tunes, CD covers, etc. that it owns. The A & R Administrator might be responsible for applying for any mechanical rights licenses that are necessary. He or she must make sure that all this is on file.

The A & R Administrator must be very organized. He or she must keep excellent records. The individual is responsible to different people and department heads depending on the company. He or she might be responsible to one of the company's vice-presidents in charge of A & R, or might be responsible to an A & R administrator supervisor.

Salaries
Salaries for A & R Administrators will vary depending on the size of the record company and the qualifications and duties of the individual. Earnings can range from $25,000 to $55,000 plus per year for individuals in these positions.

Employment Prospects
The A & R department is one of the most popular departments in which to work. There are more people who desire jobs in this area than there are openings.

Record companies often promote from within. If an individual is considering a position in an A & R department, he or she may have to enter through a lower-paying job in a different department.

Possibilities for employment also exist at smaller, independent labels that are springing up throughout the country.

Advancement Prospects
An individual who has obtained a position as an A & R Administrator probably will have the opportunity to move into an A & R coordinator position. He or she, of course, must be energetic, enthusiastic, and excellent at his or her current job.

Openings do occur as people change jobs and labels. As noted throughout this section, most record companies prefer to promote from within.

Education and Training
Many record companies require a college degree for this position. Others just ask for a high school diploma. It depends on the label.

College courses or majors that might prove useful include business, accounting and administration. There are colleges around the country with curriculums in the music business.

There are also many seminars, programs, and workshops put together by record companies, associations, organizations, and colleges that are helpful both for their educational value and for the opportunity they provide to develop contacts.

Experience, Skills, and Personality Traits
The individual working in A & R administration must have the ability to plan budgets for recording artists. Certain acts that the company feels will sell more records will have bigger budgets. Newer or lesser known acts must have budgets developed for them that are considerably smaller.

Since most of the job is budgeting or checking bills, the ability to work with numbers is a must. Other parts of the job require the individual to write reports and to keep other departments of the company informed. The A & R Administrator, therefore, must also be able to communicate both on paper and verbally.

Unions and Associations
A & R Administrators may belong to the National Academy of Recording Arts and Sciences (NARAS) as associate members. They might also belong to the Country Music Association (CMA) or the Gospel Music Association (GMA), depending on their musical interests.

Tips for Entry
1. Record companies promote from within. If you want to work in the A & R department, try to get a job in a record company doing any type of work you can. Be enthusiastic and ask questions.
2. Read the trades and any other material you can lay your hands on regarding trends in the music business, record deals, etc.
3. If you are in college, see if the school has a summer internship program with a record company for which you can get college credit.
4. There are some minority training programs available at some record companies that can help you get your foot in the door. Check with the personnel departments of individual record companies.

PROMOTION MANAGER

CAREER PROFILE

Duties: Supervise promotion department of a record label; obtain airplay for label's records

Alternate Title(s): Promotion Director; Director of Promotion

Salary Range: $25,000 to $90,000+

Employment Prospects: Fair

Advancement Prospects: Fair

Best Geographical Location(s) for Position: New York City, Los Angeles, and Nashville for larger labels; other cities throughout the country for smaller labels

Prerequisites:

Education or Training—High school diploma, minimum for most positions; some jobs require college background or degree

Experience—Working as a promotion rep or in promotion or related department in record company

Special Skills and Personality Traits—Ability to sell; communications skills, knowledge of music; supervisory skills

CAREER LADDER

```
┌─────────────────────────────────┐
│  Vice President of Promotion or  │
│    Promotion Manager in a        │
│  Large, Prestigious Company      │
└─────────────────────────────────┘

┌─────────────────────────────────┐
│       Promotion Manager          │
└─────────────────────────────────┘

┌─────────────────────────────────┐
│   Regional Promotion Person      │
└─────────────────────────────────┘
```

Position Description

The Promotion Manager of a record company supervises all the employees in the promotion department. The prime function of everyone in this department is to obtain airplay for as many of the record label's singles and albums as possible.

This is not an easy task. Hundreds of new records are released each week. The promotion department must bring new tunes to radio stations and ask them to review them in hopes of having them added to stations' playlists. As a rule, stations only add a few new songs to their list each week. Most stations play the hits of the week interspersed with a limited number of other songs. These other tunes that are aired may be oldies or potential new hits. The promotional people vie to place their new releases in these slots.

Music television is now also a very viable venue for selling records. The promotion department is in charge of attempting to obtain airplay for music videos, too.

In order to get the stations to listen to and play the label's tunes, the Promotion Manager works with the regional and local representatives who call and visit the program directors or music directors of the radio stations. The Promotion

Manager is in charge of deciding where a record should be "broken." It is up to this individual to outline a plan of action. Should the record be broken in New York City or should it be tried out first in a key market in the South? The individual must know what areas are good for what types of songs. The person must also be aware of what formats are available at which radio stations in all given markets.

The Promotion Manager is responsible for devising any type of promotion that he or she feels will help get the records aired. The individual may work with other departments in putting these together. These might, for example, include the merchandising department. Using this department, the Promotion Manager could have T-shirts, tour jackets, bumper stickers, pins, etc., designed and made up on behalf of an act or its album. The Promotion Manager might arrange interviews, television appearances, promotional appearances, or press conferences through the publicity department.

The Manager of this department may also work with the advertising department. This, too, is an important method of getting potential airplay. The Promotion Manager may feel that a group needs a little extra push that could be gained through some advertising exposure. The department heads decide together how much should be spent on this project, how to go about the task, and the route they want to take in gaining the exposure.

The Manager of the promotion department is in charge of scheduling regular meetings with the staff. At these meetings, any problems will be discussed and suggestions given for rectifying difficulties. This may also be the time when statistics on the label's records are given out, for example, how many of which records are selling, which record was added to what stations' playlists, reviews of records in the trades, etc.

In this position, the individual will work closely with, and reports to, the vice-president of the department. In smaller companies, the person might also be the vice-president and be responsible to the president or CEO. Together they create overall promotional campaigns that can be put into motion. They also discuss which methods of promotion have worked and which have failed.

Success in this position is shown by how many of the label's records are on major stations' playlists. The Promotion Manager at a record label works long hours trying to attain this success, often under quite a bit of stress.

Salaries

Annual earnings of Promotion Managers will differ depending on the size, prestige, and location of the record label as well as the experience and duties of the individual. Salaries can range from $25,000 at one of the new, smaller independent labels to $90,000 plus at a large, well-known one.

Employment Prospects

It is difficult to obtain a position as a Promotion Manager at one of the very large, well-known labels. Those who aspire to do this must first work as promotion reps and regional managers for these labels.

It is possible to locate a position, however, after a bit of experience in some of the smaller independent labels that are springing up. While the salaries are low, the experience gained can make it worthwhile.

Advancement Prospects

Advancement possibilities are fair for Promotion Managers in record companies. The most frequent career path taken is usually that of finding a similar position in a larger, more prestigious company. Other possibilities for career advancement for the Promotion Manager include becoming the vice-president of the promotion department or heading up a related department.

Education and Training

Educational requirements vary from label to label. The minimum educational requirement for a Promotion Manager at most labels is a high school diploma. Depending on the position and the label, that might be sufficient. Jobs at major labels usually require a college degree.

Experience, Skills, and Personality Traits

The Promotion Manager must know not only how to do his or her job, but also how to supervise others in the department. This individual is often in charge of many people. He or she must have the ability to guide them and direct their work.

Most Promotion Managers in this field are good salespeople. They know how to persuade people at radio and music television stations to listen to their records and watch their videos. They also know how to convince stations to add those records to their playlist.

In this job, the individual must stay well-informed on all types of music, other records, target markets, etc. The Promotion Manager should also be creative and personable.

Unions and Associations

A Promotion Manager in a record company may belong to a number of organizations and associations. He or she may be a member of the Country Music Association (CMA) or the Gospel Music Association (GMA), among others. The individual might also be an associate member of the National Academy of Recording Arts and Sciences (NARAS).

Tips for Entry

1. Many of the larger record companies, as well as a number of the smaller ones, have internship programs. Ask to work in the promotion department.
2. If there is not an internship program at the label of your choice, call or write to the promotion manager or vice president of promotion to see if you can create one. Keep in mind that the pay in an intern program is minimal, if there is any salary at all. You might, however, be able to get college credit.
3. Colleges with music merchandising and music business programs often have work-study programs within the industry. This is another excellent way to get experience.
4. Employment agencies in larger cities that host some of the better-known labels often seek out personnel for these types of positions.
5. Openings may be advertised in any of the trade magazines or in local newspaper display or classified sections. Look under heading classifications of "Music," "Records," or "Promotion."

PROMOTION STAFFER

CAREER PROFILE

Duties: Visit and call radio station program directors; try to get airplay for the label's albums

Alternate Title(s): Promotion Man (or Woman); Regional Staff Promotion Person; Local Promotion Person; Record Promoter; Promotional Representative

Salary Range: $24,000 to $60,000+

Employment Prospects: Fair

Advancement Prospects: Fair

Best Geographical Location(s) for Position: New York City, Los Angeles, and Nashville for positions with major record companies; other locations for independent promoters (reps may work in various locations)

Prerequisites:

Education or Training—High school diploma; college degree may be required or preferred

Experience—Sales jobs helpful; working in music business, radio, etc., useful

Special Skills and Personality Traits—Ability to sell; music knowledge; aggressiveness; communications skills

CAREER LADDER

```
┌─────────────────────────────────┐
│       Promotion Manager         │
└─────────────────────────────────┘

┌─────────────────────────────────┐
│       Promotion Staffer         │
└─────────────────────────────────┘

┌─────────────────────────────────┐
│   Local Promotion Person (Rep)  │
└─────────────────────────────────┘
```

Position Description

A Promotion Person working at a record company has one prime function: to get airplay for the label's albums and/or music videos. To accomplish this, the Promotion Person or representative visits and calls radio and music station program directors and music directors.

Promotion People may be assigned a certain category of music—for example, R & B, pop, gospel, rap, etc. They are also assigned territories. There are a number of different markets in which Promotion People generally work. This is where they hope to "break" records.

The Promotion People work closely with program directors, music directors, and disc jockeys in these markets. The first thing the Promotion Person does is to set up appointments with these station people. When the label's Promotion Person goes on appointments he or she will bring a number of the label's new releases. The Promotion Person also brings along a supply of promo or press material and videos about the artists who made the albums.

The individual will sit with the radio station personnel and listen to the new releases. The Promotion Person hopes that the program director or the music director will like the song well enough to add it to the station's playlist. The rep may leave copies of the records with the radio station staff to listen to at their leisure. Promotion People will visit a number of stations in each area covered.

In this position, the individual might do quite a bit of socializing. Promotion People often take key radio and music television personnel out to lunch, dinner, or for drinks. They might also bring a program director to a club to listen to a group play a song live and gauge audience response.

The individual must do research in order to get stations to play records or music videos. He or she may talk to Promotion People in other markets to determine how a specific tune is doing. The Promotion Person must also check with various record stores to see what kind of sales an album has in a specific area. The Rep may check into the total sales of the record in the label's sales department. Any number of other methods to develop information on the reason a radio station should play a record may be employed.

At certain times, the Promotion People will use the phone and mail to reach disc jockeys, program directors, and music directors. This system of mailing promotional copies of records, videos, and press material to stations and then following up with phone calls is frequently used in smaller areas. These smaller locations usually do not have the market potential to justify visits, but may be important just the same.

Salaries

Salaries for Promotion People will vary depending on the size of the record company and the experience and duties of the individual. Salaries range from $24,000 to $60,000 plus annually.

Employment Prospects

Employment prospects are fair for those people who can obtain entry into a record company. There are usually quite a number of Promotion People working for each major company. Individuals who have built up a good reputation in other record companies working in this position generally will not find any problem getting a job. Other individuals may gain entry in local promotion positions.

Advancement Prospects

A person who is a Promotion Representative has a number of options for career advancement. An individual who has a good track record for getting records listened to and put on playlists can usually obtain a better job at a larger record company. A Promotion Person may also move into the job of director of promotion.

Education and Training

As with many jobs in the recording industry, there is no major educational requirement other than a high school diploma. There are Promotion People who hold degrees and those without them. Degrees might help an individual feel more confident about holding a job, but they do not necessarily help one obtain a job. A degree may, however, help an individual to advance his or her career.

Experience, Skills, and Personality Traits

People working in the promotion field are generally interested in music, records, and radio. Some of these individuals have worked in one of these three areas at a prior time while others have been involved with product sales or a variety of different positions.

People in this field need to be able to sell. While they may not be selling a product directly, they are selling the sound of a record. Promotion People are judged on how many records or videos they can get radio or music television stations to add to their playlists. In order to do this, it is necessary for the Promotion Person to stay on top of the music and the record industry and be well-informed about all phases of it. The Person must additionally be aggressive and articulate.

Unions and Associations

Promotion People may belong to the Gospel Music Association (GMA), the Country Music Association (CMA), or other similar associations depending on the type of music they promote. Additionally, they may belong to the National Academy of Recording Arts and Sciences (NARAS) as associate members.

Tips for Entry

1. There are internship programs available in many record companies. Check directly with the various companies.
2. It helps to have contacts to get into a position in a record company. If you have any, this is the time to use them.
3. There are minority training programs available in some record companies. If you qualify, check these out.
4. Enter the record company in any way possible. Apply for a position as a secretary, receptionist, mailroom clerk, etc. These companies promote from within.

DIRECTOR OF PUBLICITY

CAREER PROFILE

Duties: Supervise record label publicity department; develop and oversee publicity campaigns

Alternate Title(s): Director of Publicity and Press Relations; Publicity Director; P.R. Director

Salary Range: $30,000 to $100,000+

Employment Prospects: Fair

Advancement Prospects: Poor to Fair

Best Geographical Location(s) for Position: New York City, Los Angeles, and Nashville are music capitals

Prerequisites:

Education or Training—College degree in public relations, communications, journalism, or music merchandising may be preferred for some positions

Experience—Positions in publicity and journalism helpful

Special Skills and Personality Traits—Ability to write and communicate well; understanding of publicity and promotion; creativity; ability to work under pressure; knowledge of music and record business; media contacts

CAREER LADDER

```
┌─────────────────────────────────────┐
│ Vice President of Press Relations and│
│ Publicity; Director of Publicity in a│
│ Large, Prestigious Record Company;   │
│ Music Oriented Publicity or Public   │
│ Relations Company Owner              │
└─────────────────────────────────────┘

┌─────────────────────────────────────┐
│ Director of Publicity                │
└─────────────────────────────────────┘

┌─────────────────────────────────────┐
│ Staff Publicist                      │
└─────────────────────────────────────┘
```

Position Description

The Director of Publicity in a record company is in charge of the entire publicity and/or press relations department of the label. As Director, he or she supervises all the work that is performed by the staff of the department.

The Director assigns to the staff publicists the various acts that the label has signed. He or she then works with the act, its management, and the staff publicists, developing a viable publicity campaign.

Once the campaign is put into motion by the staff publicist, the Director oversees all aspects of that campaign. In certain cases, the Director of Publicity will handle personally the publicity requirements of a number of the label's "top" artists.

With the current influx of smaller, independent record labels in the music industry, the Director of Publicity may be the only person in the publicity department or may work with a secretary and/or an administrative assistant. In these cases, the individual will handle all publicity functions.

The Director of Publicity meets regularly with members of the publicity staff, discussing strategies, media, and problems that have occurred. The Director also meets regularly with other department heads of the record label to talk about publicity campaign strategies for various acts on the label. The Director often works closely with the label's marketing and artist relations departments as well as the A & R and promotion departments.

The Director of Publicity gathers information from staff members in the form of publicity reports concerning each act they are assigned to. These reports are then submitted to various executives of the company.

At times, the Director of Publicity will work with an act's private publicist or public relations firms, trying to produce as much good press as possible together.

The Director of Publicity is in charge of approving major expenditures for publicity projects such as major press parties, photo sessions, press giveaways, etc. Depending on the structure of the company, these expenditures must usually be approved for the Director of Publicity by other department heads.

As Director of Publicity, the individual will ensure that all campaigns are on schedule. He or she might see that an act is not receiving as much publicity as it should. In this case, the Director must determine why. Perhaps the act is uncooperative. Possibly the publicist assigned to the act is not doing a good job. There are any number of problems that may arise. It is the Director's job to identify the difficulty and resolve it. The favorable publicity each act receives helps achieve the ultimate goal of selling records.

The Director of the Publicity Department will often attend press parties and other functions for both the label's artists and others as well. In this way, the Director can mingle and talk with the press on a range of subjects.

A Director of Publicity must evaluate persons working on the publicity staff. If one of the staffers is not working up to par, the Director may find it necessary to fire the individual (or recommend that the person be let go). On the other hand, the Director might also have the authority to promote (or recommend for promotion) a talented individual.

The Director of Publicity at a record company works long hours. After everyone else has gone home, he or she might still be making calls to publicize the label's acts.

Salaries

Salaries for Directors of Publicity or Press Relations working in a record company will vary greatly depending on the size and the prestige of the label. Individuals working for very small individual labels might earn from $30,000 to $37,000 annually. Those working in larger companies with more and better-known acts will earn between $40,000 and $48,000 per year. The Director of Publicity who is employed by a major record label can earn between $50,000 and $100,000 plus per year.

Employment Prospects

Competition for all jobs in record companies is high and this position is no exception. Prospects are better because of the many independent labels springing up around the country. It is not easy to find a position as the Director of Publicity for a major record label without some type of experience. Major record companies want to have people on staff in this position who have proven themselves either at their company or at another.

Those who seek this position will have an easier time breaking in at smaller or independent labels. These companies are springing up throughout the country.

Advancement Prospects

Advancement prospects for the Director of Publicity in a record company range from limited to fair, depending on the career path the individual takes. He or she may move up the career ladder by being promoted to the position of company

Vice President of Press Relations and Publicity. This would mean more responsibility as well as a higher salary. The individual may also be promoted to any of a host of other top executive positions.

Other possibilities for advancement for the Director of Publicity include finding employment in the same type of position in a larger, more prestigious record company. The individual may also open up his or her own publicity firm, handling publicity and public relations for music industry clients.

Education and Training

Different labels have different educational requirements. Many, especially some of the newer, independent labels, do not specify the necessity of a college degree, although most Publicity Directors have attended college.

A degree or courses in public relations, communications, publicity, marketing and/or music merchandising is useful. There are also a number of seminars and/or courses offered in public relations and publicity by colleges and organizations such as the Public Relations Society of America (PRSA).

Experience, Skills, and Personality Traits

Directors of Publicity for record companies usually worked in publicity positions prior to their appointment. A great deal of the time, they worked in a publicity department of a record company. Many Publicity Directors also worked as music critics, journalists, or for independent publicity or public relations firms.

The Publicity Director at a record label must have the basic public relations and publicity skills of writing and communicating. He or she must also have the ability to supervise others.

It is helpful to enjoy the type of music that the label's clients play (although it is not a necessity) because the individual has to listen to so much of it.

Unions and Associations

Directors of Publicity at record companies are not usually members of any union. They might, however, belong to a number of organizations and associations. One of these is the Public Relations Society of America (PRSA). There are also a number of music associations that the individual might join, including the Country Music Association (CMA), the Gospel Music Association (GMA), and the National Academy of Recording Arts and Sciences (NARAS). These groups all work to promote a specific type of music. Some of them provide internships, scholarships, seminars, and other practical help.

Tips for Entry

1. Positions are often advertised in the classified sections of newspapers in the major music capitals. Look

under "Music," "Records," or "Public Relations" heading classifications.

2. Get experience at a small, independent record label where it is easier to get your foot in the door. You might be the only person in the department, but it will give you wide-ranging experience in the field that will look impressive on your résumé.

3. Send your résumé and a cover letter to record company personnel departments. If a position isn't open at the time, request that your résumé be kept on file.

4. If a job requirement specifies experience with a record label publicity department and you don't have it, don't let that discourage you from applying for the job. You must, however, have something to spark the interest of the person who might interview you or accept your application. For example, you might bring a portfolio of press clippings for an act you worked with in a private firm or while you were self-employed.

5. Openings may be advertised in the classified section of trade publications such as *Billboard*.

6. Don't forget to check for openings on-line. Record label websites often list job openings.

STAFF PUBLICIST

CAREER PROFILE

Duties: Handle the publicity and press needs of acts signed to a label

Alternate Title(s): Press Agent

Salary Range: $25,000 to $80,000+

Employment Prospects: Fair

Advancement Prospects: Fair

Best Geographical Location(s) for Position: New York City, Los Angeles, and Nashville are music capitals; smaller labels located throughout the country

Prerequisites:

Education or Training—College degree or background in journalism, communications, music business, or music merchandising helpful

Experience—Positions in music- or nonmusic-oriented publicity and public relations

Special Skills and Personality Traits—Ability to write; creativity; persuasive manner; ability to work under pressure; enjoyment of music

CAREER LADDER

```
┌─────────────────────────────────┐
│      Director of Publicity       │
└─────────────────────────────────┘

┌─────────────────────────────────┐
│        Staff Publicist           │
└─────────────────────────────────┘

┌─────────────────────────────────┐
│ Music- or Nonmusic-Oriented      │
│ Publicist; Music Journalist      │
└─────────────────────────────────┘
```

Position Description

Publicists on staff in record companies perform many different functions. The main goal of the department is to get as much good publicity for the artists signed to the label as possible. Publicity helps the label sell records and that is the primary way the company produces income.

A beginning Publicist may do just clerical types of work, such as assembling press kits. He or she may start by gathering information for the press kits or by writing simple press releases.

As the Publicist gains more experience, he or she will be writing more creative press releases. Eventually the Publicist will work with the act on developing publicity strategies for their press campaign.

As a Publicist, an individual must be able to get an artist's name in the news (magazines, trades, TV, radio, online, etc.) as often as possible. This is accomplished by writing press releases, sending them to the correct media, talking to media about acts, arranging interviews, etc.

The Publicist often arranges a series of print interviews, radio interviews, and TV appearances in conjunction with the release of a new record.

He or she may either keep the information on the group going to the media in a shotgun approach or release information selectively. This would depend on the type of campaign that has been chosen for the act prior to the record's release.

When Publicists have something very important going on with one of their artists, they usually plan a press party or press conference to announce it. These press parties and conferences must only be used for special events. If this caution is not heeded, the media might not be interested on the next occasion, although the Publicist may really have something important to unveil. In addition, because of the great expense of these press functions, executives usually like them limited in frequency.

Publicists are on the phone a great deal of the time, calling media and trying to interest them in what is happening with their acts. When they are not on the phone or writing releases, Publicists are often at parties or functions meeting with the press and other people important to their clients.

Publicists are usually the first ones to send out promotional copies of new records and other important materials to the media. After a new record is released, the Publicist might work with the A & R department or the promotion department on a showcase booking of the group. The Publicist might then decide that this is the proper time for an all-important press party.

The Publicist working for a record company often works closely with an act's personal publicist or P.R. firm. (Acts hire personal publicists and P.R. firms because they want more attention than a label Publicist can give them.) Label Publicists often work with up to 10 acts each. As a rule, label Publicists zero in on creating publicity that will potentially sell more records. Personal Publicists work to create an image for the artist that will help to sustain him or her in the business longer.

The Publicist's hours are not the regular 9 to 5 most people work. Publicists work a long regular day and then go out to parties, clubs, and other functions to mingle with the press or to listen to acts they represent.

It is also the Publicist's job to set up interviews and appearances with the media when the act goes on tour. During big tours the Publicist works with a tour publicist and other tour personnel, coordinating tour publicity.

The Staff Publicist is usually responsible to the Director of Publicity at the label. All the Staff Publicists meet regularly with this individual to map out strategies and handle any problems that come up.

Salaries

Salaries for Staff Publicists vary depending on the size of the record label one is working for and the amount of experience the Publicist has. Salaries can range from $25,000 for a beginning Publicist or a Publicist at a small label, to $55,000 at a bigger label. Salaries for Publicists can go up to $80,000 or more yearly if the Publicist is experienced, working at a big label, and has a great deal of responsibility. This salary level is rare, though. The average salary range for a Publicist would be from $30,000 to $50,000 annually.

Employment Prospects

If an individual can write well and is creative, he or she has a decent chance of landing a position in the publicity department at a record label.

There is a fairly high turnover of people in this department because individuals move around to various record labels. Bigger labels sometimes have an entry-level position in publicity. However, the individual might only fill press kits. As one gets more experience, he or she is usually given less tedious work and more interesting projects.

It is sometimes easier for an individual to find a job as a Publicist in a record company (because you can start out in an entry-level position and move out of it fairly quickly), than as a Publicist in a music-oriented P.R. firm.

Advancement Prospects

As noted throughout this section, most positions in the record business allow for advancement fairly routinely. This is especially so in nonsupervisory capacities.

Publicists who do well at their jobs move into better positions in the department, such as supervising others or handling more prestigious clients.

Publicists with a proven track record at one label can usually find a job at another label without too much trouble.

Publicists also often gain experience at a label and then strike out on their own as independent Publicists or with a P.R. firm.

Education and Training

Different positions in publicity require different amounts and types of education. Not all positions at record companies require college degrees or backgrounds. However, these applicants are often preferred.

College courses or majors that might prove useful in this type of position include public relations, marketing, advertising, music merchandising, journalism, and communications.

In addition, there are a number of seminars offered by different organizations, associations, and colleges on publicity, promotion, and public relations as related to the music business.

Experience, Skills, and Personality Traits

A Publicist working in a record company must be able to work under pressure, as deadlines must be met on a constant basis.

Publicists must have the ability to write well. Creativity is a plus; it helps to come up with new angles for acts. The Publicist must constantly make new media contacts, as these people can make or break an act.

As the Publicist must go out after working hours quite frequently, he or she must have a lot of stamina and not mind having a business life and social life wrapped in one. Enjoying and appreciating music, especially the music of the acts being promoted, is helpful, too.

Unions and Associations

Staff Publicists working in a record company may belong to the Public Relations Society of America (PRSA). This organization is one of the best-known in the publicity and public relations field. It offers seminars, booklets, a magazine, and other helpful information to members.

The individual might also belong to the National Academy of Recording Arts and Sciences (NARAS) as an associate member.

Tips for Entry

1. Find out if the record company has an internship program and try to get into it. It's worth working for nothing (or a small salary) or even college credit for a summer or a short period of time if you can gain entry into one of these programs. Not only is the experience worthwhile, but you also have an excellent chance of being hired after the internship ends.

2. Prepare your résumé and a few samples of your writing style. Send these with a cover letter to personnel departments or publicity directors of record companies.

3. There are a number of employment agencies specializing in public relations and publicity jobs. Call or write to them about openings in the record companies.

4. There are also a limited number of employment agencies specializing in jobs in the music business. Check these out.

5. If you have any contacts in the record business, this is the time to use them. See if they will help you get your foot in the door.

6. Openings are often advertised in trade publications such as *Billboard.*

7. Check out record label websites for employment openings.

ARTIST RELATIONS AND DEVELOPMENT REPRESENTATIVE

CAREER PROFILE

Duties: Act as a liaison between a record company and one or more of their signed artists

Alternate Title(s): Artist Relations and Development Staffer

Salary Range: $25,000 to $65,000+

Employment Prospects: Poor

Advancement Prospects: Fair

Best Geographical Locations for Position: New York City, Los Angeles, and Nashville are music capitals; smaller labels may be located throughout the country

Prerequisites:

Education or Training—High school diploma minimum; college degree may be preferred

Experience—Experience in public relations, publicity, or artist management helpful

Special Skills and Personality Traits—Knowledge of music and record business; ability to deal effectively with people

CAREER LADDER

```
┌─────────────────────────────────┐
│     Artist Relations and        │
│     Development Director         │
└─────────────────────────────────┘

┌─────────────────────────────────┐
│     Artist Relations and        │
│   Development Representative     │
└─────────────────────────────────┘

┌─────────────────────────────────┐
│  Publicist/P.R. Counselor; Intern │
└─────────────────────────────────┘
```

Position Description

The Artist Relations and Development Representative is a position that is not present in every record company. Certain companies either are too small to retain people in this position, or they delegate the responsibilities normally taken care of by the Artist Relations and Development Rep to other departments.

Duties of the Artist Relations and Development Representative differ, too, depending on the company. If the record company does have this department, most often it is the Representative's responsibility to act as a liaison between the company and its artists. The Representative makes sure that the artist feels that the record company is treating him or her specially. For example, the Artist Relations and Development Rep might send roses on behalf of the record company to a singer whose record just went gold. The Rep might make sure that a group is sent champagne before kicking off a prestigious tour. In essence, the Artist Relations and Development Representative makes sure that

there is a good relationship between the artists and the record company, not only businesswise, but socially, too. The record business is unique in that business life and social life often blend into one.

The Artist Relations and Development Representative keeps in close contact with the act and its management. He or she listens for potential problems that might involve the record company. When the individual hears of any developing problems, he or she takes care of them (or, if unable to solve the problems, brings them to the attention of someone who can).

The Artist Relations and Development Representative works with the act and its management to help build the act's career. The Reps work with all the different departments of the record company, such as planning promotional concert tours in conjunction with record releases. The Rep makes sure that the tour coincides with the record release. If it turns out that a tour has to begin three weeks later than anticipated, the Rep might discuss with the record company executives the option of holding up the release for a short time.

The Artist Relations and Development Representative might also work with the publicity department or the group's P.R. firm in coordinating television, radio, and promotional public appearances.

At times, the individual will attend an act's concert and review the performance. He or she might make suggestions on how the act could improve the performance or stage presentation.

The Artist Relations and Development Representative usually becomes quite friendly with the act and its management team. He or she might remain friends with the act long after its recording contract has expired and the group has moved on to another company.

This is another position in the record industry in which long, irregular hours are maintained. To be successful at this job, an individual must really love both music and people.

Salaries

An Artist Relations and Development Representative has a salary range of $25,000 to $65,000 or more annually. The salary of the individual will depend on the size of the record company he or she is working with. Salary is also dependent on the individual's duties and qualifications.

Employment Prospects

Since not every record label has this position, it is often difficult to find openings. Once again, there are many people who want to work in this department of a record company and a limited number of positions.

Individuals who cannot find work in this position might want to look for jobs in publicity and public relations. Then, when an opening is located, the individual will already have experience in the field.

Advancement Prospects

As in most positions in a record company, once an individual gets his or her foot in the door, there is a fair chance for advancement and promotion. In order to be promoted, there must be an opening in an advanced position. Individuals may direct their careers into other departments for advancement.

Education and Training

Although often there is no educational requirement above a high school diploma, a college degree or background might be the thing that separates one applicant from another.

Courses in publicity, promotion, journalism, English, and communications might be helpful. There are also degrees offered by various colleges in music merchandising and the music business.

It is also wise to take part in any seminar or program available where you can learn, as well as develop contacts.

Experience, Skills, and Personality Traits

Most individuals who work in the artist relations and development department have had some type of experience in promotion, publicity, or public relations. Others have worked in artist management.

The successful Artist Relations and Development Representative must have a knowledge of both music and the record business. He or she must attend many shows and concerts, concentrating on other acts and their stage appearances, concerts, performances, etc.

He or she must not only have the ability to deal with people, but like to do so. Since record companies cannot comply with every request an act has, the Rep must have the ability to deny some requests and still keep the group relatively happy.

Unions and Associations

The Artist Relations and Development Representative in a record company might belong to the Country Music Association (CMA) or the Gospel Music Association (GMA), depending on the variety of musical artists he or she represents. The individual may also be an associate member of the National Academy of Recording Arts and Sciences (NARAS).

Tips for Entry

1. Attend as many seminars and programs as you can to learn the business and develop contacts.
2. As with many other record company jobs, you might have to accept an entry-level position to get to the position you want. People are promoted if they have the drive and the qualifications.
3. Try to find a record company with either a summer internship program or a college internship program and request to be placed in this department. This way you will have an "in" when you finish school.
4. You might also want to check into label-sponsored minority training programs.
5. Check out record label websites for possible job openings.

MARKETING REPRESENTATIVE

CAREER PROFILE

Duties: Oversee specific markets; report sales of records to radio stations and trades

Alternate Title(s): Marketing Staffer

Salary Range: $25,000 to $50,000+

Employment Prospects: Fair

Advancement Prospects: Fair

Best Geographical Location(s) for Position: New York City, Los Angeles, and Nashville; record company may send rep to various other cities

Prerequisites:

Education or Training—High school diploma, minimum requirement; college degree may be preferred or required

Experience—Intern position helpful but not necessary

Special Skills and Personality Traits—Communications skills; understanding of and knowledge of music and record business; ability to work with numbers

CAREER LADDER

```
┌─────────────────────────────────────┐
│   Regional Director of Marketing;    │
│        Regional Representative        │
└─────────────────────────────────────┘

┌─────────────────────────────────────┐
│    Local Marketing Representative     │
└─────────────────────────────────────┘

┌─────────────────────────────────────┐
│      Field Merchandiser; Intern;      │
│   Clerical Position in Record Company │
└─────────────────────────────────────┘
```

Position Description

A Marketing Representative for a record company may work on a local or regional level. The prime function of the marketing department in the record company is to develop various ways to market and sell the company's records. The Marketing Representative will help execute this function.

Depending on the position held, the Marketing Representative oversees marketing activities in a certain area. A local Rep will oversee specific markets. The regional Rep will oversee entire regions. For example, a local Rep may be in charge of the marketing in Philadelphia. The regional Marketing Representative or Director would be in charge of the entire northeast section of the United States, which would include Philadelphia.

Regardless of territory, the individuals have the same function and duties. The first, mentioned above, is to oversee the marketing of the records. To accomplish this, the Reps will work under the supervision of the director of marketing to assist in implementing such marketing strategies as delivering displays for a number of the label's hot acts to record shops or setting up window displays in the record stores. Other ideas might not involve stores directly. The concepts might revolve around radio station giveaway contests with the label's new records or T-shirts, bumper stickers, posters, etc., as prizes. The marketing department often offers radio stations and record shops in a specific area joint promotions, such as promotional appearances in a record shop by a hot group combined with radio station album giveaways. Similarly, the marketing department may work on promotions with various music-oriented websites or online stores.

The Marketing Representative is also responsible for calling and/or visiting record stores in a specific area to make sure that they have sufficient products on hand to meet possible demands. This often occurs after a group has won an award or a gold record or before a concert in the city.

The Marketing Representative gets reports of record sales from the various shops and stores in the specific market. He or she will call these in to the radio stations, music television stations, major trades, and tip sheets. This is the method many record stores and radio stations use to develop the music charts.

The Marketing Representative reports directly to his or her supervisor; in most cases, that is the director of marketing. The local Rep may also report to the regional director of marketing. Hours are irregular. There is often a great deal of travel associated with this job.

Salaries

Salaries for Marketing Representatives vary according to the positions they hold and the companies they work for. A Marketing Rep can expect $25,000 to $50,000 or more annually.

Employment Prospects

Employment prospects are fair for those seeking positions as Marketing Representatives. Major record labels hire a fairly large number of people in this position. One of the better ways of getting a job in the marketing department is by working as in intern for the department.

Advancement Prospects

Marketing Representatives can advance their careers by becoming regional Reps or regional directors of marketing. The individual may be promoted to the position of marketing director or a specific type of music, such as country or adult contemporary music, gospel music, etc. The Rep can further advance his or her career by becoming the national marketing director of a label.

Education and Training

The minimum education usually required to be a Marketing Representative is a high school diploma. Many labels may prefer or require a college degree or background. Courses in marketing, business, advertising, etc., will be useful. There are a number of colleges offering music business or music merchandising degrees. Keep in mind that these degrees do not guarantee a job, but are helpful in preparing for one.

Experience, Skills, and Personality Traits

Experience in a record company is useful for work in this field. One of the best ways to get this experience is to look for an intern position in the department. These jobs give the individual an invaluable hands-on learning experience.

Marketing Representatives must also be literate, articulate, and good with numbers. Creativity is a plus. Understanding of the music business and a complete knowledge of the record industry is essential.

Unions and Associations

Marketing Representatives may belong to a number of associations. These include the Country Music Association (CMA), the Gospel Music Association (GMA), the National Academy of Recording Arts and Sciences (NARAS), and a host of others.

Tips for Entry

1. Try to find an internship in a record company's marketing department. This opportunity might come through either the record company or a college.
2. If you already have a job in a record company, possibly in the clerical end, volunteer to do some work for the marketing department. Learn the business.
3. Get a job in a large record store and make contacts with Marketing Representatives who visit and/or call the store. They might be able to get you an appointment for an interview.
4. Positions are often advertised in trade publications such as *Billboard*.
5. Openings may also be listed on record label websites.

CONSUMER RESEARCHER

CAREER PROFILE

Duties: Research and analyze consumer buying practices for the record company

Alternate Title(s): Market Researcher; Market Analyst

Salary Range: $24,000 to $45,000+

Employment Prospects: Fair

Advancement Prospects: Fair

Best Geographical Location(s) for Position: New York City, Los Angeles, and Nashville offer the most opportunities

Prerequisites:

Education or Training—Bachelor's degree in business usually preferred; master's degree sometimes required

Experience—Working as a research assistant or trainee in any field; conducting interviews and opinion polls

Special Skills and Personality Traits—Knowledge of research and analytical methods; ability to write reports; knowledge of music business and record industry

CAREER LADDER

```
┌─────────────────────────────┐
│      Marketing Staffer       │
└─────────────────────────────┘

┌─────────────────────────────┐
│     Consumer Researcher      │
└─────────────────────────────┘

┌─────────────────────────────┐
│  Research Assistant or Trainee │
└─────────────────────────────┘
```

Position Description

The marketing and/or sales departments of record companies hire Consumer Researchers. These people have interesting jobs. Their main function is to research consumer buying practices for the record company. After the data have been compiled, they must be analyzed by the Consumer Researcher. With this information the marketing and/or sales department can develop a better understanding of the various types of records people want to buy through examination of what has been previously purchased.

The Consumer Researcher—or Market Researcher, as he or she is sometimes referred to—may secure information on the record-buying public in a number of ways. The first step the individual usually takes is to decide the method or methods that will be used in finding information. The Consumer Researcher may collect facts from the record company and its various departments. Information sought out includes the types of records that have sold previously; the number of records of each style that were sold during a certain time period (e.g., pop, classical, country,

adult contemporary, etc.); and the geographical location in which each variety sold well.

The individual might then research facts about records that were sold on other labels. This is usually much more difficult, as companies seldom like to disclose sales information to their competitors. However, the Consumer Researcher may talk to distributors, record shops, rack jobbers, etc., to gather such data.

Another method of checking out consumer buying practices is to prepare a survey. An interview might be given by the individual directly, or he or she might train a number of people in a variety of markets to handle the project. The Consumer Researcher might also choose to interview consumers by phone on their buying habits. Today many companies do research by surveying people's music buying habits on the Web. All of the different methods may be used to secure results.

After the surveys or the interviews have been completed, the Consumer Researcher will have to tabulate and analyze the data collected. From these surveys, the individual very often can obtain information about customer opinions and tastes in record buying. This tells the marketing and/or sales department what type of records to market, the best sales locations, and more effective ways to do the job.

The Consumer Researcher in a record company must be very knowledgeable about records, target markets, the music business, and the recording industry in order to know the types of questions to ask in a survey or opinion poll. Individuals in this field work closely with the marketing director and the department staff. The Consumer Researcher may recommend test marketing of certain records in specific areas. In other situations, the individual may recommend for or against the release of a certain record in an area because of his or her test marketing. The head of the marketing department has the option of listening to recommendations or ignoring them. The amount of authority the Researcher has, of course, depends on the position and the structure of the department.

Salaries

Consumer Researchers working for record companies may earn $24,000 to $45,000 plus annually. Salaries will depend on the size of the record company, its location, and the qualifications and duties of the Consumer Researcher.

Employment Prospects

Those who are qualified have a fair chance of obtaining a job as a Consumer Researcher in a record company. Marketing and/or sales departments of major labels usually hire a good number of Consumer Researchers. Smaller labels frequently hire a limited number, too.

There is competition in every phase of the record company, especially in larger labels. The more qualified an individual is for this job, the better his or her chances for employment.

Advancement Prospects

Consumer Researchers may advance their careers in a number of ways. The individual may assume responsibility for bigger and better projects. He or she might move into a supervisory position in the research department. Another possibility for advancement is for the individual to become a member of the marketing staff—a marketing coordinator or vice president of marketing. As in all positions in record companies, advancement really depends on the individual and on the structure of the company.

Education and Training

A good education is necessary for this type of job. A bachelor's degree is usually required. A master's degree is sometimes preferred. Majors may be in business administration, marketing, or any related field. Courses in computer technology or data processing are extremely helpful.

Experience, Skills, and Personality Traits

Individuals who aspire to get into the marketing end of the recording industry may be interested in consumer research. Those who become Consumer Researchers need the know-how to delve into consumer buying habits. The Consumer Researcher must know how to analyze the data and render an understandable final report for supervisors. In order to excel at this type of job, a thorough knowledge of the music business and recording industry is essential.

Unions and Associations

Consumer Researchers may belong to advertising associations, such as the American Advertising Federation (AAF) or the American Marketing Association (AMA). Both of these organizations provide information and assistance to people in this field.

Tips for Entry

1. Get experience in consumer research in any field.
2. Become a pollster for a new product, a corporation, a new service, etc.
3. This is one of the jobs in which a good education really helps. The more qualified you are, the better your chance of employment.
4. These jobs are often advertised in the classified sections of newspapers in the major music capitals.

ADVERTISING ACCOUNT EXECUTIVE

CAREER PROFILE

Duties: Develop advertising campaigns for a record label's products

Alternate Title(s): Account Representative

Salary Range: $28,000 to $50,000+

Employment Prospects: Fair

Advancement Prospects: Fair

Best Geographical Location(s) for Position: New York City, Los Angeles, and Nashville offer the most opportunities

Prerequisites:

Education or Training—College degree in advertising, marketing, or a related area preferred

Experience—Copywriter; advertising executive in non-music-related agency

Special Skills and Personality Traits—Creativity; ability to work under pressure; knowledge of advertising skills and technology; cognizance of music and record industry

CAREER LADDER

```
┌─────────────────────────────────┐
│     Director of Advertising     │
└─────────────────────────────────┘

┌─────────────────────────────────┐
│  Advertising Account Executive  │
└─────────────────────────────────┘

┌─────────────────────────────────┐
│     Advertising Copywriter;     │
│ Advertising Account Executive in│
│    Nonmusic-Oriented Agency     │
└─────────────────────────────────┘
```

Position Description

An Advertising Account Executive in a record company develops advertising campaigns for the label's products. The main purpose of the advertising campaign is to make the public aware that a certain album has been released and is in the stores. If people know about an album, it is hoped, they will buy it.

The Advertising Account Executive or Representative, as he or she may be called, is usually assigned a certain number of acts and/or records to work with. This assignment generally comes from the director of the advertising department.

A lot of work goes into planning an advertising campaign for a new album. The Account Executive may study other campaigns used for the specific artist and/or record or might look over other programs. The individual will consider the act's public image and decide what type of people the advertising should target. For example, if the Account Executive is developing a campaign for a rap recording act, the individual will gear the advertising to young people. If an act has put out a hard rock album, the Account Executive will gear the advertising to that audience.

Depending on the size and the structure of the record company, the Account Executive may not only have to develop advertising campaigns for the new records, but may also have to do the artwork and/or copywriting, too. The Advertising Representative may also have to negotiate contracts for advertising space or air time.

The Advertising Account Executive in the record company must have a total understanding of the recording industry and the acts and/or records for which he or she is developing campaigns. The individual needs to work with many of the other departments in the record company to obtain useful information and ideas for an advertising program. For example, the Account Representative may work with the promotion or publicity departments, putting together a total campaign that includes advertising, promotional appearances in record stores, and television and radio interviews.

In this position, the individual must have the ability to know which types of advertising will be most effective for the money. He or she must decide whether ads should be run on TV or radio, in newspapers, magazines, or trades, or on billboards, etc. Decisions must also be made as to which ads should be run locally and which ads should be run nationally. Often, when a large record store or chain advertises a specific record or group of records, the label picks up the cost of the ad. With more and more on-line stores selling CDs and records, the Internet must also be considered a viable advertising medium.

It is very important for the Advertising Account Executive to be able to stay within the budget allocated to each record.

Account Executives have frequent meetings with the director of the department. During these sessions new concepts, problems, and budgets are discussed. It is also during these times that the effectiveness of the campaigns are evaluated.

The individual in this job works long hours. He or she is responsible to the director of advertising.

Salaries

Advertising Account Executives in a record company earn from $28,000 to $50,000 plus annually. Salaries vary depending on the size of the record company and the experience and duties of the individual.

Employment Prospects

Employment prospects are fair for an individual who is trained and qualified in this area. Those who are knowledgeable about both advertising and the recording industry have better prospects. The Advertising Account Executive who has proven him- or herself in this field should be able to find employment. Large and mid-size record companies usually have advertising departments. Many of the smaller labels use the services of an outside advertising agency.

Advancement Prospects

Prospects are fair for an Advertising Account Executive working in a record company. To move up the career ladder, the individual can seek out the same type of position in a larger, more prestigious company. This type of advancement means more responsibility and a higher salary. The individual may move into the position of director of advertising in a record company. Many Advertising Account Executives obtain jobs in advertising agencies not affiliated with music.

Education and Training

A college degree in advertising, marketing, or a related area is usually preferred by most record companies. Degree programs in these fields may be found in many colleges and universities around the country.

There are many seminars, workshops, and additional courses in advertising and the music and recording industry that are beneficial to an Advertising Account Executive.

Experience, Skills, and Personality Traits

The person working in this position must be very creative. He or she must have the ability to come up with unique, effective advertising campaigns for new records. The Account Executive must be knowledgeable about all advertising skills and technology, including copywriting, the use of audiovisuals, graphics, etc. An ability to work under intense pressure is necessary.

Many record companies prefer that the staff of their advertising department has prior experience in the field. Other companies prefer to train staff themselves.

Unions and Associations

Advertising Account Executives working in record companies may belong to the National Academy of Recording Arts and Sciences (NARAS) as associate members. Individuals might also belong to the American Advertising Federation (AAF).

Tips for Entry

1. Look for an internship in the advertising department of a record company. This is one of the best ways to learn about the business. Chances of landing a paying job with the label after the internship are good, too.
2. Get a good education or solid training. Many of the things you will need to know for this type of position are taught in a school setting. You're better off making any major mistakes working on an advertising project for school than directly on the job.
3. If you can't find a job in a record company's advertising department, look into an advertising job in a non-music-oriented advertising agency. After you obtain some experience, try the record labels again.
4. Openings are often advertised in the classified section of newspapers located in areas hosting record labels.

REGIONAL SALES MANAGER

CAREER PROFILE

Duties: Supervise the selling of the label's albums to whole-salers and/or retail outlets; create sales campaigns and policies; oversee staff of department and/or region

Alternate Title(s): Regional Director of Sales; District Sales Manager

Salary Range: $35,000 to $85,000+

Employment Prospects: Fair

Advancement Prospects: Poor

Best Geographical Locations for Position: New York City, Los Angeles, and Nashville; may also work and/or live in major market target cities such as Atlanta, Philadelphia, Chicago, Detroit, etc. This depends on the company's structure.

Prerequisites:

Education or Training—High school diploma mini-mum; major labels may require or prefer college degree

Experience—Retail and/or wholesale sales experience; salesperson for record company

Special Skills and Personality Traits—Superb sales techniques; cognizance of record industry; knowledge of music business; ability to lead and direct others; ability to work under pressure

CAREER LADDER

```
┌─────────────────────────────┐
│   National Sales Director   │
└─────────────────────────────┘

┌─────────────────────────────┐
│   Regional Sales Manager    │
└─────────────────────────────┘

┌─────────────────────────────┐
│        Salesperson          │
└─────────────────────────────┘
```

Position Description

A Regional Sales Manager of a record company is in charge of selling the label's products to wholesalers and/or retail out-lets in the specific region assigned. Depending on the struc-ture of the company, regions might be divided into different segments of the country. The most popular divisions include the northeastern region, the southeastern region, the south-western region, the midwest region, and the western region. It is in these markets that the greatest concentration of selling occurs. The popularity of new on-line outlets has also created major new sales opportunities. Depending on the company, on-line outlets may be considered part of a geographic region or may be assigned a specific sales manager.

The Regional Sales Manager must see to it that a specific amount of merchandise is sold each month. These sales quotas can run into hundreds of thousands of dollars. This "demand"

selling can lead to a lot of pressure. In order to meet these huge quotas, the individual must work closely with both the national sales director and the salespeople in the region.

In this position, the individual is in charge of creating sales campaigns for his or her region. The Regional Sales Manager designs these campaigns with the help of the national sales director. Together, all the Regional Sales Managers and the national director work out the sales poli-cies they will use in selling the product. These programs include merchandise return policies, the number of records one is required to buy in order to qualify for discounts, etc.

As a Regional Sales Manager or Director of Sales, the person may be responsible for interviewing, hiring, and training salespeople. Each company has different methods and techniques for selling their product, and new employees must be instructed accordingly.

The Regional Sales Manager must keep a close watch on how salespeople in his or her region are producing. The region usually consists of a number of cities; for example, the northeast region might include Baltimore, Boston, Hartford, New York City, Philadelphia, and surrounding areas. The Regional Sales Manager must supervise each salesperson in each of these cities.

If sales activity slacks off in any particular area, the individual must check into it, find out what is wrong, and correct the situation. It may be that the city requires additional promotion. In that case, the Regional Sales Manager would contact the promotion department. It could be that a certain record needs more of an advertising push in a specific area. The individual must know whom to contact in case of a problem and do so rapidly. Loss of sales for even one week will negatively affect the monthly sales quotas.

At times, the Regional Sales Manager may feel that the salespeople in an area just aren't doing a good job. It is up to him or her to talk to the individuals, give them some pointers or a pep talk, and get them selling again.

The Sales Manager is also responsible for making sure that the salespeople in the various areas are servicing all accounts. That means that all accounts must be called upon on a regular basis, phone calls returned, and orders filled rapidly. If this is not happening, the Sales Manager is not doing a competent job.

The Regional Sales Manager works long hours, travels extensively, and works under a great deal of pressure to meet sales quotas.

Salaries

The Regional Sales Manager of a major recording company will do quite well financially. In addition to a regular salary, the individual often receives commissions on the products sold in his or her region.

Those working in smaller companies will earn considerably less than their counterparts from the major labels.

The Regional Sales Manager earns $35,000 to $85,000 plus per year.

Employment Prospects

Employment prospects for Regional Sales Managers in major record companies are limited. There are only a few major record companies and each has only a certain number of Sales Manager positions. Jobs are difficult to come by, but are obtainable.

Opportunities are better with smaller companies or independent labels located throughout the country.

Advancement Prospects

Advancement is slow. To move up the career ladder, one would probably want to become the national sales director of a label. These jobs are more limited than Regional Sales Manager positions.

Another advancement opportunity might be a similar position at a bigger or more prestigious label. One may also obtain a better and bigger region as a form of career advancement.

Education and Training

There are many Sales Managers of record companies with just a high school diploma. It is really all that they require. There are some positions, however, that require a bachelor's degree. For those who are currently planning on attending college, thought should be given to the new courses and degrees in music business and/or music merchandising. These degrees and courses will not obtain a job for the individual, but they will certainly help with some background and knowledge about the industry. This extra know-how might prove helpful. Many of the schools also offer internships in cooperation with record companies.

Experience, Skills, and Personality Traits

A Regional Sales Manager for a record company must be familiar with the entire record industry and have a basic knowledge of the music business. The individual must have proven that he or she was a superb salesperson. An ability to lead and direct others is necessary to succeed in this business. The individual must also be able to work effectively under pressure, as it is a constant in this position.

Unions and Associations

Sales Managers working for record companies may belong to the National Association of Recording Merchandisers (NARM). This organization provides a forum for people in the recorded music industry. Individuals might also be members of the Country Music Association (CMA) and/or the Gospel Music Association (GMA).

Tips for Entry

1. These positions are generally not advertised. As a rule, the Regional Sales Managers are chosen from the ranks of salespeople working for the company. The first step to take is to obtain a job in the sales department.
2. This is another of the jobs in which contacts help. If you have them, use them to help you get an interview.
3. Sales experience in any field will be beneficial.

SALESPERSON

CAREER PROFILE

Duties: Sell the company's albums; service accounts

Alternate Title(s): Sales Representative

Salary Range: $25,000 to $48,000+

Employment Prospects: Fair

Advancement Prospects: Fair

Best Geographical Locations for Position: New York City, Los Angeles, Nashville, Atlanta, Chicago, Philadelphia, Jacksonville, Miami, Detroit, etc.

Prerequisites:

Education or Training—High school diploma minimum; some positions require bachelor's degree

Experience—Retail and/or wholesale jobs helpful

Special Skills and Personality Traits—Good sales skills; aggressiveness; reliability; knowledge of music and records; ability to work under pressure

CAREER LADDER

```
┌─────────────────────────────┐
│   Regional Sales Manager    │
└─────────────────────────────┘

┌─────────────────────────────┐
│        Salesperson          │
└─────────────────────────────┘

┌─────────────────────────────┐
│   Salesperson in Related or │
│      Unrelated Field        │
└─────────────────────────────┘
```

Position Description

A Salesperson at a record company sells the label's records, tapes, CDs, DVDs and videos. He or she does this by physically visiting accounts, mailing out letters and other information, and/or making phone calls. The person's accounts may include retail stores, on-line outlets, rack jobbers, and one-stops. In order to meet the sales quota usually imposed by Regional Managers, the Salesperson must constantly service his or her accounts competently.

The individual should be totally knowledgeable about the company's catalog. Although a good number of records, tapes, CDs, etc., sold are new releases, the Salesperson must be aware of the label's older releases, too. This is especially true as older releases come out on CD. The retailer, rack jobber, on-line store, and one-stops might ask the Salesperson questions regarding a new release's sales in other areas of the country. The individual, therefore, should stay informed about as many record-related matters as possible.

After discussing any questions the buyer might have and talking about the new releases available, the Salesperson will take the order. He or she will let the purchaser know what the costs are, the types of discounts available, and how much of the product it is necessary to purchase in order to qualify for the discounts. The Salesperson may also talk about any special promotions that are available to the retailer.

The Salesperson will probably visit a number of accounts each day. Certain days may be set aside for handling correspondence and/or phone work. Depending on the structure of the company, the Salesperson might have other duties in retail shops. These duties might include taking inventory of the company's records, tapes, CDs, and videos, suggesting which products should be reordered, setting up in-store displays or window displays, etc.

Once a Salesperson has received an order, the individual must call it in to be filled. The individual must check back periodically to make sure that orders have been received on time. If they have not, the individual must bring the matter to the attention of the regional sales manager and have it taken care of.

The Salesperson talks to and/or sees the regional sales manager on a regular basis. The Salesperson must attend periodic sales and strategy meetings.

Salaries

Salespeople are compensated in various ways. They may earn a straight salary, a salary plus a commission on sales made, or a commission against a basic salary.

It is difficult to estimate the yearly earnings of a Salesperson in a record company because of the different salary structures, the sizes of various record companies, and the amount of product sold.

Generally, earnings for a Salesperson working for a record company might range from $25,000 to $48,000 plus.

Employment Prospects

Employment prospects are fair for those interested in working as a record company Salesperson. Good Salespeople are hard to find in any industry, and this includes the record business. The opportunities for people to work for major companies in locations other than the three major music capitals expands the prospects. Major and independent record companies employ large numbers of Salespeople in all the music markets, which include New York City, Los Angeles, Nashville, Memphis, Atlanta, Philadelphia, Chicago, Jacksonville, Miami, Detroit, Baltimore, and a host of others.

Advancement Prospects

If a Salesperson shows superior selling skills, he or she may be promoted to Regional Sales Manager or another supervisory position. Selling skills are proven to management when Salespeople meet and exceed their monthly quotas, obtain new accounts, and service old ones well.

Education and Training

A high school degree is the minimum educational requirement for a Salesperson in a record company. Many positions, however, may require a bachelor's degree. Courses that can be useful include marketing, sales, music merchandising, finance, and others in related areas.

Experience, Skills, and Personality Traits

Salespeople working for record companies need many of the same skills and/or experiences found in other sales jobs. The person may find that retail and/or wholesale selling experience is helpful.

A good Salesperson has good sales and interpersonal skills. He or she should be aggressive, articulate, and reliable. The individual needs to be able to work under heavy pressure to meet sales quotas. The person working in this situation also needs a knowledge of music and records to be effective on the job.

Unions and Associations

Salespeople working for a record company might be members of the National Association of Recording Merchandisers (NARM). NARM is an association that provides a forum for those in the recorded music business.

Tips for Entry

1. Apply to a field office of a major record company. These may be located in Philadelphia, Jacksonville, Miami, Chicago, Detroit, Baltimore, or one of a host of other cities, depending on the structure of the record company.
2. Send a résumé and a cover letter directly to the record company. You might want to send one to the national sales director and one to the personnel department to make sure the proper person sees it.
3. If you do send your résumé or a letter, try to find out the person's name to whom you are sending it. Try to send it to a specific name, such as Mr. John Jones, Director of Sales, etc.
4. Remember to include all your sales achievements, not just music-oriented ones. If you had a 90% conversion rate selling vacuum cleaners door to door, chances are you will be a great Salesperson for any product.
5. Visit record label websites to see if they list employment opportunities.

FIELD MERCHANDISER

CAREER PROFILE

Duties: Distribute and explain merchandising promotions to record shops and departments in specific markets

Alternate Title(s): Merchandising Rep; Field Rep

Salary Range: $25,000 to $40,000+

Employment Prospects: Fair

Advancement Prospects: Fair

Best Geographical Locations for Position: Major markets are New York City, Los Angeles, and Nashville; the individual may also work in other cities, including Atlanta, Memphis, Miami, San Francisco, Philadelphia, Boston, Chicago, Detroit, and others

Prerequisites:

Education or Training—High school diploma minimum; major labels may require a college degree

Experience—Some type of sales experience helpful

Special Skills and Personality Traits—Pleasant personality; knowledge of music and/or the record industry; communications skills; good rapport with people

CAREER LADDER

```
┌─────────────────────────────────────┐
│     Merchandising Coordinator;       │
│ Salesperson; Marketing Representative;│
│    Merchandising Representative      │
└─────────────────────────────────────┘

┌─────────────────────────────────────┐
│         Field Merchandiser           │
└─────────────────────────────────────┘

┌─────────────────────────────────────┐
│       Intern; Clerical Position      │
└─────────────────────────────────────┘
```

Position Description

A Field Merchandiser works for the record company in the marketing, merchandising, sales, or promotion department, depending on the structure of the company. The individual in this position travels to record stores and the record departments of stores in his or her territory. The Field Merchandiser distributes promotional displays, posters, contests, and merchandising aids to these locations. Displays might include record, tape or CD holders, posters, window displays, pictures, or album covers. Additional possibilities would be contest entry blanks, T-shirts, buttons, bumper stickers, and other merchandising items relating to the label's acts.

The individual may physically set up the displays or just give the owner or manager of the shop or department advice on how to set it up, describe where it would be most effective, etc. If there is a promotion under way, such as an album giveaway, the Field Merchandiser will explain the promotion in detail to the manager or owner. If the record company has set up an in-store appearance or a promotional concert in the area, the individual may bring in concert tick-

ets, flyers, posters, or other items and make sure that everything is moving according to schedule.

The Field Merchandiser travels for the majority of his or her working days. The individual keeps in close contact with the supervisor of the department. The Field Merchandiser is also required to attend staff meetings. At these meetings, new promotions and merchandise are discussed. The talk may also turn to which retailers are using the merchandising displays and which ones are not. Ideas are often exchanged concerning better methods to entice shop owners and managers into using the merchandise.

The individual in this position may also check the store's inventory of the label's merchandise while attending to other tasks. If a supply is low, the Field Merchandiser will contact the salesperson or sales manager responsible for servicing the area.

Salaries

Field Merchandisers can expect to earn a salary of $25,000 to $40,000 or more per year. Salaries will vary for individuals depending on the size of the record company, the location, the experience of the Field Merchandiser, and his or her exact duties.

Employment Prospects

Employment prospects are fair for Field Merchandisers. The individual has opportunities to work not only in the major markets of New York City, Los Angeles, and Nashville, but in other regions as well. These might include Atlanta, Memphis, Miami, San Francisco, Philadelphia, Boston, Chicago, Detroit, Baltimore, and Houston, among others.

Advancement Prospects

A Field Merchandiser may move up the career ladder to be a marketer, a merchandising coordinator, a salesperson, a sales manager, etc. The possibilities are limitless.

Education and Training

There is no specific educational requirement for this job. A high school degree is sufficient in some positions. If the individual wants to advance his or her career, additional training may be useful. In many companies, this position is considered an entry level job. A background in business, marketing, or music merchandising may prove helpful.

Experience, Skills, and Personality Traits

It helps a Field Merchandiser to have some type of sales experience prior to taking the job, although it is not always necessary. Possessing a pleasant personality and establishing a good rapport with people makes the job easier. Being articulate is a plus. A knowledge of the music and/or record industry is essential.

Unions and Associations

Field Merchandisers may belong to the National Association of Recording Merchandisers (NARM). This organization represents people who work in recorded music. While regular membership is open to record shops, distributors, rack jobbers, etc., associate membership is open to others who work in the industry.

Tips for Entry

1. Try to obtain a job in a large record store in a major market for a short time. In this position, you will often have the opportunity to meet Field Merchandisers, salespeople, promotion people, etc. Get to know them and ask about the proper person to talk to about a job in the company.
2. If you do work in a record shop or department that deals directly with record company personnel, your boss (the store owner or manager) might be able to help you. Ask the management person whether they would make a call on your behalf to the company person they deal with from the record label to inquire about setting up an interview for you.
3. If there is an opportunity open to obtain an internship in the marketing or merchandising department of a record company, grab it.
4. Send your résumé and a short cover letter to the director of personnel of record labels.

INTERN

CAREER PROFILE

Duties: Perform tasks in specific departments of a record company while learning the business under the direction of management

Alternate Title(s): Trainee

Salary Range: $0 to $15,000 (college credit is often offered)

Employment Prospects: Fair

Advancement Prospects: Good

Best Geographical Locations for Position: New York City, Los Angeles, and Nashville

Prerequisites:

Education or Training—High school diploma, minimum; other requirements depend on position

Experience—No experience required

Special Skills and Personality Traits—Eagerness to learn; desire to enter record industry; brightness; aggressiveness; knowledge of music and/or recording business; other skills dependent on specific position

CAREER LADDER

```
┌─────────────────────────────┐
│   Staffer in Department     │
└─────────────────────────────┘

┌─────────────────────────────┐
│          Intern             │
└─────────────────────────────┘

┌─────────────────────────────┐
│  Clerical Position; Student │
└─────────────────────────────┘
```

Position Description

An Intern working in a record company will perform many of the same duties as other people on staff. The Intern works under the direction of a department head, manager, or director. One of the advantages of obtaining an Intern position in a specific department is that the individual has the opportunity to learn the ropes from experienced people.

There are Interns in almost every department of a record company. In certain companies, one becomes an Intern in a specific department. In others, the individual's internship involves working in various departments of the company. Duties will depend on the department to which one is assigned. For instance, an Intern working in the publicity/press relations department may address envelopes for invitations to press parties, make calls to check whether various people will be attending press parties, and help make arrangements for the press function. As he or she gains experience the Intern might begin writing press releases, attending meetings to work out publicity campaigns, calling the media to discuss a good story, etc.

An Intern working in the marketing department might work on consumer research surveys, tabulate data, and/or call radio stations and the trades with information about the number of records sold in a specific market. As time goes on, the Intern may learn to develop marketing campaigns, go out with field reps, or help the director create a sales incentive program.

The Intern usually begins by handling a lot of the tedious work that no one else wants to do. As he or she becomes more experienced, the individual learns how to perform more difficult tasks. Only the simplest of projects is performed without direct supervision.

Whether or not the Intern is getting paid a salary, he or she is expected to function like a paid employee. This includes arriving at work on time and not taking time off unnecessarily. It is to the Intern's advantage to learn as much as possible through instruction, asking questions, and just working in a hands-on situation.

The individual is responsible to the supervisor or department head to whom he or she is assigned. If the Intern is using the program as part of a college credit experience, a paper on the work experience might be expected.

A good Intern has a fairly good chance of becoming a member of the company staff after internship has concluded.

Salaries

Interns may work and not earn a penny. If they do earn a salary, it is usually quite small. An individual who has obtained an internship through a college might get college credit for his or her work. If the person is working as an Intern and is lucky enough to receive a salary, it probably would range from $5,000 to $15,000.

Employment Prospects

Despite the low pay or even lack of a salary, many people want to work as Interns. Individuals seeking internships can find them in almost every department of every major record company. Smaller labels tend to offer fewer opportunities.

Although many of these internship programs may be located directly through the record company, there are a number that can be obtained through schools and colleges in return for college credit and hands-on experience.

Advancement Prospects

One of the major reasons so many people try to become Interns in this industry is that it almost guarantees a job in the record company. After all the training and instruction given to the individual, the company most likely will want to keep the intern in its employ. The person must, of course, be a good employee and learn the trade. Interns can advance their careers very quickly in most departments. They may first be promoted to staffers, and then become coordinators, supervisors, or directors in various departments.

Education and Training

To become an Intern in a record company the only educational requirement may be a high school diploma. If an individual is currently in college, he or she may be able to have the school set up an internship program with a company for college credit. The person may be working toward a degree in any subject that can be made relevant to a semester or summer in a record company. Majors might include business, advertising, music, communications, journalism, the social sciences, pre-law, etc.

Experience, Skills, and Personality Traits

Interns do not really need any experience. What is required is the desire to enter the record industry and an eagerness to learn all about it.

Individuals who are chosen to be Interns generally are bright and aggressive and have pleasant personalities. A knowledge of music and/or the recording business is a plus.

Unions and Associations

Interns do not usually belong to any union while working in a record company. They may, however, join associations relevant to the department in which they are working.

Tips for Entry

1. If you are in college, the school may know of some Intern positions in record companies. If the school has a music business or merchandising degree or offers courses in one of these areas, they might have an internship program already established with a record company.
2. Contact record labels to see if they conduct intern programs or if you can develop an internship.
3. If you live in one of the music capitals, you might want to visit the record companies personally to see if you can get an internship in one of the departments.
4. Interns are often chosen from the ranks of clerical workers in the office. Talk to the head of the department with which you want to work.
5. Internship openings may be advertised in *Billboard,* or other trade publications.

CAMPUS REPRESENTATIVE

CAREER PROFILE

Duties: Promote record label's products on campus for students

Alternate Title(s): Student Representative; Label Representative; College Representative; Campus Rep

Salary Range: $1,700 to $6,500+

Employment Prospects: Poor

Advancement Prospects: Good

Best Geographical Location(s) for Position: Major campuses around the country

Prerequisites:

Education or Training—Working toward a bachelor's degree

Experience—Working with campus concerts; member of student activities or union board

Special Skills and Personality Traits—Enjoyment of music; ability to work without direct supervision; responsibility; knowledge of music and/or recording industry; desire to get into music business

CAREER LADDER

```
┌─────────────────────────────────┐
│     Record Company Intern;       │
│  Staff Member in Record Company  │
└─────────────────────────────────┘

┌─────────────────────────────────┐
│     Campus Representative         │
└─────────────────────────────────┘

┌─────────────────────────────────┐
│            Student               │
└─────────────────────────────────┘
```

Position Description

A Campus Representative is a student who is hired by a record label to promote that label's products on the campus. The student may work with or without pay. Products promoted may include the company's records, merchandising material, or concerts.

The student usually does his or her work in the campus bookstore, record shop, or student union. The individual will set up a display provided by the record company. There are a variety of displays or booths the Representative might set up. One might be a merchandising booth. This would be loaded with merchandising material related to the label's acts. It might include T-shirts, bumper stickers, pins, buttons, and posters. Another type of display might be a point-of-purchase exhibit. This might be set up in a record store or bookstore and contain the label's records, tapes, CDs, etc. These displays are often quite elaborate.

The student may be responsible for checking the inventory of the records in the campus shop or in the shop's surrounding area. When stock gets low, the Rep notifies the distribution department. Conversely, if stock is not moving, the Representative might let the label know, so they can do some extra promotion in the area.

There are many other functions the individual might perform. These all depend on the specific label. At times, the Campus Rep may interview other students to find out how they feel about the label's records, acts, etc. This information would be relayed back to the correct department of the company.

Another duty of the Campus Representative may be to sell concert tickets for the label's acts when they perform on campus or in the immediate area. He or she might also put up posters or flyers in the area to promote the show. The individual may line up interviews with specific media personalities for the acts when they come to the college for a concert. The Rep could even interview the act him- or herself for the campus paper, a local paper, or a radio station.

The job of Campus Representative is sought out by individuals aspiring to get into the recording industry. A position like this allows a person to pay dues while still in school. The position almost guarantees entry into a record company.

Salaries

Campus Representatives may work with or without payment. When they do earn a salary, it usually isn't very high. A salary for a student in this position runs between $1,700 and $6,500 or more a year.

The reason most people vie for this type of job is that it often leads to a position in the record company after graduation.

Those individuals who do not receive a salary will usually get free CDs, tapes, T-shirts, posters, and concert tickets.

Employment Prospects

The position of Campus Representative is not easy to obtain, but it's possible. The problem is that not all labels use the services of such individuals. Once one finds a company that has a college department, though, prospects get better.

A person may also try to create a position such as this with any record company, even if it does not currently have Campus Representatives.

Advancement Prospects

Advancement prospects are fairly good for those who are Campus Representatives. Once a person works for a label, he or she has an excellent chance of obtaining a job after graduation. The label feels that the person has proven him- or herself and is part of the company.

People who have worked in this job may advance to almost any position in the record company. It is important to remember that the hard part of getting a job in a record company is getting in. Advancement is easier to accomplish, especially if the individual is bright and aggressive and wants to move up the career ladder.

Education and Training

Campus Representatives, as a rule, are concurrently attending a college or university and earning a degree. There are many different fields an individual might be studying; majors helpful for a career in this field include communications, music, business, finance, journalism, advertising, marketing, or music merchandising.

Experience, Skills, and Personality Traits

Record companies usually choose bright, aggressive people to fill these positions. As many of these jobs pay either nothing or only a small salary, the person must really want to get into the record business. A knowledge of the industry and the music business, even if only basic, is helpful. An ability to work without direct day-to-day supervision is necessary.

Unions and Associations

Students interested in the music business often belong to the student union or activity board of the college, work on school concert committees, and might represent the school at the National Association for Campus Activities (NACA). This organization works to help all parties involved in booking concerts on campuses.

Tips for Entry

1. Campus Representative jobs may be obtained through the record company's college department. Call or write and inquire about these positions. If you do call, follow up with a letter and your résumé.
2. If the company does not have a college department, write to the public relations department, personnel director, or president of the company asking about Campus Representative positions.
3. In the event that a label does not use the services of a Campus Rep, don't let this stop you. Call, write, and/or set up an appointment for an interview to create a job for yourself. It sometimes works.

ARRANGER

CAREER PROFILE

Duties: Determine voice, instrument harmonic structure, rhythm, tempo, etc. of a song; arrange songs for musical artists

Alternate Title(s): Adapter; Transcriber; Transcripter

Salary Range: $18,000 to $200,000+

Employment Prospects: Fair

Advancement Prospects: Fair

Best Geographical Location(s) for Position: New York City, Los Angeles, and Nashville for recording positions or music positions; other cities for other positions

Prerequisites:

Education or Training—Training in music theory, orchestration, composition, harmony, etc., required

Experience—Writing music; playing one or more instruments; copying charts

Special Skills and Personality Traits—Ability to read music; good musical "ear"; proficiency as a musician

CAREER LADDER

```
┌─────────────────────────────────────┐
│   Arranger for More Prestigious Acts │
└─────────────────────────────────────┘

┌─────────────────────────────────────┐
│              Arranger                │
└─────────────────────────────────────┘

┌─────────────────────────────────────┐
│              Musician                │
└─────────────────────────────────────┘
```

Position Description

An Arranger's main function is to arrange the various parts of a musical composition. This is accomplished by determining voice, instrument, harmonic structure, rhythm, tempo, and tone balance to achieve the desired effect.

A talented Arranger can take a song and, through creative arranging, turn it into a hit tune. A good Arranger will be aware of current music trends.

One of the functions of the Arranger is to transcribe a musical composition for an orchestra, band, choral group, or individual artist in order to adapt the tune to a style different from the one in which it was originally written.

The Arranger may, in addition to working on new tunes, work on new arrangements of some old hits or classics. Arranged well, these tunes (sometimes called "cover records") often outsell the original versions.

The Arranger who works for a recording artist will work closely with the act and the producer. He or she will be on hand before recording even begins to hear how his or her arrangements sound in rehearsals. Last-minute changes are not uncommon.

In addition to working with recording artists, Arrangers may work with artists arranging music for concerts. Other Arrangers work with such services as Muzak, which arranges and orchestrates much of the music heard in dentists' offices, doctors' offices, and department stores.

Music Arrangers who work for music publishers are responsible for developing new and/or different ways to write and play music. The music Arranger might even go into television. In this type of job, the individual might be responsible for putting together music for skits or musical guests on comedy or variety shows.

As a music Arranger one might get into the motion picture business, scoring and/or arranging music for the title tune and the music throughout the film. The opportunities are endless once the Arranger gets in the door.

Most Arrangers work freelance. Therefore, the more jobs they get, the more they earn. Hours for this type of position are extremely irregular. Recording sessions do not usually go from nine to five (although they might run from 9:00 P.M. to 5:00 A.M.).

Staff Arrangers employed by music publishers have a more regular workday.

Arrangers are usually musicians first. Many Arrangers perform with an act and arrange much of the act's material. They might also write much of the music the act records.

Salaries

Arrangers who have not yet hit stardom and success may make so little arranging that they must work other jobs to make ends meet. Once an Arranger gets his or her foot in the door, he or she can expect to make from $18,000 to $25,000 yearly.

Others who have attained more success in arranging may earn up to $45,000 annually. Salaries depend, of course, on how much work one gets. Fees for Arrangers of movies, television, or recordings are usually paid to the scale set by the American Federation of Musicians (AFM).

In some instances, Arrangers are paid a royalty on each piece of music or record sold, in addition to their fee.

Top Arrangers may demand and receive fees well over scale payments, as well as royalties. These people can earn between $75,000 and $200,000 plus yearly.

Employment Prospects

It is not difficult for an Arranger to break into the profession on a small scale. Arranging tunes for groups who have not yet made it is a good example of the work one may do. Money for this type of employment is usually low. It does give the aspiring Arranger a start, though.

Arrangers have opportunities to work for the recording industry, TV, motion pictures, shows, music publishers, or print-music licensees. Other opportunities include working for individual artists or groups of artists, arranging materials for recordings or concerts.

Advancement Prospects

Advancement as an Arranger comes in working for more prestigious acts. As the individual's talent is recognized, he or she will have more opportunities. Composing and arranging one's own material for a Broadway show or a top group is probably a situation most Arrangers hope for.

Education and Training

No formal education is required to become an Arranger. Some type of training is usually necessary, however. This training can be garnered in a conservatory or college or through private study.

The Arranger must be knowledgeable and be able to implement all phases of orchestration. He or she must be educated (either formally or informally) in areas of composition, harmony, arranging, and theory.

Most people aspiring to be an Arranger have studied at least one instrument, privately, at conservatory or in college classes, or through a combination of both.

Experience, Skills, and Personality Traits

Arrangers begin as musicians. They need to play at least one instrument well. The ability to play more than one is a plus.

Quite frequently, Arrangers have tried composing on some level, either amateur or professional. The Arranger must have the ability to read and write music. Talented Arrangers—those who become most successful—are creative individuals who can develop their ideas into musical arrangements.

A good musical "ear" is a necessity, as are versatility and familiarity with current musical trends.

Unions and Associations

Arrangers may belong to the American Federation of Musicians (AFM). This is a bargaining union that sets payment scales for arrangements.

Arrangers may also be members of the National Academy of Recording Arts and Sciences (NARAS). This organization gives out the Grammy awards each year.

Many Arrangers additionally belong to the American Society of Music Arrangers.

Tips for Entry

1. As a member of the American Federation of Musicians (AFM), you will receive their publication, *International Musician*. This paper has a number of opportunities and openings listed in it.
2. Hanging around recording studios might help you learn about the profession and develop contacts.
3. Write as much music as you can. Write for up-and-coming groups, yourself, etc.
4. You might want to arrange some tunes and try sending them to publishers.
5. You might want to form your own group and arrange for them.
6. Any type of experience in this field helps. Consider donating your talent (writing and arranging) to a local production or school or college musical.

RECORD PRODUCER

CAREER PROFILE

Duties: Produce records for recording acts; help select songs to be recorded; supervise recording sessions

Alternate Title(s): None

Salary Range: $25,000 to $1,000,000+

Employment Prospects: Fair

Advancement Prospects: Fair

Best Geographical Locations for Position: New York City, Los Angeles, and Nashville offer the most opportunities

Prerequisites:

Education or Training—Music training useful; recording school helpful

Experience—Studio experience helpful

Special Skills and Personality Traits—Good musical "ear"; knowledge of music business; musical creativity; love of music; ability to select hit tunes

CAREER LADDER

```
┌─────────────────────────────────┐
│         Major Producer          │
└─────────────────────────────────┘

┌─────────────────────────────────┐
│         Record Producer         │
└─────────────────────────────────┘

┌─────────────────────────────────┐
│  Musician; Arranger; Talent Scout │
└─────────────────────────────────┘
```

Position Description

The Record Producer's main job is to produce a record or CD. If the individual is very successful and lucky, he or she will come out of a recording session with a hit album. There are a number of different responsibilities within this job classification, some creative and others business-oriented.

The Record Producer first helps a group or artist select the tune or tunes to be recorded. Once an act has rehearsed and is ready to record, the Producer will locate a suitable studio in which to record and arrange for studio time. The Producer may then choose an engineer, hire an arranger, and contact a contractor who will find background musicians and vocalists for the job.

The Producer will make sure that all those hired arrive at the studio on time. The individual is also in charge of making sure that those who have been hired are paid promptly.

During the recording session the Producer will work closely with the engineer. The person in this position advises the engineer of any specific sounds or feelings he or she is trying to create. The Producer will supervise the entire recording session, making decisions about when to do a take over, what takes to use, etc.

The Producer usually adds a personal touch to the recording. This is sometimes a special sound effect or the way a tune is ended. Often, it is a blend of instruments or vocal harmony. It is not unusual for a Producer to place his or her trademark on records.

It is up to the Producer to try to keep the recording within the budget agreed upon. Going over budget often costs the label or artist thousands of dollars extra.

After the recording has been made, the Producer is often in charge of "mixing" it to perfection. Although the Producer doesn't always do this job personally (special engineers or mixers are often hired), he or she always supervises this function. Success or failure in the mixing process can be what makes or breaks a record.

If the tunes recorded are for an album, the Producer may help choose the order in which they are placed on the LP. He or she will also help to choose the single from the album.

The Producer is involved with all aspects of the record. When the recording and mixing have been completed, the Producer's job does not end. Though the creative process is almost over, the Record Producer must attend to many of the business aspects of producing.

The Producer is responsible for clearing mechanical licenses, making sure that all copyrights are checked, and providing completed consent forms and releases from artists, engineers, photographers, etc., who worked on the project (if they are to receive credit on the record). At this point the Producer must also submit receipts and paid bills to the record company.

The Record Producer may work on staff for a label or be an independent Producer, freelancing his or her talent. The Producer on staff at a record company is responsible to the A & R department head. The Producer who freelances may be responsible directly to the label or to the artist. This depends on the arrangement made beforehand.

Salaries

Record Producers on staff at a record company may earn a salary plus royalties on records produced.

Producers who freelance as independents are paid a fee for their services by either the label or the artist. In addition, they are always paid royalties on works they produce. The amount of the royalties differ from Producer to Producer. Successful Record Producers can negotiate for larger royalty payments. This money is often advanced to the individual.

Staff Producers may earn $25,000 to $75,000 plus, depending on the label. Very successful independent Producers may earn up to $1,000,000 or more annually.

Employment Prospects

All records and CDs have Producers. They are sometimes produced by a member of the group recording them. At other times, records may be produced by the engineer. Records and CDs may also be produced by a staff Producer working at a record company or by an independent Producer who freelances his or her talent.

On some records there is more than one producer. For example, there may be an executive Producer and a coproducer. Another possibility is for an artist to produce part of the record in conjunction with the executive Producer.

There are quite a few possibilities for employment in this field. However, one must first get in the door.

Advancement Prospects

The way a Producer advances in the recording industry is by working on records that become hits. As a Producer's efforts yield records that hit the charts, he or she becomes more valuable.

When a Producer attains success, many different options open. The Producer may go to a position at a better label, demand more money, work with more prestigious acts, or freelance as an independent Producer.

Education and Training

There is no college requirement to become a Producer, although many Producers do possess college degrees. Music training is useful. Some people attend a sound recording school for a short period to learn more about the recording process.

This is another of the careers in which a knowledge of the music business is quite helpful, as it makes it easier to get into the industry. This knowledge can be obtained through formal education or by working in various jobs in the music business.

Experience, Skills, and Personality Traits

The most important qualification for a Record Producer is the ability to pick hit tunes. Every recording group or artist wants a number one song; that is how they gain recognition and make money. Record Producers who can, indeed, pick the tunes and have a proven track record doing so will be successful.

Record Producers must have a good musical "ear" and the ability to know what will sound good. Naturally, the Producer must love music, as he or she will be listening to it for a good part of the day.

The Record Producer must be able to hear raw talent and have the ability to foresee how it will sound if properly arranged and recorded.

Unions and Associations

Record Producers may be active or associate members in the National Academy of Recording Arts and Sciences (NARAS). This is the association that gives out the Grammy awards each year.

Record Producers might also belong to any of the music associations, including the Country Music Association (CMA) and the Gospel Music Association (GMA).

Tips for Entry

1. Try to find a job in a recording studio as a floor manager, engineer, studio set-up worker, receptionist, etc. to gain opportunity to watch Producers at work.
2. One way of getting into producing is to find a group with a song they want to record. Put some of your own money into the recording of a master you produce and try to sell both the record and the group to a major label.
3. As with many careers in the music business, you should check with some recording studios or even a major label to see if you can intern or apprentice in return for learning the skills.

RECORDING ENGINEER

CAREER PROFILE

Duties: Operate the sound board and other electrical equipment during the recording of music

Alternate Title(s): Mixer, Recording Assistant

Salary Range: $25,000 to $150,000+

Employment Prospects: Fair

Advancement Prospects: Fair

Best Geographical Locations for Position: New York City, Los Angeles, and Nashville

Prerequisites:

Education or Training—College or technical school background in sound engineering or recording technology; apprenticeship in studio in lieu of schooling

Experience—Experience in studio necessary

Special Skills and Personality Traits—Good musical "ear"; electronic and mechanical inclination; appreciation of music; stamina; ability to work under a great deal of pressure

CAREER LADDER

> **Top Freelance Recording Engineer; Engineer-Producer; Chief Engineer**

> **Recording Engineer**

> **Recording Assistant**

Position Description

It is the Recording Engineer's job to operate the sound board and all the other electrical equipment necessary when making a recording.

This is not, however, the only responsibility of the Recording Engineer. In a large studio there are usually a number of engineers working on a session. These include the Recording Assistant or Set-Up Worker, the main Recording Engineer, and possibly another Engineer who helps with the mixing after tracks have been recorded.

Prior to a recording session, one of the Engineers (usually the Recording Assistant) prepares the studio before the act arrives. As recording time is booked by the hour (and it is very expensive), no one wants to waste time waiting for the instruments to be set up or the mikes to be placed, turned on, and checked.

The Recording Engineer must discuss with the act and/or his or her producer how they want the end product to sound. It then becomes the Engineer's responsibility to make the record into the sound image the act wants.

He or she does this during the recording session by operating the sound board and the other electrical equipment and

electronic devices. The different audio controls used create different sounds.

After a track has been recorded, the Engineer plays it back. The Engineer, the act, and the producer then discuss the recording and any changes they would like. For example, the recording might need more base, more treble, a faster or slower tempo, etc. This information is noted for later use.

After all the tracks have been recorded, the Engineer will mix them down to either two or four tracks. Mixing is not just a skill, but an art the Recording Engineer must learn. He or she decides how loud or soft a specific track should be and then balances it correctly. The individual might feel that another instrument is needed. The Engineer would talk over this suggestion with the producer to get his or her opinion. If the producer agrees, another track with the instrument is recorded. This new track is then mixed down with the others to become, eventually, the master tape.

Through the entire recording process the Recording Engineer works closely with the producer and the act. He or she discusses the sound with these individuals and tries to put their ideas into the final product.

In certain studios, the Recording Engineer must not only know how to work the equipment, but also how to repair it when it breaks down. As a rule, many Recording Engineers know how to take apart and put together most of the equipment they work with.

Engineers keep up with the latest electronic and recording technology. They are constantly striving to improve their talent in the engineering process.

Recording Engineers work long, irregular hours. Many Engineers begin work at 9 or 10 P.M. and work until the next morning with one act. In the afternoon, they often have to return to the studio with another client. The job requires a lot of stamina.

Recording Engineers must have the ability to work with people with whose musical ideas they disagree. The Recording Engineer is usually responsible directly to the producer and act or to the chief Engineer in the studio.

Recording Engineers can be on staff at a record company or a recording studio. They can also work by the hour. Better-known Recording Engineers work freelance. Their business is obtained through word-of-mouth.

Salaries

Salaries vary for Recording Engineers according to the situation for which they have been hired. Recording Engineers who are just beginning (called Recording Assistants or Studio Set-Up Workers) usually make close to the minimum wage.

As the Recording Engineer gains experience he or she will be better compensated. A lot depends on whether the individual is on staff, paid by the number of hours per week that he or she works, or a freelance Engineer.

Salaries for those individuals who are on staff range from $25,000 to $50,000 per year. Recording Engineers who are well-known and freelance often make up to $75,000 yearly. In addition to being paid a fee by the act or record company he or she is working with, the individual is also usually paid a percentage of the monies given to the recording studio for renting the studio time. This percentage varies.

Top Recording Engineers who work with popular recording acts can make $150,000 plus annually.

Employment Prospects

As with most jobs in the recording industry, things are very competitive. However, if an individual doesn't mind starting at the bottom, he or she may eventually get a job in a recording studio. A person with talent, personality, patience, and perseverance may obtain a position as a Recording Engineer, or at least as an assistant.

Advancement Prospects

It is often necessary to knock on a lot of doors, make a great number of calls, and mail many résumés before you get your foot in the door. Once this is done, however, a person who works hard and has a lot of talent and a little bit of luck will advance his or her career.

Engineers select different roads for advancement. One is to become a chief Engineer. This individual is in charge of the entire studio and supervises all recordings that take place in that studio.

Another method of advancement is for the individual to become a top freelance Recording Engineer. Top recording groups, record companies, and producers will usually seek such a person out to work with them on sessions.

Another method of advancement selected by Engineers is to become an engineer-producer. This individual will produce records as well as engineer them.

Education and Training

There are a variety of ways to train for a position as a Recording Engineer: through college courses in sound engineering, for example, or in a technical or training school course in sound engineering or recording technology.

A third method of training for this position is to work as an apprentice in a recording studio. Many times, the individual in this position does not get paid or is paid a minimal salary. He or she learns the business from the bottom up. By being in this environment and asking questions, he or she will pick up the major engineering methods. Eventually, he or she will become a recording assistant and learn even more.

Experience, Skills, and Personality Traits

As noted above, experience in a studio is one method to becoming a Recording Engineer. In addition, the Engineer must have a good musical "ear" to be effective at his or her job.

The ability to work under a great deal of pressure is important to the Recording Engineer. He or she might have to work with three or four different recording acts a day. Each act usually is set on how the record should sound. The Engineer must be able to communicate and translate their verbal ideas into tape.

Unions and Associations

Recording Engineers may be active members of the National Academy of Recording Arts and Sciences (NARAS). This is the association that gives out the Grammy awards each year.

Depending on the type of music the individual works with, he or she might be a member of the Country Music Association (CMA) or the Gospel Music Association (GMA). These associations work to promote their specific variety of music.

Recording Engineers may represent a recording studio as a member of the Society of Professional Audio Recording Studios (SPARS).

Tips for Entry

1. If you can afford to, you might consider offering your services free to a recording studio in exchange for learning the business. When they feel you know enough, they might put you on salary.
2. Check to see what organizations are offering in the way of seminars for Recording Engineers. These seminars might help you make important contacts as well as learn more about the industry.
3. Check with various record companies (the larger ones) to see if they offer an internship program in the recording engineering department. It isn't uncommon for the record company to hire an intern after the internship ends.
4. Look for minority training programs sponsored by record labels.

RECORDING STUDIO SET-UP WORKER

CAREER PROFILE

Duties: Arrange sound recording equipment in studio before recording begins

Alternate Title(s): Recording Assistant; Assistant Engineer

Salary Range: $18,000 to $25,000+

Employment Prospects: Fair

Advancement Prospects: Fair

Best Geographical Location(s) for Position: New York City, Los Angeles, and Nashville offer the most opportunities

Prerequisites:

Education or Training—Technical school background in sound recording may be helpful, but not required; on-the-job training

Experience—Prior work with electrical equipment useful

Special Skills and Personality Traits—Knowledgeable in electronics; dependable; mechanically inclined; appreciative of music; able to get along with people

CAREER LADDER

```
┌─────────────────────────────────────┐
│             Engineer                 │
└─────────────────────────────────────┘

┌─────────────────────────────────────┐
│   Recording Studio Set-Up Worker     │
└─────────────────────────────────────┘

┌─────────────────────────────────────┐
│      Clerk in Recording Studio       │
└─────────────────────────────────────┘
```

Position Description

Recording Studio Set-Up Workers do as the name implies—they set up equipment. Individuals employed in this type of position have the responsibility of physically setting up the recording studio before a recording session takes place.

As recording time is usually very expensive, companies and/or individuals renting the studio do not want to waste their own time setting up their instruments, mikes, etc. The Studio Set-Up Worker handles this task.

Once a block of time is booked by an act, the Recording Studio Set-Up Worker goes to work. He or she receives work orders indicating which instruments will be used, where they will be placed, how many mikes will be needed, etc.

Using this work order as a guide, the Set-Up Worker begins. In addition to setting up the instruments and mikes, the individual must position other pieces of equipment, such as consoles, isolation booths, tape machines, amps, music stands, and chairs.

Some of this equipment is moved by hand. The rest is loaded onto dollies and handtrucks. Each piece must be in the correct position before the recording session begins.

The Studio Set-Up Worker helps connect all the equipment to the correct electrical lines, following instructions. If there is a breakdown of any particular piece of equipment during the session, the Studio Set-Up Worker will replace it or fix it as quickly as possible. If there is a short in any of the electrical lines, the Set-Up Worker may help repair the problem.

After the recording session is completed, the Set-Up Worker dismantles all the equipment, instruments, and mikes and puts them in their proper places. If anything has broken or is not in good working order, he or she either fixes it or reports it as broken so that it can be repaired or replaced.

In some studios the Set-Up Worker is also responsible for maintaining the tape library. In this job, the Set-Up Worker needs to be totally organized. A lost tape can create a real problem for a studio.

The Studio Set-Up Worker may assist the engineer during a recording. He or she is usually responsible to that individual.

Salaries

Salaries for Recording Studio Set-Up Workers are considerably lower than those of engineers. The Set-Up Worker often earns only a minimum salary. Beginning Set-Up Workers may only earn around $18,000 yearly. With added experience, the individual may earn up to $25,000 annually. Salaries do not usually go much over this figure.

Employment Prospects

A Studio Set-Up Worker may find it easier to obtain a job in a studio than an engineer would. In some small studios, Set-Up Worker positions are considered entry level. In others, individuals must begin as clerks, receptionists, or gofers.

Advancement Prospects

If a Recording Studio Set-Up Worker watches what is going on in the studio and asks questions, he or she has a reasonable chance for promotion to an assistant engineer or engineer. The main thing that is necessary for advancement is skill.

Education and Training

People spend a great deal of money to rent recording time and do not always want to use their time and money to train an aspiring engineer. Many individuals in the industry feel that because a certain degree of training and skill are required, the person who wants to get into engineering should attend a technical school or college in order to learn the basics of the craft.

There are others who feel that on-the-job training is the best way to learn. A Studio Set-Up Worker with virtually no experience in recording may obtain a job in a studio and by watching and asking questions receive the same, if not better, training.

Experience, Skills, and Personality Traits

Many Studio Set-Up Workers first walk into a studio and obtain jobs as receptionists, secretaries, gofers, etc. After

a short time, if someone leaves and a position opens, the person who is in the right place at the right time gets the job. Others enter the engineering field as Studio Set-Up Workers.

Set-Up Workers do need to know the basics of electronics and to be mechanically inclined. As they are around music on a constant basis, an appreciation of music helps. Dependability and getting along well with those who book studio time can help the Studio Set-Up Worker advance his or her career.

Unions and Associations

Recording Studio Set-Up Workers do not usually belong to any union or specific trade association at this point in their career.

Tips for Entry

1. Check different studios to see if the opportunity to learn the business can be gotten in exchange for working free in the studio. After you have learned enough, they may put you on salary.
2. Some of the larger recording companies offer internship programs in recording. If you are a beginner, they'll start you as a Set-Up Worker, and you can move up the career ladder from there.
3. Certain recording associations and organizations give seminars on different facets of the recording business. Check this out.
4. Positions may be located in the classified section of newspapers in areas hosting recording studios. Look under headings such as "Studio Set Up Worker," "Recording Studio Set-Up Worker," or "Recording."
5. Knock on the door of as many recording studios as you can. Be persistent.

ORCHESTRATOR

CAREER PROFILE

Duties: Transpose music from one instrument or voice to another in order to accommodate a particular musician or group; write scores for an orchestra, band, choral group, individual instrumentalist, or vocalist

Alternate Title(s): None

Salary Range: Earnings depend on how much orchestrating is done; it is impossible to estimate earnings

Employment Prospects: Fair

Advancement Prospects: Fair

Best Geographical Location(s) for Position: New York City, Los Angeles, Boston, and other cultural and/or metropolitan areas

Prerequisites:

Education or Training—Training in music theory and notation

Experience—Experience copying music and/or arranging

Special Skills and Personality Traits—Knowledge of music theory; ability to transpose music; accuracy; reliability; neatness; understanding of music

CAREER LADDER

```
┌─────────────────────────────────┐
│   Orchestrator with Many Clients │
└─────────────────────────────────┘

┌─────────────────────────────────┐
│          Orchestrator            │
└─────────────────────────────────┘

┌─────────────────────────────────┐
│     Musician and/or Composer     │
└─────────────────────────────────┘
```

Position Description

An Orchestrator's prime function is to write the scores for an orchestra, band, choral group, individual instrumentalist, or vocalist. In this position, the person transposes the music from one instrument or voice to another to accommodate a particular musician or musical group. For example, an Orchestrator might be asked to transpose a score for a song into a key more suited to a vocalist.

When accomplishing this function, the individual does not usually alter the musical quality, harmony, or rhythm. He or she just scores the composition so that it is consistent with the instrumental and vocal capabilities of the artists. This is sometimes done with special computer software.

Although many Orchestrators work with the compositions of composers and arrangers, sometimes the individual is asked to work as the arranger. For instance, the Orchestrator may be asked to transcribe a composition while adapting it to another style of music. An example is when an individual changes the style of a pop tune to an "easy listening" instrumental version. This type of work often requires additional knowledge or training.

The Orchestrator may also function in the capacity of a copyist, transcribing musical parts onto staff or manuscript paper from a score written by an arranger. The individual performing as an Orchestrator can work full-time or part-time. He or she may be responsible for orchestrating, arranging, and/or copying as part of a job.

Salaries

Salaries for Orchestrators will vary depending on how much work they do and under what conditions. Orchestrators belonging to the American Federation of Musicians (AFM) will be paid minimum rates according to fees set by the union. In certain situations, the individual may be paid by the hour. These situations include work where the Orchestrator must do adjustments, alterations, additions, or takedowns of the score. Time rates are also used when page rates are not practical.

Individuals are urged to contact the AFM for specific rates.

Rates will vary for work done by the page depending on the type of arrangement orchestrated and what needs to be done.

Employment Prospects

Employment prospects are fair for Orchestrators. They may work for orchestras, bands, choral groups, individual instrumentalists, or vocalists. Individuals may work for, with, or as arrangers in the recording field. They may also do orchestration for television, films, and theater.

Advancement Prospects

Advancement for an Orchestrator may occur when the individual becomes so well known that he or she is constantly busy. People in this job may become successful composers and musicians in their own right. They may also go on to work in the music publishing field as music editors.

Education and Training

As in many music jobs, there is no formal education required in order to become an Orchestrator. The individual must know how to write scores for orchestras, bands, choral groups, etc., and/or how to transpose them from one instrument to another. This knowledge might be acquired at a conservatory, college, or university, or through private study. The skills needed might also be self-taught.

Experience, Skills, and Personality Traits

As an Orchestrator, an individual must have a thorough knowledge of music theory. He or she needs the ability to transpose music. The person must be accurate and have neat handwriting. As noted previously, Orchestrators may perform their job with the help of computers and special software; computer literacy is therefore becoming necessary. Reliability is a must for success in this job. Additionally, the Orchestrator must have a good understanding of music.

Unions and Associations

Orchestrators may belong to the American Federation of Musicians (AFM). This union sets the minimum rate scale for Orchestrators.

Tips for Entry

1. These positions are often advertised in the classified section of newspapers in major cultural centers.
2. Put up your business card or a flyer in music and instrument repair stores.
3. Talk to the orchestra(s) in your area to see if they have part- or full-time work.
4. If you are just beginning, volunteer to do some work for a local theater putting on a musical. It will give you invaluable experience and will add to your résumé.
5. Join the American Federation of Musicians.

COPYIST

CAREER PROFILE

Duties: Transcribe musical parts onto staff paper from scores

Alternate Title(s): None

Salary Range: It is impossible to estimate salary; earnings vary depending on the amount of copying done

Employment Prospects: Good

Advancement Prospects: Fair

Best Geographical Location(s) for Position: Major cultural and music centers for most jobs; other cities may also have positions

Prerequisites:

Education or Training—Training in music notation and theory

Experience—Music background useful; writing music helpful

Special Skills and Personality Traits—Knowledge of music notation; knowledge of music theory; neatness; accuracy; computer skills

CAREER LADDER

```
┌─────────────────────────────────────┐
│  Copyist with Many Clients; Successful │
│  Arranger, Composer, or Orchestrator   │
└─────────────────────────────────────┘

┌─────────────────────────────────────┐
│              Copyist                  │
└─────────────────────────────────────┘

┌─────────────────────────────────────┐
│  Musician, Composer, or Orchestrator  │
└─────────────────────────────────────┘
```

Position Description

A music Copyist transcribes musical parts onto staff or manuscript paper from a score. This score may have been done by an arranger, composer, or orchestrator. The Copyist reproduces the various parts of instruments and/or voices.

The individual utilizes his or her knowledge of music notation and experience and background in music to accomplish this task. The function of the Copyist is to make it easier for the musician or vocalist to play or sing his or her part. It is important for the person copying the music to do so neatly and accurately. If not, it will be extremely difficult for the artist to perform properly. In many cases Copyists now utilize computer hardware and software to do this job.

At certain times, the individual will be asked to copy a corrected or changed score. At other times, the individual may copy various parts for different instruments. A very talented individual may be asked to write the music from a record or tape onto paper without seeing a copy of the music. This is a very difficult feat and requires a thorough knowledge of music theory, notations, harmony, composition, and orchestration.

The music Copyist may work full-time, either independently or for a music publisher, or part-time. As a music Copyist, the person is responsible to the individual or organization using his or her services. If that person or organization feels that the work is inaccurate, messy or illegible, or is not done on schedule, the music Copyist will not be hired again. As the amount of music work in any given area is limited, the word will get around and the individual will not be able to obtain more copying work.

Salaries

The American Federation of Musicians (AFM) sets minimum fees and wages for music Copyists. There are different fees depending on the type of work done.

Copyists are usually paid by the page copied in relation to the score page. They are usually remunerated per page and a half produced. Rates vary depending on the parts copied.

In certain situations, the Copyist may be paid by the hour. Individuals are urged to contact the AFM for current rates.

Employment Prospects

Employment prospects are good for music Copyists. There are opportunities for individuals who can perform this function in major music and cultural centers as well as in smaller cities. There are many groups, writers, composers, arrangers, and orchestrators who require this service.

Many Copyists do the job part-time while pursuing a career as a musician, singer, composer, etc. There are also many students who perform copying services while in school.

Advancement Prospects

Copyists may advance their careers by becoming well-known arrangers, composers, orchestrators, singers, etc. There are Copyists who go on to become music editors for music publishing companies.

Many individuals prefer to stay in copying and develop a clientele.

Education and Training

There is no formal educational requirement to become a Copyist. Individuals must know how to transcribe musical parts onto manuscript paper. They must have a knowledge of music notation, music theory, etc. This knowledge may be obtained in high school or college or at private music lessons. It might also be a self-taught skill.

Experience, Skills, and Personality Traits

As noted above, the Copyist must know how to transcribe music parts onto manuscript paper. The person must know and understand music notations and should be cognizant of music theory. The individual must write neatly and be accurate. Copyists who perform their job with the help of computers and special software will need computer skills.

Many Copyists are musicians and aspiring songwriters and arrangers. The person performing this function usually has a great interest in music.

Unions and Associations

Copyists may belong to the American Federation of Musicians (AFM) and/or the American Society of Music Copyists.

Tips for Entry

1. You may wish to advertise your skill in a newspaper or entertainment magazine in your area.
2. Put up signs in the music stores, record shops, and showcase clubs in your area.
3. Occasionally there are positions requiring the skill advertised in the help wanted sections of newspapers.
4. You may consider talking to local acts and groups and letting them know you provide this service. They might be interested.
5. Join the American Federation of Musicians. It is a valuable resource to your career.

WEBMASTER

CAREER PROFILE

Duties: Design website for record labels; create content for site; manage and maintain site

Alternate Title(s): Website Administrator

Salary Range: $28,000 to $150,000+

Employment Prospects: Good

Advancement Prospects: Good

Best Geographical Location(s) for Position: Major label headquarters are in cities such as New York, Los Angeles, and Nashville; other areas throughout the country hosting record labels will offer additional opportunities

Prerequisites:

Education or Training—Education and training requirements vary

Experience—Experience designing, creating, and maintaining websites necessary

Special Skills and Personality Traits—Creative; computer skills; Internet savvy; knowledge of HTML and other programming languages; graphic and layout skills; understanding of music industry

CAREER LADDER

```
┌─────────────────────────────────────┐
│  Webmaster for Large, Prestigious    │
│  Record Label or Music-Oriented      │
│  Company; Webmaster Consultant       │
└─────────────────────────────────────┘

┌─────────────────────────────────────┐
│  Webmaster, Record Label             │
└─────────────────────────────────────┘

┌─────────────────────────────────────┐
│  Webmaster in Other Industry         │
└─────────────────────────────────────┘
```

Position Description

Most companies today have a presence on the World Wide Web. Record labels are no exception. Websites are an important part of the way labels promote themselves and their artists.

The individual in charge of creating and putting together the website is called the Webmaster. The record label Webmaster has many responsibilities. Depending on the situation, he or she may work alone or may assign tasks to assistants, content producers, copywriters, graphic artists, etc.

One of the first things the Webmaster must do is find a host for the site. In order for a label (or any company) to have a website, they must rent a space or location on the Web. This may be done by obtaining a host. The label pays the host for the right to place their site on-line on the host's space. In some instances, the label and the host are one and the same.

In order for individuals to be able to locate the record label's website, it must have a Web address. This is called the domain name. The Webmaster works with the label management to develop a Web address that people can remember and that is available. Most often the Web address is the label's name.

The Webmaster's duties depend to a great extent on the size and structure of the label, the importance it puts on the website, and whether or not the website has already been set up.

The Webmaster is expected to discuss the direction the label wants the website to take and the goals of the website. Does the management just want a website to maintain a Web presence? Do they want people to be able to buy products while on-line? Will there be separate sites for each recording artist? Should website visitors be able to listen to snipets of songs or watch music videos on-line? Does the label want to sell advertising to other companies to increase revenue? Once the Webmaster understands what label management wants, he or she can get to work.

The Webmaster is responsible for developing and creating the label's website on the World Wide Web. He or she must design the site so that it is exciting and easy to use. The Webmaster must be sure that each webpage on the site opens easily and quickly. If they do not, people will often leave the site and surf to another location.

The Webmaster will develop the site, adding photos of the label's artists, and products; animations or other graphics; and perhaps sound. In creating the site, the Webmaster may manipulate images to the proper size and format. If this is not done correctly, an image may either be too large, slowing down the loading of a webpage, or too small, making it difficult to see clearly.

The Webmaster develops the site's search function so that people can search for something specific on the site. He or she may program pop-up windows, features, shopping carts, secure payment systems, the ability to hear artists' songs or see their videos, and a variety of other functions. The Webmaster may also build in technology so the label knows how long people stay on a specific webpage, which part of the site is most popular, how many hits the site gets, etc. Developing and designing the website is just one part of the job of the Webmaster. He or she is additionally responsible for the continued management and maintenance of the site. In order to keep a website fresh and timely, the Webmaster may change the homepage and update other parts of the site. Sometimes the site content changes daily. The Webmaster must make changes and remove out-of-date content.

Websites are created in special languages so they can be displayed on the Internet. Text, for example, is converted into a language called HTML, or Hypertext Markup Language. Other languages may be used as well. The Webmaster must know how to format the special languages. Part of the job of the Webmaster is to monitor the site on a continuing basis. Every time new content or a link is added, the individual or one of his or her assistants must be sure everything on the site is working and all links are accurate.

The record label Webmaster is expected to make sure that the site is user-friendly. When there are problems with the site, the individual is responsible for handling them. This may include responding to inquiries from browsers having problems with the site.

Salaries

Earnings for Webmasters working for record labels may vary from approximately $28,000 to $150,000 or more annually. Variables include the geographic location, size, and prestige of the label and the specific site, as well as the responsibilities, experience, and reputation of the individual.

Webmasters who have a proven track record for developing creative sites that attract attention will earn the highest salaries.

It should be noted that some smaller labels hire consultants to handle their websites. These individuals may earn between $50 and $200 or more per hour.

Employment Prospects

Employment prospects for Webmasters aspiring to work at record labels are good. Depending on experience, individuals may work for major labels or may find employment at smaller independent labels. As noted, in some cases, individuals may work on a consulting basis.

Advancement Prospects

Webmasters who build websites that consistently attract visitors will have no trouble climbing the career ladder. Webmasters working for record labels may advance their careers in a number of ways. The most common method is locating similar positions with larger or more prestigious labels. This results in increased responsibilities and earnings. Some Webmasters decide to strike out on their own and start a consulting firm.

Education and Training

Education and training requirements vary for Webmasters working at record labels. Many Webmasters are self-taught. Some have taken classes. Others have college backgrounds or degrees in computers, programming, languages, graphics, web authoring, and the Internet.

However it is learned, Webmasters must know HTML. It is also necessary to know other programming languages, such as Cold Fusion, PERL, and Active Server Pages. Knowing how to integrate databases is a plus.

It is essential that Webmasters update their skills by self-study and/or classes, seminars, and workshops to keep up with changes in technology.

Experience, Skills, and Personality Traits

Experience requirements depend, to a great extent, on the size and prestige of the label. Smaller independent labels just starting a website may not require Webmasters with a great deal of experience as long as they can prove that they can do an effective job. Larger, more prestigious labels will generally want their Webmasters to have a proven track record and experience.

Webmasters need excellent communications skills, both verbal and written. Creativity is essential. A knowledge of the music industry is helpful.

Individuals must have a total competence with web dynamics, HTML authorship, and other programming languages. While some graphics work is outsourced or done by graphic designers within the company, graphic talent is necessary.

Unions and Associations

Individuals interested in learning more about careers in the field may obtain additional information by contacting the Internet Professionals Association (IPA) and the National Association of Webmasters (NAW).

Tips for Entry

1. Look for internships at record labels. These will give you on-the-job training, experience, and the opportunity to make important contacts. Contact labels to see what they offer or talk to your college adviser.

2. Positions may be located in the classified section of newspapers. Look under heading such as "Webmaster," "Record Label," "Music Industry," "Web Careers," etc. Also look for ads under specific record label names.

3. Many labels also advertise openings on their websites. You might want to check them out.

4. Look for a job on-line. Start with the more popular job sites, such as www.hotjobs.com and www.monster.com, and go from there.

5. Get experience putting together websites for not-for-profit organizations or civic groups. Don't forget to add your name as the creator and Webmaster.

6. Send your résumé and a short cover letter to record labels at which you are interested in working. You can never tell when an opening exists.

7. Don't forget to read trade publications. *Billboard* often has advertisements for labels with openings in this area.

WEBSITE MARKETING MANAGER

CAREER PROFILE

Duties: Develop and implement marketing plans and campaigns for record label's website; handle day-to-day marketing functions; plan and implement special events; oversee advertising and public relations program

Alternate Title(s): Website Marketing Director

Salary Range: $24,000 to $55,000+

Employment Prospects: Good

Advancement Prospects: Fair

Best Geographical Location(s) for Position: New York City, Nashville, Los Angeles, and other large cities for major labels; other areas hosting record labels will provide additional opportunities

Prerequisites:

Education or Training—College degree

Experience—Marketing, merchandising, publicity, public relations, advertising, and Internet experience necessary

Special Skills and Personality Traits—Creativity; good verbal and written communications skills; Internet savvy; understanding of music industry

CAREER LADDER

```
┌─────────────────────────────────────────┐
│   Website Marketing Manager for Large,   │
│      Prestigious Record Label;           │
│      Marketing Director at Label;        │
│   Marketing Director in Other Industry   │
└─────────────────────────────────────────┘

┌─────────────────────────────────────────┐
│         Website Marketing Manager,       │
│              Record Label                │
└─────────────────────────────────────────┘

┌─────────────────────────────────────────┐
│   Assistant Website Marketing Manager    │
│    or Assistant Marketing Manager        │
│           in Other Industry              │
└─────────────────────────────────────────┘
```

Position Description

The music industry is very competitive. Record labels, like most other businesses today, need to find as many ways as possible to market their company and their products. As a result most record labels are now utilizing the Internet as a marketing tool.

A record label's website can be a very effective way to promote the label as well as the label's artists. The end result of a successfully marketed website can be thousands, if not millions, of products sold. This means money in the pocket of the label and the recording artist.

The music industry has changed from the day when the only way to get exposure for a new tune was to listen to the radio. While radio is still a huge way to push a new album, many people also listen to the "radio" via the web. Others watch music television. Marketed correctly, fans will use the site to get information on their favorite artists, new CDs, and appearances.

With on-line buying becoming more and more popular, label websites can additionally generate income by selling the label's product's directly with no middleman. Additional income is often earned through selling commercial space to other complimentary companies on the site.

There are literally thousands of websites on the Internet. Some are companies who had well-known names and reputations prior to their Internet presence. Others are less well known. With so many sites available, how does any website attract visitors? As in traditional business, a website must market its presence.

The Website Marketing Manager for a record label has an important job. He or she is responsible for finding ways to market the site, the label, and its artists to current and potential fans.

Responsibilities may vary, depending on the size and structure of the label and its website. At some labels, a marketing director and one or two assistants handle all the marketing functions, including the website. Increasingly, however, record labels are hiring Website Marketing Managers whose sole job is marketing the label's website. The individual in this position can mean the success or failure of the site.

The Website Marketing Manager is responsible for developing the concepts and campaigns that will determine how the site will be marketed. The individual is expected to determine the most effective techniques and programs to market the site and its contents. To do this, the individual will work closely with the label's marketing director.

As part of this job, the Marketing Manager must plan and coordinate the site's marketing goals and objectives. How will people know the website is on-line? How will they know its Web address? Who will the site be marketed toward? Who is the label trying to attract? Marketing a website is slightly different than marketing a traditional business. Visitors to on-line sites can come from virtually anywhere in the world.

Additionally, many record labels have mini-sites within the main site for each of the label's artists. In these cases, the Marketing Manager may be responsible for marketing each mini-site as well.

It is essential that the Marketing Manager find ways to include the Web address in as many places as possible. This includes all CDs, artist promo material, advertising, etc. The more people hear a Web address, the more likely they are to remember it and visit to see what's happening on the site. The label's Web address must be added to all television commercials, print advertisements, billboards, stationery, etc. This helps keep the name and address of the label in the public eye.

The Marketing Manager is often expected to do research to obtain information about people visiting the site. He or she may prepare questionnaires or surveys to be placed on the site. In order to entice people to answer questionnaires, the website may offer a gift or entry into a sweepstakes.

Often Website Marketing Managers advertise their site on other websites via banner ads. An individual need only click on the banner ad to be taken to the site of the advertiser. In many instances, the label Website Marketing Manager partners with another company to obtain more exposure. For example, a record label may partner with record store chains, radio stations, etc.

Record label Website Marketing Managers are expected to develop innovative ideas to try to attract new fans and visitors to the site. In many situations, the Website Marketing Manager may work with the label's promotion department to develop contests, sweepstakes, and other promotions which can be entered on-line. People will then have an incentive to go to the label website. The more people who visit the website, the more exposure for the label's artists, which results in more sales.

Once people log on to a label's website to enter contests, the hope is they will return to the site to browse, read about an artist, find out about appearances, or buy products. To accomplish this, many Marketing Managers run sweepstakes that individuals can enter daily. This means visitors have an incentive to visit the label's website daily and hopefully be attracted to something of interest on the site.

Another reason Website Marketing Managers use sweepstakes is to help build mailing lists. When people enter sweepstakes, they usually provide their name, address, phone number, age and e-mail address. Additional information may be gathered as well, which may be helpful in targeting specific visitors to the site and finding ways to sell CDs, T-shirts, photographs, videos, tickets to shows, etc.

Marketing Managers also use sweepstakes to build lists for e-mail newsletters. These newsletters are useful for informing fans about new CDs, videos, artist events, and appearances. Sometimes these lists are also used when new videos are being shown on music television.

Many label Website Marketing Managers create on-line fan clubs and chat rooms. The idea is to keep a constant interest in the label's artists.

The Marketing Manager who can come up with innovative and creative ideas might get the attention of media journalists or others doing stories on interesting websites. Depending on which media show a story appears, the exposure can lead to thousands of website hits.

Depending on the size and structure of the label, the Website Marketing Manager may work with the label's main marketing, advertising, public relations or promotion department. In some situations, the Website Marketing Manager may also be responsible for handling the public relations and advertising functions of the website as well.

Salaries

Annual earnings for record label Website Marketing Managers can range from approximately $24,000 to $55,000 or more. Variables affecting earnings include the geographic location, size, and prestige of the specific label and its website, as well as the experience and responsibilities of the individual.

Employment Prospects

Employment prospects for this position are good. In addition to major labels located in music capitals such as New York, Los Angeles, and Nashville, there are many independent labels located throughout the country. Websites give independent labels, or "indies" as they are often referred to, an opportunity to gain local and global exposure for their artists.

Advancement Prospects

Record label Website Marketing Managers have a number of options for career advancement. Some individuals get experience, prove themselves, and move on to similar positions at larger or more prestigious labels. This results in increased responsibilities and earnings.

Other individuals may climb the career ladder by moving into positions as label marketing directors. Still other individuals strike out on their own to start a marketing firm.

Education and Training

Generally larger, more prestigious, or well-known labels will require their Website Marketing Managers to hold a minimum of a four-year college degree. Good choices for majors include public relations, advertising, business, journalism, marketing, liberal arts, English, communications, and business. While smaller, lesser-known labels may prefer a college degree, it might not be a requirement.

Courses and seminars in marketing, public relations, publicity, promotion, the music industry, and Web marketing are also helpful.

Experience, Skills, and Personality Traits

Record label Website Marketing Managers must be Web savvy. Communications skills, both written and verbal, are essential to success in this field. Individuals should be creative, innovative, ambitious, articulate, and highly motivated. Marketing Managers also need the ability to handle many details and projects at one time without getting flustered and stressed.

A knowledge of publicity, promotion, public relations, and advertising as well as research techniques is also necessary.

Unions and Associations

Record label Website Marketing Managers may belong to a number of trade associations providing support and guidance. These include the American Marketing Association (AMA), the Marketing Research Association (MRA), and the Public Relations Society of America (PRSA). Individuals might also belong to the National Academy of Recording Arts and Sciences (NARAS) or genre-specific associations, such as the Country Music Association (CMA) or the Gospel Music Association (GMA).

Tips for Entry

1. Positions may be advertised in the classified section of newspapers. Look under headings including "Marketing," "Marketing Manager," "Website Marketing," "Record Label Marketing," "Recording Industry," and "Record Label Marketing Manager."
2. Send your résumé and a cover letter to record labels at which you are interested in working. Ask that your résumé be kept on file.
3. Look for jobs on-line. Check out popular sites, such as www.hotjobs.com and www.monster.com, to get started. Go from there.
4. Take seminars and courses in marketing, promotion, public relations, publicity, and Web marketing. These will give you an edge over other applicants as well as help you hone your skills and make valuable contacts.
5. Many labels advertise openings on their websites. Check them out.

WEBSITE CONTENT PRODUCER

CAREER PROFILE

Duties: Develop and create content for record label website; research and write articles for website

Alternate Title(s): Website Content Editor

Salary Range: $28,000 to $75,000

Employment Prospects: Fair

Advancement Prospects: Good

Best Geographical Location(s) for Position: Music capitals such as New York City, Los Angeles, and Nashville for major record labels; other areas hosting record companies

Prerequisites:

Education or Training—College degree required

Experience—Writing and editing experience necessary

Special Skills and Personality Traits—Good command of the English language; excellent writing skills; creative; understanding of the music industry; Internet savvy

CAREER LADDER

```
┌─────────────────────────────────────┐
│  Website Content Producer for Large, │
│  Prestigious Record Label or         │
│  Company in Other Industry; Publicist│
└─────────────────────────────────────┘

┌─────────────────────────────────────┐
│  Website Content Producer,           │
│  Record Label                        │
└─────────────────────────────────────┘

┌─────────────────────────────────────┐
│  Journalist or Writer                │
└─────────────────────────────────────┘
```

Position Description

Websites give a record label exposure on the Web and another avenue for showcasing their artists. Just as print newspapers and magazines need writers and editors, many websites have Content Producers.

The main function of the Website Content Producer is to create and develop interesting and unique content for a label's site. Individuals in this position are responsible for researching and writing engaging articles and blurbs in a variety of areas. Depending on the specific label and the structure of the site, there might be artist bios, stories about upcoming tours, announcements regarding new CDs, and features about label artists.

If the record label website is large, there may be more than one Content Producer. For example, one Content Producer may handle the webpages of two or three of the label's major artists, while another might handle the content on the webpages of the label's newer artists. One may handle events or be responsible for developing the copy for on-site contests and promotions. Another may be responsible for the content on the home page.

Labels hosting large websites often have a senior or executive Website Content Producer. He or she may be responsible for overseeing the work of the other Content Producers.

The label Website Content Producer often oversees on-staff copywriters and graphic artists. Some Content Producers are also responsible for finding and retaining freelancers to write articles on specific subjects. A Content Producer in charge of an entire label website may, for example, find writers to do stories in cities where one of the label's artists is touring. Once stories come in, the Content Producer edits them and gets them ready for the Webmaster to put on-line.

The record label Website Content Producer may be responsible for interviewing label artists and obtaining photos to make the on-line stories interesting. He or she may develop eye-catching headlines for each article or blurb.

One of the great things about the Internet is that it can be interactive. The Content Producer may develop surveys, questionnaires, or other pieces to involve those visiting the site. In this manner, the label can gather information such as what track fans like best of a new CD. The Content Producer may also develop on-line chats, where fans get a chance to talk in cyberspace to their favorite artists.

The Website Contest Producer works closely with the label's promotion and publicity department in order to get as much important information out as possible. With the Internet, items can be posted on-line almost instantly. If news breaks, the Content Producer need only develop a story and get it on-line.

The Website Content Producer is often responsible for acquiring pictures, animation, and other graphics to make the content more appealing. He or she may utilize the services of graphic artists, photographers, or others to accomplish this task. The individual may work with the webmaster to find just the right images which will look good, but not affect the ease of opening the site.

It is essential for record labels to keep their websites fresh, or else they risk losing return visitors. The Website Content Producer is often responsible for daily updates. He or she may post artist events or daily news.

Salaries

Annual earnings for record label Website Content Producers can vary from approximately $28,000 to $75,000 or more annually. Variables include the geographic location, size, and prestige of the label and the specific site, as well as the responsibilities, experience, and reputation of the individual.

It should be noted that some smaller labels hire consultants to handle the content on their websites. These individuals may earn between $15 and $50 or more per hour or may be paid on a per-project basis.

Employment Prospects

Employment prospects are fair for record label Website Content Producers and are getting better every day. Depending on the experience of the individual, he or she might work for a major label or an independent label in cities throughout the country.

An interesting fact to note is that due to the nature of the Website Content Producer's job, some employers may allow individuals to telecommute all or part of the time. Individuals may also find part-time or consulting positions.

Advancement Prospects

Record label Website Content Producers may advance their careers in a number of ways. The most common method of advancement is locating a similar position at a larger, more prestigious record label, resulting in increased responsibilities and earnings. Individuals who are working on a specific area of a label's website may be promoted to executive Content Producer. Some Website Content Producers find similar positions in other industries. There are also some Website Content Producers who move into positions in the publicity or public relations department of the label.

Education and Training

Most record labels require that people in this position have a minimum of a four-year college degree. Good choices for majors include journalism, communications, English, public relations, marketing, and liberal arts.

While it may not be required, individuals who know HTML may have a leg up on other candidates. Courses, workshops, and seminars in public relations, writing, promotion, journalism, and the music industry will be helpful in honing skills and making new contacts.

Experience, Skills, and Personality Traits

Website Content Producers working for record labels generally need some type of writing and editing experience. Some individuals have journalism backgrounds, while others have worked in publicity or public relations. Experience requirements depend on the size and prestige of the label.

Website Content Producers should have a good command of the English language, great writing skills, and creativity. Editing skills are also necessary. A knowledge of the music industry is helpful.

Website Content Producers should have the ability to multitask and work under pressure without getting flustered. People skills are mandatory in this position. Those who are Web savvy will have an advantage.

Unions and Associations

Individuals interested in learning more about careers in the field may obtain additional information by contacting the Internet Professionals Association (IPA) and the National Association of Webmasters (NAW). Record label Website Content Producers may also belong to various music-related associations, such as the National Academy of Recording Arts and Sciences (NARAS) or genre-specific associations, such as the Country Music Association (CMA) or the Gospel Music Association (GMA).

Tips for Entry

1. Internships at record labels are a great way to get your foot in the door, learn skills, and make important contacts.
2. Positions may be located in the classified section of newspapers. Look under headings such as "Record Label Website Content Producer," "Website Content Manager," "Record Labels," and "Web Careers."
3. These types of jobs may be found on-line. Many labels advertise openings on their websites. Also check out the more popular job sites, such as www.hotjobs.com and www.monster.com.
4. Get as much writing experience as you can. Consider a part-time job with a local newspaper. If you are still in school, get involved in your school newspaper and/or website.
5. Don't forget to read trade publications. *Billboard* often has advertisements for labels with openings.
6. Send your résumé and a short cover letter to record label personnel departments. Ask that your résumé be kept on file if there are no current openings.

RADIO AND TELEVISION

PROGRAM DIRECTOR

CAREER PROFILE

Duties: Select format, programs, and schedule for radio station; may also act in the capacity of the music director

Alternate Title(s): P.D.

Salary Range: $25,000 to $100,000+

Employment Prospects: Fair

Advancement Prospects: Fair

Best Geographical Locations for Position: Local communities for small market stations; New York City, Los Angeles, Chicago, Atlanta, etc., for major market stations

Prerequisites:

Education or Training—Some stations may prefer college degree or broadcast school training

Experience—Hands-on training in radio station helpful

Special Skills and Personality Traits—Knowledge of radio stations; understanding of music industry; ability to supervise, hire, and fire; responsible

CAREER LADDER

```
┌─────────────────────────────────┐
│   Program Director in a         │
│   Large, Prestigious Station    │
└─────────────────────────────────┘

┌─────────────────────────────────┐
│        Program Director         │
└─────────────────────────────────┘

┌─────────────────────────────────┐
│   Music Director or Disc Jockey │
└─────────────────────────────────┘
```

Position Description

The Program Director of a radio station holds a very important position. He or she is responsible for selecting the station's format and programs. The individual is also responsible for scheduling the programs at times when they will reach the largest audience.

In certain stations, the Program Director also works as the music director, selecting music for the playlist. The Program Director might also have his or her own show, working as a disc jockey or an on-air personality.

Most Program Directors begin their career in radio as disc jockeys, although there are a small number of individuals who move into the position having had other jobs at a radio station.

The Program Director or P.D., as he or she is sometimes referred to, is responsible for everything that is said or played at the station. If a station is sold or is not doing well, the Program Director may have to revise the station's format. There are a number of formats that can be selected, including Top 40, MOR (middle of the road), A/C (Adult contemporary), oldies, classical, talk, news-oriented, jazz, country, dance-oriented music, U/C (Urban contemporary), or a combination.

The Program Director must have a thorough knowledge of the community his or her station serves and must recommend the type of format likely to attract the most listeners. The larger the audience, the higher the ratings. Ratings determine advertising and commercial rates, which is how radio stations derive income.

The Program Director decides what kind of public-service shows should be aired, who should host them, and when they should be on. The P.D. also decides how many times the news, weather, and community affairs announcements will be read and when they will air.

The P.D. is often responsible for hiring, supervising, and firing disc jockeys. It is his or her job to communicate to the disc jockeys the image the station wants to project.

One of the more important responsibilities of the Program Director is to develop a segue. The segue is the way that records are rotated in relation to other records, commercials, and announcements. For instance, a station might play a ballad, then a Top 40 tune, have a commercial, another Top 40 tune and an oldie-but-goodie; then the cycle would start over again. A good segue can keep an audience interested and excited. A boring segue can prompt listeners to switch to another station.

P.D.s also spend time with record promotion people, who visit the station in hopes of getting their clients on the station's playlist. The program director usually makes up a new list every week or two.

In general the P.D. is responsible to the station manager or owner. He or she will usually work long hours. There are many times when a P.D. must come in early, work late or come in on days off because of special station promotions. However, a special sense of pride can be derived from boosting a station's ratings.

Salaries

Salaries for Program Directors vary depending on the size of the station, its location, its popularity, and the experience and responsibility of the individual. Salaries can range from $25,000 to $100,000 plus annually. The lower salary would be for an individual without a great deal of experience working in a small station. The higher salary would go to those working in large stations in major markets.

Employment Prospects

Almost every radio station in the country has a Program Director. However, the Program Director's job might be combined with that of music director or disc jockey.

Employment prospects are fair for an individual seeking a position in a small station in a sparsely populated community. Experience helps attain a job in a middle or major market, although finding such a position becomes more difficult relative to the station's size and audience.

Advancement Prospects

Opportunities for advancement are fair. The best career path to advancement in this type of position is for the individual to seek a job as Program Director at a larger, more prestigious station, which will in turn provide a higher salary and more responsibility. The Program Director might also advance his or her career by moving into the position of the station's general manager. Opportunities for this type of career advancement, however, are poor.

Education and Training

Educational requirements vary for positions as Program Director. Some stations prefer a college degree in communi-

cations or broadcasting, but that will not guarantee an individual a job.

There are a number of radio broadcasting vocational or trade schools located around the country. Many of these schools are good ones. It is wise to look into the school through the state's Attorney General's office and/or the Department of Consumer Affairs.

Experience, Skills, and Personality Traits

Most Program Directors begin their careers as disc jockeys. Often they have had experience working at college radio stations or other stations before obtaining their position.

Program Directors must have the ability to understand the type of market their station is trying to reach.

The Program Director must have a great deal of knowledge about music and be up on trends. He or she is responsible for the station's programming and cannot let personal music preferences affect decision making.

Unions and Associations

Program Directors may belong to the National Association of Broadcasters (NAB). They may also be members of the American Federation of Television and Radio Artists (AFTRA). As Program Directors, individuals may also belong to the National Association of Broadcast Employees and Technicians (NABET).

Tips for Entry

1. Work in a college radio station and/or a local station as a disc jockey to gain experience.
2. Certain larger stations have college credit internship programs. It is not unusual for a station to hire an intern after graduation.
3. There are positions advertised in most of the radio and record-oriented trades, including *Radio and Records, Billboard,* and *Broadcasting,* to name a few.
4. Openings and positions are also often advertised in the classified sections of newspapers. Look under "Radio," "Broadcasting," "Program Director," and "Music" heading classifications.

MUSIC DIRECTOR

CAREER PROFILE

Duties: Select music for specific programs on radio station

Alternate Title(s): MD

Salary Range: $25,000 to $95,000+

Employment Prospects: Fair

Advancement Prospects: Fair

Best Geographical Locations for Position: Local communities for small market stations; New York City, Los Angeles, Chicago, etc. for major market stations

Prerequisites:

Education or Training—High school diploma, minimum requirement; college degree or broadcasting school training may be preferred, hands-on training in a radio station helpful

Experience—Working as a disc jockey for a period of time

Special Skills and Personality Traits—Knowledge of music; ability to supervise; responsibility

CAREER LADDER

```
┌─────────────────────────┐
│    Program Director      │
└─────────────────────────┘

┌─────────────────────────┐
│     Music Director       │
└─────────────────────────┘

┌─────────────────────────┐
│      Disc Jockey         │
└─────────────────────────┘
```

Position Description

The Music Director of a radio station is responsible for selecting music for specific programs aired on the station. The individual works closely with the program director. In certain stations, the Music Director is also the program director. The Music Director might also have his or her own show, working as a disc jockey.

Music Directors as a rule began their careers in radio as disc jockeys. During the time they were D.J.'s they proved that they had expertise in selecting records and putting shows together.

The Music Director's duties vary depending on what type of format is being used by the station and the duties of the program director. He or she may spend time with the record promotional people, screening tunes for the program director to listen to. The two then discuss the records that could potentially hit when they air them in their market.

Music Directors assist the program director in most music-oriented activities. The individual helps the P.D. research the market, determine the kind of audience the station plays to, learn what the people want to hear, and get a feel for station listeners' likes and dislikes.

The individual often meets with or talks to the managers of major record stores in the area. Through these meetings, he or she can find out what's hot in record releases.

The Music Director, along with the program director, might help train new disc jockeys and help them adjust to the station's procedures. This is often done by listening to air checks, which are short tapes of the different on-air personalities recorded at various times.

The Music Director is responsible directly to the program director. He or she works long hours. When the station is short of on-air personnel, the program director might assign the Music Director to take another shift. In addition, the Music Director often takes part in special appearances or promotions. These special shows usually take place during a weekend or at night.

Salaries

Salaries for Music Directors vary depending on the size of the radio station, its location, its popularity, the duties of the Music Director, and his or her experience. Salaries tend to be highest in major markets, such as New York City, Los Angeles, Chicago, etc.

Music Directors' salaries can range from $25,000 to $95,000 or more annually. In addition, many jobs offer other benefits.

Employment Prospects

Employment prospects are fair for Music Directors. It should be noted that in some stations the job of Music Director is combined with the job with that of the program director.

The best place to look for a position is in a small to mid-sized station. The individual can then gain experience, making it easier to find a position at a bigger station.

Advancement Prospects

A Music Director can advance to the position of program director at a radio station. The individual may also advance his or her career by becoming a Music Director at a better or bigger station.

Education and Training

There is no formal educational requirement for a job as a Music Director. Many stations prefer or require a college degree or broadcasting school training. If the individual does attend college, he or she should take courses in communications, journalism, music, and broadcasting. He or she should also work on the school's radio station. This will give the individual hands-on training.

There are many radio broadcasting vocational and trade schools located around the country. Although a majority of these schools are good ones, some are not. Check into the school's reputation through the state's Attorney General's office and/or the Department of Consumer Affairs.

Experience, Skills, and Personality Traits

Most Music Directors begin working in radio stations as disc jockeys. If they've been to college, they also have experience working on their college radio stations.

Music Directors, as a rule, like music. They enjoy listening to records and have the knack of knowing what will be hot.

Individuals in this position must be responsible people who have the ability to supervise others.

Unions and Associations

Music Directors may belong to the National Association of Broadcasters (NAB). Depending on the job situation, they might also belong to the American Federation of Television and Radio Artists (AFTRA). Music Directors may additionally belong to the National Association of Broadcast Employees and Technicians (NABET).

Tips for Entry

1. Work in a college radio station and/or a local station to gain experience.
2. Certain larger stations have college credit internship programs. It is not unusual for a station to hire an intern after graduation.
3. Openings and positions are often advertised in the classified sections of newspapers.
4. There are also positions advertised in most of the radio- and record-oriented trades, including *Radio and Records, Billboard,* and *Broadcasting.*

DISC JOCKEY

CAREER PROFILE

Duties: Introduce music, commercials, and news on radio station

Alternate Title(s): D.J.; Deejay; Jock; On-Air Personality

Salary Range: $25,000 to $1,000,000+

Employment Prospects: Fair

Advancement Prospects: Fair

Best Geographical Location(s) for Position: Major market stations are located in New York City, Los Angeles, Chicago, etc.; small market stations are found in towns and cities around the country

Prerequisites:

Education or Training—Educational requirements vary; college or vocational background in communications or radio broadcasting may be preferred or required

Experience—Position on school or college station helpful

Special Skills and Personality Traits—Enjoyment of music; good speaking voice; ability to project personality over the air

CAREER LADDER

```
┌─────────────────────────────────────┐
│        Program Director;             │
│  Disc Jockey at Major Market Station │
└─────────────────────────────────────┘

┌─────────────────────────────────────┐
│             Disc Jockey              │
└─────────────────────────────────────┘

┌─────────────────────────────────────┐
│          Student; Intern             │
└─────────────────────────────────────┘
```

Position Description

A Disc Jockey's main responsibility is to introduce the records, commercials, news, and public announcements that are aired on a station. The Disc Jockey is expected to have some sort of style or personality to project over the air waves. This personality is what makes a Disc Jockey successful and gives him or her a following.

Disc Jockeys work in time shifts. Shifts vary, but usually range from three to five hours in length. D.J.'s are usually assigned the same shift every day. Popular Disc Jockeys receive the most listened-to shifts, such as the morning drive, afternoon drive, or early evenings slot.

Depending on the size of the station and its makeup, the Jock has additional responsibilities. Sometimes the D.J. is responsible for picking out the music for his or her show. This usually occurs in small market stations that have small staffs. They must, however, choose records from an approved playlist put together by the station's program or music director.

Sometimes the Disc Jockey is also the acting music or program director. This, once again, depends on the size of the station and how it is staffed. If the station is small, the Disc Jockey might also be responsible for putting the records on the turntable and working the sound controls.

During the course of his or her shift, the D.J. sometimes comes up with comments, ad libs, the weather, or information about the records he or she is introducing.

Disc Jockeys have other activities besides performing on the air. As the Disc Jockey becomes a celebrity of sorts (even in small markets), he or she may make public appearances for store promotions, station promotions, or charity events. He or she also might do voice-overs on commercials for radio or television. In addition, Disc Jockeys might act as live jocks at clubs or discos, or even host concerts in large or small facilities.

The Disc Jockey is responsible to the program director, music director, or station manager.

Salaries

Salaries for Disc Jockeys vary according to a number of factors, including the size of the station, the market, the experience of the Jock, and his or her appeal.

Salaries can start at approximately $25,000 a year for a beginner in a small market station. A Disc Jockey who is very popular may earn $225,000 plus annually. In addition, Disc Jockeys may make additional income from personal appearances, voice-over commercials, and doing club D.J. work. There are some Disc Jockeys who earn $1,000,000 or more through a combination of salary, personal appearances, and endorsements.

Employment Prospects

Employment prospects in small market stations are fair. There is a large turnover at many of these stations because pay is so low and people want to move on to better positions.

Employment prospects get tougher as the station's market gets larger.

Advancement Prospects

The Disc Jockey at a small market station has an opportunity to advance to the position of program director or music director at that station or a similar station. He or she also has the option of trying to locate a position at a better station in a bigger market.

Education and Training

Educational requirements vary for the position of Disc Jockey. Many stations prefer or require their employees to have a college degree, background, or vocational training. If the individual is considering college, courses in communications and broadcasting are useful. Working on the college radio station is also valuable experience. This gives the individual hands-on training.

If the person is planning on attending a broadcasting vocational or trade school, he or she should check out the reputation of the school. This can be accomplished through the state's Attorney General's office and/or the Department of Consumer Affairs. Although most of these schools have good reputations, some do not.

Experience, Skills, and Personality Traits

Many Disc Jockeys begin their careers by participating in a high school radio club. They then move on to a college station and learn many additional radio jobs.

A Disc Jockey must have a good speaking voice and the ability to project his or her personality over the air.

The Disc Jockey must be responsible and dependable. He or she must consistently show up on time for his or her air shift.

Disc Jockeys must obtain a license from the FCC (Federal Communications Commission). This is obtained by having a letter sent to the FCC by the prospective employer stating that the individual has a job in the broadcasting field. An application must also be filled in and submitted.

Unions and Associations

Disc Jockeys may be members of the American Federation of Television and Radio Artists (AFTRA). Individuals might also belong to the National Association of Broadcasting (NAB) or be an associate member of the National Academy of Recording Arts and Sciences (NARAS). Disc Jockeys may additionally belong to the National Association of Broadcast Employees and Technicians (NABET).

Tips for Entry

1. Positions may be advertised in the classified sections of newspapers. Look under key words such as "Disc Jockey," "Radio," or "Music."
2. Other openings may be advertised in the radio and record trades, such as *Billboard, Broadcasting,* and *Radio* and *Records.*
3. See if you can get into a college internship at a radio station.
4. Work on your high school or college radio station for experience.
5. Make a demo tape and send it along with your résumé to a station's general manager or personnel director (depending on the station size). Make sure you make a few copies of the tape and always keep one.

VIDEO JOCKEY

CAREER PROFILE

Duties: Introduce music videos on television; discuss videos; host video show

Alternate Title(s): V.J.; Video Jock; Vee-Jay

Salary Range: $25,000 to $500,000+

Employment Prospects: Poor

Advancement Prospects: Fair

Best Geographical Location(s) for Position: Entry-level positions may be found in smaller markets throughout the country; major music video markets located in large cities, such as New York City, Los Angeles, Washington, D.C., and Nashville

Prerequisites:

Education or Training—No formal educational requirements; college background or degree may be preferred

Experience—Experience with television industry, radio, and/or music industry helpful

Special Skills and Personality Traits—Pleasant appearance; articulate; comfortable around television cameras, microphones and lights; understanding of television studio; knowledge of music industry and trends

CAREER LADDER

```
┌─────────────────────────────────┐
│       Video Jockey at a         │
│   Large, Prestigious Station    │
└─────────────────────────────────┘

┌─────────────────────────────────┐
│         Video Jockey            │
└─────────────────────────────────┘

┌─────────────────────────────────┐
│         Disc Jockey;            │
│  On-Air Position in Television  │
└─────────────────────────────────┘
```

Position Description

Video Jockeys are similar in many ways to radio disc jockeys. The main difference is that instead of introducing records on radio, the Video Jockey introduces music videos on television.

Previously, it took a certain amount of time for new tunes to become hits. Today success can be almost instantaneous. Now a new tune can be aired via a music video to the entire country on network and/or cable television. Within minutes, radio stations will start getting calls to play the record and a hit is made.

Video Jockeys, or V.J.'s, as they are often called, are the people who announce to the viewing audience the music videos they will be seeing. The individuals may talk about the video or its performers.

The V.J. is expected to project a particular style or personality. It is this style and personality which will determine the success and popularity of the individual. Very successful V.J.'s can develop followings which in turn may lead to better show slots or opportunities at larger, more prestigious stations.

Video Jockeys have varied responsibilities depending on the size of the station or the popularity of the show that they are involved with. The Video Jockey may work in specific time shifts if he or she is hosting a live show or may tape a number of video shows in a given period of time.

The Video Jockey may be expected only to introduce music videos or may have additional duties. For example, the individual may host an entire show during which he or she interviews music acts, reviews new videos, lists Top 10 videos, etc. The V.J. may be in charge of choosing which videos will be shown on his or her show or may just comment on videos that have been suggested by a program director.

Major music video networks will usually have a program director or station executive view new videos and decide when and if they should be included on the station's playlist.

If the V.J. is hosting a show on a local or cable station (i.e., not on a music video network, such as VH1 or Country Music Television) the individual may be responsible for reviewing videos to see if they fit the format of the particular show.

Video Jockeys, even those appearing on small market or local cable stations, often become celebrities in their viewing area. They may be expected to make public appearances for station promotions, functions, or charity events. In some situations, the Video Jockey may also work as a D.J. on a radio station or at a live event. The individual might also be asked to host concerts or act as M.C. for acts touring the city.

At smaller stations the Video Jockey may be expected to fulfill other obligations in other areas. He or she may, for example, be asked to help with the copywriting of scripts for commercials or even to sell advertising. The individual may also be the entertainment or music reporter for the station. In larger stations, the individual usually would not have to perform these tasks.

The Video Jockey may be responsible to the program director or the station's general manager. He or she may work regular hours or may tape all his or her shows in a given time period. Many V.J.'s working in small local or cable stations do just one or two shows a week.

Salaries

Salaries for Video Jockeys can range greatly depending on a number of variables. These include the size of the television station, its location, and the type of show. Other variables include the experience and responsibilities the individual has, as well as his or her popularity. At certain stations the Video Jockey will be represented by a union. In these cases, the union will set minimum earnings that individuals may be paid. Stations in smaller markets will usually have the lowest salaries because individuals in these positions are just entering the job market. Individuals working on music television oriented stations or those working for major market stations or networks will be earning the most. Salaries can range from $25,000 for those who have shows on small local stations to $250,000 plus a year for V.J.'s who have large followings. Individuals may also earn additional income by doing personal appearances and endorsements. These individuals may earn $500,000 or more.

Employment Prospects

Employment prospects for individuals seeking jobs as Video Jockeys in television are poor but are increasing. With the current surge in new local, syndicated, and cable television stations around the country, there will be more and more employment opportunities in the coming years. Opportunities will present themselves as more local and cable television shows begin to air music video shows.

It is easier for individuals with little or no experience to enter the job market in smaller stations. In these situations they may often get the job just by suggesting a video show as a possibility for a program format.

Advancement Prospects

Advancement prospects are poor for Video Jockeys but are getting better as music expands. Individuals may climb the career ladder in a number of ways. The V.J. may obtain a following and command a higher salary or he or she may look for employment at a larger, more prestigious station.

The individual may find that he or she can find better employment in radio and become a disc jockey at a larger station, thereby increasing his or her earnings. The individual might also go into broadcast news or reporting outside the realm of the music industry.

Education and Training

While no formal education may be required to obtain a position as a Video Jockey, it must be remembered that the music and broadcast industries are extremely competitive. Those who aspire to become successful may want to be as prepared as possible. A college degree with a major in television, broadcasting, or the music business may be helpful in climbing the career ladder.

Experience, Skills, and Personality Traits

A Video Jockey should have a pleasant or distinctive appearance. This is important because the V.J. will be seen by an audience. The individual should be comfortable around television cameras, microphones, and lights.

The Video Jockey should have a good speaking voice and be articulate. He or she should be personable and have the ability to project his or her personality over the air.

An understanding of television production is useful. Knowledge of camera angles, directions, lighting, etc., is helpful, but may not be necessary, depending on the situation.

The Video Jockey should have a good understanding of music and keep abreast of current trends, acts, etc. It is imperative that the V.J. is responsible and dependable. He or she must be punctual. For those who are scheduled to host live broadcasts, being late can be a disaster. Arriving late for a taping can cause problems in scheduling and will cost the station additional funds, as well.

Unions and Associations

Depending on the situation, station, and the responsibilities of the individual, the Video Jockey may be a member of the American Federation of Television and Radio Artists (AFTRA), the National Association of Broadcast Employees and Technicians AFL-CIO (NABET), or be an associate member of the National Academy of Recording Arts and Sciences (NARAS).

Tips for Entry

1. Try to choose a college with a television station, and get involved in as many facets of its operation as possible.
2. If your college does not have a television station, get involved with the school radio station. You need experience on the air.
3. Consider working as an intern or a secretary at a local station part time or for the summer. Hands-on experience in the field is helpful.
4. Positions in this field may be located in the display or classified section of newspapers under "V.J.," "Broadcasting," or "Television" heading classifications.
5. Larger stations often offer training programs or internships. Try to locate these opportunities.
6. A job in radio as a disc jockey will help you make valuable contacts.
7. Have a short video demo made to show your talent to potential station managers.
8. Keep an eye out for casting calls for V.J.'s often advertised on music television.

ON THE ROAD

TOUR COORDINATOR

CAREER PROFILE

Duties: Coordinate the many facets of an act's tour

Alternate Title(s): None

Salary Range: $35,000 to $175,000+

Employment Prospects: Poor

Advancement Prospects: Fair

Best Geographical Location(s) for Position: Most major tours are planned from booking agencies or management firms in New York City, Los Angeles, and Nashville

Prerequisites:

Education or Training—No formal educational requirement; college background helpful

Experience—Travel and touring experience with music acts as road manager, tour publicist, etc.

Special Skills and Personality Traits—Ability to assert authority; responsibility; organization; freedom to travel; communications skills

CAREER LADDER

```
┌─────────────────────────────────────┐
│  Tour Coordinator for Major Tour;    │
│  Personal Manager; Booking Agent     │
└─────────────────────────────────────┘

┌─────────────────────────────────────┐
│          Tour Coordinator            │
└─────────────────────────────────────┘

┌─────────────────────────────────────┐
│    Road Manager; Tour Publicist      │
└─────────────────────────────────────┘
```

Position Description

The position of Tour Coordinator is one of the most important jobs on the road. The individual in this position is responsible for coordinating all of the many facets of an act's tour. He or she oversees everything that is done by all members of the tour staff while the act is on the road. It is the duty of the Tour Coordinator to supervise not only the road personnel but the act as well.

The Tour Coordinator's job starts well before the tour leaves for its first destination. He or she works with the act's management, booking agents, and publicists. The individual maps out the location of concerts and their dates and times. He or she then discusses with the publicist or tour publicist other appearances that have to be made, including radio interviews, television spots, print media interviews, special promotions, stops at record shops, etc. These are added to the list of times, dates, and locations.

The Tour Coordinator may work out what transportation will be used by which members of the entourage. Often, for example, the singers travel by plane, the musicians by private bus, and the equipment crew by truck. In instances where the group must travel 2,000 miles in a day, the logical transportation would be an airplane, probably a chartered jet. The Tour Coordinator finds the best routes to take, makes reservations at hotels, and rents cars, limos, buses, and planes. As a rule, the Tour Coordinator tries to make the best arrangements as economically as possible.

The Tour Coordinator also plans the tour day by day—sometimes hour by hour—to use time as well as possible. He or she tries to get everyone where he or she is supposed to be with the least amount of effort. The road gets grueling, and sometimes the Tour Coordinator must weigh the price of flying against traveling a cheaper way and having the act come in too exhausted to put on a good show.

Once the tour leaves, the Tour Coordinator really goes into action. He or she must coordinate all the activities of the entourage. The problems of the entourage, the act, and the promoters often become the problems of the Coordinator.

The Tour Coordinator works closely with the Tour Manager, as many of their responsibilities are interchangeable. Sometimes he or she is also the road manager. Tour Coordinators also keep in close contact with the act's management and agents. He or she lets them know if everything is going according to schedule or if the act will be late for a particular date.

If a car or bus breaks down, it is the Tour Coordinator's responsibility to make sure another means of transportation is found. If a member of the backup band gets sick while on the road, the Tour Coordinator must find a replacement. If the act has a major problem during the tour, the individual must deal with it or at least delegate someone to handle the situation.

Tours can be long (no matter how short they really are). Life on the road is not for everyone. The Tour Coordinator must be able to deal with the responsibilities of the job and the road while everyone around is under tremendous pressure. Most tours average six to eight weeks, although there are shorter and longer ones; hours are long and irregular. The Tour Coordinator is always on call, not only for the act and the entourage, but also from management, agents, the act's family, etc.

Tour Coordinators often come off the road and are so physically and mentally exhausted that they must take a few weeks off and do nothing.

The one thing all Tour Coordinators, road managers, and road personnel have in common is a love of music and of life on the road.

Salaries

Salaries of Tour Coordinators are usually high. An individual could start at $700 per week. However, the remuneration is usually much higher. The average is between $850 and $2,000 per week plus either expenses or a per diem.

Experienced Tour Coordinators who work on prestigious tours often earn $3,500 or more per week plus expenses and bonuses.

Tour Coordinators are not always on staff and therefore may not work every week. There are some situations where the Tour Coordinator is paid a reduced salary while a group is not actively working in order to retain his or her services.

Employment Prospects

The outlook is not good for Tour Coordinators. There are few jobs in this area and more potential Tour Coordinators than positions.

With the current high price of touring, there are tours that go out with fewer personnel, using road managers instead. Those who prove themselves may find opportunities with major acts as well as lesser known acts who are on the way up.

Advancement Prospects

As a Tour Coordinator, an individual can advance his or her career by becoming a Tour Coordinator for a better-known group or for a major, prestigious tour.

There are a few Tour Coordinators who go into personal management or booking after their experience as Tour Coordinators.

Education and Training

There is no formal educational requirement for this position. However, a college background often helps with the job. Courses in accounting, bookkeeping, psychology, publicity, and the music business are useful.

Experience, Skills, and Personality Traits

Many Tour Coordinators were roadies, road managers, and publicists prior to their current position. There are Tour Coordinators who worked as travel agents or travel escorts but always had a love of music.

The most important trait a Tour Coordinator can have is a love of the road and travel. The individual in this position has to like living out of a suitcase. He or she also must be responsible, dependable, and able to supervise an entourage of people. The Tour Coordinator must be organized. A disorganized person can make a shambles of a tour. He or she must also have the ability to deal effectively with a crisis.

Unions and Associations

There is no union or association specific to Tour Coordinators.

Tips for Entry

1. This is another of the positions in the music business that you get through contacts. If you have any, use them. If you don't, develop some.
2. Advertise your availability in a small display or classified ad in one of the music trades.
3. Experience helps. If you have put together a tour for anyone, even an unknown show group, put it on your résumé.
4. Send your résumé to the personnel department of major record labels.

ROAD MANAGER

CAREER PROFILE

Duties: Handle problems that occur while act is traveling; supervise equipment, sound, and light personnel

Alternate Title(s): Tour Manager

Salary Range: $25,000 to $125,000+

Employment Prospects: Fair

Advancement Prospects: Fair

Best Geographical Locations for Position: Major tours are usually planned in New York City, Los Angeles, and Nashville; positions may be available throughout the country

Prerequisites:

Education or Training—No formal education required

Experience—Positions as roadie or equipment manager helpful

Special Skills and Personality Traits—Responsibility; ability to work under pressure; dependability; ability to supervise; freedom to travel; ingenuity

CAREER LADDER

```
┌─────────────────────────────┐
│      Tour Coordinator        │
└─────────────────────────────┘

┌─────────────────────────────┐
│      Road Manager            │
└─────────────────────────────┘

┌─────────────────────────────┐
│   Equipment Manager; Roadie  │
└─────────────────────────────┘
```

Position Description

The Road Manager of a group is the group's management representative while the act is on the road. He or she is responsible for handling many of the problems that occur while an act is traveling. The main job is to get everybody and everything where they are supposed to be and on time. Everything must be accomplished as easily as possible with the fewest problems possible.

The Road or Tour Manager is directly responsible to either the tour coordinator, the group's management, or the group itself, depending on advance arrangements made.

At times the Road Manager is also the tour coordinator. In these situations, he or she is responsible for all the problems on the road and for supervising not only the equipment, sound, and light personnel, but also the tour publicist, the tour photographer, the musicians, the security, and anyone else working on the tour.

It is the Road Manager's duty to make sure that the act is up in the morning, gets to any public appearances, inter-

views, or television or radio spots. He or she must make sure they arrive at rehearsals and concerts on time.

He or she is responsible for getting the equipment to the concert hall on time and getting it set up properly. The Road Manager supervises the sound checks, light checks, and security checks for the performances.

The Road Manager is often the liaison between the act and the promoter of a concert or club date. He or she has the responsibility of collecting any monies owed to the act before and/or after the show. The individual must make sure that riders have been followed and the promoter satisfied.

He or she may be in charge of paying the entourage and all bills on the road. The Road Manager must keep all receipts, vouchers, etc., from the tour to give to the group or its management. All money must be accounted for.

The Road Manager often has to deal with problems between members of the entourage or help a member of the entourage take care of personal problems. Long road tours put stress on most people. The Road Manager must be the one who keeps a cool head no matter what happens.

If an individual has responsibilities that must be dealt with at home, Road Managing is definitely not the job to look for. Road Managers must like travel and must be free to be away from home for weeks or even months at a time.

Hours are long. Road Managers may work twenty hours or more a day. They are always on call. While most of the entourage is fast asleep, the Road Manager is often working throughout the day and long into the night.

Salaries

Salaries of Road Managers vary greatly according to the popularity and success of the groups they work with. Road Managers are usually paid weekly salaries. They may, however, be paid a flat rate for each tour they complete. In addition, Road Managers are paid a per diem for living expenses while on tour. In some groups, the Road Manager's room and board are paid for and the per diem is used for personal expenses. In other situations, the Road Manager's room and board must be paid out of the per diem.

A Road Manager for a touring (but not recording) group might make approximately $400 per week. A Road Manager for a top recording group often makes $1,500 to $2,500 per week or more plus bonuses. Road Managers' salaries are often reduced by a percentage when the act is not working. This reduction keeps the Road Manager under salary with the group. Some Road Managers do not receive any salary when their act is not on tour, and may work for other groups.

Employment Prospects

Although most touring groups employ Road Managers, positions often go to nonmusical friends of a group. The Road Manager position is one for which you have to be at the right place at the right time. In addition, you need a lot of contacts in the business to find open positions. Groups and their management tend to use individuals who have a proven track record in road management for major tours.

Individuals may find employment with lesser known groups, recording acts, touring acts, and other types of entertainers.

Advancement Prospects

Road Managers advance either by moving into the position of tour coordinator or by acting as Road Manager for a more prestigious tour. Often an individual has more clout as Road Manager for a prestigious tour than he or she would have as tour coordinator for a tour starring lesser-known musicians.

To advance, the Road Manager must prove him- or herself. Management has to be totally convinced that the Road Manager is completely reliable, responsible, and effective as their representative on the road.

Education and Training

There is no formal educational requirement for the position of Road Manager. There are Road Managers who have not even completed high school. The more successful Road Managers, however, have. There are also Road Managers who have college degrees in everything from business to psychology.

Experience, Skills, and Personality Traits

Most Road Managers start out as roadies. Some begin their careers as equipment personnel or tour publicists.

The Road Manager must be able to deal with problems effectively, especially when he or she is under pressure. He or she must have the capability to supervise not only the group's road crew, but also union crews present in many concert halls.

The most important trait that a Road Manager can have is responsibility. It is his or her responsibility to get personnel and equipment where and when they are supposed to be. In addition, the Road Manager must be dependable.

Unions and Associations

There are no major associations specific to Road Managers.

Tips for Entry

1. This is a position most often gotten through contacts. If you have any, use them.
2. You might want to try to get a position by putting a small ad in one of the music trades.
3. Many groups starting out have a nonmusical friend act as Road Manager. This might be a way to gain experience.
4. Check the trades to see what tours are going out. These are usually printed well in advance. Send résumés to these groups, their management, and/or their record companies.
5. Send your résumé to the personnel department of record companies.

TOUR PUBLICIST

CAREER PROFILE

Duties: Publicize an act's tour to both fans and the media through press releases, press conferences, and special promotions

Alternate Title(s): Publicist

Salary Range: $25,000 to $100,000+

Employment Prospects: Poor

Advancement Prospects: Fair

Best Geographical Location(s) for Position: Major tours are usually planned in the music capitals of New York City, Los Angeles, or Nashville; tours may leave from other locations

Prerequisites:

Education or Training—College degree in communications, English, journalism, public relations, or music merchandising preferred

Experience—Prior position in music or nonmusic-oriented publicity

Special Skills and Personality Traits—Willingness to travel; writing skills; national media contacts; ability to work under pressure; creativity

CAREER LADDER

```
┌─────────────────────────────────┐
│  Independent Tour Publicist;     │
│  Tour Coordinator/Manager        │
└─────────────────────────────────┘

┌─────────────────────────────────┐
│        Tour Publicist            │
└─────────────────────────────────┘

┌─────────────────────────────────┐
│          Publicist              │
└─────────────────────────────────┘
```

Position Description

A Tour Publicist is a trained publicist who goes on tour with a recording act or artist. He or she is in charge of making sure that both the act's fans and the media know that the group or artist is coming to town to perform a concert.

Certain Tour Publicists set up media interviews with local television, radio, newspaper, and magazine editors before the group leaves their home base. They might also arrange press parties and press conferences. Other times a staff publicist takes care of these details. The Tour Publicist's main function occurs on the road. When the group leaves on tour, the Tour Publicist is automatically part of the entourage.

On the road, he or she attends all interviews, photography sessions, concerts, press parties, and press conferences along with the act. In addition, the Tour Publicist accompanies the act to all radio interviews or television appearances. The Tour Publicist usually spends a few minutes with the show's

producer, talent coordinator, or host to discuss what he or she would like the act to talk about during the interview.

At concerts, it is the Tour Publicist who is responsible for issuing press passes to disc jockeys, music editors, photographers, etc. He or she also issues the important backstage passes. All interviews and photo sessions must be approved in advance by the Tour Publicist. He or she usually sets a specific time before or after each show for additional interviews and photo sessions.

The Tour Publicist works closely with any sponsoring radio or television stations. He or she tries to make sure the employees of the station are happy. This might entail arranging special interviews or autograph sessions, presenting records or T-shirts, etc.

The Tour Publicist, who works for a record company or publicity firm, usually calls his or her office at least once a day. The Tour Publicist is responsible to his or her superiors at the record company or the publicity firm. An independent

Tour Publicist is responsible directly to the act and its management team.

Tour Publicists work for the duration of the tour. It is not a nine-to-five job. While the act is still sleeping at 10:00 A.M., the Tour Publicist has already been up for a few hours making calls and discussing arrangements for the upcoming day. The Tour Publicist might still be up at 3:00 A.M. at a party thrown in the act's honor. The Tour Publicist must have a lot of stamina and a great love for the job to survive on the road.

Salaries

The salary for a Tour Publicist is usually higher than that for a home-based publicist because he or she must travel for long periods of time. Tour Publicists who work for a record company or publicity firm generally receive a weekly salary plus a daily or weekly stipend to cover personal expenses. Travel expenses are paid by the act or its management firm.

Independent Tour Publicists receive a weekly or monthly fee plus all expenses. These expenses may include food, lodging, phone, and other amenities. All work-related expenses, such as printing, long-distance phone calls, mailings, etc., are paid for by the group, record company, etc.

Salaries for Tour Publicists vary according to the employer, the act, and the amount of experience that the Tour Publicist has. A beginning Tour Publicist usually makes no less than $500 per week plus expenses. An average salary for a Tour Publicist working for a fairly established music group is between $40,000 and $85,000 or more per year plus expenses. There are Tour Publicists who are very much in demand who can command $2,000 and up per week for certain tours.

Employment Prospects

With the expenses of traveling going up many groups cannot go on tour as often as they used to. There are also few groups that can afford the services of a Tour Publicist. These positions are available, but only on a very limited basis. However, there are not many people who like to or can travel constantly.

Advancement Prospects

A good Tour Publicist can advance to the position of Tour Coordinator or Tour Manager. If the Tour Publicist has worked for a major record company or has experience working with a publicity firm, he or she has the option of becoming an independent Tour Publicist.

Education and Training

A Tour Publicist position usually requires much the same training as a home-based publicist. A college degree with a major in communications, journalism, English, public relations, or music merchandising is preferable. Seminars on music-oriented publicity are also helpful.

Experience, Skills, and Personality Traits

The Tour Publicist must have the ability to travel and must enjoy being on the road for long stretches at a time. Tour Publicists work under more pressure than home-based publicists. Road tours sometimes create stress for people. Toward the end of a tour, for example, the entire entourage may get jumpy. They just want the tour to end. The Tour Publicist must make sure that this attitude is not displayed to the media or the fans.

The Tour Publicist must maintain a list of national media contacts to call upon while his or her client is touring.

Unions and Associations

There are a number of organizations and associations Tour Publicists can belong to. The best known is the Public Relations Society of America (PRSA), which has local chapters in major cities in the United States.

Tips for Entry

1. Place an ad in one of the music trades (classified or display) describing the type of position you're looking for. Professionals in the business read these trades and might be looking for someone to fill this type of position.
2. Openings for this type of position might also be advertised in the trades, such as *Billboard*.
3. If you're working in a music-oriented public relations firm or a record company, talk to your superiors about this position. Often they need someone for this position. Many publicists in a company may not be free to travel for great lengths of time.
4. Send your résumé with a cover letter to record companies or music-oriented public relations firms asking about openings for Tour Publicists.

SOUND TECHNICIAN

CAREER PROFILE

Duties: Work the sound board for an act on tour; take care of sound equipment

Alternate Title(s): Audio Technician; Sound Person; Sound Man or Woman

Salary Range: $20,000 to $50,000+

Employment Prospects: Fair

Advancement Prospects: Poor

Best Geographical Location(s) for Position: Major tours are usually planned in New York City, Los Angeles, or Nashville, although they leave from various cities; other tours are planned from cities around the country

Prerequisites:

Education or Training—No educational requirements; training in electronics or sound

Experience—Experience working sound boards and other sound equipment

Special Skills and Personality Traits—Good musical "ear"; love of music; knowledge of electronics; knowledge of sound board; freedom to travel

CAREER LADDER

```
┌─────────────────────────────────────┐
│   Sound Technician for Top Act;      │
│         Road Manager                 │
└─────────────────────────────────────┘

┌─────────────────────────────────────┐
│         Sound Technician             │
└─────────────────────────────────────┘

┌─────────────────────────────────────┐
│  Sound Technician Assistant; Roadie  │
└─────────────────────────────────────┘
```

Position Description

The Sound Technician working on the road has a good deal of responsibility. The main area he or she must be concerned with is good quality sound during a show.

The Sound Technician usually arrives at a concert hall or club earlier than the performers. Along with the rest of the road crew, he or she unloads, sets up, and positions the equipment and the instruments. (In certain union situations, such as union halls, union employees must unload the equipment. In cases like this, the Sound Technician will supervise placement of equipment.)

The equipment and the instruments must be placed on the stage in such a way that the sounds of the instruments and the vocals will blend well. In addition, everything must be situated so that the sound is good and those on stage can both see and hear what goes on during the show.

After everything is set up, the musicians and the vocalists will arrive. The Sound Technician must then prepare for the all-important sound check. During this time the Sound Tech-

nician works with the talent. Each person will play his or her instrument or sing, and the Technician must listen to determine whether the sound is coming through properly. Sometimes this takes a great deal of time because acoustics are different in every hall. During this period as many adjustments as possible are taken care of. Minor adjustments will take place just before the show when the hall fills up.

During the show the Sound Technician works the sound board. He or she can adjust the volume of voices while changing the volume of instruments. Instruments can be made to sound more bass, treble, etc. The sound must constantly be balanced so that all the instruments and vocals blend together. The Sound Technician is usually situated somewhere in front of the stage during the performance. This is where the true sound can be heard the best.

After the show, the Sound Technician may be responsible for watching the loading and packing of the sound equipment. Big tours sometimes have an entire truck designated to haul only the sound equipment.

The Sound Technician might also be responsible for checking out the equipment after a show to see what needs repair or replacement. Many Sound Technicians know how to fix much of the equipment they work with. This is a plus, especially if the equipment breaks down just before or during a show.

Sound Technicians are responsible to the head road manager or tour coordinator. It depends on the acts they work with.

Sound Technicians do not always work on a constant basis. They might work a six week tour with one act and have a month off before the next tour starts with another group. There are instances where the Sound Technician might go on a reduced salary while not on tour in order to make sure that he or she is available to a particular group.

Sound Technicians who work on the road must have the freedom to travel. In addition, they must be able to deal with long periods on the road and living out of a suitcase.

Salaries

Salaries for Sound Technicians vary greatly. Sound people working for a local band on its way up may make minimum wage or less. They may get the same percentage of the pot as each of the band members.

As Sound Technicians move up and work for better-known acts, their income increases. Salaries run from $20,000 to around $50,000 plus yearly. The higher salary would, of course, go to a Sound Technician on the road with a very well-known act.

Sound Technicians working on the road usually receive a per diem to pay for living expenses while traveling.

It is important to note that if the Sound Technician freelances, he or she will probably not work 52 weeks a year.

Employment Prospects

A Sound Technician has a fair chance of finding employment with a local or well-known regional band. Possibilities of finding work decrease as the popularity of the group with which one aspires to work increases.

Advancement Prospects

Advancement is difficult for Sound Technicians. They may find work with a more popular band or act, but this is not easy.

Sound Technicians may also advance to the position of road manager or tour coordinator if they exhibit sufficient drive, responsibility, and competence.

Education and Training

No formal education is required for the position of Sound Technician. Many individuals in this job picked up the basics by watching someone else work the board.

Other people do have some training in electronics or sound, possibly from attending a recording or broadcasting school.

Experience, Skills, and Personality Traits

As noted above, many Sound Technicians pick up the basics of the work from watching someone else do it. They might occasionally assist or ask questions of a working Sound Technician.

Talented Sound Technicians usually have gathered a lot of experience. The more they work on the sound board, the better they get at balancing the sound.

As individuals in this field usually have to travel extensively, it is a must for the person to have the flexibility to travel and to enjoy it. Not everyone likes living out of a suitcase for weeks on end.

Certain Sound Technicians start out as roadies, helping or filling in with sound work along the way. Eventually they either fill an opening or apply for a job as a Sound Technician with another group.

Unions and Associations

Touring Sound Technicians do not usually belong to any union, although they could be members of the International Alliance of Theatrical Stage Employees (IATSE).

Tips for Entry

1. If you are interested in working in this field, hang around clubs and bars that provide live entertainment. Most of the Sound Technicians working in this type of atmosphere will answer any questions you have. You might even offer to work for nothing. The experience you gain may pay you back with a job.

2. Working as a roadie for a short stint might not only train you, but also land you a job when the Sound Technician leaves.

3. You might consider taking out an advertisement (classified or display) in a trade magazine or a newspaper read by acts or managers requiring sound services. (The *Village Voice* in New York City frequently runs such ads.)

4. Positions may be advertised in the classified section of newspapers. Look under headings such as "Sound Technician," Sound Man," "Sound Woman," and "Audio Technician."

ADVANCE PERSON

CAREER PROFILE

Duties: Arrive ahead of the act to prepare for a concert; assist tour coordinator or road manager with details prior to show

Alternate Title(s): Advance Agent; Advance Man; Advance Woman

Salary Range: $23,000 to $48,000+

Employment Prospects: Poor

Advancement Prospects: Poor

Best Geographical Locations for Position: Positions are located in cities where major management and booking agencies are, such as New York City, Nashville, and Los Angeles

Prerequisites:

Education or Training—No formal education required

Experience—Nonmusic Advance Person; roadie experience helpful

Special Skills and Personality Traits—Freedom to travel; enjoyment of traveling alone; organization; dependability

CAREER LADDER

```
┌─────────────────────────────────┐
│          Road Manager           │
└─────────────────────────────────┘

┌─────────────────────────────────┐
│         Advance Person          │
└─────────────────────────────────┘

┌─────────────────────────────────┐
│ Nonmusic-oriented Advance Person; │
│             Roadie              │
└─────────────────────────────────┘
```

Position Description

The Advance Person goes out on the road before a tour. He or she leaves the home base before any of the entourage does and always arrives before the group; usually the Advance Person is gone by the time the act or group arrives at the destination.

When an Advance Person gets to a city in which an act is booked to perform, he or she will make sure that everything is set up as planned. He or she will check to see that posters and billboards are up. If they aren't, he or she might put them up or hire a crew to do it.

The Advance Person may bring in concert tickets. This happens rarely, though, because most concert halls utilize the services of a ticket service agency, such as Ticketron or Ticket Master. The Advance Person might bring in and hand-deliver any press passes issued by the publicist and/or management team.

The Advance Person will also hand-deliver press packages, photos, and promotional copies of records to press and promoters in each city.

Often the Advance Person checks out the acoustics of the hall or auditorium where the concert is to be held. He or she checks to see the location of electric outlets and types of electrical service available. This information is relayed back to the tour manager or coordinator. The Advance Person might also check out seating and exits and entrances of halls, making diagrams for the road personnel to use later.

Depending on the position, the Advance Person might measure mileage and check routes between concert cities. He or she might see what options are available for transportation in each city. All this information is relayed back to the tour manager, coordinator, or management office.

Certain groups have tremendous fan clubs that organize events in honor of the act's arrival in town. The Advance Person might contact the fan club president and deliver press passes or group memorabilia.

To be an Advance Person, an individual must be very dependable and responsible. No one is looking over the individual's shoulder. He or she must be able to structure his or her own day in order to get everything accomplished.

He or she must also be personable and articulate. Much of the job involves talking to people about the concert tour. As an Advance Person, an individual represents the group or act he or she is working for. The Advance Person must also like to travel and not mind being alone most of the time.

The Advance Person is responsible to the management, booking agency, or act that retained his or her services.

Salaries

Salaries vary depending on the group or management team that the Advance Person is working with.

Salaries usually start at about $400 per week and go up to $900 or more weekly. Advance People always receive either a per diem or reimbursement for their traveling expenses.

Advance people are usually paid by the week for the time that they work. Weeks that they are not on the road, they might have a reduction in salary, no salary, or might be kept on a retainer.

Employment Prospects

Employment prospects for this position are poor. With the new overnight delivery systems, many management firms just mail what they need delivered and make phone calls for any information. Furthermore, not every act uses an Advance Person.

Advancement Prospects

If a person does obtain a position as an Advance Person, he or she might eventually become a road manager or even a tour manager. It all depends on the type of organization the individual works with.

The Advance Person also has the option of working for bigger acts and better, more prestigious tours.

Education and Training

There is no formal educational requirement for this position. The individual might, however, be required to have a driver's license.

Experience, Skills, and Personality Traits

The Advance Person must like to travel and must not mind traveling alone. Advance People in the music business often have held positions as Advance People in other parts of the entertainment industry or for convention management.

The individual in this job must be extremely organized. He or she should be responsible and dependable. The Advance Person should also be personable and articulate.

Unions and Associations

There is no major association specific to Advance People.

Tips for Entry

1. This is a position you either get by contacts or by being in the right place at the right time. Pass along the word to musicians, groups, management, and booking agencies that you're looking for this type of job.
2. Advertise your availability in a small display or classified ad in one of the music trades.
3. Experience helps, whether it be experience as a non-music-oriented Advance Person or a travel agent, roadie, etc. Put in your résumé everything that might be of value to a potential employer.

MUSIC RETAILING
AND WHOLESALING

MUSIC SHOP MANAGER

CAREER PROFILE

Duties: Manage and run a music shop; buy and/or order instruments, sheet music, equipment, etc.

Alternate Title(s): Music Store Manager; Music Department Manager; Instrument Store Manager

Salary Range: $25,000 to $48,000+

Employment Prospects: Good

Advancement Prospects: Fair

Best Geographical Locations for Position: Any city or community that has a music shop

Prerequisites:

Education or Training—High school diploma, minimum; college degree or background often required

Experience—Retail sales experience; music shop salesperson

Special Skills and Personality Traits—Understanding of business management; knowledge of wide variety of instruments; ability to manage

CAREER LADDER

```
┌────────────────────────────────┐
│        Music Shop Owner         │
└────────────────────────────────┘

┌────────────────────────────────┐
│       Music Shop Manager        │
└────────────────────────────────┘

┌────────────────────────────────┐
│ Music Shop Assistant Manager;   │
│    Music Shop Salesperson       │
└────────────────────────────────┘
```

Position Description

The position of Music Shop Manager can be an exciting one for a person who likes to be around musical instruments. The main function of the individual in this job is to manage and run a retail music shop. There are many duties within the job classification.

Naturally, the Manager must oversee the day-to-day activities of the music shop. He or she is responsible for hiring and supervising employees. The Manager is in charge of putting together a work schedule for those who are employed by the shop. The individual assigns staff to perform specific duties and trains them, if necessary.

The Music Shop Manager works closely with the store owner (or he or she may be the store owner). Together, they decide what policies will be used for the store regarding payment, layaway, instrument returns, special orders, music lessons, etc. They may work out a marketing, advertising, or promotional campaign together, too.

The Music Shop Manager is in charge of seeing that instruments are ordered and purchased. The individual will select the equipment, supplies, and/or sheet music the store will stock. He or she is responsible for making sure that

orders come in, bills are paid on time, and internal problems with distributors or sales representatives are minimized.

If there is a problem with an instrument or piece of equipment that a customer has purchased in the music store, it is up to the manager to resolve the difficulty. The Manager must try to keep customers happy and uphold the reputation of the store.

The Music Shop Manager may act as a salesperson, selling instruments, equipment, or other supplies to customers. The individual may be called on to explain in detail differences in quality or variations among instruments.

He or she assumes the responsibility for maintaining operating records of all daily transactions. Cash income must be reconciled with the day's receipts.

This type of position usually has fairly regular retail hours. The Manager is responsible to the store owner or department store manager.

Salaries

Those who manage music shops or departments may expect salaries ranging from $25,000 to $48,000 plus yearly.

Salaries may consist of weekly salaries, bonuses, commissions, etc. The larger earnings go to individuals who are very experienced in managing music shops. The salary of a Music Shop Manager is also dependent on the location and size of the store.

Employment Prospects

Employment prospects for people seeking to be Music Shop or Department Managers are good. There are many opportunities for individuals in all sections of the country. People may find work in large stores, small shops, music store chains, or the instrument/sheet music department of a variety store.

Advancement Prospects

Music Shop or Department Managers move up the career ladder in a number of ways. They may advance by obtaining a job in a music store instead of a music department. An individual might move to a position in a larger, more prestigious store as a means of advancement. The other opportunity for a Music Department Manager is to open his or her own music shop.

Education and Training

Music shops often prefer their Managers to hold bachelor's degrees or at least have some type of college background. The exception would be an owner of a music shop who is also managing it. Even in such a situation, however, people find it helpful to have an education.

Music Shop Managers often hold degrees in business, liberal arts, music, retailing, music education, or music performance. A music background is necessary to successfully run a music store. This background may be obtained through the standard educational process, such as college or conservatory training, or might come from experiences dealing in music.

Experience, Skills, and Personality Traits

The Music Shop Manager needs to have an understanding of retail business management. He or she must possess the ability to hire, fire, and train personnel. The Manager will have to supervise the shop and the staff on a day-to-day basis.

The individual in this position needs knowledge of a wide variety of musical instruments. The person should be capable of playing or demonstrating most instruments in the store, or should find someone else who can handle this part of the enterprise.

Unions and Associations

Music Shop Managers may belong to the National Association of Music Merchants (NAMM).

Tips for Entry

1. Jobs for Music Shop Managers are advertised in the classified sections of newspapers. Look under headings such as "Music Shop Manager," "Manager-Retail," and "Retail Opportunities."
2. Job openings may also be posted in shop windows.
3. People working in music shops are often promoted. Many Music Shop Managers started working as salespeople in the shop they currently manage.
4. Send résumés and cover letters to music shops and request that they keep them on file.

MUSIC SHOP SALESPERSON

CAREER PROFILE

Duties: Sell instruments, musical accessories, equipment, supplies, and sheet music to customers in a retail store

Alternate Title(s): Music Shop Clerk; Instrument Shop Clerk

Salary Range: $15,000 to $25,000+

Employment Prospects: Good

Advancement Prospects: Fair

Best Geographical Location(s) for Position: Any city or area with music shops

Prerequisites:

Education or Training—High school diploma minimum; some positions require college background or degree; musical training

Experience—Retail sales experience helpful

Special Skills and Personality Traits—Knowledge of musical instruments; ability to play instruments; ability to work well with people; salesmanship

CAREER LADDER

```
┌─────────────────────────────────┐
│      Music Shop Manager          │
└─────────────────────────────────┘

┌─────────────────────────────────┐
│     Music Shop Salesperson       │
└─────────────────────────────────┘

┌─────────────────────────────────┐
│ Musician; Student; Retail Salesperson │
└─────────────────────────────────┘
```

Position Description

A Music Shop Salesperson sells instruments, musical accessories, equipment, supplies, and/or sheet music to customers in a retail store. The individual may specialize in selling brass, percussion, stringed, or woodwind instruments.

The Salesperson might act as a cashier, making a sale, totalling up the customer's purchases, arranging for layaways, taking money, and giving change.

The Music Shop Salesperson may perform a wide spectrum of other duties, depending on the job. A specific duty might be to assist customers in choosing the correct instruments for their needs. For example, someone may come into the store to buy a guitar. The Salesperson must find out a few things about the individual: Is the guitar going to be used for pleasure or to play in a band? Is the band a school group or a famous recording act? Does the customer want an electric guitar or an acoustic instrument? What size guitar: standard, three quarters, or child's size? What price range and brand is the customer considering? These are some of the questions the Salesperson needs answered in order to help a customer choose an instrument.

In this sales position, the individual might demonstrate a few different instruments to help a customer decide which has a better tone, sound, etc. The Salesperson talks to the potential buyer about the variables in the instruments versus the prices.

Salespeople or clerks in music shops may clean or repair instruments in addition to their sales duties. Depending on a person's talent, he or she might tune pianos, too.

The Salesperson in a music shop will take special orders for instruments not in stock. The individual often talks to schools in the area about their musical requirements and may try to solicit orders.

Salespeople in music shops frequently receive commissions on instrument sales as well as salaries. This gives them extra incentive to try to make additional sales.

Depending on the range of duties, the Salesperson may take inventory of existing merchandise and keep a list of what has been sold. He or she might send to call orders in to instrument sales representatives or companies.

In certain stores, the Salesperson also gives music lessons on various instruments. This depends on the competence of the individual teaching. The person is usually paid extra for this duty.

In a music shop, the Salesperson either works regular store hours or a particular shift. The job can be full- or part-time. The individual in this position is responsible directly to the store owner or manager.

Salaries

Salespeople working in music shops may be paid in a number of ways. The Salesperson may receive a straight salary, a commission on instruments sold, or a combination of the two. The salary range for Music Shop Salespeople is approximately $15,000 to $25,000 plus yearly. The lower figure represents the earnings of an individual working in a small shop with little or no experience. The higher figure is for a person who is working in a large music store in a city. That person probably has quite a bit of experience in the field.

Music Shop Salespeople who have the ability to play certain instruments well and can teach may make extra money by giving lessons.

Employment Prospects

Employment prospects for Music Shop Salespeople are good. Those who have the ability to play more than one instrument and can demonstrate them to prospective customers may have even better prospects. Opportunities for work exist in major cities, smaller cities, and large towns. Individuals may find work in large stores, small shops, or in the music sections of department stores.

Advancement Prospects

Individuals might find openings as Salespeople in larger stores. Working in a larger shop could mean that the Music Shop Salesperson would be earning a higher salary and/or commissions.

Those working as Music Shop Salespeople might climb the career ladder by advancing to Music Shop Managers or music department managers.

The Music Shop Salesperson may get experience, learn the business, and then open his or her own store.

Education and Training

Those working as Salespeople in music shops must usually hold at least a high school diploma. In larger, more presti-

gious music stores, management and/or owners may require that their staff have college degrees or backgrounds. Individuals who hold music degrees are often hired in these shops.

It is helpful for the Salesperson to be trained to play at least one instrument, preferably more than one. It is also useful for the person to have a knowledge of music theory and be able to read music. This training may be obtained in school, conservatories, colleges, through private study, or be self-taught.

Experience, Skills, and Personality Traits

The Music Shop Salesperson generally has had some type of retail sales experience prior to obtaining the music shop position. He or she must work well with people, making them feel comfortable purchasing in the store. The Salesperson must not pressure customers, but should be helpful and give honest, concise information about instruments and accessories.

The Music Shop Salesperson who can play and/or demonstrate various instruments is a valuable commodity in a music shop. The individual may also teach students who have purchased instruments from the store. Therefore, an ability to teach is a plus.

The individual must understand how the instruments work and be able to identify their various parts.

Unions and Associations

Depending on the store where an individual works, a Music Shop Salesperson may or may not belong to a bargaining union. The union might be an in-house union or may be a union that encompasses the job classification.

Music Shop Salespeople or the shops they work in might also belong to the National Association of Music Merchants (NAMM). This trade organization provides educational materials, training sessions, conferences, etc., for its members.

Tips for Entry

1. Jobs for Music Shop Salespeople are advertised in help wanted sections. Keep an eye on such headings as "Salesperson Wanted," "Instrument Sales," "Music Shop Clerk," etc.
2. Jobs are often posted in shops' windows.
3. You might consider sending résumés with cover letters to a number of stores. Follow up with a phone call.
4. Ask to see the store owner or manager and ask to fill out an application to be kept on file.

RECORD SHOP (OR DEPARTMENT) MANAGER

CAREER PROFILE

Duties: Manage and run a record shop or department on a day-to-day basis

Alternate Title(s): Record Store Manager

Salary Range: $23,000 to $48,000+

Employment Prospects: Excellent

Advancement Prospects: Good

Best Geographical Locations for Position: All locations have possible positions available

Prerequisites:

Education or Training—High school diploma minimum; some positions require or prefer college degree or background

Experience—Retail sales experience, preferably in record store or department

Special Skills and Personality Traits—Salesmanship; good administration; knowledge of retail record business; cognizance of customers' musical tastes

CAREER LADDER

```
┌─────────────────────────────────┐
│        Record Shop Owner;        │
│    Record Shop Chain Manager     │
└─────────────────────────────────┘

┌─────────────────────────────────┐
│  Record Shop/Department Manager  │
└─────────────────────────────────┘

┌─────────────────────────────────┐
│        Record Shop Clerk         │
└─────────────────────────────────┘
```

Position Description

Record Shop Managers work in record shops or in department stores in the record department. Their basic function is to manage and run the record shop or department on a day-to-day basis. The Manager may work for a private store owner, a record chain, a department store, or may be the actual shop owner.

Daily duties for the Record Shop Manager include the supervision of other employees in the store or department, development of work schedules, and assignment of employees to specific duties. He or she may be responsible for the hiring and firing of personnel.

The Record Shop Manager works in close contact with other employees, pitching in where needed. He or she may perform sales duties on a regular basis or assign these duties to clerks. The individual is responsible for taking care of any problems that arise with customers. These might include faulty merchandise, questions about orders, or difficulties with store personnel. It is up to the Manager to deal with problems and complaints in a fair manner but according to store policy. At times, the Manager may feel the need to go against store policy in order to keep a customer or to maintain good store relations. This is the individual's prerogative.

As the Record Shop Manager, the person is in charge of ordering merchandise. To do this, he or she must know what is hot. Managers of record shops must keep up with the current musical trends and customers' musical tastes.

The Record Shop Manager must take and/or supervise inventories of stock on hand. Certain CDs, videos, records, and tapes sell out as soon as they come in. Requisitions must be prepared to replenish the stock. Merchandise that does not sell can often be returned to the distributor. Data must be kept on what comes in, from what distributor, and on what date.

A variety of other merchandise and products may be ordered in addition to records, tapes, cassettes, and CDs. These might include music videos, blank cassettes, music magazines, posters, etc.

It is the responsibility of the Record Shop Manager to make sure that operating data are kept, daily postings of transactions are prepared, and cash is reconciled with sales receipts.

Depending on the store, the Manager may have to coordinate sales promotion activities and prepare advertisements and merchandising displays. The Record Shop Manager may perform any of these functions or supervise or direct other employees to do so.

The Record Shop Manager's hours vary, but are usually fairly regular. The Manager is responsible to the storeowner, record chain supervisor, or department store manager. If the Manager owns the store, he or she is responsible only to him or herself and to any investors.

Salaries
Salaries for Record Shop Managers fluctuate, depending on the size of the store, the location, and the experience of the individual.

Starting salaries are usually around $23,000 per year. Earnings for more experienced record shop managers of very large stores may range from $30,000 to $48,000 annually. Monies can come in the form of salaries, commissions, and/or bonuses.

Many Record Shop Managers own the shop they run and receive a percentage of the profits.

Employment Prospects
There are openings for Record Shop and Record Department Managers across the country. Individuals who have had sales experience in record shops and know how a store works are qualified for the many positions available.

With the great demand for CDs, cassettes, etc., there are more and more shops opening. There is hardly a city or town in the country that does not have at least one store, and most have more than one.

Advancement Prospects
Advancement prospects for Record Shop Managers are good. Individuals may upgrade their careers in a number of ways.

One method is to obtain a position at a larger store with additional responsibilities and greater earnings. Others advance their career by moving from a job at a department store as a Manager of the record department to a job as Manager of a record shop. There are individuals who begin

as Record Shop Managers and go on to manage whole chains of record stores. Of course, there are those people who promote themselves by buying their own record shops.

Education and Training
Record Shop Managers must usually have a minimum of a high school diploma. Some positions require or prefer a college degree or background. There are degree programs available in retailing, business administration, and music merchandising that can prove useful.

Experience, Skills, and Personality Traits
Record Shop Managers generally have worked in a retail sales position previous to their appointment. Usually, they have worked in a record store as a clerk for a period of time. The duration of this experience varies from person to person. However, Managers generally have worked long enough in a clerical position to learn how the retail record business is run. Depending on the geographical area of the record shop, Managers must know the type of customers they will be servicing and what their musical tastes are. The Record Shop Manager must be reliable, honest, and hardworking. Besides this, he or she must be a good administrator, capable of hiring and firing employees.

Unions and Associations
Record Shop Managers or the shops they manage may be members of the National Association of Recording Merchandisers (NARM). This organization is a trade association for people in the recording business.

Tips for Entry
1. These positions are often advertised in the help wanted sections of newspapers.
2. There are employment agencies that occasionally look for people to fill jobs as Managers of record shops. Depending on the agency and the job, you might have to pay a fee if you obtain a position. Check it out first.
3. Many record stores like to promote from within. If you are working as a clerk in a store and impress the owner, you may be able to advance your career.
4. Record shops often advertise openings on their front window. Keep a lookout for these signs.

RECORD STORE CLERK

CAREER PROFILE

Duties: Sell records and tapes in record shop or department; assist customers

Alternate Title(s): Record Shop Clerk; Record Shop Salesperson

Salary Range: $15,000 to $25,000+

Employment Prospects: Excellent

Advancement Prospects: Good

Best Geographical Location(s) for Position: Positions may be located nationwide

Prerequisites:

Education or Training—High school diploma (or high school student)

Experience—Retail sales experience helpful, but not required

Special Skills and Personality Traits—Sales ability; ability to work well with others; dependability; enjoyment of records and music

CAREER LADDER

```
┌────────────────────────────────┐
│      Record Store Manager      │
└────────────────────────────────┘

┌────────────────────────────────┐
│      Record Store Clerk        │
└────────────────────────────────┘

┌────────────────────────────────┐
│  Student; Other Retail Sales Job │
└────────────────────────────────┘
```

Position Description

Record Store Clerks work in record stores or departments selling CDs, cassettes, records, tapes, and assorted music-oriented merchandise to customers. Other goods might include blank cassettes and CDs, cassette and CD cases, recording maintenance equipment and supplies, music videos, posters, and music magazines.

The Record Store Clerk or salesperson may perform a variety of functions. One of these is to assist customers. Patrons may need help locating records, deciding what album would be suitable for a gift, or deciphering price codes on CDs.

The Clerk may be responsible for totalling a customer's purchases, taking money, giving change, and packaging or wrapping the merchandise. The salesperson will take down information for special orders that are not in stock. The Clerk will pass the information on to the store manager to order.

Under the supervision of the record shop manager, the Clerk may receive new stock into the store from distributors. He or she may count and sort the merchandise and verify receipt of items on invoices. The individual will check that the items arriving are indeed the merchandise that was ordered.

The Clerk may take inventory of existing merchandise, maintaining lists, and informing the manager of those records selling well and those that have not moved. He or she may pack up items that are being sent back to the distributor.

The Clerk might stamp, mark, or attach price tags to goods in the store. At times, he or she may stock bins, shelves, etc. Depending on the situation, the individual may help the manager set up advertising displays or arrange merchandise in a manner that will promote sales.

Sales Clerks work different shifts. They may work full- or part-time. Individuals in this position are responsible to the shop manager.

Salaries

Earnings for Record Store Clerks vary depending on the experience of the person, the size of the store, and the geographical location. Salaries begin at or slightly above the minimum wage. Clerks working in record shops can expect to earn $15,000 to $25,000 plus yearly. Sales Clerks may earn straight salaries or salaries plus commissions on each sale made. Sales Clerks might also receive bonuses.

Employment Prospects

Employment prospects are excellent. This particular job is one in which almost anyone can enter the music business. There are virtually thousands upon thousands of positions open in record shops, record chains, and department stores in every section of the country.

This is an entry-level position. Young people still in high school or college often apply for jobs in record shops to learn about the record business.

Advancement Prospects

Those who wish to advance have good prospects. Record Store Clerks are often promoted to record department managers, record shop managers, or other management positions in the store or chain.

As noted above, many individuals begin working in a record shop as a way of entering the music field. Learning about record sales helps prepare those aspiring to enter the recording industry. It affords them a positive means of entry.

Education and Training

Those working in record shops as clerks are usually required to hold at least a high school diploma. However, most stores will hire young people who are high school students as part-time workers or for summer jobs.

Experience, Skills, and Personality Traits

Although some retail sales experience is helpful, it is often not required. What is required is that the Record Store Clerk be pleasant and helpful to customers. A knowledge of the current records and trends is useful.

Record Store Clerks must work well with others and be dependable and reliable.

Unions and Associations

In very small record shops, Clerks usually do not belong to unions. Clerks often belong to unions in larger record shops or while working in the record department of a department store. The union may be an in-house union or a local union that encompasses the job classification.

Tips for Entry

1. Positions for Record Store Clerks are often advertised in the classified sections of newspapers. Look under key words such as "Record Store," "Retail," "Music," or "Clerk."
2. Openings are also often noted in shop windows or on bulletin boards.
3. You may consider going into a record shop and asking to see the manager. This individual will usually let you fill out an application and keep it on file for future reference.

INSTRUMENT SALES REPRESENTATIVE

CAREER PROFILE

Duties: Sell musical instruments to dealers

Alternate Title(s): Sales Rep; Rep; Manufacturer's Representative

Salary Range: $22,000 to $75,000+

Employment Prospects: Good

Advancement Prospects: Good

Best Geographical Location(s) for Position: Instrument manufacturers are located in various areas of the country

Prerequisites:

Education or Training—High school diploma minimum; some positions require college background or degree

Experience—Some sales experience (either wholesale or retail) helpful

Special Skills and Personality Traits—Sales ability; communications skills; knowledge of music and instruments; ability to play instrument helpful

CAREER LADDER

```
┌─────────────────────────────────────┐
│          Sales Manager              │
└─────────────────────────────────────┘

┌─────────────────────────────────────┐
│  Instrument Sales Representative    │
└─────────────────────────────────────┘

┌─────────────────────────────────────┐
│         Nonmusic Sales Job          │
└─────────────────────────────────────┘
```

Position Description

An Instrument Sales Representative sells musical instruments to shops, dealerships, and schools. Usually a Sales Rep has a specific territory. This area (sometimes called a region or district) may consist of a few cities, counties, or states, or an entire section of the country.

As a Sales Rep, the individual must know as much as possible about the instrument(s) and the manufacturer. Additionally, it is important for the person to know about instruments manufactured by competing companies. With this information, the individual can speak knowledgeably to dealers about comparisons. Actually, the more knowledge the Sales Rep has, the better qualified that person is to come up with a good sales pitch. Knowing about the weaknesses of a particular instrument (even if it's made by one's own company) helps prepare the individual to field questions on the subject.

In this position, a person may make sales calls either in person or on the phone or combine the two methods. The individual is responsible for visiting established accounts, seeing what they require and what has been sold since the last visit. The Sales Representative will probably talk to the dealer for a short while, discussing any problems with instruments sold and under warranty. He or she may review new instruments, products, trends, etc. By the time the Sales Representative is ready to leave, he or she should have developed a large order for the company.

The Rep may also seek out new accounts (places to sell the instruments). To do this, the individual may call in advance to try to set up an appointment, send a letter and some product brochures, or just drop in. The dealer may not buy from the Sales Representative the first time, but may after a relationship has been established.

As an Instrument Representative, the individual may call or visit schools to find out about their band and orchestra instrument needs. Making a sale in this area could mean a big order. Schools, both public and private, may create a new market for the Sales Rep.

The Instrument Sales Representative has duties other than selling. He or she must telephone established and new accounts, send letters and brochures, keep up on all the newest instrument technology, and maintain good records. Losing an order or forgetting to call back a potential buyer may mean not only a lost sale, but possibly a lost job.

The Sales Representative is usually directly responsible to the sales manager of the organization. Hours for this type of position vary. Some jobs offer more flexibility in working hours than others.

Salaries

Remuneration for Sales Representatives may be made in a variety of ways. Reps may be paid a straight salary, a commission, or a combination of the two. Instrument Sales Representatives additionally may receive bonuses and fringe benefits, including cars, traveling expenses, etc.

Earnings for Sales Representatives in the musical instrument field range from $22,000 to $75,000 plus. Individuals working on commission basis can do quite well financially. The sky is the limit as far as earnings are concerned.

Employment Prospects

Employment prospects for this field are good. There are many openings for aggressive, talented Sales Representatives. Those who have a background in music and have the ability to play an instrument or group of instruments have an advantage.

Many positions require the individual to sell in large geographic areas. Those who don't mind traveling will find even greater opportunities.

Advancement Prospects

Advancement prospects for an Instrument Sales Representative are generally good. If the individual has done a good job, met sales quotas, maintained good relationships with shop owners and dealers, and opened new accounts, he or she may be promoted to a sales manager position. This position may be on a local, regional, national, or possibly even international level.

Education and Training

Educational requirements differ with each position. Many companies just require their Sales Reps to have high school diplomas. Others prefer that their sales staff have college backgrounds or degrees.

Some type of music or instrument training is useful for a better understanding of the product being sold.

Experience, Skills, and Personality Traits

A person who works for a major music manufacturer as a Sales Representative will usually have had some type of retail or wholesale sales experience. The individual might have had other types of selling jobs unrelated to the music business.

The ability to come up with a good sales pitch is essential. The Rep must be aggressive without being annoying. It helps immensely if the individual has the ability to be articulate both on the phone and in person. It is also useful for the Sales Representative to be knowledgeable about music and about the instrument being sold. The ability to play one or more instruments can also be helpful.

Unions and Associations

Instrument Sales Representatives may belong to the National Association of Music Merchants (NAMM). Depending on the type of instruments the individual sells, he or she may also belong to the Guitar and Accessories Marketing Association (GAMA).

Tips for Entry

1. Get some experience selling before you apply for a job as a Sales Rep. You might consider finding a job in a music instrument shop. This will give you an opportunity to talk to Sales Representatives to find out more about the job.
2. When you do apply for a job with a company, know as much about the company, their instruments, etc., as possible. This will help to impress the interviewer with your capabilities.
3. If you do play an instrument, try to find some manufacturers in that family of instruments. The ability to play that instrument is a plus when looking for a job of this type.
4. You might want to look for a job on-line. Check out company websites as well as some of the on-line job sites.

RACK JOBBER

CAREER PROFILE

Duties: Supply compact discs, cassettes, records, and tapes to shops whose main business is not the sale of records

Alternate Title(s): Subdistributor

Salary Range: $24,000 to $48,000+

Employment Prospects: Fair to Good

Advancement Prospects: Fair

Best Geographical Location(s) for Position: Positions may be located in most cities across the country

Prerequisites:

Education or Training—High school diploma

Experience—Selling experience (both wholesale and retail) helpful

Special Skills and Personality Traits—Good business skills; knowledge of music market; good salesmanship; ability to work with figures and calculations

CAREER LADDER

```
┌─────────────────────────────────────┐
│   Owner of Record Shop; Record       │
│ Company Distribution Representative   │
└─────────────────────────────────────┘

┌─────────────────────────────────────┐
│            Rack Jobber               │
└─────────────────────────────────────┘

┌─────────────────────────────────────┐
│   Rack Jobber Field Representative   │
└─────────────────────────────────────┘
```

Position Description

A Rack Jobber supplies compact discs, cassettes, records, and videotapes to shops that are not primarily in the record/tape business. Many of the record displays that are seen in supermarkets, department stores, automotive shops, discount stores, book stores, and drug stores are put together by Rack Jobbers. A Rack Jobber, incidentally, may have a number of people working in the business or may work alone.

As a Rack Jobber, the individual selects CDs, cassettes, etc., to display and sell in a section of someone else's store or market. He or she receives space and in return either pays a rental fee, a leasing fee, a percentage of record sales, or a combination of these.

The job of a Rack Jobber is much like that of owning a retail record store. However, in this instance, the merchandise is in a space that already draws a stream of customer traffic. The Rack Jobber may have space in more than one store.

The Rack Jobber buys records from a distributor. Since he or she has limited space, it is impossible to stock every CD and cassette, as a conventional record shop does. The most important records are those that have a high rating on the charts. The charts, in turn, are compiled in part by reports from Rack Jobbers on sales of specific records.

Rack Jobbers offer the store a record department. If an item doesn't sell, the Rack Jobber takes it back. This is a no-risk situation for the store's management.

It is the Rack Jobber's responsibility to select the CDs and cassettes and place those that he or she feels will sell. After making sure that they get to the store, the individual must also make sure that they are displayed properly. This display should be pleasing to the eye and make people want to look at and purchase merchandise. The Rack Jobber periodically comes into the store and takes inventory. He or she takes back merchandise that isn't moving and brings in better sellers.

Depending on the situation, the Rack Jobber must either hire a staff of salespeople (if it is a lease situation) or train and supervise members of the store's existing staff who will be working in the record department. In this instance, a rental fee or percentage may be paid to the store by the Rack Jobber.

In addition, the Rack Jobber supplies the store with advertising and promotional material to help sell the records. The Rack Jobber is in charge of keeping inventory and accounting records for his or her space.

As a Rack Jobber, the individual will get to know the distributors from many of the major record companies. This will enable the Rack Jobber to develop contacts within the recording industry.

The Rack Jobber must keep the stores happy and satisfied or they will not renew their contracts.

Salaries

Salaries for Rack Jobbers vary, depending on the company, its location, how many records are sold, and the type of salary received.

Earnings may be in the form of a straight commission or may be a guaranteed salary against a commission.

Salaries range from $24,000 to $48,000 plus.

Employment Prospects

There are many stores and shops that have record displays and/or record departments serviced by Rack Jobbers. The prospects are fair to good for people who want to find jobs in this field. A person may take over an entire rack jobbing operation or be a field representative. The field representative, incidentally, acts under the instructions of the main Rack Jobber, performing most of the same functions.

Advancement Prospects

Individuals who work as Rack Jobbers or Rack Jobber field representatives have a fair chance of moving ahead in their careers. If they decide that they like the business, they might open up their own record shops. A Rack Jobber may increase the size of his or her business immensely by broadening the base of operation.

As Rack Jobbers meet and work closely with distributors of major recording companies, they frequently make good contacts in the record industry. As a result, many of these individuals obtain jobs in the distribution department of large labels.

Education and Training

No educational background is required to be a Rack Jobber or to work for one, except possibly having a high school diploma. Individuals who do prefer to go to college will find that courses in business, marketing, merchandising, and related fields will be useful. There are also music merchandising and music business majors available in many schools; these can be useful for individuals desiring to work in this field.

Experience, Skills, and Personality Traits

A Rack Jobber needs a good head for business. He or she must have the ability to sell and to be aggressive in a nice way. Knowledge of the current music market, trends, and the record business is essential to success. Being organized is also helpful.

Unions and Associations

Rack Jobbers may belong to a number of associations. These include the National Association of Music Merchants (NAMM) and the National Association of Recording Merchandisers (NARM). Both these organizations sponsor conventions, meetings, seminars, and conferences for their members. The associations also offer books, pamphlets, and other information useful to those selling or distributing records and cassettes.

Tips for Entry

1. If you're looking for a job as a Rack Jobber/field representative, visit various drug stores, department stores, supermarkets, etc. Find out who their Rack Jobbers are. Get addresses and phone numbers and set up interviews.
2. Many of the major department stores around the country have record departments serviced by Rack Jobbers. To begin with, get a job as a clerk. Move up from there.
3. Call the distributor department of a major record company. Try to find out names and addresses of Rack Jobbers in your area. Send them your résumé and a cover letter, and try to arrange an interview.

THE BUSINESS END
OF THE INDUSTRY

PERSONAL MANAGER

CAREER PROFILE

Duties: Represent act; oversee and guide all aspects of an artist's career

Alternate Title(s): Artist's Representative; Manager

Salary Range: 10% to 50% of artist's earnings ·

Employment Prospects: Good

Advancement Prospects: Poor

Best Geographical Locations for Position: Managers for major acts are usually located in New York City, Los Angeles, or Nashville; managers for lesser known acts may be located anywhere in the country

Prerequisites:

Education or Training—No educational requirement; college background helpful; courses or seminars in business and music industry useful

Experience—Any type of experience in any phase of the music business is valuable

Special Skills and Personality Traits—Music industry contacts; aggressiveness; knowledge of music industry; ability to see raw talent; ability to work under pressure

CAREER LADDER

```
┌─────────────────────────────┐
│   Personal Manager for      │
│   Top Recording Act         │
└─────────────────────────────┘

┌─────────────────────────────┐
│   Personal Manager          │
└─────────────────────────────┘

┌─────────────────────────────┐
│   Entry-Level Position;     │
│   Assistant to Personal     │
│   Manager                   │
└─────────────────────────────┘
```

Position Description

The main job of the Personal Manager is to represent one or more musical groups or artists. In doing this, the Manager oversees all aspects of an act's career.

The Personal Manager, in essence, deals with and advises the act on all business decisions and many of the creative decisions artists must make. In this manner, the Manager attempts to guide an artist's rise to the top.

The Manager begins by hearing and/or seeing an artist he or she feels has talent. After discussions with the act, a Manager may feel he or she has something to offer the act. The Manager should have the know-how to direct a musical career. If a bargain is struck, the two parties usually sign a contract. It is then the Manager's job to begin to plan for stardom.

In this position, the Manager is the single most important person (talent notwithstanding) helping the act attain stardom or success. Soon after signing the contract, the Manager will begin looking for a record label that is interested in the act. This is accomplished in a variety of ways, including talking to personal contacts, showcasing the act, and/or providing demo tapes and videos.

When the Manager finds a label interested in the act, he or she may negotiate a recording deal or recommend a music industry attorney to negotiate on behalf of the group.

The Manager seeks out booking agents to find engagements for the act. If the act is just starting out, the Manager may book dates him- or herself. However, it is illegal in a number of states for an individual to act as both a Manager and a booking agent. In other words, the Manager cannot usually take both a percentage of the artist's earnings for managing and an additional percentage for booking the act.

The Manager might help the artists polish their act by reviewing tunes, choreography, costumes, and backup musicians. He or she might also help choose musical personnel, producers, engineers, etc., for a recording date.

Representing the artist at all times, the Manager advises the act about other personnel to hire and/or fire. Personnel might include both business and talent people. Some examples of support personnel are: public relations firms, publicists, road personnel, producers, musicians, accountants, security people, and merchandisers.

As the Manager, the individual is responsible for advancing the act's career as much as possible. He or she must oversee all the personnel and their jobs in relation to the act. At times, the Manager might have to audit books or act as a Road Manager or even as the heavy in a dispute with a promoter.

A Manager must be willing to work hard for the success of the client. Working hard, however, doesn't always mean the artist will be successful. It is helpful for the Manager to have industry contacts. These contacts sometimes help the artist get to the top.

Managers are often given power of attorney for their clients. In some cases, the power of attorney is complete; in others, it is limited. Whatever the case, the Manager usually is given authority to approve concert dates and places, monies for concerts, publicity materials, etc.

The individual an act chooses to be its Manager must be compatible with the act. He or she must be available on a day-to-day basis to discuss any problems the artist has. In addition, the two parties must meet on a regular basis to discuss new ways to advance the career of the act.

In many cases, the Manager puts up money to finance the group or artist hoping to make the money back later. In other cases, the Manager might find a financial backer for the group.

The Personal Manager works closely with all members of the act's team. He or she may spend a great deal of time with the act's publicity or public relations firm working on building the image of the act.

The Manager will also be in constant communication with the act's booking agent or agency. The Manager must make sure that the act is always well represented by others.

The Manager is responsible directly to the act. Although the terms of each artist-manager contract are different, most run for a specified number of years. Some have option clauses that the Manager can pick up if he or she desires.

The lifestyle of a Personal Manager in the music business is a busy one. Long hours are spent with the act. More hours are used up dealing on the group's behalf. If a Manager is with an artist who makes it financially, he or she usually enjoys the success, too. Since Managers can handle more than one client (although they don't usually handle vast numbers at any one time), they can make out quite well financially.

Salaries

Personal Managers receive a percentage of the artist's earnings. This percentage varies with the individual and the manager. It can range from 10% to 50%. The usual amount is 15% to 20% of artist earnings. In certain situations, the percentage goes up as an artist makes more money. For example, the Manager may make 10% of all earnings up to $100,000 and 15% on all monies after that.

Managers receive these fees off the top. Fees are received on monies from personal appearances, concerts, television, recording, etc. In some cases, the Manager also takes a percentage of merchandising paraphernalia sold (T-shirts, posters, bumper stickers, pins, etc.).

A Manager working with a band just starting out may earn the same amount of money as the band members until they get on their feet financially. The Manager may opt to take nothing until the group starts doing reasonably well.

The Manager often puts up money for the act in excess of his or her salary, temporarily losing money. The Manager hopes that the money will be recouped later when the band is successful. (On the other hand, the band may break up or never get anywhere, and the Manager may incur a loss.)

A Manager working with a top recording group can make $500,000 plus. Managers often handle more than one act at a time.

Employment Prospects

Employment prospects are good for Personal Managers. As almost anyone can become a Manager, all one has to do is find acts to sign up. This is not to say that everyone can be a *good* Manager. In order to be successful, the Personal Manager must have contacts and guide the act's career.

There are many groups that are not yet signed with anyone. An individual with an eye for raw talent can certainly enter this field.

Advancement Prospects

There are many Managers around the country and the world. Most of them, however, do not handle major acts. In order to attract a top recording act, a Manager must have proven him- or herself in the past. This usually means having a top act or an up-and-coming act signed. One other excellent method is for the Personal Manager to start with a new act and work with them, guiding their career until stardom. Unfortunately, though, as groups begin to attain success they often try to get out of their contracts with smaller Managers and sign with better known Managers.

Education and Training

There is no formal educational requirement to qualify one for a position as a Manager. A college background is helpful, however. There are currently degrees and courses offered in the music business and music merchandising. Other useful majors and/or courses are business, law, communications, journalism, and marketing.

Experience, Skills, and Personality Traits

A very broad knowledge of the entire music business is necessary for success as a Manager. Many new Managers (those starting out with local acts, for instance) learn the ropes as they go. It is important for the individual to acquire as many useful music contacts as possible. This allows the Manager to help an act.

Successful Managers are hard-working individuals, always making efforts on their group's behalf. A Personal Manager should have the ability to see raw talent and work with it until it is polished to perfection.

Many Managers begin their careers as musicians and find they enjoy the business end of the industry more. Personal Managers should be adept at all the business facets of an entertainer's career. The ability to give positive, constructive advice on the creative end is a plus.

Unions and Associations

Personal Managers may be members of the Conference of Personal Managers. This organization sets standards for the conduct of Personal Managers.

Tips for Entry

1. Try to break into management on a local level. There are many acts waiting for someone to help them.
2. You might consider working for a management agency as a secretary or assistant to learn the ropes.
3. There are often ads placed in the classified sections of newspapers and trades by groups seeking management. Some of these acts need management to find a backer. Some will want the Manager to be the backer, while others may just need to have someone notice their talent. Check it out.
4. Look for an internship program in any aspect of the industry to give you a good background and the opportunity to make contacts.

BOOKING AGENT

CAREER PROFILE

Duties: Secure engagements for musical artists and groups

Alternate Title(s): Booking Manager; Theatrical Agent; Booker; Agent; Booking Representative

Salary Range: $20,000 to $1,000,000+

Employment Prospects: Fair

Advancement Prospects: Fair

Best Geographical Location(s) for Position: New York City, Los Angeles, and Nashville for major agencies; other cities may have opportunities

Prerequisites:

Education or Training—No educational requirement

Experience—Experience in various facets of music business; sales jobs; buying talent for college concerts

Special Skills and Personality Traits—Ability to communicate; knowledge of music business; knowledge of routing; ability to talk on phone for great lengths of time; good salesmanship

CAREER LADDER

```
┌─────────────────────────────────────┐
│      Booking Agency Owner;           │
│   Booking Agent for Major Talent     │
└─────────────────────────────────────┘

┌─────────────────────────────────────┐
│           Booking Agent              │
└─────────────────────────────────────┘

┌─────────────────────────────────────┐
│    Agent for Local Bands; Musician   │
└─────────────────────────────────────┘
```

Position Description

Booking Agents are also known as Booking Managers, Theatrical Agents, Bookers, Agents, and Booking Representatives. Whatever name the individual goes by, he or she performs one main job: secure engagements for musical artists and groups.

The Booking Agent works in a number of ways. To start with, an Agent needs the talent to book. He or she may send out literature, brochures, pictures, etc., to a variety of clubs and concert halls to obtain bookings for a client. The Booking Agent usually follows up with many phone calls to these places.

If an Agent is dealing with a recognized talent (for example, a group with a Top 40 record on the charts) things are different. Under these circumstances, the Agent is usually called by clubs and promoters who want the act to appear in their venues. The Booking Agent works very closely with the act's Manager and knows what fee to charge. The Agent will often negotiate with a promoter or club who wants the act for a lower price.

After a deal has been struck on the phone, the Agent sends out copies of contracts to be signed by the promoter or club owner. These contracts include all the information required by the promoter for the show or concert. Included is the name of the group, the date of the concert, the times of the shows, how many performances are required, how much money will be paid for the performance, and in what manner it will be paid. Agents, as a rule, require a percentage of the money up front. This amount varies, but is usually about 50%. The money is due when the contract is signed. The Agent collects the money, takes his or her percentage, and pays the group. The rest of the money is usually paid at the performance.

The contracts Agents send to people employing their acts may also have a rider attached that stipulates any extras the group is to receive. These extras might include expense money, hotel rooms, food, limousines, or instrumental augmentation, among other things.

In large agencies, Agents are often separated into categories. For instance, one Agent may handle classical acts, another rock acts, still another R & B acts. Other agencies may handle just one variety of artist.

Agents representing top artists may set up complete concert tours for the acts and deal with promoters all over the country. During these tours, the Agent works with the artist's manager and record company, deciding where concerts will be most effective.

In many states, booking agencies and Agents must be licensed. These licenses, like those of other employment agencies, are usually obtained through state agencies.

Agents often audition new talent that comes to them seeking representation. In addition, many Agents attend showcases, local clubs, etc., looking for talent to book.

Agents may represent a client exclusively or nonexclusively, depending on the circumstances. The Agent may also represent a client exclusively in one field (e.g., concerts) and nonexclusively in another (e.g., personal appearances).

Agents can represent as many clients as they can handle. They often book artists who compete with one another in the marketplace. Agents strive to build up a roster of clients. In addition, Agents aspire to have clients who command large fees.

The Agent is responsible to the artist and his or her manager. An Agent may sign an artist for a specified number of years.

Most of the working day of an Agent is spent on the phone trying to sell the acts, talking about the acts, negotiating for the acts, etc. Most Agents spend seven to eight hours a day on the phone and use the phone as the vehicle to success.

Salaries

Booking Agents are paid a commission. They receive a percentage off the top of the artist's fee. Commissions vary, but usually range from 10% to 20% of the act's gross income per show.

Agents working in agencies may be paid a salary plus a percentage of the monies they bring into the agency. Agents who make the most money usually handle more than one act. The most successful Agent may earn $200,000 to $1,000,000 or more per year. Individuals just starting out in the industry make much less. The variables are too great to estimate the average salary.

Employment Prospects

It is extremely difficult to break into booking on a major scale. Entering on a local level, however, prospects are much brighter. Many aspiring agents begin by booking local talent (or possibly even their own band) in local clubs and bars.

There are also agencies located in most cities. These agencies do not usually book major talent. Instead, they book regional talent. Entry into such an agency is another possibility for the individual looking for a job as an Agent.

Most booking agencies that book major talent are located in New York City, Los Angeles, and Nashville. Many of these agencies have offices in other cities around the country.

Advancement Prospects

Agents may advance in a number of ways. They may begin booking a local band that gains some notoriety and go up the success ladder with it.

Another way an Agent may advance his or her career is to gain entry into a regional agency. After obtaining experience, the Agent might be able to move into a major agency.

Agents frequently become talent buyers for concert halls, clubs, arenas, etc. Other Agents build up enough of a client roster to start their own talent agency. There is no one way to advance a career like this. There are a number of Booking Agents and agencies around the country who are making a fortune booking acts on a regional level. Some of these people earn more than Agents who work in a major agency in a music capital.

Education and Training

There is no educational requirement to work as a Booking Agent. There are seminars, workshops, and courses available in booking entertainment. Courses in business may be useful. There are also classes and seminars in contracts and/or contract law offered in many colleges.

Experience, Skills, and Personality Traits

A Booking Agent, in effect, sells a group or an artist. Therefore, first and foremost an Agent must possess sales ability.

In order to be a successful Agent, one must be aggressive. Much of the selling of acts is done on the telephone. Agents of major groups may stay on the phone pushing their acts for seven to eight hours a day or even more.

As in most jobs in the music industry, Agents must be able to work under extreme pressure. Acts constantly call to see if they have new jobs. Managers call to tell the Agent they want more money for their acts. Clubs call to negotiate for an act for less money. Even after everything is set up, the group might cancel. The Agent must be able to keep his or her cool under these conditions.

Unions and Associations

Major Booking Agents may work under a union contract, such as that of the American Federation of Musicians (AFM), the American Federation of Television and Radio Artists (AFTRA), the American Guild of Variety Artists (AGVA), the Screen Actors Guild (SAG), or the American Guild of Musical Artists (AGMA). These unions specify what percentage an Agent can get from an act, how long contracts can run, etc.

Tips for Entry

1. Start booking groups in your area. All groups need work and most can never find enough jobs. Make sure the groups you book know that you will be taking a percentage. This money won't make you rich, but it will give you an opportunity to gain valuable experience in this type of position.

2. You might consider calling clubs in your area, too. Try to set up a meeting with the owner or club manager to see if they need entertainment for their clubs. Indicate that you will hire the entertainment under their direction, taking into account their budget, style of music, etc. Then place an ad for bands looking for work. Always keep a list of possibles in case an act cancels out.

3. In both of the above instances, try to use some form of contract as protection for yourself so that you get your commission.

4. If you want to work in a major agency, you might have to accept an entry-level position as a secretary, receptionist, or mailroom clerk. Once you get in, ask questions and be interested.

5. If you are familiar with the business and have some experience, keep knocking on doors and calling major agencies. They often feel that if you can sell yourself to them, you can certainly sell the acts.

6. Look into the training programs some of the bigger agencies have established. There is a list of major agencies in the appendix.

CONCERT PROMOTER

CAREER PROFILE

Duties: Present talent in concert, club, or festival settings; oversee every aspect of putting on a show

Alternate Title(s): Talent Promoter

Salary Range: $0 to $1,000,000+

Employment Prospects: Poor

Advancement Prospects: Poor

Best Geographical Location(s) for Position: Large cities for major concerts; smaller cities for other types of shows

Prerequisites:

Education or Training—No educational requirement

Experience—Music business background helpful; booking acts on any level; working as an assistant to a concert promoter or in a promotional company is helpful

Special Skills and Personality Traits—Ability to finance shows; knowledge of music business; knowledge of area where concert is being promoted; stamina; contacts within the industry

CAREER LADDER

```
┌─────────────────────────────────────┐
│   Concert Promoter of Major Talent   │
└─────────────────────────────────────┘

┌─────────────────────────────────────┐
│          Concert Promoter            │
└─────────────────────────────────────┘

┌─────────────────────────────────────┐
│    Assistant to Concert Promoter     │
└─────────────────────────────────────┘
```

Position Description

The Concert Promoter is responsible for putting concerts together. As a Promoter, the individual has many duties.

The first thing a Promoter needs to do is secure the money required for the venture. In some cases, the Promoter raises and invests the money and is the backer him- or herself. In other situations, the Promoter finds others who share the expenses and profits.

The Promoter must have a definite plan of action. In what city will the concert take place? Which hall (or club, arena, etc.) will be used? When will the show be? How many shows will be promoted? Who will headline?

Creation of a preliminary budget is one of the most important tasks the promoter will undertake. Underbudgeted, the Promoter will lose money; overbudgeted, he or she is in a better position. The extra budget funds will often take care of situations that don't go according to plan. The preliminary budget will be reworked after negotiations for the main act have taken place.

Once the Promoter has completed the negotiations, signed the headliner and a supporting act, and rented a venue, he or she must go to work to sell tickets.

The Promoter generally must advertise. He or she will decide where the advertising dollar buys most—on radio or TV, or in the print media. The Promoter will buy advertising space, keeping in mind the money allocated for advertising in the budget. If, near the show date, and ticket sales are low, the Promoter might put extra money into advertising.

The Promoter will have posters, flyers, etc., printed and put up around the area. He or she will also need a place for tickets to be sold. This might be the box office of the concert hall, a ticket selling agency, or record stores in the area.

The Promoter may work with the act's record company or the act themselves putting together interviews, publicity stunts, press conferences, etc., in order to build momentum before the concert. The Promoter may hire a publicist or public relations firm to help orchestrate these things or may do them him- or herself. The Promoter or the publicist also sees that the press releases, press kits, and free tickets are delivered to media people prior to the event.

The Promoter is in charge of supervising any workers, specialists, etc., who have been hired. Depending on the circumstances under which the hall is rented, the Promoter may be responsible, additionally, for hiring and/or supervising stage managers, ushers, security guards, lighting technicians, sound technicians, and people to move equipment.

The night of the concert the Promoter will go over the final box office receipts, often with the act's manager or road manager in attendance. At this time, the act is usually paid the monies that were not advanced to them on signing the contract.

After the show, the Promoter will make sure that the hall is in proper order. At this point, many Promoters throw parties, either for the act or for the people who helped pull the event together.

After checking the expenses and the box office receipts, the Promoter can tell whether he or she lost money, made money, or broke even on that show. The Promoter, incidentally, may promote an act's entire tour or just one concert. This individual may also promote in more than one area.

This career is best suited to those in a position to take financial risks. The Promoter must also have incredible stamina and enthusiasm in order to pull off a successful event or try another promotion after one has failed.

Salaries
There are a great many variables that influence the earnings of Promoters. These include the area where they promote shows, the kind of talent used, how successful the talent is, and luck.

If the show is successful, Promoters wind up with a percentage of the profits. It is not unheard of for Promoters to lose money on shows they put together. Breaking even is sometimes thought of as a blessing by those in the business.

Promoters who are successful in the business can earn a great deal of money—sometimes hundreds of thousands of dollars a year. The top promoters have earnings topping $1,000,000.

Employment Prospects
It is very difficult to break into the world of concert promotion. Most areas are locked up by Promoters who have proven track records in the business. Turnover of these Promoters is very slow.

Many agents do not want to take chances and work with new Promoters, especially with their major acts.

It is sometimes easier, though, to break into the smaller promotional field of halls and clubs with up-and-coming acts.

Advancement Prospects
It is difficult to advance in the concert promotion field. As noted above, there is not a high turnover of successful Promoters in an area, and in order to promote, agents prefer those with a proven track record. It turns into a "Catch 22" situation.

Advancing by promoting an up-and-coming act which does rise to the top is one method of moving upward in this profession. If one has a great deal of money to promote shows and a lot of good contacts in the industry willing to take a chance, possibilities for success increase.

Education and Training
There is no educational requirement for a Promoter. There are those in the business who have no education whatsoever, and those who hold graduate degrees from leading colleges and universities.

It does help to have some type of business background, either from formal education or from practical experience. Learning the basics of music promotion from a college course or music seminar might help, too.

Experience, Skills, and Personality Traits
The successful Concert Promoters—those who make money most of the time—often have a background in the music business. They have built up a list of contacts and friends in the business with whom they can work.

The most important thing a Concert Promoter needs to get any show off the ground is money. Sufficient funds are required so that if the show loses money or breaks even, the Promoter can learn from the experience and try again.

Unions and Associations
Concert Promoters do not belong to any union, although they probably work with a few unions when putting together a concert.

Many Concert Promoters are associate members of the National Academy of Recording Arts and Sciences (NARAS), the organization that gives out the Grammy awards.

Promoters may also belong to other associations, such as the Country Music Association (CMA) or the Gospel Music Association (GMA).

Tips for Entry
1. Try finding a position with an established concert promotion company as an assistant, receptionist, secretary, etc. Watch what is going on in the company and learn the ropes.
2. If you decide to promote on your own, start small. Promote a concert with a small outlay of money instead of an enormous one.
3. Try promoting on someone else's money. Donate your services to a school, church, or organization that will put up the money and give you help. You book the show and take care of the details. You might not make any money (you won't lose any either), but you will gain invaluable experience.
4. Get on your school's or college's entertainment or concert committee. This is a great way to learn about concert promotion.
5. There are organizations and associations dealing with concert promotion in colleges. They sometimes offer apprenticeships, workshops, or conferences on concert promotion.

MUSIC PUBLISHER

CAREER PROFILE

Duties: Publish music; negotiate royalty agreements with composers; screen songs; print music; acquire copyrights; distribute music; find material

Alternate Title(s): None

Salary Range: $0 to $1,000,000+

Employment Prospects: Fair

Advancement Prospects: Fair

Best Geographical Location(s) for Position: New York City, Los Angeles, and Nashville

Prerequisites:

Education or Training—Educational requirements vary according to position; some jobs require bachelor's degree

Experience—Working in all facets of music business useful

Special Skills and Personality Traits—Understanding of music industry; ability to hear hit tunes; knowledge of copyright laws; business orientation; contacts in music business

CAREER LADDER

```
┌─────────────────────────────────┐
│       Top Music Publisher        │
└─────────────────────────────────┘

┌─────────────────────────────────┐
│        Music Publisher           │
└─────────────────────────────────┘

┌─────────────────────────────────┐
│ Song Plugger/Professional Manager;│
│     Songwriter; Musician         │
└─────────────────────────────────┘
```

Position Description

Individuals working as Music Publishers are responsible for acquiring the copyrights to songs and publishing them. People in this profession may work in a variety of job situations. They might work for a very large music publishing company and perform one or two specific duties of a Music Publisher. They may work for a relatively small firm and fulfill a variety of functions. Another option for an individual in music publishing is to become an independent Music Publisher, with one's own music publishing firm.

The Music Publisher has many responsibilities. The first is to obtain music to be published. In order to do this, a Music Publisher must listen to demos that are sent or brought into the office. The Music Publisher may also visit clubs, cabarets, showcases, and concerts to locate new material. The purpose is to find potential hit songs. This function may be accomplished by or with a song plugger or professional manager.

In this position, the individual must decide which materials are good and which ones are not. Bad songs must be

rejected. Writers of good songs are offered contracts. If the songwriter (or owner of the song) has had prior hits, the Publisher may negotiate a contract that is acceptable to both parties. Once the contract is signed, the publisher has the rights to the song. His or her main concern then is to sell it in as many ways as possible. This may mean getting a group to record it, having it used for motion picture music, sheet music, etc. Every time that musical piece is used in any way, the Music Publisher will make money. This process is called "exploiting the work (or copyright)."

In order to sell the song, the Music Publisher must have a demo to bring or send to potential buyers. The Publisher should have contacts in the business. These might include recording groups, record producers, managers, agents, etc. The Music Publisher tries to get as many people as possible to listen to the demo in the hope that he or she will find someone to record it. If a Music Publisher has a song in the catalog that has been recorded previously, that individual will try to get it recorded again and again, in an attempt to turn it into a standard that everyone will want to record.

The Music Publisher will prepare printed music (sheet music, songbooks, etc.) and have it distributed. Before this occurs, the Publisher must make sure that the music is technically correct, proofed, and printed. This is another method by which the Music Publisher can collect fees. Before the record industry became as large as it is today, Music Publishers made most of their earnings publishing printed editions.

An important function of the Music Publisher is to file copyright forms on behalf of the song. As the Publisher, he or she is responsible for making sure that there is no copyright infringement and/or unauthorized use of the material.

In the position of Music Publisher, the individual may also seek to subpublish any of the music from his or her catalog out of the country. This may be done through a subsidiary of the Music Publisher in a different nation or through a different publishing company in the other country.

Publishing companies make money by exploiting songs. The more the song is recorded, played, distributed as sheet music, etc., the more income the Music Publisher earns. As a Music Publisher, the individual is in charge of collecting fees for the use of the songs. Publishers may collect fees or royalties from a variety of sources. These include performance fees (fees for each time a song is played on the radio, TV, etc.), mechanical royalties (from the sale of each record or tape), printed edition royalties (from songbooks, sheet music, etc.), synchronization fees (from the use of a Publisher's song in a movie), and ancillary income (from commercials, advertisements, music boxes, and on such merchandising paraphernalia as toys, clothes, greeting cards, T-shirts, bumper stickers, etc.).

People in this field work under a great deal of pressure, constantly trying to sell songs from their catalogs. Hours depend on the work situation but are often flexible.

Salaries

It is difficult to estimate the earnings of a Music Publisher. Incomes vary widely, depending on the songs the Publisher has in his or her catalog, how often they are recorded, the size of the catalog, etc. A Music Publisher who has just one song that hits the top of the charts can make a fortune. Conversely, there are Music Publishers who never have a hit tune in their catalogs. One of the exciting things about music publishing, though, is that a good song can become a hit anytime. This means that a Music Publisher can bring in thousands of dollars anytime. It does take luck, perseverance, and, of course, a good song.

Music Publishers' earnings can range from almost nothing to a million or more dollars a year.

Employment Prospects

Employment prospects for Music Publishers are fair. If an individual cannot find a job, it is not uncommon for him or her to become an independent Music Publisher. Entering this field without experience or knowledge may not be the best idea in the world, but it sometimes works.

Those seeking employment in established firms must have extensive knowledge and experience in the business. Individuals with a good working knowledge of the copyright laws may have a better chance of getting in the door.

Advancement Prospects

The more background in the business one has, as noted above, the better the chances of not only getting into music publishing, but moving up.

The individual who has a proven track record in music publishing will probably have no trouble finding a job. Many people advance their careers in this field by becoming independent Publishers or owners of large music publishing companies.

The difficulty in moving ahead in this field, however, is that it is hard to know what will turn into a hit song. Locating these hits and acquiring the copyrights on them is the real key to advancement.

Education and Training

There are many different sizes and kinds of publishing companies. Education for this career varies. There seems to be a correlation between the size of the firm and the educational requirements. The bigger the company, the more education usually required. This stems from the fact that in smaller companies, an individual may perform a variety of functions, while in larger firms, individuals usually perform one or two tasks.

Some publishing companies require their people to hold bachelor's degrees. Others don't care much about the education an individual has as long as he or she has had experience in the music industry and/or music publishing.

There are some schools that offer a major in the music business or music merchandising. These schools usually have courses in music publishing. There are also a number of seminars given on the subject. All these information resources will prove helpful to the aspiring Music Publisher.

Experience, Skills, and Personality Traits

A total understanding of the music industry is needed by a Music Publisher. Contacts in the business are vital, too. The individual must have extensive knowledge of copyright laws and business in general.

As a Music Publisher, one of the most important qualifications is the ability to hear a hit song before it is a hit. The individual must be aggressive enough to sell a song and/or get appointments for it to be listened to. The Music Publisher must also be organized in business. Records must be kept accurately in order for songwriters to be paid properly.

Unions and Associations

Music Publishers may belong to the Music Publishers' Association of the U.S. (MPA) and/or the National Music Publishers' Association. Individuals in this field might also be associate members of the National Academy of Recording Arts and Sciences (NARAS). This is the organization that gives out Grammy awards each year.

Tips for Entry

1. Positions in this field are not usually advertised. If you want to get into this type of work, put together a good résumé, including all experience in the music field. Send it with a cover letter to a number of the larger music publishing companies. These firms are more apt to have openings.

2. You can open your own music publishing firm. However, try to get some experience beforehand. Knowing the ropes can not only make you money, but also save you money.

3. There are a number of music publishing companies owned by record companies. As indicated throughout this book, many of these record companies have internships and minority training programs.

4. Try to be as knowledgeable about the subject as possible. If you can find a course or seminar in music publishing, take it.

PROFESSIONAL MANAGER

CAREER PROFILE

Duties: Persuade acts to record other writers' tunes; acquire songs to plug

Alternate Title(s): Song Plugger

Salary Range: $25,000 to $100,000+

Employment Prospects: Fair

Advancement Prospects: Fair

Best Geographical Location(s) for Position: New York City, Los Angeles, Nashville

Prerequisites:

Education or Training—No educational requirement

Experience—Working in music industry in any capacity helpful

Special Skills and Personality Traits—Perseverance; a feel for the right song and act; knowledge of music business; contacts in the industry; salesmanship

CAREER LADDER

```
┌─────────────────────────────────┐
│  Major Buyer of Tunes for Music │
│  Publishers; Professional Manager│
└─────────────────────────────────┘

┌─────────────────────────────────┐
│     Professional Manager        │
└─────────────────────────────────┘

┌─────────────────────────────────┐
│  Entry-Level Position; Musician;│
│         Songwriter              │
└─────────────────────────────────┘
```

Position Description

A Professional Manager, or song plugger, works for a music publisher. Depending on the size of the publishing company, the publisher might also act as the song plugger. This happens most frequently in one-man operations.

In the Professional Manager capacity, an individual has a number of duties. One of these is to perform the administrative functions of the publishing office.

In this role, the Professional Manager must find possible hits to add to the publisher's catalog. Naturally, in order to be good at the job, the individual must have a feel for a good song. The Professional Manager may look for material by attending concerts, clubs, showcases, etc. The Professional Manager also goes through material sent to the publishing company, listening to a piece of each song until one clicks.

The individual also is responsible for finding acts to record songs from the publisher's catalog. The catalog contains all tunes to which the publisher has the rights. Each time the song plugger gets a singer or group to record a tune from the catalog, money is made for the publishing company.

After songs are recorded by one group, the Professional Manager will often try to get the tune covered by another. A tune that is covered enough becomes a standard. Standards make publishers wealthy. A Professional Manager who is good at his or her job is in great demand.

Most song pluggers use to get songs recorded and/or rerecorded through personal contacts. These contacts can make or break a Professional Manager and/or publisher. By contacting people in the industry (such as recording acts, record producers, A & R personnel, personal managers, etc.), the Professional Manager often can get his or her song listened to. A good tune is useless to a Professional Manager or a publisher if it sits idly in the catalog.

The Professional Manager often assists artists with tunes he or she believes in by helping them make professional-sounding demos. These demos help the individual sell the tune. The demos are either delivered in person or mailed to the key people noted above. As a rule, if the Professional Manager is not mailing or dropping off the demo to someone he or she knows, making a phone call and writing a brief note to accompany the tape are customary. It is very rare for a Professional Manager to send a demo tape completely unsolicited.

Salaries

Salaries for Professional Managers vary widely according to a number of factors. These include the size of the music publishing company, the number of songs recorded, and the songs' popularity.

Professional Managers usually receive a weekly salary. When they are successful in getting tunes recorded by known acts, they may also receive bonuses. Individuals in this field earn between $25,000 and $100,000 plus annually.

Employment Prospects

There are innumerable groups looking for material to record and many songs that need to be published. Technically, an individual has a fair chance of becoming a Professional Manager.

The hard part is getting a foot in the door. If one can find the way in, there are quite a few jobs in this field.

Advancement Prospects

Advancement for a Professional Manager comes only when the individual has attained some success. Success means that the Professional Manager or song plugger has picked up one or more tunes that have become hits or that the person has matched a tune in the publisher's catalog with an act that has turned it into a hit. After this happens, the Professional Manager is in a very good position.

Many Professional Managers become the major buyers of songs for prestigious music publishers. Other individuals strike out on their own and form new publishing companies. Individuals who have been acting as Professional Managers in their own companies find success through increased earnings.

Education and Training

Professional Managers are not required to have any specific education. Many people in the profession are former musicians. Other individuals have degrees in areas ranging from business to music to broadcasting.

Professional Managers who desire to move into other phases of the industry would be wise to have some business background. Any seminar or course on music publishing would also prove useful.

Experience, Skills, and Personality Traits

The most successful Professional Managers have had experience in many different phases of the music industry. Over time, they have made innumerable personal contacts. These contacts are what help the Professional Manager attain success.

The individual must have a feel for the right song and the ability to put songs and artists together in an effort to get the song recorded. If a person has a good song and believes in it, he or she must have the perseverance to work with it until someone else believes in it, too.

Unions and Associations

Professional Managers may belong to the Music Publishers' Association of the United States (MPA) and the National Music Publishers' Association (NMPA). The organizations provide programs, conferences, seminars, etc., on all aspects of music publishing. The Professional Manager may be an associate member of the National Academy of Arts and Sciences (NARAS).

Tips for Entry

1. Music publishing companies can be small or very large. Send your résumé to some of the larger companies. Make sure you include all your experience in the music business, from writing tunes to working in a record store.
2. Some individuals form their own publishing companies. As indicated above, you can act as a Professional Manager while being a music publisher. Remember, just forming a company does not make money. Acquiring songs and getting them recorded does.
3. Learn which organizations, associations, and schools are putting on seminars or giving courses in music publishing. You should know as much as possible about the entire business, especially if you do not have a lot of experience in the music industry.

BUSINESS MANAGER

CAREER PROFILE

Duties: Manage the financial affairs of musicians and entertainers

Alternate Title(s): Business Agent

Salary Range: $20,000 to $1,000,000+

Employment Prospects: Fair

Advancement Prospects: Fair

Best Geographical Location(s) for Position: New York City, Los Angeles, and Nashville are music capitals; other cities may have additional opportunities

Prerequisites:

   Education or Training—No educational requirement; most individuals have degrees in business administration with concentration in accounting or management

   Experience—Accounting experience helpful; dealings in entertainment or music industry useful

   Special Skills and Personality Traits—Knowledge of negotiating; accounting skills; awareness of investments; thorough knowledge of tax laws

CAREER LADDER

```
┌─────────────────────────────────────┐
│        Top Business Manager         │
└─────────────────────────────────────┘

┌─────────────────────────────────────┐
│          Business Manager           │
└─────────────────────────────────────┘

┌─────────────────────────────────────┐
│ C.P.A.; Assistant to Business Manager │
└─────────────────────────────────────┘
```

Position Description

A Business Manager handles financial affairs for singers, musicians recording artists, and other entertainers. A person in this position may have one or more clients. Acts that hire Business Managers are usually doing quite well financially.

The Business Manager (or agent, as the person is sometimes called) must oversee the finances of an act or individual in order to maximize the earning potential. The individual is responsible for collecting all monies due and paying all the bills.

The Business Manager performs a number of duties as part of the job. The Business Manager may negotiate with agents and/or representatives for contracts and appearances. He or she might negotiate with union officials, motion picture studios, television producers, concert halls, record companies, merchandising firms, or publishing companies. The Business Manager may seek out firms, companies, and corporations that will pay the artist for endorsements or sponsor a large concert tour. After the act has performed a service, the individual will make sure they are paid in a timely fashion.

The individual is in charge of checking all bills for accuracy. If bills are in order, the Business Manager pays them. The person may be responsible for paying employees of the act, such as road personnel, secretaries, musicians, vocalists, publicists, public relations firms, lawyers, etc. The Business Manager may also pay the artist's personal bills. He or she must keep records of all monies taken in and paid out.

Depending on the requirements of the act, the Business Manager may plan budgets for the group or for individual members. The individual may work with the record company or the booking agent and personal manager in designing budgets for various projects.

The Business Manager might act as a financial or business advisor, counseling the act and its members on good investments, taxes, legal matters, or other income interests.

If the act is experiencing differences concerning contractual rights and obligations with their representatives, the Business Manager may act as a liaison during these difficulties. The Business Manager may also request audits of firms with which the act is or has been doing business. The individual might hire a C.P.A. to conduct these audits.

The person hired as a group's or individual's Business Manager will regularly summarize and send statements of investments, property, and financial status to the client. He or she will also be available for meetings with the act or their representatives to discuss investments, problems, audits, etc.

Salaries

The earnings of a Business Manager vary from individual to individual and from year to year. Individuals just starting out may earn only $20,000. Persons doing well can earn $1,000,000 or more. Variables include the number of clients one has, how well each of them is doing financially, geographical location of the Business Manager, and his or her experience and expertise.

The Business Manager makes money by charging clients fees. Fees can be obtained in a variety of ways. The most common is to charge a percentage of the act's total gross income. This percentage varies from 3% to 10% or more. The individual can also charge a flat retainer or an hourly fee. Some Business Managers charge a combination of a minimum fee against a commission on total monies earned by the client.

It is important to remember that a Business Manager may (and usually does) service more than one client.

Employment Prospects

A qualified individual has a fair chance of becoming a successful Business Manager. The person seeking this type of job will probably have to work in or near one of the music capitals to obtain clients. There are many offices in which a person can work as an administrative assistant to a Business Manager and learn the ropes. Once again, these are usually located in one of the music cities—New York City, Los Angeles, or Nashville.

An individual might also work as a Business Manager or accountant for nonmusic-oriented clients and then actively seek music clients. Most of the time, this must be accomplished through contacts in the music business, although there are Business Managers who advertise in the music trades.

Advancement Prospects

The way a Business Manager advances his or her career is by obtaining more clients. Conversely, the Business Manager can take fewer clients, if they are large ones.

More prestigious clients are obtained by word of mouth. If a Business Manager can advise well and help the act save and make money, that individual will probably become successful.

Education and Training

Although there is no educational requirement for a person in this field, most individuals do have college degrees in business administration, finance, or accounting. Persons who are very successful as Business Managers usually have gone through a graduate program in one of the above fields.

There are some business managers who are C.P.A.s and others who are not. Business Managers might retain the services of C.P.A.s when needed.

Experience, Skills, and Personality Traits

Business Managers should be cognizant of all types of investments. The individual may advise the client on investments outside of the music industry, which are often thought to be safer. The Business Manager must have the ability to negotiate with people in all phases of business. He or she should have a total understanding of the music business in order to negotiate efficiently.

The individual in this position must also have a good knowledge of tax laws. It is beneficial to be able to advise the act how to save money on taxes. The ability to help the artist make money through investments, endorsements, etc., is another valuable commodity.

Unions and Organizations

Business Managers may belong to a number of associations. If they are accountants, they might belong to the American Institute of Certified Public Accountants (AICPA), or the National Society of Public Accountants (NSPA).

Individuals might also be members of the Institute of Certified Financial Planners (ICFP).

If the individual is also a personal manager, he or she could belong to the Conference of Personal Managers (COPM).

Tips for Entry

1. Try to locate some successful Business Managers and apply for a position as an administrative assistant.
2. Make sure you are qualified for a position like this. Big acts will not go near a person who has not yet proven him- or herself. Smaller, lesser-known acts might.
3. This is a position in which contacts in the music business help. Let people know what you are doing (or trying to do).
4. Take seminars on business management, investments, tax shelters, etc. These courses need not be specific to the music business. Many of the investments you advise your clients to make will not be music-oriented. You need to be well versed in a full range of investments.

INSTRUMENT REPAIR, RESTORATION, AND DESIGN

MUSICAL INSTRUMENT BUILDER/DESIGNER

CAREER PROFILE

Duties: Build and/or custom design instruments for sale privately or through a shop or factory

Alternate Title(s): Musical Instrument Master Craftsman (or Craftswoman); Custom Instrument Builder

Salary Range: $15,000 to $100,000+

Employment Prospects: Good

Advancement Prospects: Poor

Best Geographical Locations for Position: Larger cities may have more positions in factories and shops; many custom Instrument Builders/Designers work from their homes in any town or city

Prerequisites:

Education or Training—Training or an apprenticeship in instrument building and designing

Experience—Working with wood and metal (depending on family of instruments the individual designs and/or builds)

Special Skills and Personality Traits—Knowledge of instruments; woodworking; metal working; good musical "ear"; mechanical ability

CAREER LADDER

```
┌─────────────────────────────────────┐
│  Master Craftsperson; Self-Employed  │
│      Instrument Builder/Designer     │
└─────────────────────────────────────┘

┌─────────────────────────────────────┐
│  Musical Instrument Builder/Designer │
└─────────────────────────────────────┘

┌─────────────────────────────────────┐
│  Musical Instrument Builder/Designer │
│              Apprentice              │
└─────────────────────────────────────┘
```

Position Description

The Instrument Builder/Designer is a creative person. He or she not only loves instruments but loves to touch them and find new ways they can be shaped or built.

The individual's main function is to take materials and turn them into functioning instruments. He or she does this by watching other Instrument Builders work, examining other instruments, reading books on the subject, and visiting museums that have collections of instruments from other eras. By noting how these instruments are constructed, the Builder/Designer can often develop interesting, usable ideas for instruments of today.

The Instrument Builder/Designer usually knows how to play at least one instrument. Sometimes he or she knows how to play almost an entire family of instruments. It is usually that family of instruments that the individual artisan yearns to build and/or design.

The Builder/Designer has a number of options as to where he or she can work. He or she might choose a position on staff in a music factory or store or the individual might design and build instruments on speculation or from custom orders in his or her workshop.

Instrument Builders/Designers are usually handy people. They have an interest in handcrafts as well as in musical instruments. The ability to work with the hands is essential. They are not only creative, but usually extremely inventive as well.

Although almost any instrument can be built and designed, there is a great market for violins, guitars, dulcimers, harpsichords, banjos, and flutes that are finely crafted and have excellent tones. Many self-employed Instrument Builders/Designers find that they sell as many instruments as they can make, and often they cannot keep up with their orders.

Once Instrument Builders/Designers have been trained as master craftspeople in their field, they are also qualified to teach others who aspire to learn the art.

Salaries

Salaries vary according to the instruments built or designed. The highest salaries go to Builders/Designers of rarer instruments. Salaries run from $15,000 for a beginner to $100,000 plus yearly by Builders/Designers in large musical instrument companies. Individuals can also custom design and build instruments for skilled classical musicians and pop/rock stars. Skilled craftsmen may sell their works of art for $2,500–$50,000 plus per instrument. Yearly salaries depend upon the number of custom instruments an individual completes and sells.

Employment Prospects

There are always openings for qualified Instrument Builders/Designers. These individuals can work in factories, shops, or companies or on their own.

Once a Builder/Designer is qualified, he or she can usually find work and make a good living.

It should be noted that with the current influx of electronic instruments, there is a budding new field that is waiting to be tapped.

Advancement Prospects

As indicated above, qualified individuals can usually find work in the field. However, depending upon the individual, it may take years to become a skilled master craftsman (or woman).

Education and Training

There are courses and technical schools around the country that teach the fine art of building and designing musical instruments. However, they are often difficult to locate.

The best training might be available through working for a qualified Builder/Designer as an apprentice. To enter into

an apprenticeship, one needs a degree of knowledge in woodworking skills. This can often be picked up in high school through industrial arts programs or at an extension course from a community college or other institution. Some knowledge of instrument technology is also useful.

Experience, Skills, and Personality Traits

Instrument Builders/Designers must usually go through an apprenticeship. This apprenticeship helps hone the skills needed for this type of career. The Instrument Builder/Designer needs to know all there is to know about the type and family of instruments he or she is working with.

The individual must also be creative enough to come up with unique ways to put instruments together. A good musical "ear" is necessary. Knowledge of woodworking and/or metalworking is also required.

Unions and Associations

There are no unions for Instrument Builders/Designers. Depending on the types of instruments the individual works with, he or she might belong to the Acoustical Society of America, the National Council of Acoustical Consultants, The Piano Technicians' Guild, or the Electronic Industry Association.

Tips for Entry

1. To find a person with whom to apprentice, contact a manufacturer of the type of instrument you would like to work with. Tell them what you are looking for and ask for their help.
2. There are a number of associations dealing with specific families of instruments. These associations—the Acoustical Society of America, the National Council of Acoustical Consultants, the Piano Technicians' Guild, and the Electronic Industry Association— might also be able to help you find training in your area. In addition, they may know of any seminars or training programs scheduled around the country.
3. Go into your local instrument shop and see if you can get a job for the summer. Try to learn as much as possible about instruments.

INSTRUMENT REPAIR AND RESTORATION SPECIALIST

CAREER PROFILE

Duties: Repair and restore instruments that are damaged, broken, or not in correct working order

Alternate Title(s): Instrument Repair & Restoration Expert

Salary Range: $15,000 to $75,000+

Employment Prospects: Good

Advancement Prospects: Fair

Best Geographical Locations for Position: Large cities have more opportunities

Prerequisites:

Education and Training—Training in instrument technology

Experience—An apprenticeship in instrument repair and restoration lasting from two to five years is usually necessary

Special Skills and Personality Traits—Interest in instruments; good musical "ear"; knowledge of woodworking and/or metalworking; mechanical ability

CAREER LADDER

```
┌─────────────────────────────────────┐
│  Private or Self-Employed Instrument │
│   Repair and Restoration Specialist  │
└─────────────────────────────────────┘

┌─────────────────────────────────────┐
│        Instrument Repair and         │
│        Restoration Specialist        │
└─────────────────────────────────────┘

┌─────────────────────────────────────┐
│        Instrument Repair and         │
│  Restoration Specialist Apprentice   │
└─────────────────────────────────────┘
```

Position Description

An Instrument Repair and Restoration Specialist usually loves instruments. He or she likes to hear them, play them, and work with them. His or her main function is to take instruments that are damaged, broken, or not in correct working order and repair and/or restore them.

The Instrument Repair and Restoration Specialist can specialize in string and fretted instruments, pianos, organs, brass instruments, percussion instruments, or a combination of the above.

The individual must be familiar with the various parts of many different instruments. In addition, he or she must know where they belong in the instrument and how to get them there. Many parts for older instruments are not even made today. In cases such as this, the Repair and Restoration Specialist must often create and build new parts.

Repair and Restoration Specialists usually enjoy music and instruments during their school years. Most like woodworking and other industrial arts subjects in high school.

Many Repair and Restoration Specialists know how to play a variety of instruments. This musical knowledge is helpful in repairing or restoring an instrument to its original state.

The Repair and Restoration Specialist can work on staff in a music store, factory, or school. He or she might also work for a museum, restoring instruments from earlier time periods. If on staff, the Specialist may be paid a weekly salary, a commission, or a combination of the two.

As the individual becomes more proficient, he or she might decide to work as a self-employed Instrument Repair and Restoration Specialist. Eventually, he or she might also take on an apprentice and help that individual hone his or her skills.

In areas where the Instrument Repair and Restoration Specialist does not have sufficient work to make a full-time living, the individual might also build, design, or supervise the production of instruments for manufacturers, shops, or individuals.

Salaries

As there is a tremendous shortage of Instrument Repair and Restoration Specialists, salaries can get quite high. Salaries depend on the experience level of the Repair and Restoration Specialist and where he or she works.

Depending on whether the Specialist works for him- or herself or is on staff at a music store or factory, the individual may earn between $15,000 and $75,000 plus annually.

Those who work on instruments that are more difficult to repair and for which there are fewer trained specialists command higher wages, some earning over $200 per hour.

Employment Prospects

As noted above, there is a shortage of qualified Instrument Repair and Restoration Specialists. The prospects of finding a job in this field after apprenticeship are good. The individual would probably have to live in a culturally active location, however, or he or she would not be able to locate work.

Advancement Prospects

After training in the craft of instrument repair and restoration, the individual must find a skilled craftsman (or woman) to work with as an apprentice. Depending on how quick he or she learns, the individual might apprentice for two to five years.

Usually, the Repair and Restoration Specialist works in a shop or factory for a few years after the apprenticeship. After this, he or she may stay in a shop or factory setting or move on to a self-employed situation.

Education and Training

A successful Specialist needs the appropriate training in instrument technology and repair. These courses are given in schools and colleges or through private instruction.

The position also requires a knowledge of woodworking and/or metalworking, depending on the type of instrument in which one specializes. This is often acquired in high school courses. Additional training is available at many technical schools and colleges.

A good Instrument Repair and Restoration Specialist needs to know how to play a variety of instruments. The more instruments with which he or she is musically adept, the more flexible he or she can be.

Experience, Skills, and Personality Traits

To become an Instrument Repair and Restoration Specialist, one must go through an apprenticeship with a talented individual in the field. The apprenticeship can last anywhere from two to five years, depending on the individual. This on-the-job training is often picked up by working in instrument repair shops and factories.

The Instrument Repair and Restoration Specialist needs a good musical "ear." He or she must have a total dedication to learning the craft. The individual must also have a great deal of patience and good mechanical ability.

Unions and Associations

Depending on the type of instruments individuals work on, they can belong to the Acoustical Society of America, the National Council of Acoustical Consultants, the Piano Technicians' Guild, or the Electronic Industries Association.

Tips for Entry

1. Try to find an instrument repair and restoration shop and get a job there part-time doing anything. Watch, learn, and gain experience. If you can apprentice in a shop such as this, do so.
2. Learn to do minor repairs, such as changing or replacing strings on stringed instruments, becoming skilled in as many repairs as possible.
3. Join professional organizations. These offer opportunities to network.

PIANO TUNER-TECHNICIAN

CAREER PROFILE

Duties: Tune and repair pianos

Alternate Title(s): None

Salary Range: $23,000 to $65,000+

Employment Prospects: Fair

Advancement Prospects: Fair

Best Geographical Locations for Position: Large cities offer the most opportunities

Prerequisites:

Education or Training—Training in piano technology and/or an apprenticeship

Experience—Apprenticeship with Tuner-Technician or in shop or factory

Special Skills and Personality Traits—Interest in piano; knowledge of instrument; mechanical ability; good musical "ear"; patience

CAREER LADDER

```
┌─────────────────────────────────────────┐
│  Independent Piano Tuner-Technician      │
└─────────────────────────────────────────┘

┌─────────────────────────────────────────┐
│  Piano Tuner-Technician                  │
└─────────────────────────────────────────┘

┌─────────────────────────────────────────┐
│  Piano Tuner-Technician Apprentice       │
└─────────────────────────────────────────┘
```

Position Description

A Piano Tuner-Technician's main job is to tune pianos and keep them in tune. After deciding to become a Piano Tuner-Technician and getting the proper training, an individual must usually apprentice in order to hone his or her skills to perfection.

The Piano Tuner-Technician must know the piano inside and out. He or she must recognize the 6,000 to 8,000 different pieces of each instrument. The Tuner-Technician must know what each of these parts is, where it belongs in the instrument, and what it does.

The individual adjusts the piano strings so that they will be in proper pitch and sound musically correct. There are approximately 220 strings in a standard 88 key piano. After muting the strings on either side, the Tuner-Technician uses a tuning hammer to tighten or loosen the string being tested until its frequency matches that of a standard tuning fork. The Piano Tuner-Technician tunes the other strings in relation to the starting string. A good musical "ear" is essential in order to attain a perfect pitch, tone, and sound.

The Piano Tuner-Technician often works with electronic tuning devices. These devices are relatively new in the field. Old-time master craftsmen usually do not use these aids and don't encourage their apprentices to use them, either. With these electronic devices, however, Piano Tuner-Technicians can usually take care of more pianos in a shorter period of time. This is important if the individual is being paid per instrument tuned.

The Tuner may make minor repairs, such as replacing worn or broken hammers in the piano. He or she may also detect and correct other problems in the instrument that affect its sound. More serious problems that the Piano Tuner-Technician may take care of include realigning hammers that do not strike the strings just right and replacing the felt on hammers. The Piano Tuner-Technician may have to dismantle the piano to find out what is wrong with it and fix the problem.

The Tuner-Technician may also teach piano to supplement his or her income.

Salaries

Salaries for Piano Tuner-Technicians vary according to the types of jobs they hold. A Piano Tuner-Technician working in a piano factory can earn between $24,000 and $45,000 per year. Tuners working for music dealers can average between $23,000 and $45,000 plus annually.

Tuner-Technicians are often self-employed or independent. These individuals charge fees for each piano they work on. Fees vary according to whether or not the individual is a member of the Piano Technicians' Guild.

A Tuner can obtain contracts with music conservatories, universities, studios, and/or music groups. Independent Piano Tuner-Technicians, working full time, can earn $65,000 or more annually. Tuner-Technicians who are self-employed must pay their own expenses. These might include tools, travel expenses, etc.

Employment Prospects

Piano Tuner-Technicians have the opportunity to work full-time or part-time, for themselves or on staff for dealers, factories, music schools, conservatories, universities, colleges, music shops, or music groups.

Clients can be obtained by advertising or word of mouth. Satisfied clients can make an independent Piano Tuner-Technician successful.

Large cities with many stores, factories, dealers, etc., offer the best opportunities for Tuner-Technicians. In smaller communities with limited music outlets, Piano Tuner-Technicians often do other piano-related work, including teaching.

Advancement Prospects

Piano Tuner-Technicians who have been trained well and have apprenticed with skilled Tuner-Technicians can usually get a position as a staff Tuner. After a few years, many individuals find that they prefer to work on their own as self-employed or private Piano Tuner-Technicians. They then have the opportunity to build as large a business as they can handle.

Education and Training

A training program and/or an apprenticeship is required to become a Piano Tuner-Technician. The best type of course to take is one endorsed by the Piano Technicians' Guild.

Check the appendix for a list. A good course of study will usually take two to three years to complete.

The individual might opt to take an apprenticeship with a skilled Piano Tuner-Technician. These opportunities are often difficult to locate for those without experience. After completing a training program, however, the individual will probably need to apprentice with an individual or a shop or in a factory.

Experience, Skills, and Personality Traits

To become a Piano Tuner-Technician, an individual must have experience as an apprentice. The Tuner must have a good musical "ear." He or she should have a great interest in the piano, a knowledge of the instrument, and the ability to play it.

The Piano Tuner-Technician must have a mechanical ability and dexterity. In addition, he or she must have an enormous amount of patience to obtain a perfect pitch, tone, and sound.

Unions and Associations

Piano Tuner-Technicians may belong to the Piano Technicians' Guild. This association is open to Tuner-Technicians who pass an exam given by the guild. After becoming a member, the Piano Tuner-Technician's fees are set by the guild. Nonmembers are free to charge lower fees.

Tips for Entry

1. Prepare well by obtaining good training. Your best bet is to go to a school the Piano Technicians' Guild endorses.
2. Try to find the most skilled person possible to apprentice with. It is during this apprenticeship that you pick up much of the craft.
3. If you are trained in the profession, put your business card up in music stores, record shops, and on supermarket bulletin boards.
4. Remember to check out websites of piano factories and music dealers for openings.

BOW REHAIRER AND RESTORER

CAREER PROFILE

Duties: Rehair stringed instrument bows and restore old or damaged bows

Alternate Title(s): Bow Restorer; Craftsman

Salary Range: $25 to $150+ per bow

Employment Prospects: Fair

Advancement Prospects: Poor

Best Geographical Location(s) for Position: Major cultural centers, such as New York City, Boston, Cleveland, Philadelphia, Chicago, Los Angeles, etc., offer the most opportunities

Prerequisites:

Education or Training—Training at workshops or seminars on subject; apprenticeship

Experience—Hands-on experience in craft is necessary

Special Skills and Personality Traits—Fine craftsmanship; dexterity; ability to work with detail; patience; desire to develop the craft

CAREER LADDER

```
┌─────────────────────────────┐
│  Bow Rehairer and Restorer   │
│      with Many Clients       │
└─────────────────────────────┘

┌─────────────────────────────┐
│  Bow Rehairer and Restorer   │
└─────────────────────────────┘

┌─────────────────────────────┐
│  Apprentice; Workshop Student │
└─────────────────────────────┘
```

Position Description

Bow Rehairers and Restorers replace the bow hair of stringed instrument bows. They also restore old and/or damaged bows and put them back in working condition.

The work is done using hand tools such as small knives, chisels, short- and long-nose pliers, scissors, and a comb. The individual must disassemble the bow and remove the spent or used hair. (Most bows are made of the hair of horses' tails.) The person then examines the bow to see what condition it is in, check for damage, etc. The Rehairer also cleans the various bow parts.

If the bow is old and/or damaged, the individual may restore it. The Bow Rehairer and Restorer may concentrate on a broken bow tip, a cracked frog, or the timber. This restoration, too, is done with hand tools.

People in this line of work require a great deal of manual dexterity. They may have to hand-carve replacement wedges and/or plugs to fit the bow. These parts must fit exactly or it will affect the quality of the sound produced by the bow.

The Bow Rehairer must select new hairs for the bow. Once this is done, the individual will bind one end with special threads. This bound end will be secured into one end of the bow with the hand-carved wedges.

The Bow Rehairer will comb the hair neatly and bind the remaining loose ends with the special thread. This end will then be secured with wedges.

The quality of construction and rehairing of the bow affects the quality of tone and sound of the stringed instrument. The Rehairer is totally responsible for this task. There are Rehairers who are famous for their craft and skill.

The Rehairer may work full- or part-time at this job, depending on how many customers he or she can obtain. Many people in this position contact schools, colleges, conservatories, and orchestras to obtain contracts to perform all the rehairing required for the group's stringed instruments.

Hours are flexible. Many rehairers are working or aspiring musicians, usually with an ability to play a stringed instrument.

Salaries

It is impossible to estimate the yearly salary of a Bow Rehairer and Restorer. Individuals who perform this work often do so on a part-time basis while pursuing performance or teaching careers, or careers in instrument building or instrument repairing and/or restoring.

People who rehair and restore may get contracts to take care of all the stringed instruments in a school, college, conservatory, or orchestra. The normal charge for bow rehairing ranges from $25 to $150 or more per bow. Fees for restoring bows depend on the amount and type of damage done to the bow. Restoration fees range from $25 to $150 or more per item.

Employment Prospects

As there are not many people who know how to correctly rehair and/or restore bows, individuals who do have a fair chance of locating work. There are opportunities in the major cultural cities, such as New York City, Boston, Cleveland, Philadelphia, Chicago, and Los Angeles. These locations have symphony orchestras, chamber music groups, etc., that use a large number of stringed instruments. Individuals looking for work in the Bow Rehairing field might have to relocate to one of these major cities.

Advancement Prospects

Advancement as a Bow Rehairer and Restorer is difficult to achieve. The best way to do it is to obtain a lot of clients. People in this field may open their own music or repair shop.

Education and Training

There is no specific educational requirement for a Bow Rehairer and Restorer, but people must be trained in the craft. This may be accomplished in workshops or seminars given on the subject or through an apprenticeship with a master craftsman.

Experience, Skills, and Personality Traits

To perfect this craft, a person needs hands-on experience in bow rehairing. This may be acquired through an apprenticeship.

The individual doing this type of work needs manual dexterity. The person must also be extremely patient and capable of working on details.

Many who perform this job are aspiring or working musicians who love the sound of good music.

Unions and Associations

If individuals are performing musicians as well as Rehairers and Restorers, they might belong to the American Federation of Musicians (AFM). Individuals may also belong to the Acoustical Society of America and/or the National Council of Acoustical Consultants.

Tips for Entry

1. Teachers of violin often know of workshops in the art of rehairing bows.
2. Violin or other string players usually know of people in this field. Talk to a Bow Rehairer and inquire about an apprenticeship.
3. If you already know how to rehair bows, go to schools, colleges, and orchestras to obtain clients.
4. Put up signs, posters, or business cards on the bulletin boards in music stores.

PUBLICITY

PUBLIC RELATIONS COUNSELOR

CAREER PROFILE

Duties: Create an image for a musical group, artist, product, place, or company; write press releases; compile press kits; arrange press conferences

Alternate Title(s): Publicist; P.R. Counselor

Salary Range: $23,000 to $175,000+

Employment Prospects: Fair

Advancement Prospects: Fair

Best Geographical Locations for Position: New York City, Los Angeles, Nashville, Philadelphia, and Chicago offer the most opportunities; other areas may have additional possibilities

Prerequisites:

Education or Training—College degree in communications, journalism, English, advertising, marketing, or public relations

Experience—Some type of music or nonmusic-oriented publicity position; journalism experience

Special Skills and Personality Traits—Good writing skills; knowledge of music business; creativity; aggressiveness; ability to work under pressure

CAREER LADDER

```
┌─────────────────────────────────┐
│   Public Relations Director;    │
│  Public Relations Agency Owner  │
└─────────────────────────────────┘

┌─────────────────────────────────┐
│   Public Relations Counselor    │
└─────────────────────────────────┘

┌─────────────────────────────────┐
│    Public Relations Trainee     │
└─────────────────────────────────┘
```

Position Description

The main function of Public Relations (P.R.) Counselors in the field of music-oriented public relations is to create an image for a group or artist. If the counselor is working in a radio station or concert hall, his or her function is to create a good image of and for the business.

The Public Relations Counselor must begin by evaluating the public's perception or image of the client. Sometimes the client is well-known but has a poor image. In this case, the Public Relations Counselor is often retained to help change this public perception. Sometimes the client is an act or a club that is just starting out and is not known. In this case, the Public Relations Counselor must start from scratch, building the client's image.

The counselor might begin by outlining a campaign for the client. This campaign will vary according to any image problems and to the budget available to accomplish the task.

The P.R. Counselor must know how to write press releases, compile press kits, arrange press conferences and parties, etc. In addition, the counselor must know how to find an angle to arouse media interest.

P.R. Counselors usually spend a great deal of time with a client getting pertinent information. During this period, he or she usually learns some interesting facts about a client that may be unrelated to the music business. For example, a club might have been the place a famous president stayed during a war. This theme might be the basis of a feature article about the club. Another example is a singer whose hobby is cooking. The counselor could expand the client's image from singer (in music magazines) to singer who likes to cook (gourmet cooking magazines). This gives the singer a more rounded personality. In essence, the P.R. Counselor works on creating a fuller image for clients.

P.R. Counselors usually have a large list of media contacts to call upon and use when they require press for their clients. When calling on this press, the counselor must always try to remain as credible as possible; otherwise, he or she won't be able to use the press effectively.

As with all positions in promotion and publicity, public relations people must be able to work under a great deal of pressure. There are constant demands by clients, deadlines to meet, things to accomplish, and parties to attend.

As a rule, the Public Relations Counselor working in a P.R. firm is directly responsible to his or her supervisor. On occasion, he or she might be responsible to the client. A counselor working in a radio station is usually responsible to the general manager of that station. P.R. Counselors or directors working in concert halls or arenas are generally responsible to the concert hall director or manager.

The Public Relations Counselor must be willing to work behind the scenes and not expect any public recognition. A successful campaign for a client will yield only personal satisfaction. An unsuccessful campaign will often yield an unhappy client who blames the Public Relations Counselor.

Salaries
Salaries for Public Relations Counselors vary depending on the firm or company, geographical location, and type of job held.

A Public Relations Counselor in a music industry firm can earn anywhere from $23,000 to $175,000 plus. In addition, P.R. Counselors often earn 10% to 15% of all income from clients they bring to the firm. This can add up to thousands of dollars.

A radio station Public Relations Counselor or director might make from $23,000 at a small station to $45,000 plus at a larger station.

A Public Relations Counselor or Director working at a concert hall or auditorium would be at the same income level as the P.R. person working at a radio station. Once again, salaries vary according to the size of the business and the location of the company.

Employment Prospects
There are only a limited number of music-oriented public relations firms. Competition for jobs in the field is very heavy.

There are, however, a fair number of positions as Public Relations Counselors and directors at businesses that are music-oriented. Some of these include radio stations, night clubs, concert halls and arenas, record companies, music stores, etc.

Advancement Prospects
A Public Relations Counselor working in a P.R. firm specializing in music will usually get more responsibility and more challenging clients as he or she gains experience. Experienced P.R. people sometimes strike out on their own and open firms.

There is usually very little advancement opportunity in a radio station or concert hall P.R. department. In smaller radio stations there is usually only one person in the P.R. department. The job, however, is often classified as P.R. Director. The individual always has the option of moving on to a bigger station or concert hall with the job of P.R. Director on his or her résumé. Having worked in radio stations, concert halls, record stores, etc., the individual has the opportunity to gain experience in the music business and move into a position in a P.R. firm.

Education and Training
A college degree in communications, public relations, journalism, English, advertising, marketing, or music merchandising is preferable. Depending on the firm the individual wants to work with, some positions require a master's degree.

There are numerous public relations seminars given around the country by colleges, universities, and the Public Relations Society of America. These are very useful to one aspiring to be in the public relations field or one who has already landed a P.R. position.

Experience, Skills, and Personality Traits
A good P.R. Counselor must have excellent writing skills. The Counselor must also be creative enough to come up with a really special campaign so the act or product will be a hit.

A good knowledge of the music business is essential to the P.R. Counselor in the music industry. He or she must understand the complexities of the industry in order to be effective in his or her client's campaign.

Many P.R. Counselors in the music industry work in non-music-oriented public relations or publicity positions prior to entering the music business. Other aspiring P.R. people work for newspapers or magazines as reporters, critics, or reviewers.

Unions and Associations
Public Relations Counselors can belong to the Public Relations Society of America (PRSA). The association is run by and for public relations people and works to keep ethics in public relations high. The association also prints a magazine and runs seminars throughout the year.

Public Relations Counselors may also belong to the Association of Theatrical Press Agents and Managers (ATPAM).

Tips for Entry
1. If you can't get the position you want, try to get some experience in the public relations department of a record store, radio station, or concert hall.
2. Attend seminars such as those given by the Public Relations Society of America. You might make some contacts with people who know of openings.
3. Attend a music industry convention. There are a number of conventions around the country throughout the year.

These conventions also offer great potential for making contacts. It could be worth the price of attending.

4. If you can't locate a position in a music-oriented field, see if you can find a job in nonmusic-oriented public relations (there are many more of these). The experience might be all you need.

5. Openings are often advertised in *Billboard* magazine and other trade publications.

6. Openings may also be located on-line. Check out music- and entertainment-oriented Public Relations company websites as well as on-line job sites, such as www.monster.com and www.hotjobs.com.

PUBLIC RELATIONS TRAINEE

CAREER PROFILE

Duties: Assist public relations counselor in servicing clients; learn basic public relations techniques

Alternate Title(s): Public Relations Assistant; P.R. Trainee

Salary Range: $21,000 to $27,000+

Employment Prospects: Fair

Advancement Prospects: Fair

Best Geographical Locations for Position: New York City, Los Angeles, Nashville, Chicago, Philadelphia, and other large cities offer most opportunities; other areas may have additional possibilities

Prerequisites:

Education or Training—College degree in public relations, journalism, marketing, English, communications, advertising, or music merchandising preferable

Experience—Writing experience; attending seminars on music business or public relations helpful

Special Skills and Personality Traits—Good writing skills; knowledge of music business; outgoing personality; creativity

CAREER LADDER

```
┌─────────────────────────────────┐
│   Public Relations Counselor    │
└─────────────────────────────────┘

┌─────────────────────────────────┐
│    Public Relations Trainee     │
└─────────────────────────────────┘

┌─────────────────────────────────┐
│        College Student;         │
│ Nonmusic-oriented Publicity     │
│   Position; Print Media         │
│          Journalist             │
└─────────────────────────────────┘
```

Position Description

A Public Relations Trainee or Assistant usually has little or no experience in public relations. In the music business, however, Public Relations Trainees often have had experience working at nonmusic-oriented publicity firms. People in music business P.R. like to train their people with the music business as a focal point.

The P.R. Trainee learns how to develop a campaign for a musical act or product. He or she learns to talk to a client, gather information, and put together press releases. Once the press release is written, it must usually be approved by the Trainee or Assistant's supervisor.

The Trainee makes the many contacts he or she needs by calling people, following up on press releases or client activities. He or she might also meet media people at a press conference or press party for a client's campaign.

The Public Relations Trainee learns how to put together these important press functions. The individual does this by handling details for the P.R. supervisor.

The Public Relations Trainee often studies previous campaigns put together and implemented by other counselors. Using these programs, he or she learns how to create an angle or "hook" for a campaign.

The P.R. Trainee sits in on many meetings with clients and throws out his or her ideas for the campaign. As the Trainee gains experience, he or she might begin to implement certain facets of the actual campaign.

The Trainee responds to many of the calls from clients dealing with details such as dates and times. The Assistant/Trainee often accompanies the client to interviews or public appearances that have been scheduled. In addition, the Trainee accompanies the client to television or radio interviews that have been arranged.

As a Public Relations Assistant, he or she attends many social functions on behalf of his or her firm or company or its clients. It is at these luncheons, dinners, cocktail parties, etc., that the P.R. Trainee has opportunities to make new contacts and meet new people in the industry.

A P.R. Trainee/Assistant working for a concert hall or auditorium might be responsible for showing the press around the facility. At a radio station, he or she might be responsible for introducing media or recording acts to the staff.

Unless the company has a clipping service, the P.R. Trainee/Assistant might also be responsible for clipping press releases, articles, feature stories, and photographs of the client from magazines, newspapers, trades, etc. These clippings are put together in a client's portfolio with tapes of interviews, advertisements, etc.

The P.R. Trainee is responsible directly to his or her supervisor, who checks most work done by the Trainee.

Salaries

Salaries for Public Relations Trainees/Assistants in the music field start low. A beginning salary might be around $21,000 for a trainee who has no public relations experience at all. The salary is usually higher for people who have previously worked in the public relations industry. Earnings for P.R. Trainees can go up to $27,000+ or more.

Employment Prospects

The job market for music-oriented public relations is competitive. Music-oriented firms are limited. There are positions for trainees in concert halls, auditoriums, radio stations, etc.

Advancement Prospects

If the trainee shows promise and talent, he or she will have the opportunity to move up the career ladder. P.R. Trainees must work very hard to move up. Often there are no positions in the company open as a public relations counselor. With the experience as a P.R. Trainee in the music field, however, the individual has the opportunity to go to other firms that have openings. Many of these companies might want the person to stay in the position of P.R. Trainee for a short time to train him or her their way.

Education and Training

The best education for a Public Relations Trainee is a college degree with a major in public relations, journalism, English, or communications. Courses in music merchandising are useful. As creative writing is one of the important skills required of a Public Relations Trainee, a variety of writing courses should be included in the curriculum.

Experience, Skills, and Personality Traits

A Public Relations Trainee needs many of the same skills as a public relations counselor or publicist. He or she must be a good writer. That skill might come from writing for a college newspaper or reviewing concerts for a local magazine or newspaper.

The Trainee must be creative and have an outgoing personality. Many P.R. Trainees in the music field work in non-music-oriented positions prior to obtaining their positions in music public relations.

A summer internship is a useful, fun way of learning the different skills needed in a music-oriented P.R. firm, as well as an opportunity to make contacts.

Unions and Associations

Public Relations Trainees may belong to the Public Relations Society of America (PRSA). This organization puts out many useful booklets and a magazine and presents communications seminars throughout the country.

Tips for Entry

1. Try to get into a summer internship position in one of the music-oriented public relations firms. Although they usually are not paid, interns might get positions as Trainees after the summer.
2. Write for a local or college paper reviewing concerts and records. Make copies of the clippings and send them with your résumé. This helps prove that you have talent. (Always keep copies of *everything* you have written that has been printed.)
3. On occasion, openings for P.R. Trainees in music oriented P.R. firms are advertised in the classified sections of newspapers.
4. Many record labels have minority training programs in this area. If you qualify, take advantage of these programs.
5. Look for opportunities on-line. Check out record label websites, music- and entertainment-oriented public relations and publicity company sites and on-line career sites.

PUBLICIST

CAREER PROFILE

Duties: Get a musical act's name better known; compile press kits; write press releases; arrange press conferences

Alternate Title(s): Press Agent

Salary Range: $25,000 to $150,000+

Employment Prospects: Fair

Advancement Prospects: Fair

Best Geographical Location(s) for Position: New York City, Los Angeles, Nashville, Philadelphia, Chicago, and other large cities offer the most opportunities; other areas may have additional possibilities

Prerequisites:

Education or Training—College degree in communications, journalism, English, advertising, marketing, public relations, or music merchandising preferred

Experience—Prior position in music or nonmusic-oriented publicity; newspaper reporter, journalist, or critic experience helpful

Special Skills and Personality Traits—Creative writing skills; persuasiveness; ability to work under pressure; knowledge of music business; love of music

CAREER LADDER

```
┌─────────────────────────────┐
│   Independent Publicist     │
└─────────────────────────────┘

┌─────────────────────────────┐
│        Publicist            │
└─────────────────────────────┘

┌─────────────────────────────┐
│    Assistant Publicist      │
└─────────────────────────────┘
```

Position Description

The basic duty of a music-oriented Publicist or press agent is to create ways to make a musical act's name, record, and video better known. The best way to get a group's or artist's name or product in the spotlight is to keep it in the public eye as much as possible. The better the act and the product are known, the more records, tapes, videos, and concert tickets will sell.

The Publicist must know how to write creative press releases that the press will use. Press kits consisting of press releases, biographies, pictures, and reprints of reviews and articles must be compiled. The Publicist must then see that the press kits are given or sent to music editors, disc jockeys, TV producers, etc., around the country.

The Publicist must know what type of event is important enough to call a press conference for, how to put one together, and how to get the right people to attend.

The Publicist must know how to get through to music editors, disc jockeys, TV producers, etc., in order to place the client on a television or radio show or have a feature story written on the act.

Many times, the press isn't interested in an act until it is so well known that publicity self-generates. In such a case, the Publicist must be creative enough to come up with a unique angle to get attention for the act from the press and/or radio and television.

There are some acts, on the other hand, that are so well known that every editor and disc jockey wants to interview them. In this case, the Publicist must be selective and decide which interviews are in the best interest of the client. The Publicist has to act as the bad guy and keep the press away from a client if he or she feels it would harm a client's image to give interviews. The Publicist must say no in such a way as to save the media contact without blaming the act.

Publicists are famous for creating hype. Hype is the practice of taking a group or record and super-selling it with media saturation and sometimes exaggeration.

Part of the Publicist's job is attending a lot of parties, luncheons, and dinners on a client's behalf or to make important contacts. The Publicist's social life and business life are frequently rolled into one.

Contacts are important for the Publicist, especially if he or she is working as an independent. One of the ways new clients are obtained is through these musical cocktail parties that "everyone" attends.

The Publicist employed by a record company generally works to help the artists sell their records, videos, and concert seats. He or she is usually responsible to a supervisor. Independent Publicists are usually responsible directly to the client and the client's management team.

A Publicist must have the ability to work under the constant pressure of deadlines. He or she must also be willing to accept the fact that if a publicity campaign is successful, the act will get the credit, while if it fails, the Publicist will most likely get the blame.

Salaries

Salaries vary according to the type of firm or company the Publicist works for and the geographical location of that firm. Firms or companies in New York City, Los Angeles, Nashville, and Chicago tend to pay more. Some Publicists start out at $25,000 per year. Others at more prestigious firms have a starting salary of $30,000. As the Publicist gains more experience and recognition in the field, he or she can make $35,000 to $50,000 per year. In addition, Publicists who attract new clients to their firms are often given 10% to 15% of all monies brought in by the new clients. Depending on what the clients pay the firm, this can add up to a great deal of money.

Independent Publicists are paid directly by their clients. Fees range from $850 per month per client to $2,500 plus per week per client. The fees depend on the status of the musical act or artist being publicized. In addition, the Publicist often earns a percentage of any monies brought in from commercials, endorsements, TV, or movies that he or she obtains for the client. Independent Publicists are usually paid their fees as a monthly retainer. They are often reimbursed for out-of-pocket expenses as well.

Employment Prospects

Music-oriented Publicists may work for record companies to promote their acts or any upcoming promotional tours. Record companies generally have a number of Publicists on staff. Although there were once many positions in this field, economic problems at record companies have resulted in the elimination of a number of these positions.

Music-oriented Publicists can also find work in firms that specialize in publicity or public relations for the music business. These positions are limited but more available than those in record companies.

Publicists may also work as independents, which means that they must get their own clients and are paid a fee instead of a salary. Independent Publicists and press agents have to be very good or they won't get clients. They must have a proven track record with clients in order to be successful on their own.

Advancement Prospects

A good Publicist will usually be promoted to better clients, more interesting projects, and less tedious work in a firm or record company. If the Publicist can deliver a good campaign, a lot of TV and radio talk shows, good placement of press releases, and a happy client, he or she will move up. Good Publicists are sought after by other companies, firms, and clients. Although the public doesn't usually know who "made" a star, group, or artist, the insiders usually find out. Competition is keen in publicity positions, so the Publicist must be the best.

Education and Training

Different positions in publicity require different amounts of education. The most qualified person has a better chance of getting the job. A college degree in communications, journalism, public relations, advertising, marketing, English, or music merchandising is helpful in honing the skills needed for a position as a music business Publicist. Courses or seminars in publicity and the music business are also useful.

Experience, Skills, and Personality Traits

A music industry Publicist must be able to work under pressure. The constant stress of deadlines and clients changing their minds about what image they want to project can take its toll.

Publicists must be creative enough to come up with an angle for a client and then be persuasive enough to make the client and his advisors like it, too. He or she must have the ability to make a news release about an ordinary subject into an exciting story the press will pick up. Many Publicists have worked with the press as reporters, reviewers, or talent coordinators. Contacts picked up from other positions are valuable. The Publicist must have a reputation for credibility, however, or all contacts will prove useless.

Unions and Associations

The best-known organization that Publicists can belong to is the Public Relations Society of America (PRSA). This organization offers seminars, booklets, a magazine, and other helpful information.

Publicists working with clients in musical theater might additionally belong to the Association of Theatrical Press Agents and Managers (ATPAM).

Tips for Entry

1. Find out if the record company or public relations firm has an internship program for Publicists. Most internships are unpaid.
2. Prepare your résumé and a few samples of your writing style and write to the record company or publicity firm where you want a job, call for an appointment, or go knock on doors.
3. Work with a local music group as an independent Publicist to get some experience for yourself and for your résumé. (You frequently have to work for a nominal fee.)
4. Openings are often advertised in trade publications such as *Billboard*.
5. Jobs may be located on-line. Check out record label sites, music- and entertainment-oriented public relations company sites, and on-line job sites.

ASSISTANT PUBLICIST

CAREER PROFILE

Duties: Assist the publicist; compile press kits; write press releases; double-check information for accuracy

Alternate Title(s): Publicist Trainee; Press Agent Trainee; Assistant Press Agent

Salary Range: $23,000 to $40,000+

Employment Prospects: Fair

Advancement Prospects: Fair

Best Geographical Locations for Position: New York City, Los Angeles, Nashville, Philadelphia, Chicago, and other large cities offer the most opportunities; other areas may have additional opportunities

Prerequisites:

Education or Training—College degree in communications, journalism, English, advertising, marketing, public relations, or music merchandising preferred

Experience—Working in music or nonmusic publicity; attending seminars on publicity and the music business

Special Skills and Personality Traits—Good writing skills; knowledge of music business; outgoing personality; aggressiveness; typing ability; computer skills

CAREER LADDER

```
┌─────────────────────────────────────────┐
│               Publicist                  │
└─────────────────────────────────────────┘

┌─────────────────────────────────────────┐
│          Assistant Publicist             │
└─────────────────────────────────────────┘

┌─────────────────────────────────────────┐
│    Nonmusic-oriented Publicist;          │
│  Secretary to Publicist; Student; Intern │
└─────────────────────────────────────────┘
```

Position Description

The main function of an Assistant Publicist is to help the head publicists in a company sell an act's name, records, and videos. The Assistant Publicist learns from watching and doing. He or she writes press releases and helps compile press kits. It is usual for all of the Assistant Publicist's work to be reviewed and checked for accuracy and content by the individual's superior.

Many Assistant Publicists sit in on meetings with clients, joining the publicist assigned to that client. They often throw in ideas for the act's publicity campaign.

However, as a rule, they are never totally responsible for originating and implementing an entire campaign.

At times, the Assistant Publicist will accompany an act to radio, television, or public appearances. He or she will also be asked to go with the act for interviews or photography sessions set up by the head publicist.

The Assistant Publicist will handle many of the details of press parties the head publicist arranges. He or she may also be responsible for extending invitations to the media and other guests who will be invited.

The Assistant Publicist might also go to dinners, luncheons, and/or cocktail parties on behalf of a client or his or her company.

Responding to a client's calls and answering questions about schedules, dates, etc., is one of the responsibilities of the Assistant Publicist. He or she also will have to do secretarial work, such as typing press releases, making phone calls, confirming appointments, checking out information, etc.

The individual might also be responsible for clipping press releases from magazines and newspapers. These clippings are put together in the client's portfolio, along with copies of advertisements, photos, and tapes of interviews.

The Assistant Publicist must be ready and willing to work overtime. Deadlines must be met, afterhours functions must be attended, and calls must be made.

Salaries

Assistant Publicist's salaries usually range from $23,000 to $40,000 or more yearly. Salaries depend on the type of firm or company at which the Assistant Publicist is employed. Salaries also vary by geographical location. The highest salaries are usually found in Los Angeles and New York City. As the Assistant Publicist gets more experience, he or she begins to make more money. Experienced Assistant Publicists working in large cities may earn up to $30,000 plus annually. Assistant Publicists who work for public relations firms specializing in music acts usually earn more than Assistant Publicists who begin at record companies. The record companies, as a rule, have better benefits.

Employment Prospects

The job market is tight for Assistant Publicists, but there are openings. Individuals may find opportunities at record companies, music-oriented publicity firms, or management companies.

Advancement Prospects

A talented Assistant Publicist will move into the position of Publicist. Assistant Publicists must show a lot of promise and be willing to put in extra effort to get promoted. Once an Assistant Publicist has some experience under his or her belt, he or she can apply for a position in another record company or P.R. firm. However, companies often promote from within in these position categories.

Education and Training

An Assistant Publicist needs a background in writing. A college degree in communications, journalism, English, advertising, marketing, public relations, or music merchandising is preferred. Courses in the music business or seminars on the subject are also useful. To achieve the position of Assistant Publicist, one may start out as a secretary to a publicist. When this is the case, the individual must also have training in secretarial skills. Courses in typing, word processing, and computer usage are always useful in the event the office is backed up and the Assistant Publicist must type a story or press release.

Experience, Skills, and Personality Traits

An Assistant Publicist needs most of the same skills as a publicist. He or she must be able to work under pressure. The individual must be able to foresee what both the head publicist and the client want.

He or she must be creative enough to write press releases and stories that will grab the attention not only of the press, but of his or her superiors, too.

Experience working in a publicity office or the publicity department of a record company helps the aspiring Assistant Publicist understand the activities of the publicity office. If a summer internship opens up, it is worth investigating. The internship is a useful tool in helping to learn different techniques and skills and in making contacts.

Unions and Associations

There are a number of organizations and associations an Assistant Publicist may belong to. The best known is the Public Relations Society of America (PRSA). The organization offers many seminars throughout the year on public relations and publicity subjects.

Tips for Entry

1. Find out if the record company or public relations firm for whom you would like to work has an internship program for publicists. (Most intern programs are unpaid positions.)
2. Certain record companies and music organizations have minority training programs. Check with the companies you would like to work with.
3. Prove yourself by presenting reviews you have written on concerts or records for local, school, or college newspapers. Send copies of the clippings to the act's record label's publicity department. Make sure you include a short letter telling them your name, address, phone number, qualifications, and the type of position you're interested in. Persistence and perseverance sometimes land a job.
4. Begin putting together a portfolio of your work to illustrate your talent and creativity.

MUSIC JOURNALIST

CAREER PROFILE

Duties: Write articles, reviews, and critiques on music acts, concerts, shows, records, videos, etc.

Alternate Title(s): Writer; Music Critic; Music Reviewer

Salary Range: $20,000 to $150,000+

Employment Prospects: Good

Advancement Prospects: Fair

Best Geographical Location(s) for Positions: New York City, Nashville, and Los Angeles for major music publications; other large cities with moderate-sized publications and smaller locations for individuals just starting out

Prerequisites:

Education and Training—College degree required or preferred for most jobs

Experience—Writing for school paper; reviewing local concerts or records for local papers

Special Skills and Personality Traits—Writing skill; knowledge of music; typing skill; computer literate; objectivity; ability to work under pressure

CAREER LADDER

```
┌─────────────────────────────────────┐
│ Music Journalist for Major Publication │
└─────────────────────────────────────┘

┌─────────────────────────────────────┐
│          Music Journalist            │
└─────────────────────────────────────┘

┌─────────────────────────────────────┐
│  Entertainment Journalist for Local  │
│  Paper; Nonmusic-oriented Reporter or│
│      Journalist; Student             │
└─────────────────────────────────────┘
```

Position Description

Music Journalists work in many different situations. A Music Journalist might be on staff at a local or small circulation weekly newspaper. In this case, he or she might write a daily, biweekly, or weekly column about happenings in the music business. The Music Journalist would also be responsible for reviewing any concerts, shows, and artists passing through the area. The Music Journalist might review new records or music products on the market. In small circulation newspapers, he or she might write about other entertainment-oriented subjects. A Music Journalist may also have to report on nonentertainment subjects. Many opportunities now exist in on-line publications or other sites on the World Wide Web.

As Music Journalists move into positions on larger papers or magazines, their jobs become more specialized. For instance, one might be a classical reviewer, a rock writer, a jazz writer, a record reviewer, etc. Some Music Journalists write columns for on-line publications or websites.

The life of a Music Journalist is often exciting. He or she is expected to be knowledgeable about the field of music being covered. Usually the individual also enjoys the music. As a Music Journalist reviewing concerts or acts, the individual might first receive a press kit on the artist. A phone interview may take place for additional background material. Music Journalists receive press passes to the shows covered.

Prior to the event, he or she may have much of the background story developed and written. After the show, the journalist writes a review of the actual act. The ability to work under pressure is a must, as the finished review may have to be completed and handed in just an hour after the show ends to make a deadline. The journalist must also be careful to be as objective as possible. For example, if the journalist is writing a review of a group of which he or she is not particularly fond, this feeling may enter the review. It must not be allowed to color the piece.

Music Journalists interview musical acts for short features or in-depth articles. The ability to delve below the surface to seek information is necessary to Music Journalists. The Music Journalist who will move up and succeed is the one who asks the questions that no one else has thought of and develops a really interesting story.

Reviewers often have to review semiprofessional concerts, such as student symphonies. The reviewer must try to write a review in which the symphony is judged on its own merits and not the same basis as a major orchestra.

Music Journalists gather material in a variety of ways. They may research prior stories about a group in other magazines or publications. They may interview the act either personally or by phone. During the interview, the Music Journalist may either take notes or record the interview session (with the permission of the act). The journalist may talk with people who are close to the act (the manager, a songwriter, family members, friends, etc.). It is important to end up with a factual and interesting story.

Music Journalists may work full-time and part-time. They can work as stringers for publications on a concert-to-concert basis or work on a freelance basis doing stories by commission or writing articles to sell.

A Music Journalist is responsible to the editor of the publication for which he or she writes. Many Music Journalists become editors after a few years in writing.

Salaries

Salaries for Music Journalists depend on where they are employed, how experienced they are, and what they do.

A beginning journalist writing reviews and/or music news for a local paper may earn approximately $20,000 yearly. As he or she gains more experience, yearly salaries go up to $25,000 or more.

Journalists writing for major publications or newspapers earn between $35,000 and $150,000 plus yearly. The higher figure, of course, is for those who have made it in the field. Salaries usually average between $35,000 and $50,000 annually for a Music Journalist working for a good publication.

Employment Prospects

Employment prospects are good for the individual who doesn't mind starting at the bottom and/or moving to a location where a job is available.

Nearly all newspapers have some type of entertainment or music section, including local newspapers and magazines. The reporter-journalist may often have other duties besides writing about music.

After one gains experience writing professionally, he or she may seek employment anywhere. Employers usually require writing samples.

Advancement Prospects

If a Music Journalist has a good writing style, is responsible, and develops good contacts and a good reputation, he or she can advance. Music Journalists generally advance by obtaining positions at more prestigious publications. For example, they can go from a job on a local paper to a position on a regional newspaper. They can advance from this point to a major city newspaper as a music reviewer, reporter, or journalist. Or they can obtain a position at a prestigious music-oriented magazine.

Education and Training

Most jobs on newspapers require a college education. Individuals might, however, be able to obtain a position on a local newspaper without a college degree, but advancement is difficult.

There are journalism degrees offered at many colleges, although this does not have to be the specific degree obtained. A general liberal arts education is usually sufficient. If individuals are interested in this type of career, they should take a variety of journalism, communications, and writing courses.

Experience, Skills, and Personality Traits

Music Journalists usually begin writing for their high school papers. During their college years, they obtain positions on their school papers or part-time for local newspapers reviewing concerts, writing music columns, and critiquing records.

The Music Journalist must have good writing skills as well as a solid knowledge of the type of music he or she is writing about. The journalist must be a responsible individual who can get things done on time. Newspapers and magazines cannot wait for someone to finish articles.

Unions and Associations

Music Journalists might belong to a number of associations or organizations depending on their interests. One of the most important is the Music Critics Association. This organization sponsors seminars, conferences, etc., for those in the industry.

Tips for Entry

1. Get experience locally reviewing music events, concerts, records, etc.
2. You may consider proposing a music column to a local newspaper or magazine that doesn't already have one.
3. Names and addresses of daily newspapers are available in the *Editor and Publisher International Year Book*. This publication is available in many libraries and larger newspaper offices. You might use this as a starting point to send out your résumés and writing samples. Pick a geographical area you want to

work in and send your résumé to all the newspapers in that region.

4. There are a number of fellowships, assistantships, scholarships, and internships available in the journalism field. You might have to begin your career in an area of journalism other than music.

5. If you are in college, try to get on the college paper. Every bit of experience is important.

6. The Music Critic Association of America sponsors seminars and other interesting programs for those in the field.

7. New opportunities may also exist for Music Journalists at on-line publications.

8. Begin putting together a portfolio of your best work to illustrate your talents.

SYMPHONIES, ORCHESTRAS, OPERAS, ETC.

CONDUCTOR

CAREER PROFILE

Duties: Prepare the orchestra for the performance; conduct the orchestra

Alternate Title(s): Musical Director

Salary Range: $15,000 to $275,000+; individuals working in small orchestras may earn $75 to $500+ per service

Employment Prospects: Poor

Advancement Prospects: Poor

Best Geographical Locations for Position: Major cultural centers and other large cities which house orchestras

Prerequisites:

Education or Training—Training in conducting; musical study

Experience—Practical experience conducting different types of orchestras and/or chamber ensembles is useful

Special Skills and Personality Traits—Ability to communicate musical thoughts; proficiency at piano and at least one other instrument; thorough knowledge of symphonic repertoire

CAREER LADDER

```
┌─────────────────────────────────┐
│  Conductor of Major Orchestra   │
└─────────────────────────────────┘

┌─────────────────────────────────┐
│          Conductor              │
└─────────────────────────────────┘

┌─────────────────────────────────┐
│      Assistant Conductor        │
└─────────────────────────────────┘
```

Position Description

The Conductor holds the top musical job in the orchestra. His or her main duty is preparing the orchestra for the finest performance it is capable of presenting. The job is stressful as well as demanding. Hours are long. The Conductor must often put many hours into rehearsals before a performance. When the orchestra is on tour in cities throughout the country or the world, he or she must travel, too.

Top Conductors possess dynamic, charismatic stage personalities. This, plus immense talent, is what makes the difference between a good Conductor and a great Conductor.

As a Conductor, an individual must be proficient in at least one instrument in addition to the piano. He or she must have the ability to sight-read. Most important, the Conductor must know how to communicate musical thoughts and ideas not only verbally during rehearsals, but also through his or her body movements while involved in a performance.

The Conductor is responsible for choosing the orchestra's repertoire. He or she studies the orchestral scores and decides how the works will be played. The same piece of music might sound different depending on which individual conducted it. Each Conductor possesses his or her own style.

A good Conductor with a unique technique is often sought out to make appearances as a guest Conductor with other orchestras. As a guest Conductor, the individual's only responsibility is to prepare for the particular performance.

With his or her own orchestra, the Conductor has many other responsibilities. In addition to preparing the orchestra for individual performances with numerous rehearsals, the Conductor must plan an entire musical season. He or she is responsible for choosing guest soloists, artists, and other conductors to guest or fill in with the orchestra.

The Conductor's job includes advising various section leaders and assisting them when auditions are held for section members. The Conductor of an orchestra is also called on for public and private appearances at fund-raising events on behalf of the orchestra. During summers, many leading Conductors teach at seminars, helping aspiring Conductors to reach their goals.

The Conductor of an orchestra is usually responsible to the board of directors of that orchestra.

Salaries

Conductors' salaries vary widely. In major orchestras the Conductor may earn up to $275,000 plus a year. There are a number of very well-known conductors who earn $1,000,000 from live performances and recording revenues. In smaller orchestras, the individual may earn between $75 and $500 per service. In between, there are orchestras where Conductors' salaries range from $15,000 to $70,000 plus annually. As a rule, Conductors negotiate their salaries with individual orchestras.

Employment Prospects

Jobs are not plentiful for Conductors. The field is very limited. To get a job as a Conductor or even as an Assistant Conductor one must have the opportunity to audition. Competition is fierce. Most Conductors work for years as musicians while studying to become Conductors.

Possibilities for work as a Conductor include all varieties of orchestras. Not all positions are full-time jobs. Many successful Conductors have agents and/or managers who seek positions for them.

Advancement Prospects

The Conductor has the top position in an orchestra. Conductors can, however, advance from one type of orchestra to another. For instance, one might obtain a job as a Conductor in a community orchestra and eventually move up to the position of assistant conductor in an urban orchestra. In this profession, advancement occurs as a result of both great talent and a degree of luck.

Education and Training

An individual might have a doctoral degree in conducting and still not land a job as a Conductor. A conservatory or college degree in conducting is not usually required, but may be helpful. Training similar to that received in an educational setting is required, whether it be through seminars or private study.

Summer seminars in conducting are extremely useful to an individual aspiring to be a Conductor. Through these seminars, one can find out if he or she has the talent to be in this field. The best seminars are led by world-renowned Conductors. A seminar given by a skilled Conductor can help an individual bring out his or her own personal style of conducting.

Experience, Skills, and Personality Traits

Any practical experience is useful in becoming a Conductor. Conducting chamber ensembles, small community orchestras, youth orchestras, etc., gives the individual needed experience. Most conservatories and music-oriented schools also offer assistant programs where the student is given an opportunity to conduct.

Summer seminars, such as those held at Tanglewood in Massachusetts, also offer individuals a chance for conducting experience.

Unions and Associations

Conductors may belong to the American Federation of Musicians (AFM) or the American Guild of Musical Artists (AGMA), depending on their situation. For example, if the Conductor plays or played an instrument, he or she probably belongs to the AFM. If the individual was a soloist, he or she might also belong to AGMA. However, many Conductors do not belong to either union.

Tips for Entry

1. Try to attend a summer seminar that has world-renowned Conductors associated with it. Aside from the excellent experience gained at these seminars you can often make important contacts. If you show exceptional talent in the art of conducting a well-known Conductor may help you and guide you up the ladder to success.

2. There are a number of orchestras that offer internships and fellowships in conducting. Check with orchestras to see what programs they offer and whether you qualify.

3. Positions are advertised in many music-oriented publications, including *The International Musician*.

4. Positions may also be advertised in the newspaper classified section. Look under key words such as "Music," "Orchestra," "Conductor," or "Symphony."

CONCERTMASTER/CONCERTMISTRESS

CAREER PROFILE

Duties: Lead the entire string section of the orchestra; solo; tune orchestra

Alternate Title(s): Section Leader; 1st Violinist

Salary Range: $25,000 to $100,000+ full time; impossible to estimate the earnings of individuals working part time and/or paid per service

Employment Prospects: Poor

Advancement Prospects: Poor

Best Geographical Locations for Position: Major cultural centers and other large cities that host orchestras

Prerequisites:

Education or Training—Extensive musical training and/or private study of violin

Experience—Performing as a section member; performing in orchestras and/or chamber music groups

Special Skills and Personality Traits—Good leadership skills; excellent musical ability; ability to deal with stress and pressure; sight-reading skills

CAREER LADDER

```
┌─────────────────────────────────────┐
│        Assistant Conductor          │
└─────────────────────────────────────┘

┌─────────────────────────────────────┐
│   Concertmaster/Concertmistress     │
└─────────────────────────────────────┘

┌─────────────────────────────────────┐
│            Assistant                │
│   Concertmaster/Concertmistress     │
└─────────────────────────────────────┘
```

Position Description

The position of Concertmaster/Concertmistress is an extremely important one in an orchestra. The person holding this position leads the entire string section of the orchestra during rehearsals and concerts.

At the beginning of every rehearsal or concert, the Concertmaster/Concertmistress is responsible for tuning the rest of the orchestra. For example, the individual will glance at the oboe player, who then gives the "A" note. The rest of the players then tune themselves before the conductor walks out on stage. This procedure takes only 15–20 seconds.

The Concertmaster/Concertmistress usually begins his or her career as a section player. Then if he or she is in the second violin section, the individual can choose to either become section leader in the second violin section or move into the first section as a first section player.

If a player moves into the first section as a section player, he or she then might strive to become the Concertmaster/Concertmistress. This person must show good leadership qualities. Coordination and leadership of the section must be subtle. It must not be obvious to the audience, only to the members of the section.

It is important for the individual to know all the solo literature (music) in the orchestral repertoire. He or she will often have to perform solo during concerts.

The Concertmaster/Concertmistress is also responsible for supervising rehearsals of the string section. The individual may be involved in preliminary auditions for new section members.

A Concertmaster/Concertmistress is directly responsible to the conductor. The job is all-encompassing. The individual is practically considered the section leader of the entire orchestra.

To attain this position, a person must be an extremely accomplished musician and a master of the violin. The Concertmaster/Concertmistress job is competitive; only the best are chosen.

Salaries

Concertmaster/Concertmistress salaries vary depending on the type of orchestra (major, metropolitan, suburban etc.), the number of weeks the orchestra is in session, and the bargaining power of the individual. Minimum earnings are negotiated by the American Federation of Musicians (AFM) local unions for musical members of an orchestra. The Concertmaster/Concertmistress might also be a member of the American Guild of Musical Artists (AGMA), as he or she may often perform as a soloist. Therefore, minimum earnings might also be set by that union.

The amount of money paid to the Concertmaster/Concertmistress over that paid to the section musicians will vary. In some orchestras the Concertmaster/Concertmistress receives from 10% to 35% over the section members' salaries. In other cases, the individual may negotiate his or her own contract directly with the orchestra management. In a major orchestra, the Concertmaster/Concertmistress may earn from $25,000 to $100,000 plus annually. In smaller orchestras the individual will earn considerably less. As many of the smaller orchestras offer only part-time work, the Concertmaster/Concertmistress may be paid on a perservice basis.

Individuals in this position may earn additional income by teaching, participating in recording sessions, or going on the lecture circuit.

Employment Prospects

There are not many opportunities for obtaining a Concertmaster/Concertmistress position with a major orchestra. Opportunities in other types of orchestras are limited too. As there is only one Concertmaster/Concertmistress in each orchestra, competition is always extreme.

Advancement Prospects

The position of Concertmaster/Concertmistress is not entry-level. Once in this position, the individual might want to advance to conductor or assistant conductor. In many orchestras, the assistant conductor position is held simultaneously by the Concertmaster/Concertmistress.

After an individual gets his or her foot in the door by obtaining an orchestral position such as section member, advancement is possible. However, if one holds the position as a Concertmaster/Concertmistress in an urban orchestra,
he or she might still have a problem obtaining a position as a Concertmaster/Concertmistress in a major or regional orchestra. The person would probably have to work as a section member in the regional or major orchestra prior to obtaining the Concertmaster/Concertmistress position in a more prestigious orchestra.

Education and Training

Extensive musical training is necessary for the Concertmaster/Concertmistress. This training may be obtained through study at a conservatory, college, with private teachers, or a combination of the above.

Experience, Skills, and Personality Traits

The Concertmaster/Concertmistress begins as a section player. Experience in many different orchestras hones skills. Playing at every opportunity possible helps the musician become more accomplished. It goes without saying that the individual must be an accomplished, talented violinist. Demonstrating leadership skills is important too, as the Concertmaster/Concertmistress leads the entire string section.

Unions and Associations

A Concertmaster/Concertmistress can belong to either the American Federation of Musicians (AFM) or the American Guild of Musical Artists (AGMA). In addition, there are a number of associations that individuals may belong to. Among them are the American Symphony Orchestra League (ASOL) and the National Orchestra Association (NOA).

Tips for Entry

1. Audition for the position of Concertmaster/Concertmistress in your college orchestra.
2. Learn the orchestra's repertoire.
3. Take as many lessons as possible, and practice, practice, practice.
4. Take part in seminars and internships that are available throughout the country.
5. Listings for positions are available through the *International Musician Magazine* (an American Federation of Musicians publication) as well as a variety of other orchestral newsletters, magazines, and publications.

SECTION LEADER

CAREER PROFILE	CAREER LADDER

CAREER PROFILE

Duties: Lead a section of the orchestra; supervise any rehearsals with the section; assign parts to players in the section

Alternate Title(s): Principal

Salary Range: $25,000 to $95,000+ in full-time orchestras; part-time or per service wages in smaller orchestras

Employment Prospects: Poor

Advancement Prospects: Poor

Best Geographical Locations for Position: Major cultural centers and other large cities

Prerequisites:

Education or Training—Extensive musical training

Experience—Performing as a section member; acting as section leader in youth or college orchestra

Special Skills and Personality Traits—Leadership skills; exceptional musical talent

CAREER LADDER

```
┌─────────────────────────────┐
│   Concertmaster (if violin)  │
└─────────────────────────────┘

┌─────────────────────────────┐
│       Section Leader         │
└─────────────────────────────┘

┌─────────────────────────────┐
│       Section Player         │
└─────────────────────────────┘
```

Position Description

Each section of an orchestra has a leader called the Section Leader or the Principal Player. The Section Leader is responsible to the concertmaster. The main duty of the Leader is to lead the section so that the sound is the best that can be produced. It is important that the Leader communicate what he or she expects of the section. This is a job that has to be done subtly. It must be obvious only to the section and never the audience.

The string Section Leader, for example, must decide where the bowing should be inserted. The individual must make a decision on the correct phrasing and on who in the section should play the individual parts.

In the wind section, the Section Leader emphasizes such techniques as correct breathing. In certain sections, like that of the oboe, the Section Leader has different responsibilities because there are so few members of that section. Those sections function much more as a personal team than the larger sections do.

To obtain a position as a Section Leader, an individual must audition. Committees are usually set up to listen to these auditions and select the best candidate.

A good stage presence and creative musical ability help place one musician above the rest. A thorough knowledge of the symphonic repertoire is essential. The Section Leader must know how to sight-read and be ready to do so at any time.

At times, the Section Leader has to be able to recognize talent. This individual is on the selection committee during auditions for the section. The Section Leader, additionally, must supervise any rehearsals within his or her section.

Certain orchestras require their Section Leaders to participate in the orchestra's chamber music group. This is usually specified in the job description.

Salaries

Salaries for Section Leaders in orchestras depend on a number of variables. These include the type of orchestra (major, metropolitan, suburban, etc.), its location, the number of weeks the orchestra is in session, and the seniority of the player.

Minimum earnings are negotiated by the American Federation of Musicians (AFM) local unions. In some orchestras, the Section Leaders receive the same amount of money as other section players. In other orchestras, Section Leaders receive a specific amount of money over the scale set for the section members. In other cases, the Section Leader's salary will be from 10% to 35% over those of section members. Certain Section Leaders negotiate their contracts directly with the orchestra management.

Section Leaders in full-time and major orchestras earn from $25,000 to $95,000 plus. Section Leaders in smaller orchestras earn considerably less. As many of the smaller orchestras offer only part-time work, Section Leaders may be paid on a per service basis.

Section Leaders may earn additional income by teaching or by participating in recording sessions.

Employment Prospects

To become a Section Leader, one must first be a section member of an orchestra. In the ladder of experience, therefore, it is usually the older players with experience in a few different orchestras who obtain these positions. The opportunity does exist, however, to become a Section Leader of a community orchestra or an urban orchestra.

Advancement Prospects

The Section Leader of the violin section can move up to the concertmaster/concertmistress position. However, these positions do not often open up.

The Section Leader of the flute or any of the wind instruments, on the other hand, cannot move up to a concertmaster/concertmistress position. They have the opportunity, though, to train to be conductors or to obtain jobs as a Section Leader or section members in more prestigious orchestras.

Education and Training

As with most symphonic positions, a college degree is not required. Conservatory training or a degree in music per-

formance may help the musician in his or her journey toward becoming a great musician and Section Leader. Years of intensive training and study in the instrument of choice are essential.

Seminars in section leading are also available and often prove to be useful.

Experience, Skills, and Personality Traits

Section Leaders must have experience as section members. Many also play in chamber music ensembles.

Section Leaders often begin playing in youth orchestras. There they gain the experience of acting as Section Leaders. Of course, a Section Leader must be an exceptional musician on his or her instrument.

The Section Leader must be a good leader, able to communicate to the section without being obvious to the audience.

Unions and Associations

Section Leaders must belong to a musician's union. Most belong to the American Federation of Musicians (AFM). This union sets the minimum pay scale for musicians.

Tips for Entry

1. This position is obtained through application and auditions.
2. Prior to applying, take part in as many different orchestral situations as possible.
3. The National Orchestral Association holds training programs for individuals entering the orchestral music field.
4. Take part in seminars and internships offered by orchestras, organizations, colleges, and associations.
5. Positions are listed in music-oriented journals and newsletters such as *The International Musician*.

SECTION MEMBER

CAREER PROFILE

Duties: Play an instrument in an orchestra

Alternate Title(s): Classical Musician; Artist; Section Player

Salary Range: Weekly earnings in orchestra of major musical production, symphony, ballet, or opera company: $800 to $2,500+; weekly earnings in smaller or less prestigious orchestra of musical production symphony, ballet, or opera company: $300 to $750+

Employment Prospects: Poor

Advancement Prospects: Poor

Best Geographical Location(s) for Position: Major cultural centers and other large cities offer the most opportunities

Prerequisites:

Education or Training—Extensive musical training

Experience—Performance in chamber music ensembles, youth, college, urban, and/or metropolitan orchestras useful

Special Skills and Personality Traits—Exceptional musical talent; dedication to music; perseverance

CAREER LADDER

```
┌──────────────────────────────┐
│      Section Leader          │
└──────────────────────────────┘

┌──────────────────────────────┐
│      Section Member          │
└──────────────────────────────┘

┌──────────────────────────────┐
│    Freelance Performer;      │
│    Conservatory Student      │
└──────────────────────────────┘
```

Position Description

The Section Members of the orchestra are the people who make up the musical portion of the orchestra. There are different numbers of Section Members in each orchestra.

To be a Section Member, an individual must have exceptional talent with his or her instrument. In addition, the individual must like to perform on stage.

The Section Member must have a full knowledge of the orchestral repertoire. He or she must know the music before going into rehearsal. Rehearsals are mainly for putting together all the parts played by the orchestra.

An important part of the Section Member's responsibility is to play with a group. This is what makes an orchestra sound the way it does.

The Section Member is responsible to his or her section leader. The musician must take cues such as where the correct bowings or phrasing should be (in the string section), correct breathing (in the brass sections), who will play what part, etc.

Section Members must continually practice their instruments and rehearse musical pieces. As a Section Member, an individual must always keep trying to better his or her musical skill.

The Section Member is under contract to perform a specific number of concerts and rehearsals per week. Any rehearsal or concert over that number (the number differs with various orchestras) and any recording the Section Member participates in qualifies the individual for additional monies.

The Section Member must be available to travel, as orchestras often tour other cities and countries. Travel expenses are paid by the orchestra management.

Section Members who work full-time in major or regional orchestras generally receive at least four weeks vacation, usually when the orchestra takes its break.

Section Members often earn additional income teaching privately. If the individual is a noted member of the orchestra, he or she may also become a speaker on the lecture circuit.

Salaries

Salaries for Section Members depend on a number of factors. These include the type of orchestra (major, metropolitan, urban, etc.), its location, the number of weeks the orchestra is in session, and, in some cases, the seniority of the player.

Minimum earnings are negotiated by the American Federation of Musicians (AFM) local union. Depending on the location, Section Members working in a major orchestra may earn between $800 and $2,500 or more per week. Annual salaries depend on how many weeks per year the orchestra is in session. Major orchestras run from 30 to 52 weeks a year. Salaries may also be contingent on seniority. In addition to salaries, Section Members receive vacation pay and other benefits.

Section Members working in smaller orchestras usually earn considerably less than those playing in major orchestras. Many of the smaller orchestras offer only part-time work. Members are paid on a per service basis. This means that they are paid for each concert in which they perform. In most cases, these individuals are also paid for each rehearsal they attend.

Section Members in youth and college orchestras generally do not get paid and play for the experience.

Section Members might earn additional income by teaching or by participating in recording sessions.

Employment Prospects

The chances of obtaining a position as a Section Member in a major orchestra are limited. There are many talented, qualified musicians vying for few positions. There is intense competition.

Prospects in the smaller and less prestigious orchestras are slightly better.

(Many orchestras now audition people in back of a screen. Using this technique, there can be no racial or sexual discrimination in the selection process. This technique came about after many years of orchestras that were dominated by white males.)

Advancement Prospects

Once a Section Member obtains a position in an orchestra, the individual has a chance of advancing to a section leader position. The Section Member must be very talented to advance in this manner. Section Members also have the opportunity to advance their careers by trying to land positions as Section Members in more prestigious orchestras.

Education and Training

No college degree is required for a position as a Section Member. However, extensive musical training is essential. This training might be acquired at a conservatory or college, or through intensive private study.

Experience, Skills, and Personality Traits

Any type of performance experience is helpful to an aspiring Section Member. Performing in youth or college orchestras or chamber music ensembles is most useful. Auditioning is useful for the experience.

Section Members must be very dedicated to their music. They must also have the perseverance to keep trying to land a position in an orchestra.

Unions and Associations

Section Members may belong to the American Federation of Musicians (AFM). This union negotiates minimum wages for the musician, maximum number of rehearsals, etc.

Tips for Entry

1. This position is obtained through application and auditions.
2. Prior to applying, take part in as many different orchestral situations as possible.
3. The National Orchestral Association holds training programs for individuals entering the orchestral music field.
4. Take part in seminars and internships offered by orchestras, colleges, and associations.
5. Positions are listed in music-oriented journals and newsletters such as *The International Musician*.

OPERA SINGER

CAREER PROFILE	CAREER LADDER

CAREER PROFILE

Duties: Sing, perform, and act in operas

Alternate Title(s): Classical Singer; Operatic Singer

Salary Range: $10,000 to $200,000+

Employment Prospects: Fair

Advancement Prospects: Fair

Best Geographical Location(s) For Position: New York City is the opera capital of the United States; culturally active cities worldwide hosting opera companies will offer other opportunities

Prerequisites:

Education or Training—Graduate of music conservatory or college or university with a major in classical music

Experience—Experience singing operatic music and other classical music necessary

Special Skills and Personality Traits—Extraordinary voice; talent; acting skills; familiarity with operas; fluency in foreign languages; physical, mental, and emotional stamina; perseverance; drive; determination

CAREER LADDER

```
┌─────────────────────────────────────┐
│   Opera Singer Performing with       │
│   More Prestigious Opera Company     │
└─────────────────────────────────────┘

┌─────────────────────────────────────┐
│          Opera Singer                │
└─────────────────────────────────────┘

┌─────────────────────────────────────┐
│   Student or Aspiring Opera Singer   │
└─────────────────────────────────────┘
```

Position Description

Opera Singers are highly trained in classical music. Individuals perform in classical theatrical productions set to music. During these performances, the dialogue is sung instead of spoken. Opera Singers must also act and move on the stage to help bring the story to life.

Traditional operas were written and performed in a number of foreign languages. Opera Singers must either know the language that the opera was written in or be able to learn his or her part in the particular language. Often, the Opera Singer may just learn the part without being able to speak or understand the meaning of the words. Modern operas, written in this country, are usually written and performed in English.

Every opera tells a story. The story is written in a libretto or little book. Operas may be elaborate productions relying on a myriad of costuming, scenery, and lighting.

Individuals may be Principle Singers in the opera singing lead, feature, or support roles. They may also sing in opera choruses.

Opera Singers usually audition to obtain jobs. Some individuals have agents or managers who obtain auditions for them. Others find out about openings in shows in a variety of ways, including word of mouth, through the union, or advertisements or notices in trade papers.

Once the Opera Singer obtains a part, he or she is required to attend show rehearsals, become familiar with the opera, and learn the part. Individuals will be fitted with costumes, and have their hair and makeup determined by stylists.

It is the responsibility of the Opera Singer to attend each rehearsal and sing at each performance. Work hours may vary depending on the schedule of rehearsals and performances. Opera Singers often work in the afternoon, evenings, and on weekends.

Salaries

Salaries can vary greatly for Opera Singers depending on a number of factors. These include the type of setting in which the individual sings, the geographic location, and level, size and budget of the opera company. Other factors include the reputation and experience of the individual and the type of part he or she is singing. Individuals may be paid by the performance or on a weekly basis, depending on their specific situation.

Opera Singers can earn between $10,000 and $200,000 or more annually. Variables affecting earnings are, among other things, based on the singer's experience, talent, and popularity.

Aspiring Opera Singers, taking part in an apprentice program, may earn a weekly salary of approximately $250 to $500 or more plus housing. Individuals with additional experience such as those involved in a Young Singer program may earn between $500 and $750 a week. (Young Singer programs are a type of program for up-and-coming young singers similar to apprentice programs.)

Opera Singers are either paid by the performance or on a weekly basis. Individuals also may earn royalties from recordings. Opera Singers working in unionized halls have minimum earnings set by the American Guild of Musical Artists (AGMA). Minimum earnings are based on the type of role an individual is singing as well as the number of rehearsals and performances required.

Employment Prospects

Employment prospects are dependent on talent, determination, and drive. Employment opportunities exist in choruses of operas throughout the country in local, regional, and national companies.

While opera companies exist in most culturally active cities throughout the country and the world, New York City is the opera capital.

Opera Singers often find employment with the help of a manager or talent agent. There are a number of agencies specializing in classical music. Most of them are located in New York City.

Advancement Prospects

Once a talented Opera Singer gets his or her foot in the door, prospects for advancement are fair. Individuals may climb the career ladder by locating a position singing with a more prestigious opera company or by obtaining a lead or solo part in an operatic production.

Education and Training

Individuals must go through years of classical singing and other training to become Opera Singers. Aspiring Opera Singers usually participate in apprenticeship programs with regional or national opera companies before becoming full-fledged Opera Singers.

Generally, Opera Singers attend music conservatories or colleges or universities with majors in classical music. This period is invaluable to individuals for the training and education as well as the opportunities and practical experience that may not be available elsewhere.

Many individuals take additional classes from private vocal coaches and teachers to supplement their training.

Experience, Skills, and Personality Traits

In order to become successful, Opera Singers must get a great deal of experience singing classical music. This may be obtained through Young Singer and apprenticeship programs sponsored by opera companies.

An Opera Singer must be very talented and have an extraordinary voice. Acting skills are also necessary. Fluency in other languages is useful when singing classic operas in foreign languages or performing in other countries. Familiarity with operas is also helpful.

Success in this field is also dependent on drive, determination, and the willingness to practice long hours. To do this, individuals must have a great deal of physical, mental, and emotional stamina.

Unions and Associations

Opera Singers working in unionized concert halls, theaters, and other venues must be members of the American Guild of Musical Artists (AGMA). This union negotiates minimum earnings for its members as well as minimum working conditions and standards.

Tips for Entry

1. Summer workshops and other similar programs with opera companies are a good way to get excellent training and experience.
2. Internship and apprenticeship programs are invaluable to this career. Contact opera companies for program availabilities.
3. Get the best training you can.
4. Make contacts and get additional experience by finding competitions in opera.
5. Get involved with your local opera company.
6. Attend live operas to learn techniques from other Opera Singers.
7. Many public broadcasting networks and cable stations have operatic productions on television. These are valuable learning tools.

MANAGING DIRECTOR

CAREER PROFILE

Duties: Oversee the administrative functions of the orchestra

Alternate Title(s): Executive Director; Chief Administrator

Salary Range: $24,000 to $90,000+

Employment Prospects: Poor

Advancement Prospects: Poor

Best Geographical Locations for Position: Major cultural centers and other large cities that house orchestras

Prerequisites:

Education or Training—College background or degree with major in business, arts administration, or music management recommended

Experience—Positions in supervisory capacities; experience in public relations helpful; orchestra manager position useful

Special Skills and Personality Traits—Management skills; supervisory skills; personability; responsibility; business ability

CAREER LADDER

```
┌─────────────────────────────┐
│   Managing Director of a    │
│      Major Orchestra        │
└─────────────────────────────┘

┌─────────────────────────────┐
│      Managing Director       │
└─────────────────────────────┘

┌─────────────────────────────┐
│     Orchestra Manager        │
└─────────────────────────────┘
```

Position Description

The Managing Director of the orchestra holds the top administrative position in an orchestra. It is his or her job to oversee all of the administrative functions of the orchestra and to supervise the administrative personnel.

The individual works closely with the orchestra manager. Together they work with and supervise the development, public relations, business, educational activities, and ticket subscriptions directors and their departments. Both the orchestra manager and the Managing Director must be knowledgeable about these departments, their internal problems, and their activities.

The Managing Director acts as a liaison between the orchestra's board of directors and the administrative departments. It is his or her responsibility to make sure that the policies set up for the orchestra are carried out. The individual attends most of the orchestra board's meetings, working with the board on many of the policies developed. He or she will also report on any administrative problems. Through these meetings, the Managing Director keeps the board members aware of all that is happening within the orchestra.

The Managing Director, or executive director, as he or she is sometimes called, takes part in all labor negotiations involving the orchestra. The individual must have the ability and the knowledge to effectively negotiate with unions.

The Managing Director of an orchestra usually works in many of the other departments of the orchestra's administration before attaining the Directorship. This experience makes the Director better qualified to handle the details of managing the orchestra.

As the Managing Director, the person is responsible for ensuring that the orchestra meets the needs of the community from a cultural standpoint. He or she might decide that the community needs more children's concerts or a summer concert series. In these cases, the individual will work with the orchestra board and the community to try to put these programs together.

At times, the Managing Director will work with the personnel director. He or she will ultimately be responsible not only for hiring administrative personnel, but also for firing individuals who don't work out.

The Managing Director must work with the development department and the business department, making up budgets and raising money for the orchestra. Some of this money is made available through foundations, corporations, and arts councils. The Managing Director is responsible for locating as much money as possible through this system and bringing it to the attention of the development department.

The Managing Director of the orchestra is responsible to the president of the board of directors and to the board members. His or her days are long, but they are challenging and exciting.

Salaries

Symphony orchestras are classified into different categories according to their size, budget, etc. Salaries will naturally depend on the size, budget, and location of the orchestra. Individuals working as Managing Directors in major orchestras earn more than those working in smaller organizations. Salaries range from $24,000 to $90,000 plus per year.

Employment Prospects

There are a limited number of major and regional orchestras. Employment prospects at that level are limited, too. Positions are more frequently available at the metropolitan and urban levels of orchestras.

Advancement Prospects

The orchestra's Managing Director may advance by obtaining the job of Managing Director with a bigger, more prestigious orchestra. The Managing Director of the orchestra holds the top position in the administrative side of the organization.

Education and Training

A college degree is not always required for this position, although it is usually preferred. Courses in arts administration, music arrangement, business, publicity, and journalism are helpful in handling the job.

Seminars on arts and orchestral administration, given by various colleges and by associations such as the American Symphony Orchestra League (ASOL), are a bonus to the individual seeking or already holding a position as an orchestra Managing Director.

Experience, Skills, and Personality Traits

The Managing Director must be an enthusiastic type of person. The individual must be personable and congenial, as he or she must deal not only with the orchestra but also with the entire orchestra administration and the board of directors.

The Managing Director must have the ability to supervise and must do so effectively. He or she must be sensitive and understanding toward both the musicians and the administration.

Unions and Associations

The Managing Director of an orchestra may belong to the American Symphony Orchestra League (ASOL). This association sponsors seminars and internship programs in addition to publishing a magazine/newsletter. Many individuals also belong to the Associated Council of the Arts and/or local arts councils.

Tips for Entry

1. Find an orchestra, school, or association that offers an internship program. Interns have a much better chance of obtaining a position.
2. Attend seminars on orchestral management. These seminars are given by colleges, orchestras, and associations such as the American Symphony Orchestra League (ASOL). These will train and educate you and help you develop important contacts.
3. Vacancies are listed in the ASOL newsletter, the Associated Council of the Arts newsletter, and many regional arts organizations' publications.
4. Take a chance and send your résumé with a cover letter to a number of orchestras. One might have an opening for an assistant.

ORCHESTRA MANAGER

CAREER PROFILE

Duties: Assist managing director in various management duties; negotiate contracts for musical orchestral personnel

Alternate Title(s): Assistant Manager; Operations Manager

Salary Range: $23,000 to $73,000+

Employment Prospects: Poor

Advancement Prospects: Fair

Best Geographical Locations for Position: Positions may be available in cultural centers or other cities that house orchestras

Prerequisites:

Education or Training—College degree preferred or recommended for most positions

Experience—Positions in supervisory capacities helpful

Special Skills and Personality Traits—Management skills; supervisory skills; personability; ability to negotiate

CAREER LADDER

```
┌─────────────────────────────────┐
│      Managing Director          │
└─────────────────────────────────┘

┌─────────────────────────────────┐
│      Orchestra Manager          │
└─────────────────────────────────┘

┌─────────────────────────────────┐
│   Director of Development;       │
│ Publicity or Public Relations Position │
└─────────────────────────────────┘
```

Position Description

The Orchestra Manager is the assistant to the orchestra's managing director. A primary duty is negotiating with the musicians union on behalf of the orchestra. An Orchestra Manager must try to get the best deal for the orchestra management from the union while keeping the players happy.

The Orchestra Manager is also in charge of arranging any concert tours for the orchestra. He or she not only arranges the details of the tour, but also tries to make it easy for the orchestra members who will be traveling. The individual is responsible for any problems that are not directly music-related. These could include anything from a musician's instrument that arrives late to an auditorium, a musician who becomes ill in the middle of the night in a strange town, or a dispute caused by hot tempers that erupt on the road. The Orchestra Manager must deal with crises that occur while traveling. With the pressures of touring, many problems are magnified.

The Orchestra Manager also oversees the orchestra's administrative employees, including the director of development, director of public relations, music administrator, business manager, director of educational activities, and director of ticket subscriptions. He or she must be knowledgeable about these positions and the problems that might occur.

The person must have a broad understanding of the needs of the community or area in which the orchestra is based. As Orchestra Manager, he or she must negotiate contracts for guest soloists and guest conductors.

The Orchestra Manager is responsible to the managing director of the orchestra. The position is not a nine-to-five job. The successful Orchestra Manager loves symphonic music. This makes the job—which involves long hours and hard work—worthwhile.

Salaries

Symphony orchestras are classified into different groups depending on size, budget, and other factors. There are major orchestras, such as the Boston Symphony or the Cleveland Orchestra; there are regional orchestras, like the Birmingham Symphony Orchestra or the Memphis Symphony Orchestra; there are metropolitan, urban, community, college, and youth orchestras. Salaries of Orchestra Managers vary according to the classification and location of the orchestra. Salaries range from $23,000 to $73,000 plus annually. Orchestra Managers of urban, community, college, or youth orchestras often work on an avocational or per service basis.

Employment Prospects

There is a limited number of major and even regional orchestras in the country. Therefore, employment prospects at this level are poor. Positions are sometimes available at the metropolitan, urban, and community levels. However, these jobs are not always full-time.

Advancement Prospects

The position of an Orchestra Manager is not an entry-level job. Positions held prior to Orchestra Manager might include public relations director, fund-raising director, business manager, or an assistant in one of these fields. Once an individual has proven him- or herself in the position of Orchestra Manager, he or she is a valuable commodity to the orchestra and has the opportunity to move up to the position of managing director or to move to an open position in a better orchestra as Orchestra Manager.

Education and Training

A college degree is preferred or recommended for most positions as Orchestra Manager. Individuals may find a few positions without this requirement. These are usually in smaller orchestras.

Courses in music management, administration, and/or business are helpful. Classes in publicity, labor negotiations, fund-raising, and psychology are useful, too. There are also seminars given around the country in arts administration. These seminars put the individual in touch with others already in the field and help develop contracts.

Experience, Skills, and Personality Traits

A good sense of business is important to an Orchestra Manager. An understanding of and sensitivity to musicians and their problems and pressures is almost equally important. To do the job well, one must be able to deal effectively with problems and people under pressure. Hands-on experience is always helpful. Many conservatories and universities have internship programs that provide practical experience. Enjoying music makes it all worthwhile.

Unions and Associations

The Orchestra Manager may belong to the American Symphony Orchestra League (ASOL). He or she might also belong to a local arts council.

Tips for Entry

1. Find an orchestra or school that has an internship in orchestral management. The American Symphony Orchestra League (ASOL) sponsors a variety of internship programs.
2. Attend seminars on orchestral management. Seminars are sponsored by various universities and orchestras in addition to the ASOL.
3. Vacancies are listed in the ASOL newsletter, the Associated Council of the Arts newsletter, and many regional arts organizations' publications.
4. Job openings may also be located on the Internet. Look for specific orchestra sites which often list employment opportunities.

BUSINESS MANAGER

CAREER PROFILE

Duties: Supervise the financial affairs of the orchestra; prepare and distribute payroll

Alternate Title(s): Controller

Salary Range: $23,000 to $73,000+

Employment Prospects: Fair

Advancement Prospects: Poor

Best Geographical Locations for Position: Major cultural centers such as Boston, Philadelphia, New York City, Chicago, etc.

Prerequisites:

Education or Training—Educational requirements vary; all positions require at least a high school diploma; many require a college degree

Experience—Bookkeeping experience, accounting positions, etc.

Special Skills and Personality Traits—Skill with figures; accuracy; responsibility; accounting and/or bookkeeping skills; cognizance of orchestral procedures

CAREER LADDER

```
┌─────────────────────────────────────┐
│  Business Manager of Major Orchestra;│
│        Orchestra Manager             │
└─────────────────────────────────────┘

┌─────────────────────────────────────┐
│          Business Manager            │
└─────────────────────────────────────┘

┌─────────────────────────────────────┐
│       Bookkeeper; Accountant         │
└─────────────────────────────────────┘
```

Position Description

The Business Manager of the orchestra is in charge of supervising all of its financial affairs. Depending on the size and the budget of the organization, the Business Manager may work alone or have an assistant and a staff.

The individual in this position must check all bills the orchestra receives. If they are correct, he or she issues checks and pays them. If they are wrong or if there is a discrepancy, the Business Manager or Controller attempts to rectify the problem. The individual is responsible for paying all bills on time. These may include rentals for music, transportation costs for out-of-town concerts, hotel bills, etc.

The Business Manager may look at comparative prices of various items to make sure that the organization is buying well. For example, the person may check the prices of music stands from four or five companies before purchasing to establish a good price. The individual may work out deals with hotel or motel chains for putting up the orchestra members while on tour. As most orchestras' budgets are extremely tight, the Business Manager will always try to save money for the group.

Accurate records must be kept on all expenditures paid out for the orchestra. Payment dates, check numbers, and lists of items purchased must be kept meticulously. If there are any guarantees or warranties on products purchased, it is usually up to the Business Manager to keep these on file.

The Business Manager is responsible for preparing the payroll and distributing it at the proper times. If a guest conductor or soloist has been employed by the orchestra, the individual must make sure that he or she are paid, too. These payments must be disbursed in accordance with union regulations. The individual must make sure that the proper deductions are taken from everyone's salary and that these monies are correctly deposited and reported to the government.

The person in this position works closely with the director of development. The Business Manager may be responsible for keeping a tally of money raised or for depositing donations. He or she might be in charge of the bookkeeping for the fund-raising department.

The Business Manager also works with the orchestra manager and the managing director in putting together a yearly budget for the organization. After the budget is approved by the board of directors, the Business Manager works to stay within its bounds.

The individual in this position works fairly regular hours. He or she may report to the orchestra's managing director or to the board of directors.

Salaries

The salary of a Business Manager working for an orchestra will vary depending on the classification, size, and budget of the orchestra. Salaries might also vary due to an individual's qualifications and responsibilities. A Business Manager working full time may earn from $23,000 to $73,000 or more annually.

Employment Prospects

Employment prospects are fair for those wanting jobs as business managers in orchestras. Almost every orchestra in the country which has any type of income and/or expenses hires at least a part-time person to fill this position. Larger orchestras may hire a full-time Business Manager and one or more assistants.

Advancement Prospects

Advancement prospects for a Business Manager in an orchestra are poor. The individual may be promoted to orchestra manager, but this may take a long time.

A Business Manager working for a smaller orchestra may, however, advance his or her career by finding employment with a larger or more prestigious orchestra. This usually means more responsibility and an increase in salary.

Education and Training

Education requirements vary greatly according to the orchestra and the position. For example, a Business Man-

ager working part-time in a small orchestra may only be required to have a high school diploma. A major orchestra might, however, require an individual to have a degree in accounting, business, finance, or a related area.

There are many people who work in all phases of the orchestral system who have music performance degrees but cannot get performance-related jobs. A good number of these individuals take jobs in non-performance areas such as Business Management just to be close to the orchestral setting.

Experience, Skills, and Personality Traits

One of the primary skills a Business Manager needs is an ability with figures. Many people in these positions have bookkeeping experience or accounting skills. Accuracy is essential.

It is helpful, too, for the individual to have a basic knowledge of orchestra procedures.

Unions and Associations

The Business Manager in an orchestral situation does not usually belong to any union. He or she may belong to a number of orchestra-related associations. The most prominent in the field is the American Symphony Orchestra League (ASOL).

Tips for Entry

1. Jobs as Business Managers of orchestras are often listed in the classified sections of newspapers. Most often these jobs open up at the end of a season.
2. Openings are listed in the American Symphony Orchestra League (ASOL) newsletter and various other arts council newsletters.
3. Send a résumé and a cover letter to a few orchestras. They may have openings coming up.
4. Check out the websites of orchestras. Many list job opportunities.

DIRECTOR OF DEVELOPMENT

CAREER PROFILE

Duties: Coordinate annual giving activities, capital campaigns, and deferred giving opportunities for donors and potential donors to an orchestra

Alternate Title(s): Fund-raising and Development Director

Salary Range: $23,000 to $90,000+

Employment Prospects: Fair

Advancement Prospects: Fair

Best Geographical Locations for Position: Any city that hosts an orchestra—New York City, Boston, Memphis, Phoenix, Syracuse, Pittsburgh, Philadelphia, etc.

Prerequisites:

Education or Training—College degree not required in all positions, but may be preferred

Experience—Fund-raising and development experience required in music or nonmusic-oriented positions

Special Skills and Personality Traits—Communications skills; creativity; enthusiasm; organization

CAREER LADDER

```
┌─────────────────────────────────┐
│       Orchestra Manager         │
└─────────────────────────────────┘

┌─────────────────────────────────┐
│    Director of Development       │
└─────────────────────────────────┘

┌─────────────────────────────────┐
│        Assistant to the          │
│    Director of Development        │
└─────────────────────────────────┘
```

Position Description

Getting people to donate money isn't easy, especially when there are so many causes and organizations soliciting. The Director of Development of the orchestra has one job: to raise money for the orchestra.

He or she does this in a number of ways. The Director of Development will coordinate the annual giving activities, capital campaigns, and deferred giving opportunities for donors and potential donors.

As part of this project, he or she might develop special events and programs to support the orchestra financially. These programs may increase attendance or develop direct financial support.

Activities of a Director of Development might include direct mail campaigns, telephone and telethon fund-raisers, balls, dinners, or cocktail parties.

In order for the Director of Development to reach people who are interested in these fund-raisers, he or she must do a great deal of research. Questionnaires and surveys are used to locate potential supporters.

The Director of Development should have strong public contacts. Through these contacts the Director learns the needs of the community in relation to the orchestra. He or she works closely with both the director of public relations and the orchestra's manager.

The Director of Development usually reports to either the Orchestra Manager or the Managing Director, as well as to the orchestra's board of directors.

The Director of Development acts as a liaison between donors, potential donors, and the orchestra's management and board of directors. He or she informs the management and the board of any occurrences affecting donors. The Development Director also works with the board projecting support programs for fund-raising projects.

At times, the Director of Development may also work with volunteers, getting them involved in such orchestra fund-raising activities as auctions, dinner-dances, etc., to benefit the organization. He or she will reach out to the community for much-needed volunteer support.

The Director of Development creates fund-raising literature and audio-visual materials such as brochures, booklets, pamphlets, programs, volunteer training films, slide shows, and tapes.

A large amount of money for orchestras is raised through grants, foundations, corporations, and endowments for the arts. The Director of Development must keep up with the latest information on these. He or she must know how to apply for grants, how to write proposals, and how to follow up in order to receive the largest gifts possible.

He or she must be an enthusiastic individual. Believing in the cause (financial support of the orchestra) is crucial to the successful Director of Development. Days are long. In addition to regular work hours, he or she must attend community meetings, volunteer meetings, and special events.

Salaries

The Director of Development's salary is commensurate with the size of the orchestra and its fund-raising goals. Directors of Development for small orchestras start out at around $23,000 annually. Individuals working with larger orchestras and with greater responsibility can earn up to $90,000 or more.

Employment Prospects

Directors of Development who can produce results are always in demand. There is a turnover of people in this field. Much of the turnover is a result of an individual's failure to satisfy the board of directors of the orchestra in fund-raising. It takes a number of years to develop a producing program and many boards are impatient, demanding immediate results.

Advancement Prospects

As noted above, Directors of Development who can produce are in demand. An individual who is knowledgeable in coordinating fund-raising and can back up that knowledge with results can move on to a development position with a more prestigious orchestra. He or she may also try to advance his or her career by becoming an orchestra manager.

Education and Training

College degrees are not always required of Directors of Development. However, they are often preferred. There might be several applicants who are qualified, and the difference between them might be a college background or degree.

There are a number of colleges around the country that offer degrees in arts administration or management. If attending a school with such a major is impossible, the individual should take courses in marketing, public relations, and business. These courses will help lay a foundation for a job in the development field.

Experience, Skills, and Personality Traits

Many people get into fund-raising by acting as chairperson for a club or organization. They find that it is a challenge to bring in money for a specific cause or organization. These individuals are enthusiastic about fund-raising and finding ways to get other people to give.

As a rule, Directors of Development are persuasive in an inoffensive way. They not only know the methods to use to bring in potential donations, they know how to get others to volunteer to help. This is important to an orchestra that depends on fund-raising to stay alive financially.

Unions and Associations

Many Directors of Development of orchestras belong to the American Symphony Orchestra League (ASOL), the Associated Council of the Arts, and/or local arts councils.

Tips for Entry

1. There are internship programs in the various positions of orchestral management, including development. These internships are made available through orchestras, colleges, or organizations.
2. There are also many seminars offered in both the development and fund-raising field and specialized orchestral development. These programs are sponsored by major orchestras, colleges, or other organizations. Look into them.
3. Vacancies are listed in the American Symphony Orchestra League (ASOL) newsletter, the Associated Council of the Arts newsletter, and many regional arts organization publications.
4. If you are interested in a position of this type, write to a number of orchestras and ask if you may submit an application to work as an assistant or trainee.

DIRECTOR OF PUBLIC RELATIONS

CAREER PROFILE

Duties: Handle press and promotion of the orchestra and its activities; possibly handle advertising (for small orchestra)

Alternate Title(s): P.R. Director; Director of Press Relations; Publicity Director

Salary Range: $25,000 to $75,000+

Employment Prospects: Fair

Advancement Prospects: Poor

Best Geographical Location(s) for Position: Cultural centers hosting major orchestras; other cities that host smaller orchestras

Prerequisites:

Education or training—College degree not always required, but sometimes preferred

Experience—Publicity and public relations experience in orchestral or nonorchestral situation

Special Skills and Personality Traits—Good writing skills; ability to work under pressure; creativity; knowledge of orchestras

CAREER LADDER

```
┌─────────────────────────────────────┐
│   Director of Public Relations for   │
│       Prestigious Orchestra;         │
│      Director of Development         │
└─────────────────────────────────────┘

┌─────────────────────────────────────┐
│    Director of Public Relations      │
└─────────────────────────────────────┘

┌─────────────────────────────────────┐
│  Assistant Public Relations Director;│
│              Publicist               │
└─────────────────────────────────────┘
```

Position Description

The Director of Public Relations for an orchestra is in charge of handling the press and promotion of that orchestra and its activities.

Throughout the season, the orchestra puts on a number of concerts. It is the job of the Director of Public Relations to see that the community and the press know of these concerts. Most orchestras also plan special activities, such as children's concerts, educational activities, holiday shows, etc. The P.R. Director must make sure that the community is aware of these events.

The way most Public Relations Directors alert the community to orchestra activities is through publicity. This is attained through press releases and advertising.

P.R. Directors must build up a media contact list to which to send out important news items. After writing a news release and sending it out, the P.R. Director's job is not complete. He or she must follow up on stories, calling the press to see if they need additional information, photos, interviews, etc.

The Public Relations Director works with the development department. When that department is trying to raise monies through an annual fund-raising drive, for example, the P.R. department will usually do a story on the activity.

The P.R. Director will also put together a number of press parties, press conferences, cocktail parties, and other functions. These affairs are used by the P.R. Director to help promote the orchestra.

The Director of P.R. might supervise the writing, layout, and printing of publications prepared for the orchestra, including those used for promotion, education, and fund-raising.

In his or her position, the Director of P.R. might also work with other organizations or corporations for tie-in possibilities. For instance, the orchestra might work with a shopping mall in a promotion for both the mall and the orchestra.

The Director of P.R. would also do publicity on the hiring of a new conductor. He or she might write press releases on new section members. The individual must put together press packages for the media to use routinely or for special events.

If the orchestra hires a guest conductor, the Director of Public Relations may do a special news release as well as setting up interviews between the conductor and media.

The Director of Public Relations is responsible to the orchestra manager or managing director, depending on the size and structure of the organization. He or she might also be responsible to the orchestra's board of directors.

The Director of Public Relations for an orchestra might supervise a number of people in the organization's P.R. department or might be the sole employee of that department. This depends, of course, on the size and budget of the orchestra.

Salaries

Salaries of Public Relations Directors for orchestras are usually commensurate with the size of the orchestra.

P.R. Directors working for small orchestras might have yearly salaries of $25,000 or more. P.R. Directors for these smaller orchestras might also work part-time or on a per project basis. Fees for specific types of P.R. projects vary.

Public Relations Directors working in larger orchestras have yearly incomes ranging from $27,000 to $75,000 or more annually.

Employment Prospects

If an individual is interested in working in an orchestral setting and can write and communicate fairly well, this may be the type of position to seek.

Most orchestras employ at least a part-time person for the position of Public Relations Director or publicist.

Larger orchestras may have five or more people working in their P.R. departments.

Advancement Prospects

There are a number of ways for a Public Relations Director to advance. The individual may seek a position with a more prestigious orchestra. These are often hard to obtain, as people in these positions do not tend to float from job to job. The individual may also move into the development department, possibly as director of development. Financially, this does not represent that much of a promotion; however, since these two jobs are often interrelated, many people do advance to these positions.

Education and Training

Directors of Public Relations in orchestras are not always required to hold college degrees, although it is sometimes preferred.

Courses in journalism, communications, public relations, publicity, and marketing help. A knowledge of the activities of an orchestra is helpful, too.

There are seminars and programs given by schools, associations, and organizations on public relations and music. These might be useful.

Experience, Skills, and Personality Traits

Any type of writing skill and experience is helpful to a Director of Public Relations. P.R. Directors often come from the ranks of newspaper and magazine journalists.

Other P.R. Directors work as assistants in the orchestra or with other companies. Still other individuals work as publicists in either music or nonmusic fields.

Whatever the experience, the P.R. Director needs sound, creative writing skills. The individual should also have built up or be able to build up a list of media contacts.

As in most jobs in P.R., the Director must have the ability to work under tremendous pressure.

Unions and Associations

The P.R. Director of an orchestra might belong to the Public Relations Society of America (PRSA). This organization works to uphold the ethics of P.R. people. In addition, the organization offers seminars, a magazine, pamphlets, and other useful information.

The individual might also belong to the American Symphony Orchestra League (ASOL). This organization, too, provides many useful seminars, workshops, and a newsletter.

Tips for Entry

1. There are numerous internship programs in various orchestral management positions, including the public relations department. These internships are made available directly through orchestras, colleges, and organizations.
2. There are vacancies listed for these positions in the ASOL (American Symphony Orchestra League) newsletter, the Associated Council of the Arts newsletter, and many regional arts organization publications.
3. Even if there is not an opening listed, you might want to contact a number of orchestras and send them your résumé plus a few samples of your writing style. Ask the personnel people to keep your résumé on file in case an opening develops.
4. Make sure you check out opportunities on-line. Orchestras often list openings on their websites.

SUBSCRIPTIONS AND TICKET SERVICE DIRECTOR

CAREER PROFILE

Duties: Obtain new subscriptions for orchestra season; renew current subscriptions; keep records of ticket sales

Alternate Title(s): Head of Subscriptions; Ticket Service Director

Salary Range: $21,000 to $45,000+

Employment Prospects: Poor

Advancement Prospects: Fair

Best Geographical Location(s) for Position: Any city that hosts an orchestra, such as New York City, Boston, Memphis, Phoenix, Syracuse, Pittsburgh, Philadelphia, etc.

Prerequisites:

Education or Training—College degree not required for all positions, but may be preferred

Experience—Volunteer work with orchestras; fund-raising; prior promotional work helpful; working in box office

Special Skills and Personality Traits—Organization; ability to write; knowledge of orchestras; bookkeeping skills

CAREER LADDER

```
┌─────────────────────────────────────┐
│       Director of Development        │
└─────────────────────────────────────┘

┌─────────────────────────────────────┐
│         Subscriptions and            │
│      Ticket Service Director         │
└─────────────────────────────────────┘

┌─────────────────────────────────────┐
│     Box Office Director; Student     │
└─────────────────────────────────────┘
```

Position Description

The Subscriptions and Ticket Service Director is responsible for selling and keeping track of tickets and subscriptions for the orchestra season.

In this position, the individual must put together programs to obtain new subscribers for the upcoming season. Although part of the income of the orchestra is derived from grants and funding, much of it comes from subscriptions. In order to procure these new subscriptions, the Director of this department often runs a variety of campaigns directed toward locating potential subscribers. These programs might include mass telephoning, mailings, or telethons. Additionally, the individual runs advertisements and sends out press releases on the subject. Some of these functions might be handled in conjunction with the public relations department.

Depending on the orchestra, the Subscriptions Director may work with a number of volunteers who help run the

above events. In a major orchestra, the director of the department may have a paid staff.

The Subscriptions and Ticket Service Director must also keep track of current subscribers. Renewal forms have to be sent out at the appropriate time. In certain instances, these renewal forms must be followed up with phone calls. At times, the Director of the department will ask a board member to make a follow-up phone call or visit a subscriber regarding a renewal.

The person in this position is in charge of coordinating the sales of individual concert tickets. Records must be kept on how many tickets are sold at each location. Tickets may be sold at the box office, schools, stores, or a ticket service. If a ticket service (such as Ticketron) is used, the Director must make sure they receive monies owed to them for ticket sales.

The individual in this job must keep precise records of everything in the department. He or she has to know at a glance who was sent what, when it was sent, when a follow-up call was made, etc. Records must also be maintained on monies arriving for subscriptions and tickets.

The Director of Subscriptions may be called upon to speak to groups or to attend functions on behalf of the orchestra. He or she usually works fairly regular hours. The Director of this department is responsible to the orchestra manager and/or the board of directors.

Salaries

Salaries range widely for Subscriptions and Ticket Service Directors. In very small orchestras, the position may be a voluntary one. In large orchestras, an individual may earn from $21,000 to $45,000 or more yearly, depending on the size of the orchestra and its budget.

Employment Prospects

Employment opportunities in this type of position are not bountiful. There are only a limited number of orchestras employing a full-time paid person to do this job.

Individuals will find that only the larger orchestras, such as major and regional ones, have these jobs. Additionally, there is not a large turnover in this department.

Advancement Prospects

Advancement is difficult but possible. Individuals in this field may find employment in the same position in larger, more prestigious orchestras, or they may advance their careers by becoming directors of development.

In order to advance in the current organization, he or she may need additional training or education.

Education and Training

As in many positions in the music industry, educational requirements vary widely. In larger major orchestras, the position of Subscriptions and Ticket Service Director may require or prefer a college background or degree.

In a smaller orchestra the individual may need only bookkeeping experience and training.

Experience, Skills, and Personality Traits

A Subscriptions and Ticket Service Director must be a totally organized individual. He or she needs the ability to keep accurate records. A good memory is a must.

Additionally, the person seeking this job should have the ability to write well and creatively. The individual must possess a talent for supervising both staff and volunteers. Knowledge of bookkeeping is essential. The Director of Subscriptions must be fully cognizant of the way an orchestra functions.

Unions and Associations

A Subscriptions and Ticket Service Director may belong to the American Symphony Orchestra League (ASOL), the Associated Council of the Arts, or any number of local arts councils.

Tips for Entry

1. If you think you might be interested in a position of this type, try volunteering. Go to an orchestra and ask if it would be possible to help out on a ticket subscription campaign.
2. Check with various orchestras and colleges to find out if they offer internships programs.
3. Openings are found in the American Symphony Orchestra League (ASOL) newsletter and various other arts council newsletters. On occasion, an orchestra may advertise an opening for a job of this type in the local newspaper.
4. Send a résumé and a cover letter to orchestras you might want to work with.
5. Check out openings on-line. Orchestra websites often advertise openings.

DIRECTOR OF EDUCATIONAL ACTIVITIES

CAREER PROFILE

Duties: Coordinate activities for students; design young people's concert series; plan learning activities relating to orchestra

Alternate Title(s): Education Director

Salary Range: $19,000 to $45,000+

Employment Prospects: Poor

Advancement Prospects: Poor

Best Geographical Location(s) for Position: Major cultural centers

Prerequisites:

Education or Training—Bachelor's degree required or preferred for most positions

Experience—Experience in orchestra administration and business helpful

Special Skills and Personality Traits—Writing skills; knowledge of orchestra & music; public relations skills; communications skills

CAREER LADDER

```
┌─────────────────────────────────┐
│   Director of Educational Activities  │
│        for Major Orchestra;      │
│    Director of Public Relations,  │
│   Fund-Raising, Development, Etc. │
└─────────────────────────────────┘

┌─────────────────────────────────┐
│   Director of Educational Activities  │
└─────────────────────────────────┘

┌─────────────────────────────────┐
│   Assistant Director of Educational  │
│    Activities; Publicist; Student │
└─────────────────────────────────┘
```

Position Description

The Director of Educational Activities in an orchestra is responsible for coordinating all orchestral activities for students and other young people in the community.

One of the main functions of this individual is to keep in close contact with the schools in the area surrounding the orchestra's base of operations. The Director may call or meet with school district music supervisors, music teachers, etc.

At times, the orchestra may offer concerts to the schools. They might bring the entire orchestra or just parts of it directly into the school to perform. Other educational activities might include offering the conductor or other orchestra members as speakers at school assemblies or at career days.

The individual in this position works closely with the music administrator, managing director, and/or orchestra manager designing young people's concerts. These concerts may be coordinated with school visits by members of the orchestra.

As the Director of this department, the individual may recommend reduced prices for student tickets. Additionally, the individual is responsible for making sure that students, parents, and administrators are aware of the special activities, ticket prices, etc. This may be accomplished by the Director designing and sending brochures or posters to the schools, placing them in the surrounding areas, sending out press releases to newspapers, and mailing notices to current subscribers. This function may be accomplished with the help of the public relations director.

The Director of Educational Activities may plan tours for students of the orchestra hall, backstage, rehearsals, and/or business offices. He or she may prepare booklets dealing with the different career opportunities in the orchestral field. This person might counsel or find appropriate people to counsel students on educational requirements and/or training needs of various positions in the field.

It should be noted that this position is not found in all orchestras. In smaller orchestras, responsibilities of this job overlap into other areas such as public relations or the ticket subscription department.

The Director of Educational Activities may be responsible to the orchestra manager, the managing director, or the organization's board of directors.

Salaries

The Director of Educational Activities in an orchestra may work on a part-time or full-time basis, depending on the size of the orchestra. Part-time workers work by the project or by the hour.

Full-time people in this position have salaries that range from $19,000 to $45,000 or more annually. Salaries vary according to the size and budget of the orchestra and the specific duties of the individual.

Employment Prospects

This is a hard position to locate. Jobs are very limited. In smaller orchestras, this job is often combined with the duties of other jobs. There are only a limited number of orchestras in the country in which to seek positions. Orchestra jobs in this specialty area are so hard to locate that there is not a high turnover rate.

Advancement Prospects

An individual in the position of Director of Educational Activities may advance his or her career in a number of ways. The person may seek a job in the same field with a more prestigious orchestra. The person may move up in the organization and become a director of public relations, development, fund-raising, etc.

Advancement opportunities are poor. There is not a high turnover rate in any of the jobs in the orchestra. This makes it difficult to advance to another position.

Education and Training

Educational requirements for the Director of Educational Activities in an orchestra vary. In some jobs—mainly in the larger major orchestras—individuals are either required or preferred to hold college degrees. Other positions—those in smaller orchestras—do not require anything over a high school diploma.

Experience, Skills, and Personality Traits

People in this position must be knowledgeable about the working of the orchestra and music in general. They must have the ability to write clearly and creatively.

Individuals working in this job must be articulate, congenial, and able to relate well to young people.

Some individuals working as Directors of Educational Activities obtain the position soon after leaving college. Other individuals work in various capacities with the orchestra or at arts councils. There are other people who work as reporters, publicists, or musicians before entering the field.

Unions and Associations

The Director of Educational Activities of an orchestra may belong to the American Symphony Orchestra League (ASOL). This association offers seminars, information, and other help to people working with orchestras.

Tips for Entry

1. Look for seminars and courses on orchestral management and administration. These are given by colleges, universities, associations, organizations, and orchestras.
2. Internships—paid, unpaid, and credit-bearing—are sometimes available. Check with your college, various orchestras, and the American Symphony Orchestra League (ASOL).
3. Openings for these positions are often listed in the ASOL newsletter as well as in various arts council newsletters.
4. If you're still in school, you might volunteer your services or look for a summer job in this career area, either in an orchestra or in a similar position with arts council projects.

PERSONNEL DIRECTOR

CAREER PROFILE

Duties: Send out notices for job openings in orchestra; screen applications; maintain files of potential job candidates

Alternate Title(s): Personnel Manager

Salary Range: $23,000 to $60,000+

Employment Prospects: Poor

Advancement Prospects: Poor

Best Geographical Location(s) for Position: Major cultural centers and other cities that house orchestras

Prerequisites:

Education or Training—Educational requirements vary from orchestra to orchestra; some positions require college background or degree, others do not

Experience—Working in personnel positions

Special Skills and Personality Traits—Knowledge of music and positions in orchestra; communications skills; ability to write; organization

CAREER LADDER

```
┌─────────────────────────────────────┐
│    Personnel Director for More      │
│   Prestigious Orchestra; Possible   │
│   Advancement to Other Departments  │
└─────────────────────────────────────┘

┌─────────────────────────────────────┐
│        Personnel Director           │
└─────────────────────────────────────┘

┌─────────────────────────────────────┐
│       Personnel Staff Member        │
└─────────────────────────────────────┘
```

Position Description

The Personnel Manager of an orchestra is responsible for all the hirings and firings of personnel in that orchestra. He or she is in charge of sending out notices whenever openings occur in either the business end or the talent end of the operation. These notices are usually sent to schools, colleges, conservatories, newsletters, associations, and organizations. In addition to notices, the Personnel Manager writes ads and places them in newspapers or magazines to alert people to these openings.

The Personnel Manager screens all applications that come to the orchestra. In the case of talent positions (section members, leaders, etc.), he or she will usually work in conjunction with the conductor, the concertmaster, and the section leaders who will be doing the auditioning.

In cases where the position is on the business side, the Personnel Manager would not only screen the applications, but also give preliminary interviews. After the first interviews are held, the Personnel Manager calls back the best candidates for further interviews.

Substitute musicians are often required by orchestras. It is the duty of the Personnel Manager to hire these substitutes. As these individuals are often needed on the spur of the moment, the Personnel Manager must maintain a list of backups for each instrument in the orchestra.

Before an individual is hired, the Personnel Manager usually explains orchestra policies, rules, regulations, and salaries. He or she must see that all forms are filled out and all information needed by the orchestra is supplied.

In the event that an individual must be fired, this job usually falls to the Personnel Manager, too. The Personnel Manager keeps track of employee attendance and, in the case of musicians, punctuality.

This individual works with all the other departments of the orchestra. He or she must have the ability to put people into jobs for which they are best suited.

Salaries

Salaries for the Personnel Director of an orchestra vary according to the size of the orchestra, its budget, and its location. Earnings will also depend on the qualifications of the individual and his or her duties. The Personnel Director has a salary between $23,000 and $60,000 plus annually.

Employment Prospects

There are only limited positions open for Personnel Directors in orchestras. Employment prospects for this job are not good. There are more and more people with personnel training that want to get into work involving music and/or orchestras, and there are not enough positions to go around. Additionally, there is not a high turnover of people in these positions.

Advancement Prospects

Advancement in this job is difficult. Finding a position as a Personnel Manager with a more prestigious organization is very hard. As competition is tough and people don't leave these jobs often, it is almost impossible.

Personnel Directors may, however, advance to other departments in the orchestra if they are qualified. Personnel Directors with the correct training may also go into labor relations and negotiating.

Education and Training

Educational requirements for the position of Personnel Director vary from orchestra to orchestra. Some do not require a college degree, while others do. Certain positions require at least some college background.

Major orchestras often require their Personnel Directors to have degrees in personnel administration.

There are colleges around the country that grant degrees in the field of personnel.

Experience, Skills, and Personality Traits

Personnel Directors need the ability to put the right people in the right jobs. In the symphony orchestra, Personnel Directors must have at least a basic knowledge of music and of the other business positions in the organization.

The individual must be skilled at interviewing potential employees, screening applications, etc.

In addition, the Personnel Director must be extremely articulate, able to communicate ideas well, and organized.

Unions and Associations

The Personnel Director of an orchestra may be a member of the American Symphony Orchestra League (ASOL), the Associated Council of the Arts, or other arts councils in the area.

Tips for Entry

1. Try to find an internship program. Internships help you get a foot in the door.
2. Openings for these positions are sometimes listed in the American Symphony Orchestra League (ASOL) newsletter, the Associated Council of the Arts newsletter, regional arts organizations' publications, and local newspaper advertisements.
3. No matter what educational requirement an orchestra has for this position, it doesn't hurt to be overtrained. It makes it easier to get a job and easier to advance if you have the education beforehand.

ORCHESTRAL MUSIC LIBRARIAN

CAREER PROFILE

Duties: Catalog and order music for orchestra; assist conductor copying scores and parts

Alternate Title(s): None

Salary Range: $23,000 to $50,000+

Employment Prospects: Poor

Advancement Prospects: Poor

Best Geographical Location(s) for Position: Cities that host larger orchestras, such as New York City, Boston, Memphis, Phoenix, Syracuse, Pittsburgh, Philadelphia, etc.

Prerequisites:

Education or Training—Bachelor's degree in music history or theory and library sciences; master's degree in music or library science often required

Experience—Position as music librarian assistant; library experience

Special Skills and Personality Traits—Interest in orchestral music; extensive knowledge of music; ability to copy musical notations; organization

CAREER LADDER

```
┌─────────────────────────────────────┐
│ Music Librarian for Major Orchestra  │
└─────────────────────────────────────┘

┌─────────────────────────────────────┐
│         Music Librarian              │
└─────────────────────────────────────┘

┌─────────────────────────────────────┐
│     Music Librarian Assistant        │
└─────────────────────────────────────┘
```

Position Description

Orchestral Music Librarians combine their skills as librarians with their love for and comprehensive knowledge of music. An Orchestral Music Librarian has many duties. He or she catalogs the orchestra's printed music. The individual is also responsible for ordering new music. If the orchestra decides not to purchase certain pieces of music, the Music Librarian is in charge of locating the music, renting it, and seeing that it gets back when it is no longer needed.

The Orchestral Music Librarian must be competent in copying musical markings. The individual often assists the conductor after he or she has looked at a piece of music and made changes in it. The Music Librarian may copy parts for the different section members, making the necessary corrections and adding bowings and/or phrasings where indicated.

During rehearsals or concerts, it is the Music Librarian's job to hand out the music to the section members. These are collected after the rehearsal or performance has concluded.

The Music Librarian travels with the orchestra when it goes on tour or performs special concerts. On the road, the individual is totally responsible for the sheet music. The Music Librarian also makes contact with any guest conductor the orchestra might be hosting. It is his or her duty to question the conductor about his or her music requirements.

The Orchestral Music Librarian has more contact with live music than a Music Librarian working at a school or a library. Although many of the responsibilities are the same, there are some differences. The Music Librarian must decide what type of setting he or she prefers.

The Orchestral Music Librarian does not work regular hours, as Music Librarians in other places of employment usually do. He or she is usually responsible to the orchestra conductor.

Salaries

As with all orchestral positions, salaries depend on the type of orchestra. A Music Librarian working for a major orchestra makes between $25,000 and $50,000 or more annually.

A Music Librarian working for a regional or metropolitan orchestra might make between $23,000 and $29,000 yearly. In local orchestras, the Music Librarian is often a section member who works gratis.

Employment Prospects

There are only a few orchestras in the country. As noted above, not all orchestras employ paid Music Librarians. The employment prospects for a position such as this are limited.

Advancement Prospects

The possibility for advancement is poor as a result of the small number of Music Librarian positions available in orchestras. There are more candidates than there are jobs to fill.

An individual in an orchestral setting might find that he or she wants to move into another type of position, such as one in a library or educational setting. However, these, too, may be limited.

Education and Training

The education needed for a Music Librarian working in an orchestra is much the same as for any Music Librarian. All positions require at least an undergraduate degree in music theory or history. Some positions require a dual major in music and library sciences. Still others require a master's degree in either music or library sciences.

Additionally, the Music Librarian in this setting needs training in copying parts and scores.

Experience, Skills, and Personality Traits

Orchestral Music Librarians often work as music librarian assistants prior to becoming full-fledged Music Librarians.

These positions are usually available only in larger symphonies. However, there are internship programs to help the aspiring Music Librarian gain experience.

The Music Librarian must have neat handwriting. The individual must also be able to copy conductor's markings on scores.

In addition, the Orchestral Music Librarian must be extremely organized and very personable.

Unions and Associations

The Orchestral Music Librarian might belong to a number of associations. These include the American Library Association (ALA), the Special Libraries Association (SLA), and the American Symphony Orchestra League (ASOL). These organizations help the individual to maintain contacts and they provide seminars, newsletters, and other valuable information. The Orchestral Music Librarian might additionally belong to the American Federation of Musicians (AFM).

Tips for Entry

1. Try to find an internship as a Music Librarian in a major, regional, or metropolitan orchestra.
2. Act as the Music Librarian of your college or school orchestra or band for experience.
3. Send your résumé and a short cover letter to orchestras. Remember to request that your résumé be kept on file if there are no current openings.
4. Openings may be advertised in the classified section of newspapers. Look under headings such as "Orchestras," "Orchestral Music Librarian," and "Music Librarian."

ARENAS, FACILITIES, HALLS, AND CLUBS

CONCERT HALL MANAGER

CAREER PROFILE

Duties: Manage concert hall; oversee all activities in venue; supervise employees

Alternate Title(s): Theater Manager; Arena Director; Facility Director; Director of Hall Operations

Salary Range: $23,000 to $85,000+

Employment Prospects: Fair

Advancement Prospects: Poor

Best Geographical Location(s) for Position: Most geographical locations have positions; cities tend to have more concert halls and/or arenas

Prerequisites:

Education or Training—High school diploma minimum; some jobs may require additional education

Experience—Working in concert halls, clubs, etc., in various positions; concert hall assistant manager experience useful

Special Skills and Personality Traits—Responsibility; ability to handle crises; knowledge of music business, contracts, etc.; cognizance of hall and theater business

CAREER LADDER

```
┌─────────────────────────────────┐
│   Manager of Large Facility or   │
│    Prestigious Concert Hall      │
└─────────────────────────────────┘

┌─────────────────────────────────┐
│      Concert Hall Manager        │
└─────────────────────────────────┘

┌─────────────────────────────────┐
│  Concert Hall Assistant Manager  │
└─────────────────────────────────┘
```

Position Description

A Concert Hall Manager is in charge of managing the hall and overseeing all activities that occur in the facility. The individual has diverse duties to perform depending on the facility and the position.

One of the functions of the Hall Manager is to supervise all employees of the facility. These workers include electricians, sound people, lighting people, ticket sellers, ushers, security, clean-up people, and a host of others. In some situations, the person might also hire a publicist, public relations firm, or advertising agency to handle hall promotion. In other circumstances, the hall owner might handle this project. As a rule, the Concert Hall Manager has the authority to hire people and fire them. In directing the activities of all these workers, the Manager tries to ensure the most efficient operations possible for the theater.

Another function of the Concert Hall Manager is to oversee the financial business of the hall. The individual must try to keep the hall or theater booked.

Sometimes the Manager will buy the talent; other times he or she will rent out the hall to various promoters. Whichever system is used, the individual must negotiate to get the best price. When promoters rent the hall, the individual must attempt to obtain the best rental fee, giving away the fewest possible extras.

The Concert Hall Manager may be responsible for payroll. In some cases, if a union is involved (and they frequently are), the individual must see that all union regulations are enforced at the hall. Unions involved might include the musicians union, the electricians union, and others.

After an event has been planned, the Manager is in charge of advertising it and publicizing it to maximize the attendance. This might be accomplished with the assistance of an advertising agency and a public relations firm. The hall may have its own in-house advertising agency and/or publicist. The Hall Manager must be knowledgeable about obtaining the most exposure for an event for the least amount of money.

It is the responsibility of the Hall Manager to make sure that the facility is in good condition and clean at all times. If there are things that need repair, the individual oversees the work. On occasion, the hall may be refurbished or completely done over. The Hall Manager, once again, is in charge of these work projects.

The Hall Manager must be ready to handle all types of crises effectively and without panicking. Potential problems include an act not showing up for a performance, union workers going on strike before a show, inclement weather on the night of a performance when tickets are being sold at the door, or a patron getting unruly during a show. There are, of course, many other things that can occur.

The Concert Hall Manager must see to it that the money that is to be paid to acts is available on the night of a show. He or she must also be sure to fulfill any contract riders exactly as they are written.

The individual must work closely with all the media in the immediate area. Most of the time these press people will be offered press passes or backstage passes. Maintaining a good relationship with the press and other media goes a long way toward helping the theater become successful.

The Concert Hall Manager works long, irregular hours. He or she is responsible to the owner of the theater, hall, or arena.

Salaries

The salary of a Concert Hall or Arena Manager or Director varies greatly depending on the size of the venue, the location, the prestige of the hall, qualifications of the individual, and the duties.

A person managing a small concert theater in an out-of-the-way location will not make as much as one who is managing a large, prestigious hall in a major metropolitan area. The individual managing a small theater might earn from $23,000 to $33,000 yearly. Those who manage larger, more prestigious halls in major metropolitan areas earn from $35,000 to $85,000 or more annually.

Employment Prospects

Employment prospects for a Concert Hall Manager are fair. There are different types of halls, a range of sizes, and various locations. Major cities have the greatest number of concert halls and/or arenas. However, it may be more difficult to obtain a job in these locations.

Smaller cities have fewer opportunities, but jobs are usually easier to obtain.

Advancement Prospects

Advancement is difficult for Concert Hall Managers. Those who seek to stay in that field usually need to find jobs in larger facilities or more prestigious halls. There seems to be a correlation between the size and prestige of a concert hall and the difficulty of obtaining a job there.

Individuals who do move into better positions, however, are usually able to continue advancing their careers.

Education and Training

Most positions as Concert Hall Managers only require a high school diploma. There are, however, jobs that require additional education. Many people who hold these positions have degrees in music, theater, or business. A good many of these individuals originally aspired to be musicians, actors, or actresses. When that fell through, they went into managing concert halls as a way of maintaining contact with the industry.

Courses that may prove useful include theater management, business, bookkeeping, accounting, communications, marketing, and other music business-oriented subjects.

Experience, Skills, and Personality Traits

Concert Hall Managers cannot just walk into a job without experience. Usually the individuals have worked in the music business or at least in some type of theater for a period of time. A job as an assistant manager of a concert hall is often extremely helpful to the individual.

Managing a concert hall, one must be adept at reading concert contracts and the long riders that sometimes accompany them. One must have the ability to handle crises effectively. The individual must also be totally knowledgeable about the music business and concert hall and arena affairs.

Being responsible and having supervisory skills are musts.

Unions and Associations

Concert Hall Managers may belong to the International Association of Auditorium Managers (IAAM). Concert Hall Managers may have to deal with a variety of unions, including the American Federation of Musicians (AFM).

Tips for Entry

1. Your chances of obtaining a job, if you are not experienced, are better in a smaller facility and/or a smaller city.
2. Jobs for theater or Concert Hall Managers are often advertised in the classified or display sections of newspapers.
3. Try to find a job as an assistant manager in a small venue. The employee turnover is higher in these halls, and you will have a better chance of promotion in a shorter span of time.
4. Many openings are advertised in a word-of-mouth fashion. Get friendly with Hall Managers in other facilities.

STAGE MANAGER

CAREER PROFILE

Duties: Supervise and oversee all activities occurring onstage in a theater, club, concert hall, arena, etc.; may be responsible for lighting, curtain changes, etc.; in charge of backstage area

Alternate Title(s): None

Salary Range: $19,000 to $58,000+

Employment Prospects: Fair

Advancement Prospects: Poor

Best Geographical Location(s) for Position: Large metropolitan cities offer the most opportunities

Prerequisites:

Education or Training—No education required; training in lighting, sound, and/or electronics helpful

Experience—Lighting technician; sound person; assistant stage manager

Special Skills and Personality Traits—Responsibility; dependability; enjoyment of music; knowledge of lighting technology; cognizance of sound and/or electronics; supervisory skills; ability to get along with people

CAREER LADDER

```
┌─────────────────────────────────────┐
│  Stage Manager in Large, Prestigious │
│  Concert Hall, Club, Theater, etc.;  │
│       Hall or Club Manager           │
└─────────────────────────────────────┘

┌─────────────────────────────────────┐
│                                     │
│           Stage Manager              │
│                                     │
└─────────────────────────────────────┘

┌─────────────────────────────────────┐
│  Sound Technician; Lighting Technician; │
│  Assistant Stage Manager; Student    │
└─────────────────────────────────────┘
```

Position Description

The Stage Manager is the individual in charge of much that occurs onstage in a concert hall, theater, arena, club, etc. Depending on the situation, he or she may work alone or oversee the work of an assistant and/or an entire staff.

The Stage Manager must be present during rehearsals and concerts. His or her duties depend on the type of venue, its size, and the kind of concert.

If the Stage Manager is working in a very large concert hall or theater, he or she might be responsible for supervising or controlling the lighting of the stage and the room. For example, during a show the Stage Manager might have the house or room lights off and the stage lit brightly. Or the stage may be dark, illuminated by a spotlight. The Stage Manager must find out during the rehearsal exactly when the act wants each kind of lighting. He or she probably will go over the show concept with the act or its management, road management, or lighting technician.

Many of the top rock acts travel with their own lighting technician and/or light show. In these instances the Stage Manager works with the act's technician, helping and advising. The Stage Manager may or may not be responsible for the lighting in these circumstances.

The Stage Manager may also be responsible for controlling the volume on the microphones. Once again, if an act comes in with its own sound people, the Stage Manager may just help and advise these people. In other situations, the Stage Manager might oversee a resident sound technician.

The Stage Manager is in charge of curtain changes. This includes making sure that the curtains are opened at the proper times and closed when there is an intermission or the show is finished.

The Stage Manager is also responsible for keeping the backstage area as clear as possible. Many times, with very well-known acts, the backstage area gets crowded and noisy. It is up to the individual to check for backstage passes and enforce any rules and regulations necessary to clear the area of unnecessary people.

At times, the Stage Manager may have the responsibility of making sure that the act has water, soda, juice, towels, etc., in their dressing room.

The Stage Manager might be the one who tells the act when to begin or when they should go onstage. He or she may also signal to the act when their show should be over.

The individual works late hours in this job. He or she is usually responsible to the facility manager or owner.

Salaries

Salaries of Stage Managers vary according to the type of venue, the geographical location, and the qualifications and duties of the individual.

Generally, the larger and more prestigious a theater, club, concert hall, arena, etc., is, the larger the Stage Manager's salary.

Individuals working as Stage Managers may earn from $19,000 to $58,000 plus annually.

Employment Prospects

Employment prospects for Stage Managers are fair. Almost every theater, concert hall, and arena hires a Stage Manager. Clubs might hire individuals for this position or may delegate their responsibilities to other people.

If an individual works in a smaller venue, he or she may be hired as a Stage Manager and also have additional duties.

Metropolitan areas tend to have more positions.

Advancement Prospects

It is difficult for a Stage Manager to advance his or her career. The individual may obtain a position in a larger or more prestigious concert hall, club, theater, etc. In some situations, the individual may go on to become a club or theater manager or talent buyer. In other situations, the Stage Manager is just working in that position to be close to the live music business. He or she may be an aspiring musician, songwriter, etc.

Education and Training

No formal education is required for the position of Stage Manager. The individual may require training in sound, lighting, electronics, etc., depending on the position. If he or she is hoping to advance to club or theater manager, the Stage Manager may consider taking some business classes.

Experience, Skills, and Personality Traits

The Stage Manager must enjoy music. He or she will probably have to listen to quite a bit of it. The individual must be dependable and reliable. He or she needs the ability to get along with others. Supervisory skills may be necessary.

The Stage Manager should also know as much as possible about electronics, lighting, and sound equipment.

The individual in this position may have been a sound technician, a lighting technician, or an assistant Stage Manager, or might just have finished school.

Unions and Associations

Stage Managers may belong to the International Alliance of Theatrical Stage Employees (IATSE). They may also belong to the American Guild of Musical Artists (AGMA) under certain conditions.

Tips for Entry

1. Stage Manager jobs are often advertised in the classified sections of newspapers.
2. You might consider visiting clubs, theaters, concert halls, etc. Speak to the manager of any of these venues. Tell him or her of your qualifications and leave a résumé. Follow up by writing a letter thanking the person for talking to you.
3. Volunteer your services as a Stage Manager in a community, school, or church concert or play. It will give you useful experience.
4. The more skills you have, the better your chances are to find a job. Learn all you can about lighting, sound, electronics, stage techniques, etc.
5. You might consider taking a theater course to learn concepts that might be helpful to you.

RESIDENT SOUND TECHNICIAN

CAREER PROFILE

Duties: Provide sound for concerts; work sound board; keep sound equipment in good working order

Alternate Title(s): Sound Man (or Woman); Audio Technician; Sound Engineer

Salary Range: $19,000 to $45,000+

Employment Prospects: Fair

Advancement Prospects: Poor

Best Geographical Location(s) for Position: Any city that houses concert halls, arenas, clubs, etc.

Prerequisites:

Education or Training—No educational requirement; formal or informal electronic and/or sound training

Experience—Experience working sound boards, sound equipment, and electrical equipment

Special Skills and Personality Traits—Ability to work with people; knowledge of electronics; knowledge of sound board; responsible attitude; good musical "ear"; enjoyment of music

CAREER LADDER

```
┌─────────────────────────────────────┐
│   Sound Technician at Major Venue;   │
│    Director of Audio Department      │
└─────────────────────────────────────┘

┌─────────────────────────────────────┐
│          Sound Technician            │
└─────────────────────────────────────┘

┌─────────────────────────────────────┐
│           Roadie; Usher              │
└─────────────────────────────────────┘
```

Position Description

The Resident Sound Technician of a hall is responsible for the basic sound engineering of a concert. The Technician may work in a club, theater, concert hall, arena, school, or any similar location. The individual may be a full-time or a part-time employee.

The Sound Technician oversees the set-up of the sound equipment. The objective is to have everything in just the right place in order to produce the best possible sound. As the Resident Sound Technician, the individual must be aware of any acoustical problems in the room. Understanding the acoustical problems is just the beginning of a Sound Technician's job. Solving the problem is the prime responsibility. The more familiar the person is with the room and its problems, the better he or she can counsel the touring technician employed by the act or the act's road manager.

In the position of Resident Sound Technician, the individual must attend all sound checks scheduled before a concert. During these sound checks, the individual will talk to the act's road manager or act members in order to determine exactly what type of sound they require. The technician will also discuss any special effects the act likes to have during the show.

The Resident Sound Technician might ask questions involving how the act wants its music balanced. The individual might advise the act on the volume requirement of the hall and should be prepared to regulate the sound.

During a concert or show the Resident Sound Technician is responsible for running the sound board. The sound board is usually set up somewhere in the middle of the front of the stage. From this location the technician can best hear the sound and make the proper adjustments.

After the concert, the Resident Sound Technician will go over the equipment and check for any problems. If repairs are required, the technician will either make them or arrange for others to take care of them immediately.

The Resident Sound Technician works closely with the act's road manager. In some cases, the act appearing at the club or hall will travel with their own sound technician.

Under these circumstances, the Resident Sound Technician will act as an advisor and overseer.

People in these positions must usually work late evening hours. Work schedules do not begin, however, until the afternoon.

Salaries

Resident Sound Technicians may work either part time or full time. On a part-time basis, they will probably be paid by the hour or the show. Rates can vary from minimum wage to approximately $85 per hour.

Sound Technicians who work full time may earn $19,000 to $45,000 or more annually, depending on the type and size of the club, hall, etc., that they are involved with. Other factors affecting earnings include the experience and responsibilities of the individual. Sound Technicians working in unionized facilities have minimum earnings set by the union.

Employment Prospects

Employment prospects for Resident Sound Technicians are fair. Qualified individuals may find employment in a variety of clubs, halls, arenas, schools, or theaters. Some of these positions may be part time. People seeking employment in this type of job category may have to relocate to areas where there are greater opportunities.

Advancement Prospects

It is difficult to advance in this career. It can be done, however. A number of Resident Sound Technicians who work in halls are picked up by major touring groups seeking a qualified sound technician.

Sound Technicians may advance their careers by locating a position at a larger, more prestigious hall. Others in this field are promoted to a director position in a theater or hall's audio department.

Education and Training

There is no formal educational requirement for a position as a Resident Sound Technician. Different halls or clubs may require that applicants have some training, either formal or informal, in electronics and sound recording. There are a variety of technical and vocational schools that teach electronics. Most people, however, pick up the basics of sound engineering by watching and listening to others.

Experience, Skills, and Personality Traits

A Sound Technician working in a hall, club, arena, etc., must be able to work well with people. Many times the Sound Technician who travels with an act will accompany the group to the hall. The Resident Sound Technician may have to advise or consult with this individual. It is imperative that the individual be a responsible type of person. He or she must be at sound checks on time to oversee things, even if there is another technician hired by the group working the sound equipment at a concert.

The Sound Technician must have a good knowledge of electronics, the sound board, and other sound equipment. The individual must have a good musical "ear" and enjoy music.

Unions and Associations

Resident Sound Technicians may belong to the International Alliance of Theatrical Stage Employees (IATSE). This is a bargaining union for individuals working in theater situations.

Tips for Entry

1. Sound Technician positions are often advertised in the help wanted sections of newspapers. Check under "Sound Technician," "Sound Engineer," and "Audio Technician."
2. Check the clubs and theaters in your area that employ Resident Sound Technicians. Talk to the managers of these clubs and theaters and tell them of your qualifications. Follow up the discussion by sending them your résumé to keep on file.
3. You might consider a short stint as an apprentice to a Resident Sound Technician. This will provide you with added on-the-job experience. The Sound Technician may leave the job or know of other openings. All this can be useful to you.

NIGHTCLUB MANAGER

CAREER PROFILE

Duties: Manage the day-to-day operations of a nightclub

Alternate Title(s): Club Manager

Salary Range: $22,000 to $70,000+

Employment Prospects: Fair

Advancement Prospects: Fair

Best Geographical Location(s) for Position: All cities have opportunities as well as many smaller locations

Prerequisites:

Education or Training—No formal education required; training in food service or the hospitality industry helpful

Experience—Working as assistant nightclub manager; positions as bartender, host or hostess

Special Skills and Personality Traits—Supervisory skills; aggressiveness; personability; knowledge of the entertainment and/or music business, booking acts, negotiating, and contracts; ability to deal under pressure

CAREER LADDER

```
┌─────────────────────────────┐
│  Nightclub Manager in Large,│
│  Prestigious Nightclub;     │
│  Nightclub Owner            │
└─────────────────────────────┘

┌─────────────────────────────┐
│     Nightclub Manager       │
└─────────────────────────────┘

┌─────────────────────────────┐
│  Assistant Nightclub Manager│
└─────────────────────────────┘
```

Position Description

A Nightclub Manager is responsible for overseeing the day-to-day (or night-to-night) functions of a nightclub. Duties may differ depending on the type of club an individual manages. In many instances, the Nightclub Manager is also the club owner.

As the Nightclub Manager, a person may be responsible for not only hiring the entertainment, but deciding what type of entertainment the club will use. For example, should the club cater to country fans, dance-music fans, or rock-and-rollers? The Manager must also decide whether the club should use live entertainment, D.J.'s, or jukeboxes. In making these decisions, the individual must often do research. Other clubs in the area may be checked out. Clubs that have been unsuccessful as well as those that are doing well may be looked into. Often, if a Nightclub Manager sees why a certain club isn't doing well, he or she knows what to avoid to make his or her club successful.

The Nightclub Manager must choose what types of advertising to use. In certain areas, radio works well. In other areas, TV advertising or the print media may work better.

The individual must develop an advertising budget and decide where his or her advertising dollar can best be spent.

The Nightclub Manager may call local media, trying to build good relationships between editors, disc jockeys, TV producers, and the club.

When the club hires live entertainment, the Nightclub Manager may be responsible for negotiating and signing contracts, or this responsibility may fall to the club owner.

The individual must run the nightclub. This includes hiring and training personnel. The Nightclub Manager may hire bartenders, waitresses, hosts, hostesses, chefs, cooks, security people, lighting technicians, sound people, etc., depending on the type of establishment.

As the Nightclub Manager, the individual may be responsible for buying food and liquor. He or she may also be in charge of controlling the liquor and making sure that all state and local alcohol laws are observed.

The Nightclub Manager must make sure that all accounts are paid. The individual may be responsible for tallying nightly totals and receipts.

If there are any problems in the club, the Manager is in charge of taking care of them. The Nightclub Manager works long hours. He or she may begin working in the afternoon and not get home until 4:00 or 5:00 A.M. The Nightclub Manager is responsible to the club owner.

Salaries

Salaries for Nightclub Managers depend on the type of club, its location, its popularity, and the experience and duties of the individual.

Salaries run from around $22,000 to $70,000 plus. If the Club Manager is also the club owner, he or she may receive a salary plus a share of profits from the club or the individual might just receive a share of the profits.

Employment Prospects

Employment prospects for Nightclub Managers are fair. The individual might have to work in a very small club, or an establishment specializing in a different form of entertainment or music than the Manager's choice. He or she might have to move to another location to find a job.

There are nightclubs all over the country. However, many of these are so small they don't use the services of a Manager.

Advancement Prospects

Advancement prospects are fair for a Nightclub Manager. After obtaining some experience in a small nightclub, an individual may move into a job as Nightclub Manager in a larger, more prestigious club. The Nightclub Manager might also open up his or her own nightclub.

Education and Training

There is no formal educational requirement to become a Nightclub Manager. Some training in business is helpful. Training in food service or the hospitality field might also be useful.

Experience, Skills, and Personality Traits

Any type of experience in running a business is a plus. Usually a Nightclub Manager has worked as either an assistant manager or a supervisor in a nightclub, bar, or restaurant.

The individual must be knowledgeable about the music business, booking talent, negotiating, and contracts. Much of this is learned on the job.

The Nightclub Manager needs the ability to deal well with people and to deal effectively under pressure.

Being aggressive and personable helps. The individual in this position needs good supervisory skills.

Unions and Associations

Nightclub Managers may work with any number of local unions, depending what variety of club they manage. Individuals may also represent their clubs in the National Federation of Music Clubs.

Tips for Entry

1. You might begin by working as a bartender, host, or hostess. Then move on to a job as an assistant nightclub manager.
2. These jobs are often listed in the help wanted sections of newspapers.
3. The more skills you have, the better your position. If you have managed a restaurant or bar and have an understanding of the entertainment business, put these things in your résumé.
4. You may consider sending a résumé and cover letter to a number of nightclubs. Ask them to keep your résumé on file.
5. Think about trying to obtain a job as a Nightclub Manager in a hotel/motel club. These clubs can be found all over the country and turnover is high. You may go directly to the hotel/motel or send a letter and résumé to the main office of a hotel/motel chain.
6. If you live in an area hosting casinos, check out openings in casino clubs.

EDUCATION

MUSIC SUPERVISOR

CAREER PROFILE

Duties: Direct and coordinate activities of teaching personnel engaged in instructing students in vocal and instrumental music in school system

Alternate Title(s): Music Administrator

Salary Range: $26,000 to $75,000+

Employment Prospects: Fair

Advancement Prospects: Fair

Best Geographical Location(s) for Position: Opportunities may be located throughout the country

Prerequisites:

Education or Training—Bachelor's degree in music education; master's degree or additional graduate courses in supervision and administration

Experience—Teaching music in school system

Special skills and Personality Traits—Ability to administer; ability to lead; enjoyment of music; tolerance; ability to relate to others on all levels

CAREER LADDER

```
┌─────────────────────────────┐
│   State Music Supervisor    │
└─────────────────────────────┘

┌─────────────────────────────┐
│      Music Supervisor       │
└─────────────────────────────┘

┌─────────────────────────────┐
│      Music Teacher;         │
│   Music Department Head     │
└─────────────────────────────┘
```

Position Description

The school Music Supervisor may work in a variety of situations. He or she may work as a School Supervisor, a District Supervisor, or a State Music Supervisor.

In this position, the individual is responsible for directing and coordinating activities of teaching personnel who are engaged in instructing students in vocal and instrumental music in a specific school or school system.

As a Supervisor, the person probably will not teach on a day-to-day basis. There are, however, positions in which the person teaches a few days a week and administers a program the remaining days.

One of the duties of a Music Supervisor is to plan and develop the music education curriculum for the school, district, or state. This is accomplished by meeting and consulting with teachers and others on the administrative staff to get input. Working closely with these people, the Supervisor can tell which programs work, which do not, and which should be eliminated.

The Music Supervisor will visit classrooms while other teachers are giving classes and observe and evaluate them.

If the Supervisor has any comments on their teaching, he or she may set up a meeting. During this meeting, the Supervisor will talk about the evaluation and recommend possible changes in teaching methods.

The Supervisor will analyze the music education program in the school, district, or state. The individual may evaluate both the instructional methods and/or the materials used in teaching.

As many schools are currently experiencing cutbacks in funds, the Supervisor may have to decide which programs to continue and which to cut out.

The Music Supervisor might order any instructional materials, books, supplies, equipment, and/or visual aids needed by the music department. In this position, he or she is authorized to order and purchase musical instruments required for instruction or for the school band.

Additionally, the school Music Supervisor would help establish interschool bands, choruses, and orchestras to represent the various schools at civic and community events.

The Music Supervisor's hours are usually regular working or school hours. He or she is responsible to either the principal, the superintendent, or the Commissioner of Education.

Salaries

Salaries of Music Supervisors depend largely on the location of the school district and the position. Supervisors generally have salaries that parallel those of teachers in the area. If, for example, teachers' salaries are low in a particular community, the supervisor's salary, too, will be low. Conversely, if the Supervisor works in a district in which teachers' salaries are relatively high, his or hers will be correspondingly higher.

The salary range for Music Supervisors runs from approximately $26,000 to $75,000 plus annually.

Employment Prospects

Employment prospects are fair for Music Supervisors. Applicants may have to relocate to another area in order to obtain a position.

There is not a high turnover rate in these jobs.

Advancement Prospects

Individuals in the position of school Music Supervisor can be promoted to District Music Supervisor. District Supervisors can be promoted to state Music Supervisor positions.

Individuals with education in supervision and administration may additionally go on to positions as assistant principal or principal.

Education and Training

Music Supervisors are required to have bachelors' degrees with a major in music education. As a rule, they would have to complete a semester of student teaching in order to become a music teacher.

Music Supervisors are generally required to have additional courses in supervision and administration and/or master's degrees depending on the state regulations.

Experience, Skills, and Personality Traits

Music Supervisors must like music. Generally, they have held positions as music teachers for a few years prior to applying for a job as a Music Supervisor.

As a Supervisor, an individual must know how to teach and be able to evaluate others. He or she must also have the ability to lead others, administer a program, and, most important, enjoy music and instructing others in it.

Unions and Associations

Music Supervisors may belong to the National Federation of Teachers (NFT). Individuals may also belong to the National Council of State Supervisors of Music (NCSSM).

Tips for Entry

1. There are specialty employment agencies that deal specifically with educational jobs. These are usually located in larger cities.
2. Openings may be advertised in the classified section of newspapers. Many newspapers have sections specifically dedicated to job openings in education.
3. Check with your local school district for openings.
4. Check out openings on-line. Start with some of the major job sites, such as www.monster.com and www.hotjobs.com, and go from there.

COLLEGE, CONSERVATORY, OR UNIVERSITY MUSIC EDUCATOR

CAREER PROFILE

Duties: Teach music instruction, theory, history, composition, and/or instrumental or vocal training and performance; coach chamber music groups

Alternate Title(s): Music Teacher; Professor; Instructor

Salary Range: $25,000 to $70,000+

Employment Prospects: Fair

Advancement Prospects: Fair

Best Geographical Location(s) for Position: Locations with colleges, conservatories, and/or universities may have positions available

Prerequisites:

Education or Training—Master's degree minimum; many positions require doctoral degree

Experience—Teaching at some level; instrumental or vocal performance experience (if applicable)

Special Skills and Personality Traits—Knowledge of many facets of music; desire to continue learning, studying, and researching; ability to communicate ideas to students

CAREER LADDER

```
+---------------------------+
|        Professor          |
+---------------------------+


+---------------------------+
|    Associate Professor    |
+---------------------------+


+---------------------------+
|    Assistant Professor     |
+---------------------------+
```

Position Description

College, Conservatory, and/or University Music Educators may be hired for a variety of different positions. They may be brought into a school as a general Music Educator to teach areas of music theory, music arranging, and/or music history, or they may teach vocal or instrumental performance. Educators are also hired to coach chamber music groups or to conduct choruses or orchestras.

Applicants for positions that require some performance skills are usually given auditions. These types of positions may include any area of instrumental instruction, coaching, or conducting.

Educators at higher learning institutions, especially those which specialize in music degrees, generally teach students who want to learn all they can. Most of these students are seriously considering professional careers in music.

It is the duty of the Educator to be as knowledgeable and informed about his or her subject matter as possible. He or she must help the students learn all they can during their educational careers.

Most Educators also delve into research areas of special interest to them. They take the research and write papers for publication. Published works help Educators advance their careers and increase the demand for their services.

Working in a school setting, the Educator may participate in many of the cultural and educational programs, events, and benefits available.

The Educator cannot walk into a classroom or lecture hall and begin teaching without preparation. Preparation for classes takes a great deal of time. This is especially true for the beginning Educator or for the individual who is teaching a course for the first time.

Educators who solely teach voice or instrumental performance or coach or conduct music groups usually require less preparation time.

The Educator must have specific hours set aside each week to meet with his or her students. He or she must read student's papers and grade any tests or exams.

The Educator working in a community college setting will probably teach about eighteen hours a week. An Educator working at a four-year university, college, or conservatory spends considerably fewer hours teaching. Teaching time usually runs from nine to twelve hours per week. Keep in mind, though, the amount of time that is spent in preparation, student meetings, and grading. Total working time may be more than 45 hours per week.

The Educator is responsible to the head of his or her department or to the administrator of the school.

Salaries

Salaries for College, Conservatory, or University Music Educators depend on the school, its reputation, and its location. Salaries also depend on the professional status of the Educator.

Salaries for assistant professors at small schools can start at $25,000 yearly. As the Educator gains more experience, earnings go up.

Professors' salaries range from $25,000 to $70,000 or more yearly. As noted above, however, salaries depend heavily on the school where an Educator is employed. A professor working at a prestigious university would undoubtedly earn more than a professor teaching at a small college.

Employment Prospects

There is a fair chance for employment as a Music Educator at a conservatory, college, or university. Applicants, however, must be willing to relocate to areas that have openings.

Applicants additionally must be willing to teach in more than one specialization.

Advancement Prospects

Educators in higher learning institutions can advance their careers in a number of ways. they can start out as assistant professors and teach for a few years. Eventually they may be promoted to associate professors. During the years as an assistant professor, the Educator is evaluated. He or she may or may not receive tenure. Associate professors can also be promoted to full professors.

The Educator can also advance his or her career by taking a position in a college and then seeking a better position in a more prestigious university.

Education and Training

The majority of positions as College, Conservatory, and/or University Music Educators require at least a master's degree. Many of the positions also demand a doctoral degree.

There are Educators currently teaching at conservatories and universities who hold no degree. Individuals such as symphony orchestra members are accepted as Educators on the basis of exceptional musical acclaim.

Experience, Skills, and Personality Traits

Most Educators have some type of teaching experience previous to their appointment at a college, university, or conservatory.

The individual must have a tremendous knowledge of many facets of music, not only his or her specialization. He or she usually has an ongoing desire to learn more, whether through study or research.

Most important, the College, University, or Conservatory Music Educator must be able to effectively communicate ideas and theories to their students.

Unions and Associations

College, University, or Conservatory Educators may belong to the College Music Society and the American Musicological Society. These organizations sponsor a number of conferences and programs during the year. They also publish newsletters.

Individuals may also be members of the College Band Directors National Association, the College Music Society, and/or the National Association of College Wind and Percussion Instructors.

Tips for Entry

1. There is a list of openings at a variety of schools, colleges, and universities called the "Music Faculty List." This list is published by the College Music Society (CMS) and the American Musicological Society (AMS). The list is available to their members.

2. Openings are usually sent to college placement offices. Keep in contact with yours.

3. Many positions are advertised in the classified sections of Sunday newspapers. Some positions are advertised in display ads within the classified section.

4. Send your résumé with a cover letter directly to colleges and universities and ask to have it kept on file in case openings occur.

SECONDARY SCHOOL MUSIC TEACHER

CAREER PROFILE

Duties: Teach instrumental and/or vocal music and theory to high school or junior high students

Alternate Title(s): High School Music Teacher or Instructor; Junior High School Music Teacher or Instructor; Instrument Teacher; Voice Teacher

Salary Range: $25,000 to $65,000+

Employment Prospects: Fair

Advancement Prospects: Good

Best Geographical Location(s) for Position: Areas throughout the country have opportunities

Prerequisites:

Education or Training—Bachelor's degree in music education; some schools require additional education for permanent certification

Experience—Student teaching

Special Skills and Personality Traits—Ability to teach; enjoyment of music; ability to play instrument(s); ability to read music

CAREER LADDER

```
┌──────────────────────────────────┐
│      Tenured Music Teacher       │
└──────────────────────────────────┘

┌──────────────────────────────────┐
│  Secondary School Music Teacher  │
└──────────────────────────────────┘

┌──────────────────────────────────┐
│         Student Teacher          │
└──────────────────────────────────┘
```

Position Description

Secondary School Music Teachers can work in junior highs or high schools and at public, private, or parochial institutions. Their duties vary depending on the type of job they are hired for.

A Secondary School Music Teacher might fill a position in instrumental teaching. This teacher would be responsible for giving lessons to students, organizing and conducting a school band and/or orchestra, and teaching basic music theory. The instrument teacher is also responsible for putting on school concerts. He or she might work with students to get them ready for competitions or auditions for summer music festivals. In addition, the instrumental Music Teacher could be in charge of putting together a marching band. In this case, he or she would not only be responsible for rehearsals and conducting, but also for performances in parades and at various events after school hours and on weekends or holidays.

A Secondary School Music Teacher might conversely fill a position in vocal instruction. This teacher would be responsible for giving vocal lessons, putting together and conducting school choruses and choirs, and teaching basic music theory. The vocal teacher is usually in charge of putting on all vocal concerts. He or she might be involved in musicals or plays put on by the school.

The vocal teacher works with students preparing them for school and state vocal competitions. He or she might also be in charge of a school glee club.

Secondary School Music Teachers, like all teachers, usually go through a period of student teaching. Through student teaching they can better evaluate what area of specialization they prefer. They get the important chance for hands-on training with students while they are still under supervision.

The Secondary School Music Teacher is evaluated after a certain number of years in a school system. If his or her evaluation is positive, he or she will receive tenure. After receiving tenure, the teacher cannot be fired from the school system under normal conditions and circumstances. This gives the job a great degree of security. The school system can, however, terminate the teacher's position and move him or her to another area of music specialization.

In addition to the Secondary School Music Teacher's teaching and leading responsibilities, he or she must be available for parent/teacher/student conferences.

He or she is responsible for making up lesson plans and grading student work.

Teachers usually work only ten months a year. If they work in summer school positions, they are paid extra. Teachers do not work during school vacations.

Music Teachers are responsible to the music department head, the school principal, or the superintendent of the school system.

Salaries

Salaries for teachers depend on the location of the school, the type of school, and the teacher's qualifications.

Teachers working in large metropolitan areas earn more than teachers in small communities.

Teachers usually start out at around $25,000 per school year. Their salary can go up to $65,000 or more annually. In addition, most school systems have fringe benefits and pension plans.

Salaries in public schools are usually paid on a system called "steps." Each time an individual reaches a certain step, his or her salary is raised. Steps relate to the amount of education (degrees, credits, etc.) a teacher has accumulated. Steps also relate to the amount of experience that a teacher has.

Employment Prospects

Employment prospects are not good, but positions may be found if the applicant is willing to relocate to other areas. Teachers who get tenure often do not leave their jobs, so school system turnover is not great. Once a teacher gets tenure, he or she is likely to stay in the system until retirement.

Advancement Prospects

Teachers advance their careers in a number of ways. First, there is the monetary advancement. This is attained through the step system noted above.

Second, teachers who have proven themselves are given tenures. This means that they cannot be fired under normal circumstances. This gives the individual a great deal of security.

Third, teachers can take additional courses and become department heads, district music supervisors, or state music supervisors.

Education and Training

Secondary School Music Teachers are required to have at least a bachelor's degree with a major in music education. They are usually required to complete a semester of student teaching.

The individual who plans on teaching in a public school must have a teaching certificate or license. These are granted to qualified individuals by state education departments.

In order to get permanent certification, many states require additional credits or even a master's degree.

Experience, Skills, and Personality Traits

Secondary School Music Teachers must like to teach and have good teaching skills.

As a Secondary School Music Teacher, an individual usually specializes in either vocal or instrumental music. However, he or she needs a broad background and knowledge of music.

He or she must also have at least a limited knowledge of conducting either a vocal or band ensemble.

Unions and Associations

Teachers may belong to the National Education Association (NEA) or the National Federation of Teachers (NFT). Both of these organizations work on behalf of the Teacher to obtain better benefits, working conditions, and salaries.

Teachers may also belong to the Music Educators National Conference, the Music Teachers National Associations, Inc., the National Association of Schools of Music, the American Choral Directors Association, and a host of others. These associations work toward good music education in the schools and offer seminars, conferences, booklets, and other information on various subjects.

Tips for Entry

1. There are employment agencies (usually located in major cities) that specialize in locating positions for teachers. Check these out.
2. College placement offices receive notices of openings at schools.
3. Get letters of recommendation from several of your professors at school as well as your student teaching supervisor.
4. Apply for summer school positions. These are often easier to obtain, and they help you get your foot in the door of a school system.

ELEMENTARY SCHOOL MUSIC TEACHER

CAREER PROFILE

Duties: Teach singing, listening, and music theory to elementary school students

Alternate Title(s): Music Instructor

Salary Range: $25,000 to $65,000+

Employment Prospects: Fair

Advancement Prospects: Good

Best Geographical Location(s) for Position: Areas throughout the country have opportunities

Prerequisites:

Education or Training—Bachelor's degree in music education; some schools require additional education for permanent certification

Experience—Student teaching

Special Skills and Personality Traits—Enjoyment of children; enjoyment of music; ability to play an instrument; ability to teach

CAREER LADDER

```
┌─────────────────────────────────┐
│     Tenured Music Teacher       │
└─────────────────────────────────┘

┌─────────────────────────────────┐
│ Elementary School Music Teacher │
└─────────────────────────────────┘

┌─────────────────────────────────┐
│        Student Teacher          │
└─────────────────────────────────┘
```

Position Description

Elementary School Music Teachers work in public, private, and parochial schools. Their duties vary depending on the school and the ages and grades they teach.

Music Teachers must often follow guidelines for what they teach students. These are set up by the school music department heads, district music supervisors, and state music supervisors.

Very young children, such as those in kindergarten and the first grade, are often taught simple things, like singing songs or rhythmic movements. This singing, clapping, and stamping is considered fun by most children. The teacher also might play records or show films about music.

As the age and grade of the children increases the Music Teacher can teach such things as music theory, singing fundamentals, and group singing. He or she might also get the students interested in instruments and possibly give lessons.

Music Teachers learn many of the teaching methods that they use as student teachers. Student teaching gives the individual a chance for hands-on training with supervision.

A Music Teacher is evaluated after a certain number of years working in the school system (usually three or four), and he or she may receive tenure. After receiving tenure, a teacher cannot be fired from the school system under normal circumstances. This gives the job a tremendous amount of stability.

Good Elementary School Music Teachers are creative and enthusiastic. They come up with unique ways of teaching. For example, the teacher might have the class make instruments out of everyday materials or have the students write their own lyrics and music for a song.

In addition to the normal teaching responsibilities, Music Teachers might also direct the school's choral group, be involved in plays, shows, concerts, etc., in the school.

Teachers usually work only 10 months a year. If they work in summer school, they receive additional remuneration. Teachers also have time off during all school vacations.

Teachers are responsible to the department head, principal, or superintendent of the school system.

Salaries

Salaries for Music Teachers depend on the location of the school, the type of school, and the teacher's qualifications.

Teachers in large metropolitan areas earn more than teachers in small communities.

Teachers usually start out at around $25,000 per school year. Their salary can go up to $65,000 or more annually.

Salaries in public schools are usually paid on a system called "steps." Each time a teacher reaches a certain step, his or her salary is raised. Steps relate to the amount of education (degrees, credits, etc.) a teacher accumulates. Steps also relate to the amount of experience a teacher has.

Employment Prospects

Employment prospects for Music Teachers are not as good as they were a few years ago. There are still positions available, however. Teachers may have to relocate to areas in which openings occur.

Teachers who get tenure tend not to leave their jobs, so the turnover in a school system is low.

Advancement Prospects

Teachers advance their careers in a number of ways. First, there is a monetary advancement. This is attained through the step system mentioned above. Second, Teachers who have proven themselves are given tenure. This means that they cannot, under normal circumstances, be fired. This provides job stability.

Third, Teachers can take additional courses and become department heads, district music supervisors, or state music supervisors.

Education and Training

Teachers are required to have at least a bachelor's degree. Most Music Teachers major in music education. Usually individuals are required to take a semester of student teaching.

As a rule, if the individual is planning on teaching in a public school, he or she must also obtain a teaching certificate or license. These are granted by state education departments to qualified individuals.

In order to get permanent certification, many states require a master's degree or additional credits in music education.

Experience, Skills, and Personality Traits

Elementary School Music Teachers must have both the ability and the patience to teach children. They are usually required to play at least one instrument, either piano or guitar.

The Elementary School Music Teacher must also be able to read music and must have a broad knowledge of the subject.

Elementary School Music Teachers must be creative and enthusiastic in order to guide children into an interest in this subject.

Unions and Associations

Teachers may belong to the National Education Association (NEA) or the National Federation of Teachers (NFT). Both of these organizations work on behalf of the Teacher to obtain better benefits, working conditions, and salaries.

Teachers may also belong to a host of associations, depending on their interests. These include the Music Educators National Conference, the Music Teachers National Association, Inc., the National Association of Schools of Music, the American Choral Directors Association, and others. These groups work toward having good music education in the schools and offer seminars, conferences, pamphlets, booklets, and other valuable information.

Tips for Entry

1. There are employment agencies (usually located in major cities) that specialize in locating positions for teachers. Check these out.
2. Colleges usually have placement offices that receive notices of openings at schools.
3. Get letters of recommendation from several of your professors at college as well as your student teacher supervisor.
4. Check out openings in the newspaper classified section as well as on-line via the Internet.

PRIVATE INSTRUMENT TEACHER

CAREER PROFILE

Duties: Instruct and teach a student how to play a specific instrument on a private or semiprivate basis

Alternate Title(s): Studio Teacher

Salary Range: $18,000 to $45,000+

Employment Prospects: Good

Advancement Prospects: Fair

Best Geographical Location(s) for Position: Cities and metropolitan areas with large enough populations to support a number of private teachers

Prerequisites:

Education or Training—Extensive training and/or study in specific instrument

Experience—Playing instrument

Special Skills and Personality Traits—Ability to teach; ability to play one or more instruments; patience; enthusiasm

CAREER LADDER

```
┌────────────────────────────────────┐
│  Owner of Private Teaching Studio  │
└────────────────────────────────────┘

┌────────────────────────────────────┐
│    Private Instrument Teacher      │
└────────────────────────────────────┘

┌────────────────────────────────────┐
│ Performer; Schoolteacher; Student  │
└────────────────────────────────────┘
```

Position Description

A Private Instrument Teacher teaches students how to play a specific instrument. Sometimes the student is eager to learn the instrument; at other times he or she is being forced to take lessons. This can be quite frustrating for the teacher.

Good instrument teachers have the ability to make the instrument exciting and make learning to play a good experience. Expertise in a certain instrument alone does not make a good teacher.

Private Instrument Teachers can teach in a number of different locations, including their home, the student's home, a music instrument store, a private studio, or a commodity room.

Private Instrument Teachers often teach groups of three or four students at one time in addition to giving private lessons to individual students. Lessons run from 45 minutes to an hour and are usually scheduled once a week. Students must be encouraged not to miss lessons and to practice in between.

Instructors may teach beginners or advanced students. There are also expert instructors who teach professionals.

Private Instrument Teachers must be reliable and dependable. Nothing hurts a new teacher's reputation more than forgetting a lesson or habitually cancelling.

If the Private Instrument teacher is self-employed (as opposed to working on staff in a studio or shop), he or she must decide how much will be charged per lesson, how and when the fee will be paid, and what policies to develop on the way his or her business will be run.

If the instructor is teaching in a studio or shop, he or she might put the students together for a group recital or a program of solo performances.

The Private Instrument Teacher is responsible directly to the student (or, in the case of children, to the parents). To be successful, the teacher must be easy to get along with, congenial, and professional, as well as being a good teacher.

Most often, a successful teacher is one who struggled through technical problems in his or her own training. These individuals have frequently developed new and easier ways to conquer these problems and can pass the methods on to their students.

Private Instrument Teachers usually have irregular working hours because of students' jobs and/or school times.

Salaries

Salaries vary depending on the instrument being taught and the expertise of the teacher. Fees usually range from $10 to $40 per hour. Fees naturally go up for experts in the field, such as jazz greats, orchestra musicians, etc. These fees can run from $30 to $200 and up per lesson.

Private Instrument Teachers are often on staff in music stores or studios. In cases such as this, the instructor is either paid a fee per student, a weekly salary, or a combination of the two. Studio teachers may earn from $15,000 to $45,000 plus annually.

Employment Prospects

A talented Private Instrument Teacher is always in demand on staff at a studio or music store or as a self-employed private instructor. Once a teacher obtains a few students who are satisfied, word travels fast.

There are many Private Instrument Teachers who work full-time as schoolteachers and part-time giving lessons after school. The individual may obtain quite a few private students as a result of the school position.

Advancement Prospects

Advancement prospects are fair for a Private Instrument Teacher. As noted above, it doesn't take long for word to travel about a good teacher.

Eventually, the teacher may have so many students that he or she wants to open a private teaching studio. The individual may employ other Private Music Teachers of the same instrument or diversify, offering instruction in other instruments. When hiring other teachers, the owner must screen the teachers carefully in order to uphold the reputation of the studio.

Education and Training

The main requirement for a Private Instrument Teacher is the ability to play an instrument well enough to show a student the techniques of playing. Extensive training and/or study in the specific instrument or group of instruments is necessary. This may be professional training from a conservatory or college, private lessons, or self-taught skills.

Experience, Skills, and Personality Traits

Private Instrument Teachers must have the ability to play an instrument or instruments and to teach it as well. If an individual plays an instrument he or she cannot always teach someone else to play it.

One of the most important traits a teacher can have is patience. Often, it takes new students a while to pick up new techniques on an instrument. The teacher must be enthusiastic enough to communicate the excitement of new techniques to the student.

Unions and Associations

Private Music Teachers do not have a union. They can belong to the American Federation of Musicians (AFM) if they are also performers.

Private Music Teachers might also belong to The Music Teachers National Association, Inc., the Music Educators National Conference, or the National Association of Schools of Music. These organizations promote music education of all varieties.

Tips for Entry

1. Talk to all the music, record, and instrument shops in the area. Discuss your credentials and the instrument or instruments you can teach.
2. Leave business cards and/or flyers in all the music, record, and instrument shops. Include information such as your name, phone number, any accomplishment with your instrument, and any other pertinent information.
3. Contact the churches, temples, and synagogues in your area as well as all the school systems and colleges. It is usually best to visit all the places in person instead of calling or writing. Have your credentials with you.

MUSIC THERAPIST

CAREER PROFILE

Duties: Use music or musical activities to treat physical, mental, and/or emotional disabilities in patients

Alternate Title(s): None

Salary Range: $20,000 to $52,000+

Employment Prospects: Excellent

Advancement Prospects: Good

Best Geographical Location(s) for Position: Positions may be found in every major city in the country as well as in smaller communities.

Prerequisites:

Education or Training—Undergraduate degree in music therapy required; master's degree may be required

Experience—Some experience working with handicapped or disabled individuals

Special Skills and Personality Traits—Ability to work with handicapped and/or disabled individuals; compassion; ability to play piano and/or guitar; emotional stability

CAREER LADDER

```
┌─────────────────────────────┐
│  Music Therapy Consultant;  │
│  Music Therapy Supervisor   │
└─────────────────────────────┘

┌─────────────────────────────┐
│      Music Therapist        │
└─────────────────────────────┘

┌─────────────────────────────┐
│      College Student        │
└─────────────────────────────┘
```

Position Description

The Music Therapist works to restore a patient's health, working with a number of other individuals. These might include doctors, nurses, teachers, physical therapists, psychologists, psychiatrists, and/or the patient's family. Together the team decides what course of action to take for the patient's therapy.

Often, when all else has failed, the Music Therapist can make a breakthrough with a patient. The Music Therapist uses different forms of music as therapy for patients who have physical, mental, or emotional disabilities or illnesses.

The Music Therapist plans musical activities for an individual or a group. For example, the therapist may teach a group of elderly patients a new song or play a record or tape of tunes that were popular when they were younger. This often helps a withdrawn nursing home patient remember and reminisce. The patient might start talking about what was going on in his or her life when the song was popular.

The Music Therapist might teach a blind child how to play an instrument. This gives the child a sense of accomplishment that he or she might not have had before. Once again, the therapist has accomplished something of value.

The Music Therapist is often responsible for selecting pieces to be used as background music in certain rooms in a facility. Through training, the therapist knows what type of music might evoke a reaction and what type might be soothing.

The Music Therapist in a hospital might put together a group of patients to sing or play instruments for hospital staff and other patients.

He or she works with a patient on either a one-to-one basis or in a group, depending on the patient and his or her needs. Conferences are often held with other members of the team. At these conferences the Music Therapist discusses the patient's needs and progress. The Music Therapist is usually happy if the patient makes even the slightest amount of progress. Progress is usually slow, and the Therapist must be extremely patient.

The Therapist hopes to reach his or her patient through music and have the patient become healthier emotionally, mentally, and/or physically.

Salaries

Salaries for Music Therapists vary, depending on experience, education, and the responsibilities of the individual. Earnings are also dependent on the size, prestige, and geographic location of the specific facility and job. A Music Therapist just entering the field usually makes from $20,000 to $29,000 yearly. A more experienced therapist at a larger institution or facility may have a salary of $26,000 to $36,000 or more yearly. Supervisory positions in the field of music therapy often offer yearly salaries of $52,000 and up.

Employment Prospects

With the growing number of health care facilities, the music therapy field is wide open. There are currently more positions than there are Music Therapists. A qualified individual should have no problem finding a job.

Advancement Prospects

Music Therapists can move up to supervisory or administrative positions. These positions, however, usually reduce the contact Therapists have with patients. They also require additional training and education.

Other Music Therapists move into research or university teaching. These positions also limit contact with patients.

Many Therapists go into private practice and consulting after working in institutions or facilities for a period of time.

Education and Training

Music Therapists need bachelor's degrees in music therapy. There are many colleges that offer this degree program. Courses usually include music theory, voice studies, instrument lessons, psychology, sociology, and biology in addition to the general courses. A Music Therapist who plans on working in a public school system must also have a teaching degree.

Many positions require a master's degree. These too, can be obtained at colleges and universities around the country.

In addition, Music Therapists must go through a six-month internship before getting their licenses. Certification by the Certification Board for Music Therapists (CBMT) requires competition of academic and clinical training approved by the American Music Therapy Association (AMTA) and passing a national, written examination.

Experience, Skills, and Personality Traits

A good Music Therapist must be able to work with handicapped and/or disabled people. He or she must have patience, compassion, and emotional stability.

A Music Therapist must be able to play the piano and/or guitar. Ability to play other instruments is a plus. He or she must also be able to teach others to either play an instrument or sing. A good knowledge of music is essential.

Many Music Therapists work at a health facility or school as a summer job or as a volunteer before deciding to become a therapist. This gives them the opportunity to gain some experience in the field.

Unions and Associations

Two associations that Music Therapists may belong to are the National Association for Music Therapy, Inc. and the American Association for Music Therapy. These organizations help place qualified Music Therapists, do research, and act as liaisons for colleges that have music therapy programs.

Tips for Entry

1. Go to the college job placement office. Often facilities or schools looking for Music Therapists will send a list of openings to colleges and universities that grant degrees in music therapy.

2. Both the National Association for Music Therapy, Inc. and the American Association for Music Therapy have registration and placement services for their members. Join the organizations. In addition, their newsletters list various openings.

3. Many positions for Music Therapists are available through the Federal Government. These civil service positions can be located through your state employment service.

4. Check out openings via the Internet.

5. There are many civil-service positions throughout the country for qualified Music Therapists. Contact state employment services for information.

MUSIC LIBRARIAN

CAREER PROFILE

Duties: Catalog music, recordings, musical books, etc.; do reference work on music-related subjects

Alternate Title(s): Record Librarian (in radio stations)

Salary Range: $19,000 to $52,000+

Employment Prospects: Poor

Advancement Prospects: Poor

Best Geographical Locations for Position: Large cities housing conservatories, symphonies, large public libraries, and many radio stations

Prerequisites:

Education or Training—Bachelor's degree in music history or theory and/or library science; some positions require a master's degree

Experience—Library assistant position

Special Skills and Personality Traits—Interest in music recordings, books, and research; extensive knowledge of music history and theory; library research training; foreign language helpful

CAREER LADDER

```
┌─────────────────────────────────┐
│   Music Library Administrator   │
└─────────────────────────────────┘

┌─────────────────────────────────┐
│        Music Librarian          │
└─────────────────────────────────┘

┌─────────────────────────────────┐
│           Student               │
└─────────────────────────────────┘
```

Position Description

A Music Librarian combines his or her skills as a librarian with an extensive knowledge of music. Duties vary depending on the type of position. Usually, however, the Music Librarian is responsible for cataloging all musical materials. These might include records, tapes, printed music, books on music-oriented subjects, etc.

The Music Librarian must do all reference work. He or she often looks up or finds information for a student, library patron, or professor. The individual must constantly be reading reviews of new music books, records, and tapes. The person in this position often writes reviews of books and music. The Music Librarian is in charge of ordering or recommending new materials for the library to purchase.

At times, the Music Librarian's duties also include arranging for courses on music-related subjects or lecturing on music. Depending on the position, the Music Librarian might also be responsible for putting together concerts, recitals, and other music-related activities or locating sponsors for these activities.

A Music Librarian may work in a library or school, for an orchestra, or at a television or radio station. At a TV station, the Librarian is not only responsible for cataloging the music, but is also often responsible for helping choose music for programs.

The Music Librarian working at a radio station must catalog all the station's records and tapes. He or she is usually responsible for pulling the records that the Disc Jockey or Program Director has chosen prior to a show. At stations that have live request shows, the Music Librarian may be on hand to pull the requested records from the library. The radio station Music Librarian is usually responsible for putting used records and tapes back in their proper places. He or she keeps track of any broken, scratched, or warped records that need replacement. In addition, the Librarian works with the program director choosing and purchasing new music.

The Music Librarian must be an extremely organized individual. His or her memory must be good enough to remember vintage tapes, records, books, etc.

The Music Librarian usually works regular hours. If the Music Librarian works in a public library, conservatory, or university library position, he or she is usually responsible to the library director. If the position is in a TV or radio station, the individual is usually responsible to the program director and/or station manager. Music Librarians working in music stores or record shops are responsible to the store manager or owner.

Salaries

A Music Librarian at a mid-sized radio station might make a starting salary of $19,000 yearly. His or her salary at a larger station might range to $38,000 annually.

Music Librarians working in libraries, schools, conservatories, etc., can make from $20,000 for a beginning position to $52,000 or more in a position that requires experience.

Employment Prospects

There are more Music Librarians than there are jobs to fill. A Music Librarian can choose from a variety of different settings, including schools, conservatories, colleges, universities, public libraries, sheet music stores, record stores, radio or TV stations, orchestras, and music research libraries.

Positions in symphonies and/or choirs are limited. There is a low rate of turnover of Music Librarians in schools, conservatories, colleges, universities, and public libraries. The best place to look for a job is in a mid-sized radio station. Individuals in these stations often leave for jobs with bigger stations.

Advancement Prospects

There is almost no possibility for advancement as a Music Librarian. The competition for jobs in this field is very tough. The main way to advance as a Music Librarian is to find a job at a bigger radio station, better college or university, or more extensive library.

Music Librarians can also be promoted to administrative positions at the facility or institution for which they work.

Education and Training

The education required of a Music Librarian varies according to the type of position desired. All positions require at least an undergraduate degree in music theory or history. Some positions require a dual major in music and library sciences. Other positions require a master's degree in either music or library sciences. Jobs at very large libraries often require a master's in both disciplines.

Experience, Skills, and Personality Traits

Most Music Librarians work in libraries before and during their training. Picking up the basic library science skills makes training for the position easier. Prior experience in a sheet music store or large record store is also helpful.

Music Librarians must like to do research and have a great interest in music, recordings, and books.

This position also requires an ability to get along with people. Depending on the type of position, some Music Librarians must also be knowledgeable in a foreign language.

Unions and Associations

There are a number of associations for Music Librarians to belong to. These include the American Library Association (ALA) and the Special Libraries Association (SLA). Music Librarians might additionally belong to the Music Library Association (MLA) and the American Federation of Musicians (AFM).

Tips for Entry

1. As competition is very stiff, secure as much education as possible.
2. In addition to required courses, take specialized classes in specific areas such as ethnic music. Become an expert in at least one specialty.
3. Try to obtain a job as a library assistant while you're still in school.
4. Check out openings on-line. www.monster.com and www.hotjobs.com are good places to start your search.
5. Jobs may also be advertised in the classified section of the newspaper. Look under headings such as "Music Librarian," "Record Librarian," "Librarian," etc.

TALENT AND WRITING

RECORDING GROUP

CAREER PROFILE

Duties: Record tunes for singles and albums

Alternate Title(s): Recording Act; Recording Artist(s)

Salary Range: It is impossible to estimate earnings

Employment Prospects: Poor

Advancement Prospects: Fair

Best Geographical Location(s) for Position: New York City, Los Angeles, and Nashville, for major record labels; independent labels located throughout country

Prerequisites:

Education or Training—No formal educational requirement; musical and/or vocal training may be helpful

Experience—Writing songs; playing music; singing

Special Skills and Personality Traits—Musical and/or vocal talent; creativity; understanding of music and recording industry; professionalism; good stage appearance; charisma; perseverance; luck

CAREER LADDER

```
┌─────────────────────────────────┐
│      Top Recording Group        │
└─────────────────────────────────┘

┌─────────────────────────────────┐
│        Recording Group          │
└─────────────────────────────────┘

┌─────────────────────────────────┐
│  Musical Artists; Songwriters;  │
│   Aspiring Recording Group      │
└─────────────────────────────────┘
```

Position Description

A Recording Group is a group that is currently recording their music professionally or one that has done so in the past. For the sake of this section, Recording Group will mean a group or an individual artist.

Recording Groups may be involved with any type of music, including rock, pop, folk, country, jazz, R&B, rap, classical, or orchestral.

The Recording Group may evolve in a number of ways. Many Groups start out as bar bands, lounge groups, show groups, etc. Other Groups begin their careers by writing music and making demos, never really setting foot on stage.

Once the Group receives a recording contract, it needs to find something to record. A Recording Group may or may not write its own material. If not, the Group must find suitable songs to record. These might be located through the help of an A & R person, a music publisher, the Group's manager, etc.

After a Group finds songs that might be potential hits, it learns them, rehearses until perfect, and records. This is done with the help of engineers, arrangers, studio musicians, and/or background vocalists.

At this point, the Group may also make a music video to help sell and market the record and the act.

The Recording Act will work with all the different departments in a record company to get ready for the release of the record. The Group and/or their representative may sit down with the publicity and press department to give them information for press kits, news releases, etc. It may work with the promotion department setting up promotional appearances. The Group may talk to the art department about ideas for the album cover.

Once the record is released, one or more members of a Recording Group may visit key radio stations and meet with program directors, music directors, and disc jockeys. A concert tour to promote the release of the record will probably be scheduled. The Group may give interviews to various print media and appear on TV talk and variety shows.

The Recording Group must set aside time for rehearsals both before concert tours and while on the road. Once it has made it, the Group must always sound their best.

As a successful Recording Group, the members may enjoy some fame and fortune. To keep the fame and build up the fortune, the Group must constantly come up with new tunes to record that become hits.

Becoming a top Recording Group is the ultimate goal for most musical artists. Staying at the top is never easy.

Salaries

Earnings for Recording Groups are impossible to estimate. There are too many factors that can influence finances: how the Group splits up the money, how popular the Group is, the type of recording contract, etc.

Many Groups do not make big money on their first recording, even if it is a hit. It depends how much was spent making the record. Record companies usually recoup their expenses from the record's profits.

Successful Recording Groups can make hundreds of thousands or even millions of dollars. Some of these monies are earned from the sale of the record. Other monies might come from concert tours, public appearances, and merchandising of the Group's name and products.

Employment Prospects

Realistically, it is very difficult to become a top Recording Group. For every Group that gets a recording contract, there are hundreds that don't. However, a Group with talent, perseverance, and a lot of luck can make it eventually. Many Groups that fail may just give up too soon.

Today, it is somewhat easier than in the past to market records with music videos. Having a music video aired on a national or even regional music television show can mean instant success for a recording act.

Advancement Prospects

Once a Group has obtained a bona fide recording contract, they have a fair chance of advancing their career. The first step in advancement for a Recording Group is getting a record on the charts. The second is moving it up the charts. Moving into the top ten on the charts is next. A Recording Group whose record holds the number one position for one or more weeks is achieving the goal. Having a string of tunes hit this position is even better.

None of this is easy, but it is possible.

Education and Training

Members of Recording Groups are not required to have any educational training, although many individuals do have a college background. Some type of music and/or vocal training is necessary. This might come through private study or schooling or be self-taught.

Experience, Skills, and Personality Traits

Members of Recording Groups should have good stage presence and charisma. This is important for the Group when they do promotional tours and appearances. Members should be talented musically and/or vocally. An understanding of the music and recording industry is necessary. An ability to deal with business situations is helpful. Perseverance, luck, and being at the right place at the right time are all factors.

Unions and Associations

Recording Groups may be members of the American Federation of Musicians (AFM). They might also belong to the National Academy of Recording Arts and Sciences (NARAS). This is the association which gives out the Grammy awards each year. Depending on the type of music the Group records, they might belong to the Country Music Association (CMA) or the Gospel Music Association (GMA).

Tips for Entry

1. Make the most professional demo possible.
2. Try to have original songs on the demo.
3. Many members of successful Recording Groups start out as session musicians. After being recognized as having talent, the individuals can strike out on their own.
4. Never send your demos out without first querying interest. Either call the record company or write them a note. Try to send your demo to a specific person, not just a title. For example, address it to "Mr. John Jones, A&R Director," not just "A&R Director."
5. Look for opportunities to showcase your act.

FLOOR SHOW GROUP

CAREER PROFILE

Duties: Perform in nightclubs, hotels, bars, concert halls, etc.; put on shows; entertain people

Alternate Title(s): Show Group; Show Band

Salary Range: $250 to $15,000+ per engagement

Employment Prospects: Fair

Advancement Prospects: Fair

Best Geographical Location(s) for Positions: Larger cities have more opportunities

Prerequisites:

Education or Training—No educational requirements; musical training helpful

Experience—Performing; working in bands

Special Skills and Personality Traits—Good stage appearance; musical and/or vocal skills; knowledge of musical trends; ability to travel; charisma

CAREER LADDER

```
┌─────────────────────────────────────┐
│  Well-Paid, Well-Known Show Group;   │
│            Recording Act             │
└─────────────────────────────────────┘

┌─────────────────────────────────────┐
│          Floor Show Group            │
└─────────────────────────────────────┘

┌─────────────────────────────────────┐
│        Bar Band; Lounge Act          │
└─────────────────────────────────────┘
```

Position Description

Floor Show Groups work in nightclubs, hotels, cruise ships, cafés, bars, and concert halls putting on shows for patrons. They not only perform, they entertain. Show Groups may perform all different types of music in their act.

Show Groups have to play a specific number of sets per night. Generally, Show Groups will be required to perform two shows. They may also have to play one or two dance sets during the course of the engagement.

The dance set will consist of popular and old tunes the group plays so that patrons can get out on the floor and dance. Shows, on the other hand, must be developed and put together. During show sets, members of the audience stay seated and watch and listen to the act on stage. The act may include any number of songs, melodies, skits, jokes, etc. The show may also contain dancers, light shows, sound effects, or any number of other special effects.

Show Groups have pizzazz. The show set is usually planned quite extensively. Ad-libs may sound like ad-libs to the audience, but they have usually been repeated time and time again. The show must be flexible. At times, a Show Group will change its opening and closing and leave the rest of the act as is. As new songs become hits, the group may

wish to take out some of their old material and replace it. Usually, Floor Show Groups have exciting finales. They wear costumes on stage. Key members of the group may change costumes for each set.

Between sets or after the engagement, the musicians and vocalists may mingle with patrons.

Floor Show Groups may work in one place for two or three weeks before moving on to the next gig.

Fees are paid weekly or semi-weekly for this type of work. Hotel rooms and, on occasion, food may be part of the deal.

The Floor Show Group travels quite a lot. If the club manager likes their show, they will be booked back again. This is how Show Groups build up followings in specific areas. Individuals must not only be free to travel, but also like living out of a suitcase for months at a time.

The Show Group must appear professional at all times. They must arrive at the correct times for their sets, dressed appropriately. Working hours are usually at night. In order to attain success, it helps for the Group to develop good working relationships with managers and agents of clubs where they work. The Group is responsible directly to the club manager. It is he or she who controls whether or not the Group is invited back. Members of Show Groups often acquire a bit of stardom, at least on the club circuit where they perform.

Salaries

It is difficult to determine a salary range for members of Floor Show Groups. There are quite a number of factors that can affect salaries: the way the group splits up fees, how popular the act is, whether they are working under a union contract, how many members are in the act, expenses, etc.

As a rule, Show Groups earn more per engagement than lounge acts. According to the American Federation of Musicians (AFM) union, leaders earn more than the other members of groups.

There are Show Groups that work sporadically and earn minimum fees (according to union contracts). There are also Show Groups that tour fifty weeks a year, zipping back and forth across the country (or sections of it) earning large fees.

Fees for Show Groups run from $250 to $15,000+ per engagement.

Employment Prospects

Once a Group attracts a following, employment prospects are fair. Until a Show Group has a following, employment is difficult. Show Groups usually work with agents who book them in specific areas of the country. Some Show Groups also try to book themselves, but this task can be extremely difficult. There are agents who work specifically with Show Groups and have contracts with various rooms around the country. Groups of this type may also open for better-known acts.

Advancement Prospects

It is difficult to advance as a Show Group. Most groups of this kind aspire to be recording artists. This transition is tough to make.

Show Groups can, however, build up a tremendous following. By doing this, they assure themselves of constant bookings and larger fees.

Advancement in any part of the music business depends on talent, the ability to persevere, and a lot of luck.

Education and Training

There are no educational requirements for members of Show Groups. What is required is the ability to play an instrument and/or sing very well. This may be acquired through high school training, college or university education, private study, or self-teaching.

Experience, Skills, and Personality Traits

Show Groups must be exciting. Their members need to have a good stage presence and charisma. It goes without saying that members of these groups must have musical and/or vocal skills.

Show Groups must not only perform, but also entertain. They need the ability to play dance sets and show sets. In order to do this, someone in the Group or their entourage must put shows together creatively. The Group needs to keep in mind the current musical trends. It is often required that the Group have a variety of different sets, enabling patrons to come back to the club, see the show, and not be bored.

Unions and Associations

Members of Show Groups may belong to the American Federation of Musicians (AFM). This union bargains for musicians on fees, terms of contracts, etc. It also helps protect the musician from being fired unjustly, treated badly, etc.

Not all musicians belong to the union. However, most major clubs work with the union and do not hire any nonunion Groups.

Tips for Entry

1. Join the union. They often know of openings. Hanging around their offices or talking to other union members helps build a contact list.
2. Be professional. If you have an interview with a club manager or agent, show up on time. If you cannot get to an interview on time, chances are you will be late for gigs.
3. Have a professional photographer take pictures of the Group. Make sure the Group is shown in the picture as they will be on stage (e.g., don't take pictures in costumes and go on stage in jeans).
4. Have the Group's name printed on the picture. Don't forget to include your agent's or manager's phone number. If you don't have either yet, use a number where you know someone will answer the phone most of the time. If you don't answer, someone else will get a call for the job.
5. Print up a list of clubs where you have worked previously. You might want to get recommendations in writing from club owners you have worked for.
6. Print up a list of tunes you can perform for both dance sets and show sets.
7. You might want to make up a small brochure (or a letter with the Group's picture) letting people know that you are available. Send this to clubs, agents, organizations, etc.
8. When you do get gigs, get the commitment in writing in the form of a contract. Make sure dates, times, monies, and any other pertinent information are included. Make sure that the contract is signed by both parties.
9. Consider utilizing the new karaoke hardware and software in your act. Successful Floor Show Groups often have a segment of their show dedicated to audience involvement.

DANCE BAND

CAREER PROFILE

Duties: Play music and sing in clubs, bars, schools, etc., so that patrons can dance

Alternate Title(s): Bar Band; Lounge Band

Salary Range: $100 to $3,000+ per engagement

Employment Prospects: Fair

Advancement Prospects: Poor

Best Geographical Location(s) for Position: Any location has possible openings

Prerequisites:

Education or Training—Musical training helpful

Experience—Performing; member of school band

Special Skills and Personality Traits—Musical ability and talent; good stage appearance; knowledge of all types of music; ability to read music helpful

CAREER LADDER

```
┌─────────────────────────────────────┐
│   Floor Show Group; Recording Act    │
└─────────────────────────────────────┘

┌─────────────────────────────────────┐
│            Dance Band                │
└─────────────────────────────────────┘

┌─────────────────────────────────────┐
│            Musician                  │
└─────────────────────────────────────┘
```

Position Description

Dance Bands may work in schools, bars, clubs, cafés, or hotels, or for private parties. The Dance Band's main function is to provide music for people to dance to and listen to.

When Dance Bands are employed by a specific person, they contract to play a certain number of sets. These sets are usually from forty-five minutes to one hour in length. The Band may play from two to five sets nightly, taking breaks in between.

Dance Bands may consist of guitarists, bass players, pianists, organists or synthesizer players, drummers, singers, horn players, etc. They may have any number of people in them.

Dance Bands usually specialize in one or two varieties of music. Rock, pop, Top 40, disco, jazz, country, swing, etc., are all possibilities. When the Band, is hired the leader, manager, or booking agent must ask what type of music will be required for the engagement.

Dance Bands must set aside specific periods of time for rehearsals. Good Dance Bands know most of the current hits in their variety of music. Additionally, most Dance Bands know an assortment of other tunes. It is important for the Dance Band to have a big playlist. This will enable them to perform sets without repeating songs.

Dance Bands may take requests from the audience. These requests may be made in a written form or face-to-face. Dance Bands often have specific parts of their sets in which they take requests. In this way, the structure of their show will not be disturbed.

It is usual for Bands to know ahead of time which songs will be played at what time during the set. There may be a group leader who calls out the songs during the show. The sets may be peppered with ad-libs by members of the group.

Dance Bands may work on either a part-time or a full-time basis. Frequently, the first paying job a musician has is in a Dance Band. Dance Bands usually work nights, although they may be hired for affairs and functions in the daytime.

Members of Dance Bands often hold day jobs or teach on the side in order to earn additional income.

When working, the group is responsible to the individual or club who has hired them. The Dance Band may work with an agent, manager, road manager, or other personnel. They may perform popular tunes as well as their own compositions.

Salaries

Salaries and/or fees for Dance Bands and their members vary greatly depending on the popularity of the group, their location, experience, etc.

Groups playing in school situations earn from $100 to $1,500 plus per engagement. Dance Bands with large followings may earn considerably more.

If the members of the band belong to the musicians union (AFM), their base pay will be set by the union.

Dance Bands working in bars earn between $100 and $1,500 plus per night. A group playing in a lounge or nightclub setting might earn from $150 to $3,000 plus per engagement.

Employment Prospects

Dance Bands looking for part-time work on weekends have a fair chance of finding gigs if they are good. These groups usually have fairly large followings within their community.

Dance Bands seeking full-time employment have a more difficult time. There are many more Bands looking for work than there are openings.

Advancement Prospects

It is very hard for a Dance Band to advance its career. The most these groups can reasonably hope for is that they will attract such a large following that they will stay booked constantly and can demand and receive bigger fees.

A group may decide to put together a show and try to work as a show group. Most groups, however, break up before this occurs.

If the band is very talented, very lucky, and in the right place at the right time, they may become a top recording group. But the odds are against this.

Education and Training

Members of Dance Bands are not required to have any type of specialized education. The ability to play an instrument or sing well is essential. Training for this may be picked up in school or in private study, or it may be self-taught.

This is not to indicate that members of Dance Bands are uneducated. Many are highly educated. Some have degrees or backgrounds in music, while others hold degrees in other majors. Some Dance Band members are still in school.

Experience, Skills, and Personality Traits

Dance Bands must have, or be able to build, large followings. The group must have musical talent and ability. Members of the group should be able to work well together, giving and taking. They must want to persevere and stay together. Dance Bands that play during their college years know that they will probably only be together until graduation. Other groups may stay together for years on end. As long as all the members want the same thing, it usually works out.

Many members of Dance Bands begin playing their instrument or singing while in school. They find that they can earn money while enjoying themselves playing in a school group for a dance or prom.

Members of Dance Bands need a good stage presence. Professional behavior at all times is important. Bands that are familiar with all types of music will have more flexibility in finding jobs.

Unions and Associations

Members of Dance Bands may belong to the American Federation of Musicians (AFM), which is a bargaining union. It helps the musician in all phases of his or her career, from setting guidelines on base salaries for performing to providing health insurance plans.

Tips for Entry

1. Openings for Dance Bands may be found in local papers in the help wanted section.
2. Other openings are learned about by word-of-mouth through members of organizations, schools, associations, firms, etc.
3. Be as professional as possible. Show up on time for all interviews and gigs.
4. Have pictures taken by a professional photographer.
5. Have the group's name, representative, and phone number printed on the pictures so that people know how to locate you for jobs.
6. Set up adequate time for rehearsals *before* a job, not during it.
7. You may consider making up a small brochure or printed piece to mail to potential talent buyers (schools, clubs, agents, etc.).
8. Try to get job commitments in writing in the form of contracts. There are standard contract forms available if you don't have one. Read the contract thoroughly before signing and make sure all information is correct.
9. Make up business cards and give them out. Tell everyone you have a group. Put cards on bulletin boards in stores, schools, malls, etc.
10. You might want to put an ad in a local paper indicating your group's availability. Make sure to put down a phone number where people can locate you or your representative.
11. Develop a press kit to give to the media and potential talent buyers.

SESSION MUSICIAN

CAREER PROFILE

Duties: Play background music for a recording artist in a studio

Alternate Title(s): Studio Musician; Session Player; Sideman or Woman; Freelance Musician; Backup Musician

Salary Range: Up to $100,000+

Employment Prospects: Fair

Advancement Prospects: Fair

Best Geographical Location(s) for Position: New York, Los Angeles, and Nashville; other cities may also have opportunities

Prerequisites:

Education or Training—Musical training helpful

Experience—Performing in bands and groups

Special Skills and Personality Traits—Proficiency in at least one instrument; dependability; ability to read music; versatility

CAREER LADDER

```
┌─────────────────────────────────────┐
│   Recording Artist; Group Leader     │
└─────────────────────────────────────┘

┌─────────────────────────────────────┐
│          Session Musician            │
└─────────────────────────────────────┘

┌─────────────────────────────────────┐
│        Musical Group Member          │
└─────────────────────────────────────┘
```

Position Description

The Session Musician may be known as a Studio Musician, a Session Player, a Sideman or woman, a Freelance Musician, or a Backup Musician. The job, however, stays the same.

The main responsibility of a Session Musician is to back up the leader of a group in the recording studio. He or she might also play music for commercials. At times, the individual may back up the leader of the group in a live concert.

It is important for the Session Musician to have the ability to sight-read. There is usually not a lot of time for rehearsals, and because of the high cost of studio personnel and time, mistakes are not tolerated.

In order for the Session Musician to get as much work as possible, it is in his or her best interest to know how to play a number of different styles and to be proficient in more than one instrument.

Session Musicians are usually hired by a contractor. This individual most often calls musicians he or she knows and has worked with before. The contractor tells the individual the date, time, and whom they will be backing up. The Session Musician either accepts the job or rejects it. After a few job rejections, the contractor probably won't call that partic-

ular Session Musician back, no matter what the reason for the rejections.

It is the responsibility of the Session Musician to play what he or she is told and in the manner that the leader of the group or the producer wants it played. He or she must be responsible, reliable, and easy to get along with, in addition to being a good musician.

Session Musicians are usually paid by the hour. Their minimum fee is set by the union (AFM). If they are in great demand, they can usually negotiate higher fees. Session Musicians often work with a number of different groups over a short time span. Each job is called a gig or a session.

A Studio Musician can make a good living. However, one thing that bothers many Studio Musicians is that this job stifles their creativity. Another problem for some is that the individual playing on the recording does not always get credit for his or her work. This means that the Studio Musician works in the shadow of another musician.

Salaries

Salaries of Session Musicians depend on a number of factors. These include the type of recording, how much work they do, their geographical location, and whether they are in great demand.

The American Federation of Musicians (AFM) specifies the minimum rate Session Musicians should receive. The union has different rates depending on the specific recording situation. Individuals are urged to check with the local AFM for specific rates.

When Session Musicians are in demand and well known, they can negotiate for more than the minimum rates. Individuals who play more than one instrument during a session will usually be paid additional monies.

Talented Session Musicians who are in constant demand may earn $100,000 or more annually. Naturally, those who are called less frequently will make considerably less.

Employment Prospects

Employment prospects for Session Musicians are fair if the Musician is extremely talented. He or she needs a lot of contacts to get his or her foot in the door. Unfortunately, talent alone doesn't make it.

Session Musicians are often hired through contractors. If an individual is hired and turns out to be not only talented, but responsible and easy to work with, too, he or she will continue receiving assignments from the contractor.

The majority of studio work is found in New York, Los Angeles and Nashville, although there are studios located all over the country.

Advancement Prospects

Session Musicians can advance their careers in a number of ways. They can become group leaders—not always an easy move—or they can become top Session Musicians. To become a top Studio Musician, one must be more talented, more versatile, and better connected than other musicians around.

Although there are many who have moved from being Session Musicians to top positions in the music business, it is a tough hill to climb.

Another option for career advancement for Session Musicians is for individuals to be called in to play for sessions more frequently, resulting in increased earnings.

Education and Training

There is no formal educational requirement for Session Musicians. Individuals have usually had extensive private study in their instruments. However, there are also many successful Session Musicians who are self-taught. The ability to read music is not always necessary, but makes the Musician more flexible.

Many Musicians have college degrees in music or an unrelated subject. This way, they feel they have something to fall back on in case they can't make a living in music.

Experience, Skills, and Personality Traits

It is essential for the Session Musician to be a great musician. Most Session Musicians begin their careers playing in local bands while in high school. Any performance experience at all is useful for a Session Musician.

As noted above, it is not always necessary to read music, but the ability to do so is a plus. Another advantage is the ability to play more than one instrument.

Unions and Associations

Session Musicians may be members of the American Federation of Musicians (AFM). This union stipulates the minimum wages that can be paid to musicians in addition to performing a variety of other functions.

Tips for Entry

1. Begin your career by working in a local band.
2. When you feel experienced enough, put an ad for work as a Session Musician in either a music-oriented newspaper or one of the trade magazines.
3. If you want to get into recording studio work and no one will let you put your foot in the door musically, try to get a job doing anything in the studio (studio assistant, receptionist, gofer, etc). You will learn a lot and make the contacts you need.
4. Join the American Federation of Musicians; your affiliation will help you locate jobs and make contacts.

BACKGROUND VOCALIST

CAREER PROFILE

Duties: Back up other singers or musicians on recordings or in live performance

Alternate Title(s): Singer, Studio Singer; Studio Vocalist; Background Singer; Chorus Member; Jingle Singer; Vocalist

Salary Range: Impossible to determine due to nature of the job

Employment Prospects: Fair

Advancement Prospects: Poor

Best Geographical Location(s) for Position: New York City, Los Angeles, and Nashville for major jobs; other locations for smaller jobs

Prerequisites:

Education or Training—No formal educational requirement; private vocal study useful

Experience—Singing or performing; working in music groups; singing in choruses

Special Skills and Personality Traits—Ability to sight-read; flexible singing style; ability to harmonize; excellent singing ability; good vocal range

CAREER LADDER

```
┌─────────────────────────────────────┐
│  Major Recording Artist; Solo Singer │
└─────────────────────────────────────┘

┌─────────────────────────────────────┐
│        Background Vocalist           │
└─────────────────────────────────────┘

┌─────────────────────────────────────┐
│   Unemployed Singer or Amateur       │
└─────────────────────────────────────┘
```

Position Description

Background Vocalists back up other singers or musicians on recordings, in jingles, on television commercials, or in live performance. Background Vocalists may have full-time jobs or may freelance.

An individual working as a Background Vocalist in a lounge or show group travels with the act to all their performances. He or she is responsible for singing background music in all the shows. The person must also learn all the songs in the repertoire and attend all the rehearsals.

Background Vocalists working in the theater may sing in the chorus. They must attend all rehearsals, learn parts, and sing in shows.

Background Vocalists who freelance on recordings, jingles, or television commercials have slightly different functions. Such an individual must build up a reputation as a great singer and be flexible, responsible, and available when needed.

The world of singing backup on recordings is unique. A Background Vocalist must be able to walk into a studio, pick up some music, go over it quickly, and be ready to record without a mistake. The Vocalist may be asked to harmonize with other singers with whom he or she has never sung. The individual may also be asked to improvise. The singer who can pick up on what the producers want and sound good is the one who will be called on again.

The Background Vocalist must be versatile. An individual may have a job in the morning doing the background vocals for a pop tune and another gig that night singing background for an R & B tune. The more flexible the singer is, the more opportunities there are.

The Background Vocalist who works on television commercials or radio jingles performs much the same as when doing a recording. Individuals in this type of work often have more time to rehearse the tunes.

People involved in singing background vocals may work long, irregular hours on some days and not at all on others. As a matter of fact, Background Vocalists who rely only on recording dates might not work for weeks or months at a time.

Jobs are often obtained through contractors or producers in the recording field. The Background Vocalist needs many contracts to become successful.

The Background Vocalist working in a group or chorus finds work either through an agent or by auditioning.

Salaries

Salaries of Background Vocalists depend on a number of variables. These include how much the singer works, what type of work he or she performs, geographical location of the singer, and general success. Base salaries of union members are set by the various unions. Background Vocalists who work as singers with bands may not belong to a union.

Background Vocalists working in recording studios are paid according to how long the finished product will be, what day and time the individual works, how long the Vocalist is in the studio, etc. Rates are also based on the number of Vocalists singing on the recording. The Background Vocalist will earn additional monies for overtime, other songs, etc. If the completed song is more than $3\frac{1}{2}$ minutes, the individual is paid extra.

It is impossible to estimate the earnings of a Background Vocalist because of the variables involved. Those who are successful may earn up to $100,000 plus in the studio.

Employment Prospects

Employment prospects are fair for a Background Vocalist working as a singer within a band. Employment opportunities become more difficult for Vocalists seeking work with very well-known acts or in recordings or jingles.

Generally, Background Vocalists must audition for a position in a major act. Competition is keen. Some Background Vocalists audition for agents who find them jobs.

Locating jobs as Background Vocalists for recordings or jingles is much more difficult. One must develop a reputation in order to get a foot in the door.

Advancement Prospects

Advancement is difficult for a Background Vocalist. One of the problems is that the individual rarely possesses the qualities needed to be a soloist. Another possible reason for poor career advancement is the lack of jobs for soloists. Many Background Vocalists aspire to become major recording artists in their own right. This is possible, but the odds are against it.

For those who get their foot in the door as Background Vocalists for recording sessions or jingles, however, there are better advancement prospects. Many of these individuals are offered more work than they can handle. Many a jingle singer has achieved financial security.

Education and Training

There is a school of thought that says that individuals who aspire to be musicians or singers should be educated in a field other than music in order to have something to fall back on. This is up to the individual.

There is no formal education needed to become a singer. Some singers have a broad background in music and others do not. Many Background Vocalists have graduated from conservatories. Still others go to vocal coaches or other private teachers. Many singers are self-taught.

Experience, Skills, and Personality Traits

A Background Vocalist needs a good voice and the ability to sing. This is not as silly as it sounds, for many great singers do not possess the confidence to sing well in front of others.

Other qualifications for a good Background Vocalist include the ability to harmonize, possession of a good vocal range, and the ability to sing all styles of music. This permits the Background Vocalist to obtain more jobs.

Although it is not always necessary, it is helpful for a Background Vocalist to be able to sight-read. Many recording jobs specify this.

Additionally, the person in this position must be reliable, show up on time for jobs, and have the perseverance necessary to make a living in this type of job.

Unions and Associations

Background Vocalists may belong to a number of different unions, depending on where they are working. If the Singer is doing a recording session or a radio jingle, he or she may belong to the American Federation of Television and Radio Artists (AFTRA). Individuals singing in theatrical jobs will belong to the American Guild of Musical Artists (AGMA) or the Actors Equity Association, commonly referred to as Equity (AEA). The singer who works on a television commercial may belong to either the Screen Actors Guild (SAG) or AFTRA. Individuals may belong to more than one union.

Tips for Entry

1. Background Vocalists often advertise their specialty in the trades or in the classified sections of newspapers.
2. Read the trades on a regular basis. See what is happening and where there are possible openings.
3. Local groups may advertise for a Background Vocalist in the newspaper's classified section.
4. The various union offices are full of information on openings. You might have to hang around there or become friendly with the people who run the office.

5. Visit different recording studios. Get to know people who book studio time, producers, engineers, etc. These people can help you find work. Make sure you tell them what you do and leave a phone number.

6. The telephone is your lifeline, especially if you are looking for freelance recording dates. Make sure someone answers your phone at all times. If this isn't possible, use voice mail, an answering service or answering machine. Don't keep the line busy with unnecessary talking if you don't have call waiting. If your number is busy, important people may call someone else for a job.

7. Sing at every possible opportunity. Get your name (and your voice) around.

SONGWRITER

CAREER PROFILE

Duties: Write lyrics, music, or both

Alternate Title(s): Composer; Lyricist; Writer

Salary Range: $0 to $1,000,000+

Employment Prospects: Fair

Advancement Prospects: Poor

Best Geographical Location(s) for Position: Any location is suitable for writing songs; staff positions are usually located in New York, Los Angeles, and Nashville

Prerequisites:

Education or Training—No formal education required; songwriter workshops, seminars, and books are helpful; music training may be useful

Experience—Writing music, lyrics, poetry, etc.

Special Skills and Personality Traits—Creativity; musical talent; knowledge of music business helpful; good work habits; persistence; perseverance; cognizance of music theory

CAREER LADDER

```
┌─────────────────────────────┐
│   Successful Songwriter      │
└─────────────────────────────┘

┌─────────────────────────────┐
│        Songwriter            │
└─────────────────────────────┘

┌─────────────────────────────┐
│    Aspiring Songwriter       │
└─────────────────────────────┘
```

Position Description

A Songwriter writes songs. He or she may write the lyrics, the melody, or both. Songwriters who work with others are called collaborators.

Songwriters work in many different ways. Some people sit down at the same time every day and try to create music and/or lyrics. Others wait until they are inspired by an idea, a person, a thought, an occasion, a feeling, etc. Some may write the music first, then try to create or find the perfect lyrics. Others develop lyrics and then try to find the perfect tune.

Songwriters may also be called composers, writers, or lyricists. Once the individual has finished a song, either alone or with another person, he or she must find a way to market it. The main goal of most professional Songwriters is to write a song that is not only recorded, but also turns into a number one hit or a standard.

Before the Songwriter does anything, he or she should make sure that the song is protected. This can be done in a number of ways. The individual can copyright the song. Another method of protection is to put the finished music and words into an envelope, address it, and send it to him- or herself via certified registered mail. Once the person receives the song back from the post office, he or she should put it away without opening it. The official postmark is a type of protection. Some individuals feel that if they are dealing with reputable music publishers these procedures are not necessary. However, it is better to be safe than sorry. Many industry professionals feel that the only real protection is to copyright.

The Songwriter must find a music publisher or recording act to work with the song. The person should use any contacts he or she has to get the song listened to. As many publishers, recording acts, producers, A & R people, managers, etc., as possible should be contacted. If the Songwriter does not know such people, he or she must make calls, knock on doors, and write letters.

In order for the song to be listened to, the Songwriter must make up a demo record or cassette. These demos should accurately showcase the song. There is no need to make a very elaborate demo, although it should be as professional as possible. After a demo master is made, copies must be made to send to the important listeners. If the

Songwriter makes his or her own demo, the individual should be sure that the tapes are clean and of good quality. Each tape should be labeled with the Songwriter's name, address, phone number, and the names and times of each song included on the demo. Incidentally, if there is more than one song on a tape, the person should note where each song ends and the next begins. There shouldn't be more than three or four songs on a tape.

It is always better to send a query letter prior to sending a demo. Many music publishers and A & R people don't accept unsolicited material. When the Songwriter does send tapes, they should always be sent first class.

The Songwriter may get lucky and have one of his or her songs accepted by a music publisher, recording group, A & R person, etc. Depending on the deal made, the Songwriter may sell the song outright or just sell the rights to it. At this point, the individual should seek the advice of an attorney to go over any details, contracts, etc.

Although the Songwriter receives credit on a record, he or she does not often receive a lot of attention for writing a song.

The individual may work long hours trying to create something unique. The Songwriter may develop a block. Some people write one hit song and are never heard from again. Others have a long stream of hits and standards. There are also many people who write good songs but are never discovered.

Salaries

Earnings of Songwriters depend on a number of factors. These include the number of songs published and/or sold, the number of times each song is played, used, etc., the general popularity of the tune, and the type of agreement made for each song. For example, songs may be sold outright, pay writer's royalties, and/or pay publisher's royalties.

Songwriters may write the tune, the lyrics, or both. If individuals collaborate on songs, monies must be shared. The split will differ depending on the individuals and the tunes.

Songwriters may write songs for years and never sell or publish them. On the other hand, one of these individuals might wake up one day, write a song, have a recording act record it, and have it turn into a monster hit. Financial success can occur at any time in this profession. Once a song is published, a Songwriter may receive royalties from it for the rest of his or her life.

Successful Songwriters can earn $500,000 plus yearly. Very successful individuals may earn over a million dollars each year.

Employment Prospects

Almost anyone can write a song. Selling it or publishing it is a different matter. Songwriters may write songs for performers to sing in concert or on records. They may write radio or television jingles or music for plays, films, or TV.

The exciting thing about being a Songwriter is that an individual can write a song that will turn into a hit at any time.

In this profession, a person can work full- or part-time. He or she might be a musician who prefers to write his or her own tunes.

Songwriters usually work for themselves or work with a collaborator. There are numerous opportunities for an individual to be employed by a record company, producer, recording group, etc., as a staff Songwriter. Competition for these jobs is tough.

Advancement Prospects

The way a Songwriter advances is by writing songs that turn into hits. As noted before, this can happen at any time in a Songwriter's career.

Education and Training

There is no formal education needed to be a Songwriter. Depending on whether one writes lyrics, music, or both, he or she might study music theory, harmony, orchestration, and/or ear training. The individual may have studied one or more instruments through private lessons or be self-taught.

The Songwriter might take courses in lyric writing. Again, this is not a requirement.

There are many Songwriter workshops, seminars, and books that may be helpful and provide inspiration.

Experience, Skills, and Personality Traits

Songwriters need to be talented, creative people. A knowledge of the music business is helpful in marketing, selling, or publishing the song. The ability to play one or more instruments and/or musical talent is helpful, although not necessary for every Songwriter.

As most Songwriters work on their own, good work habits are useful in getting things accomplished. Persistence is a must in writing new songs and selling and/or publishing them.

Luck and being in the right place at the right time are important factors.

Unions and Associations

Songwriters may belong to a variety of organizations, including the American Society of Composers, Authors, and Publishers (ASCAP), Broadcast Music, Inc. (BMI), and/or SESAC. These performing rights organizations pay Songwriters royalties for public performances of their song.

An individual might be a member of the Songwriters Guild of America (SGA). This association represents composers and lyricists. The Songwriter may be a member of the Nashville Songwriters Association International, the Country Music Association (CMA), or the Gospel Music Association (GMA). Songwriters might additionally be members of the National Academy of Recording Arts and Sciences (NARAS).

Tips for Entry

1. Write as much as you can. Practice does not always make perfect, but it helps develop the craft.
2. Try to find some songwriting workshops. These not only give helpful advice and tips, but also provide inspiration.
3. Protect your songs. Either copyright them or send them to yourself by registered, certified mail. Copyrighting is best.
4. Do not get involved with any individual who wants you to pay to publish your songs. Publishers are supposed to pay *you* for the songs.
5. Learn as much as possible about every aspect of the music business. It will help you sell, publish, and market your songs more effectively.
6. Try to get your songs listened to by as many people as possible. You might consider letting local club acts, disc jockeys, and music directors hear your tunes. Get their opinions and advice on how to better your work.
7. Have persistence and perseverance.

CHURCH MUSIC

CHOIR DIRECTOR

CAREER PROFILE

Duties: Recruit and direct choirs; develop and maintain music budget; plan music programs

Alternate Title(s): Music Director; Minister of Music; Administrator of Music Program; Church Musician

Salary Range: $21,000 to $85,000+

Employment Prospects: Good

Advancement Prospects: Fair

Best Geographical Location(s) for Position: Cities with a number of large churches tend to have more positions available

Prerequisites:

Education or Training—Bachelor's degree in church music usually required; master's degree in church music preferred

Experience—Experience working in church music situations helpful

Special Skills and Personality Traits—Ability to work well within the congregational hierarchy and politics; knowledge of choral techniques; familiarity with liturgical practice

CAREER LADDER

```
┌─────────────────────────────────────┐
│   Choir Director of Large Church     │
└─────────────────────────────────────┘

┌─────────────────────────────────────┐
│          Choir Director              │
└─────────────────────────────────────┘

┌─────────────────────────────────────┐
│            Organist                  │
└─────────────────────────────────────┘
```

Position Description

The Choir Director's prime responsibility is to prepare the church's choir for services. In some jobs, the Choir Director may be the only paid person involved in the music department of the church. In this situation, the Choir Director might not be only in charge of the choir, but might also be the organist accompanying the group during services.

In other positions, the Choir Director acts as the music director, supervising others in the music department of the church and coordinating their efforts.

As a Choir Director, an individual must conduct and lead the choir. This may include auditioning members of the congregation who would like to sing in the choir as well as soliciting potential members who would be assets to the group. The director also auditions singers to act as section leaders, assistant conductors, or soloists.

The Choir Director sets times each week for rehearsals. He or she is responsible for leading and supervising rehearsals so that time is spent most effectively.

Another duty of the director is to choose the music that will be used during services, making sure that it is appropriate to the sermon, holiday, or special occasion. As Director, the individual will be in charge of the church's music library and might recruit a volunteer to act as music librarian. The Choir Director must often recruit volunteers to care for vestments and help with music programs as well.

Special programs, concerts, and other musical activities are the responsibility of the Choir Director. He or she must plan them, orchestrate them, and rehearse them.

The Director works closely with all the members of the music department of the church as well as with the minister of the congregation. If any of them have a particular musical need, they will go to the Director. The Choir Director is, in essence, the music resource person for the church.

The Music or Choir Director must work out a budget for the music program. This budget is presented to the appropriate members of the congregation for approval. It then becomes the responsibility of the Choir Director to stay within the budget. The budget might include items such as robes for the choir, music for the group, trips for special concerts, staging for plays, etc. The Director analyzes the needs and sets budget priorities.

Certain churches have more than one choir. For example, the church may have a regular choir and a children's choir. The Director must provide leadership for both. At times, the Choir Director will be asked to have extra concerts or lead the choir at special events, weddings, funerals, etc. The Director may also be required to coordinate additional music-oriented activities in the church and community.

In addition to his or her music responsibilities, the Choir Director is usually expected to maintain office hours each week to discuss problems, work with small groups of singers, help the organist, write music, and handle administrative chores. The Music or Choir Director may be expected to attend a variety of workshops, conferences, and seminars each year.

The Choir Director is responsible to a church committee or to the minister of the church. Whatever the case, the Choir Director works very closely with the minister and the congregation to help fulfill their musical requirements.

Salaries

Salaries of church musicians vary depending on their experience, the type of position held, and the size, location, and budget of the church. Salaries for full-time Choir Directors begin at around $21,000 yearly. Salaries go up to $85,000 or more per year, and may be slightly higher at very large metropolitan churches.

Employment Prospects

Employment prospects for church musicians are good. The Choir Director must have sound training to get into any major position. A bachelor's degree in church music helps land a job; a master's or doctorate in church music makes a person even more employable in this field.

While educational qualifications are helpful, an applicant must also demonstrate an enthusiastic, positive attitude to pass the interview process many church committees require.

Advancement Prospects

Depending on the job a Choir Director holds, he or she has a fair chance of advancement. Small churches do not usually have large music departments. An individual who holds a position in such a church has limited upward mobility in that institution.

In larger metropolitan churches, however, the Choir Director may have a lot of money to put into a music program. The Director can build up the music department of the church and may gain some recognition for doing so. He

or she may then move on to a position in an even larger and more prestigious church.

This is not to say that a church musician cannot do well in a smaller church. He or she may institute and supervise a number of music programs, choirs, etc., for the church and be quite happy doing so.

Education

Education requirements for the position of Choir Director differ from church to church. Most churches, however, require at least a bachelor's degree in music with a major in church music. Some churches are now requiring that a Choir Director hold a master's degree.

Experience, Skills, and Personality Traits

Church musicians, as a rule, work in churches in one capacity or another throughout most of their lives. The aspiring Choir Director was probably a member of the choir at his or her own church.

It is important that the Choir or Music Director have the ability to work well within the politics of the congregational hierarchy. From the time the person is interviewed, and throughout his or her tenure the Choir Director will be working closely with these people.

The Choir Director must be familiar with liturgical practice. A knowledge of choral techniques and an ability to teach and/or lead is essential. Additionally, most church musicians know how to play the organ, piano, and/or guitar.

Unions and Associations

Among the helpful and useful groups a Choir Director may belong to are the AGO (The American Guild of Organists), the Choristers Guild, the American Choral Directors Association, the National Association of Pastoral Musicians, the Association of Anglican Musicians, and various other denominational groups.

Tips for Entry

1. Schools of religious music have placement centers at which graduates may register. Churches in need of musical personnel usually advise these placement agencies about openings and opportunities.
2. Your church's Music/Choir Director may know of openings in other churches. Ask around.
3. In certain positions, auditions are necessary (especially if organ playing is part of the job). Check the requirements before an interview so that you can prepare properly.
4. Positions are often advertised in the classified section of the newspaper. Look under heading such as "Choir Director," "Music Director," "Minister of Music," and "Church Musician."

CANTOR

CAREER PROFILE

Duties: Lead prayers in synagogue or temple; teach music; pastoral duties

Alternate Title(s): Hazzan; Reverend

Salary Range: $25,000 to $75,000

Employment Prospects: Excellent

Advancement Prospects: Good

Best Geographical Location(s) for Position: Any area that has synagogues and temples

Prerequisites:

Education or Training—College degree required; music major preferred; degree from a Cantorial college

Experience—Taking part in synagogue functions; participation in Jewish youth groups; involvement with junior congregational services

Special Skills and Personality Traits—Knowledge of Hebrew and all Hebraic disciplines; broad musical knowledge; possession of cultured voice; ability to get along with people

CAREER LADDER

```
┌─────────────────────────────────────┐
│  Cantor of Large Synagogue or Temple │
└─────────────────────────────────────┘

┌─────────────────────────────────────┐
│               Cantor                 │
└─────────────────────────────────────┘

┌─────────────────────────────────────┐
│          Cantorial Student           │
└─────────────────────────────────────┘
```

Position Description

The Cantor of a temple or synagogue has a very important position. The prime responsibility of the individual is to present liturgical music that will help clarify the prayers and studies of the religion. The objective is to enrich the religious experience of the worshippers.

As the Cantor of a temple or synagogue, the individual leads the congregation in prayer during services. The Cantor's cultured and melodic voice can usually be heard clearly above everyone else's.

The Cantor may teach music in the religious school of the synagogue. If the temple has a choir, the Cantor will lead them, supervise their rehearsals, etc. The Cantor is responsible for preparing the choir for all services. Special attention is given to the Jewish High Holy Days services. Any musical activity that occurs in the synagogue becomes the Cantor's responsibility.

In the Cantorial position, the individual may teach various courses in the synagogue's adult education classes. One of the main teaching responsibilities is that of preparing

youngsters to sing or chant their Bar or Bat Mitzvah services. This responsibility is often shared with other members of the synagogue, depending on how many young people must be trained at any one time.

The Cantor is, in essence, a minister of his or her faith. Although the job is structured in part by the Cantor's duties at all Sabbath worship services, it is unstructured in other ways. Many Cantors maintain schedules that give them time for additional study of the Jewish religion and liturgical music.

The Cantor works closely with the rabbi of the congregation. At times, he or she will be involved in pastoral duties, which might include visiting members of the congregation who are sick or comforting members who are in mourning. The individual may officiate at weddings and funerals as well as at regular weekly services and holidays.

Before becoming a Cantor, one usually chooses the branch of Judaism in which he or she will study and officiate. Individuals may select the Reform branch, the Conservative branch, or the Orthodox branch. Training varies slightly in the various Judaic philosophies.

The job is generally a service position in that the Cantor helps and guides people. Cantors in both small and large congregations are, in fact, public figures in the community. On occasion, they will be asked to serve on community boards, as members of associations, and as speakers at functions.

Cantors additionally have the option during their career of becoming concert artists. In this position, Cantors sing liturgical music in a variety of concert settings, ranging from local functions to full-scale concerts at major halls.

Salaries

Cantors' salaries depend on the location and size of the synagogue or temple. Salaries usually range from $25,000 to $75,000 plus yearly. Most Cantors also receive living allowances from the congregation.

Cantors may have an opportunity to earn additional income by performing at concerts.

Employment Prospects

The employment prospects for Cantors are excellent. As of this writing, there is a shortage of qualified individuals to fill cantorial positions.

As a rule, Cantors work with congregations close to their branch of Judaic preference. They may work with either Reform, Conservative, or Orthodox congregations.

Advancement Prospects

As noted above, there is a shortage of trained Cantors. Individuals who have gained experience in the cantorate can move into positions in larger synagogues or temples.

Cantors who have established themselves as great singers may become guest Cantors for special services and/or give concerts of Jewish music. There are a number of Cantors who have attained great prestige in this way.

Education and Training

In order to become a trained Cantor one must obtain a college degree. A degree in music is, of course, preferable. There are a limited number of schools available to prepare the individual for a position as a Cantor. Schools differ in the branch of

Judaism they follow. One may become a Cantor in the Reform, Conservative, or Orthodox branch of the religion.

Study in one of these schools varies in length from three to five years. As a graduate of a Cantorial college, an individual will receive a diploma certifying him or her a Cantor or Hazzan.

Incidentally, both secular and religious studies must be completed before graduation.

Experience, Skills, and Personality Traits

An individual aspiring to become a Cantor must possess a cultured voice. They must have a knowledge of Hebrew and all Hebraic disciplines. Cantors need to be adept at reading Torah.

Musical knowledge is a must and the ability to play an instrument is a plus.

Before an individual decides to become a Cantor, he or she generally participates in a variety of synagogue functions, taking part in various Jewish youth groups and junior congregational services.

Unions and Associations

Depending on the branch of Judaism the Cantor is involved with, he or she may belong to different organizations. These include the Jewish Ministers and Cantors' Association of America (JMCA) and the American Conference of Cantors.

Tips for Entry

1. Talk to the Cantor at a synagogue or temple in the branch of Judaism with which you hope to be involved. Ask questions you have about the occupation.
2. The B'nai B'rith Vocational Service has trained people to counsel you in a career as a Cantor.
3. If you require financial aid for your education in this field, there are a number of options. Check out the college of your choice for financial assistance, scholarships, etc. Local community groups and synagogues often offer financial help in this area.
4. There are part-time Cantorial positions available for Cantorial students. Check synagogues, temples, and the school you attend for positions.

ORGANIST

CAREER PROFILE

Duties: Play the organ at religious services

Alternate Title(s): Musician; Church Musician

Salary Range: $18,000 to $30,000+

Employment Prospects: Fair

Advancement Prospects: Fair

Best Geographical Location(s) for Positions: Cities with a large number of religious institutions tend to have more positions available

Prerequisites:

Education or Training—Organ training; educational requirements vary

Experience—Performance experience playing the organ

Special Skills and Personality Traits—Ability as an organ player; knowledge of religious music; ability to read and write music; ability to get along with congregation

CAREER LADDER

```
┌─────────────────────────────────┐
│     Choir or Music Director     │
└─────────────────────────────────┘

┌─────────────────────────────────┐
│            Organist             │
└─────────────────────────────────┘

┌─────────────────────────────────┐
│  Freelance Organist; Student    │
└─────────────────────────────────┘
```

Position Description

An Organist working for a religious institution provides the music during the services. The Organist may be in charge of choosing the music to accompany prayers or may work closely with the choir or music director in accomplishing this task. In some houses of worship, the individual may act as both the Organist and the choir director.

Depending on the size and the budget of the hiring institution, the job may be either full time or part time. In a small, rural church, for instance, the Organist may work only on Sunday. In a larger metropolitan church, the Organist might be responsible not only for Sunday service music, but also for accompanying choirs, rehearsals, or playing for church services for TV or radio broadcasts.

The Organist may also be required to play for special services, including weddings and funerals. If the individual is working on a part-time basis, he or she is usually paid for the extra workload.

In this position, a person may teach other students the instrument as a way of earning additional income. The Organist is usually allowed to use the organ and the space at no charge. Occasionally, the Organist will find musically talented youngsters in the congregation. It is up to him or her to encourage the students and possibly have them participate in services.

The Organist may be responsible for giving recitals. These are mainly presented as part of the institution's music program. However, it is not unusual to find Organists performing in a setting totally apart from their job.

In a full-time position, the Organist is expected to supervise the maintenance of the organ and make sure that it is always in proper working order.

As a member of the house of worship's music committee, the Organist might advise the congregation on music-related matters. He or she usually has regular office hours or at least time in which practice and rehearsal take place.

The Organist working for a house of worship may play in a church, synagogue, or temple. The individual need not be of the same religious belief as the congregation for which he or she is providing music. The Organist is responsible to the institution's music or choir director, the music committee, or directly to the minister, priest, or rabbi.

Salaries

Salaries of Organists in religious institutions vary. Some jobs are part time, some are full time. Part-time positions are usually paid by the service. Fees range from $15 to $250 per service.

Depending on duties, location of the church or temple, size of the institution, budget, etc., Organists working full-time may make between $18,000 and $30,000 or more yearly.

Employment Prospects

There are quite a few opportunities to work as an Organist in a church, temple, or synagogue. Many of these positions are only part time. (A number of churches, temples, and synagogues have Organists within the congregation who donate their services.)

Full-time positions are available in larger metropolitan areas. The more education and experience an individual has, the better opportunity he or she will have to obtain a full-time position.

Advancement Prospects

Advancement for an Organist is possible. In this position, an individual may be promoted in a number of directions. For example, the Organist may go from a part-time to a full-time position. The individual may find a position at a larger institution that pays a higher salary. An Organist might advance to the position of Organist/choir director or to that of music director.

Education and Training

Educational requirements for Organists vary according to the position. In a small town church or temple, often all that is required is the ability to play the organ well.

Conversely, Organists who are hired to work in large metropolitan houses of worship in full-time positions may be required to hold not only a bachelor's degree, but possibly a master's degree. If the Organist's position is one which also encompasses the duties of a musical or choir director, a degree will generally be required.

In lieu of college education (although training is most certainly needed), Organists may apply for an Associates Certificate. This is given by the American Guild of Organists. The organization gives a series of tests and certifies church musicians at various levels.

Experience, Skills, and Personality Traits

The Organist must be accomplished on the instrument. He or she must be able to read and write music. A knowledge of religious music is a must.

The Organist may need to know how to maintain the organ or at least be able to supervise service on it.

Organists must get along well with the congregation and be reliable.

Unions and Associations

Organists may belong to the American Federation of Musicians (AFM) if they play outside the church, synagogue, or temple. They may also belong to a number of organizations, including the AGO (the American Guild of Organists), the Choristers Guild, the American Choral Directors Association, or a host of denominational groups.

Tips for Entry

1. There are often ads in the classified sections of newspapers from religious institutions looking for organists. Most of these jobs are part time.
2. The American Guild of Organists has a placement service for church Organists. Churches let the organization know of any openings they have.
3. The music director or choir director of any institution usually knows about job openings or opportunities in other institutions. Speak to these individuals.

APPENDIXES

APPENDIX I
DEGREE AND NONDEGREE PROGRAMS

A. FOUR-YEAR COLLEGES AND UNIVERSITIES THAT OFFER
MAJORS RELATED TO THE MUSIC INDUSTRY

Although possession of a college degree does not guarantee a job in the music industry, many feel that it is in their best interest to pursue an education after high school. This gives people the opportunity to learn additional information, gain new skills, and make important contacts. Because the music industry is so competitive, a higher education may give one person an edge over another who does not continue his or her schooling.

The following is a listing of four-year schools granting degrees relating to the music industry. They are grouped by state. The author does not endorse any one school over another. Use this list as a beginning. Check the newest copy of *Lovejoy's* (found in the reference section of libraries, in guidance counseling centers, and in bookstores) for additional schools.

ALABAMA

University of North Alabama
UNA–Box 5121
Florence, AL 35632-0001
Phone: (256) 765-4100
http://www.una.edu

ARKANSAS

University of the Ozarks
415 College Avenue
Clarksville, AR 72830
Phone: (479) 979-1000
http://www.ozarks.edu

ARIZONA

Northern Arizona University
Box 4084
Flagstaff, AZ 86011
Phone: (888) MORE-NAU (toll-free)
E-mail: undergraduate.admissions@
   nau.edu
http://www.nau.edu

CALIFORNIA

Christian Heritage College
2100 Greenfield Drive
El Cajon, CA 92019-1157
Phone: (619) 441-2200
http://www.christianheritage.edu

Point Loma Nazarene College
3900 Lomaland Drive
San Diego, CA 92106-2899
Phone: (619) 849-2200

E-mail: admissions@ptloma.edu
http://www.ptloma.edu

University of the Pacific
Stockton, CA 95211
Phone: (209) 946-2211
E-mail: admissions@uop.edu
http://www.pacific.edu

COLORADO

University of Denver
2199 South University Boulevard
Denver, CO 80208-0132
Phone: (303) 871-2000
http://www.du.edu

CONNECTICUT

University of Hartford
200 Bloomfield Avenue
West Hartford, CT 06117-1599
Phone: (860) 768-4296
http://www.hartford.edu

University of New Haven
300 Orange Avenue
West Haven, CT 06516
Phone: (203) 932-7000
http://www.newhaven.edu

FLORIDA

Florida Southern College
111 Lake Hollingsworth Drive
Lakeland, FL 33801-5698
Phone: (863) 680-4111

E-mail: fscadm@flsouthern.edu
http://www.flsouthern.edu

Jacksonville University
2800 University Boulevard North
Jacksonville, FL 32211
Phone: (904) 744-3950
E-mail: admission@ju.edu
http://www.ju.edu

University of Miami–Coral Gables
P.O. Box 248025
Coral Gables, FL 33124-4616
Phone: (305) 284-2211
E-mail: admissions@miami.edu
http://www.miami.edu

GEORGIA

Berry College
2277 Martha Berry Highway, NW
Mount Berry, GA 30149-0159
Phone: (706) 232-5374
http://www.berry.edu

Georgia State University
University Plaza
Atlanta, GA 30302-4009
Phone: (404) 651-2000
http://www.gsu.edu

Shorter College
315 Shorter Avenue
Rome, GA 30165
Phone: (706) 291-2121
E-mail: admissions@shorter.edu
http://www.shorter.edu

IDAHO

Boise State University
1910 University Drive
Boise, ID 83725
Phone: (208) 426-1101
E-mail: bsuinfo@boisestate.edu
http://www.boisestate.edu

ILLINOIS

Columbia College
600 South Michigan Avenue
Chicago, IL 60605-1996
Phone: (312) 663-1600
http://www.colum.edu

Elmhurst College
190 Prospect Avenue
Elmhurst, IL 60126-3296
Phone: (630) 617-3500
http://www.elmhurst.edu

Illinois Wesleyan University
1312 North Park
Bloomington, IL 61702-2900
Phone: (309) 556-1000
http://www.iwu.edu

Lewis University
One University Parkway
Romeoville, IL 60446-2200
Phone: (815) 838-0500
http://www.lewisu.edu

Millikin University
1184 West Main Street
Decatur, IL 62522-2084
Phone: (217) 424-6211
E-mail: admis@mail.millikin.edu
http://www.millikin.edu

North Park College
3225 West Foster Avenue
Chicago, IL 60625-4895
Phone: (773) 244-6200
http://www.northpark.edu

Roosevelt University
430 South Michigan Avenue
Chicago, IL 60605-1394
Phone: (312) 341-3500
http://www.roosevelt.edu

**Southern Illinois
    University–Carbondale**
Carbondale, IL 62901-4701
Phone: (618) 453-2121
http://www.siuc.edu

**Southern Illinois
    University–Edwardsville**
Edwardsville, IL 62026-1600
Phone: (618) 650-2000
http://www.siue.edu

Wheaton College
501 College Avenue
Wheaton, IL 60187-5593
Phone: (630) 752-5000
http://www.wheaton.edu

INDIANA

Anderson University
1100 East Fifth
Anderson, IN 46012
Phone: (765) 649-9071
E-mail: info@anderson.edu
http://www.anderson.edu

Butler University
4600 Sunset Avenue
Indianapolis, IN 46208
Phone: (317) 940-8000
E-mail: admission@butler.edu
http://www.butler.edu

DePauw University
313 South Locust Street
Greencastle, IN 46135-1611
Phone: (765) 658-4800
E-mail: admission@depauw.edu
http://www.depauw.edu

Indiana State University
210 North Seventh Street
Terre Haute, IN 47809
Phone: (812) 237-6311
http://web.indstate.edu

Indiana University–Bloomington
107 South Indiana Avenue
Bloomington, IN 47405-7000
Phone: (812) 855-4848
http://www.iub.edu

University of Evansville
1800 Lincoln Avenue
Evansville, IN 47722
Phone: (812) 479-2000
http://www.evansville.edu

Valparaiso University
651 South College Avenue
Valparaiso, IN 46383-6493
Phone: (219) 464-5000
http://www.valpo.edu

IOWA

Drake University
2507 University Avenue
Des Moines, IA 50311-4505
Phone: (515) 271-2011
http://www.drake.edu

Luther College
700 College Drive
Decorah, IA 52101-1042
Phone: (563) 387-2000
http://www.luther.edu

KANSAS

Benedictine College
1020 North Second Street
Atchison, KS 66002-1499
Phone: (913) 367-5340
http://www.benedictine.edu

Friends University
2100 University
Wichita, KS 67213
Phone: (316) 295-5000
http://www.friends.edu

Sterling College
Box 98
Sterling, KS 67579-0098
Phone: (620) 278-2173
http://www.sterling.edu

KENTUCKY

Union College
310 College Street
Barbourville, KY 40906
Phone: (606) 546-4151
http://www.unionky.edu

LOUISIANA

Loyola University–New Orleans
6363 St. Charles Avenue
New Orleans, LA 70118-6195
Phone: (504) 865-2011
http://www.loyno.edu

MARYLAND

Columbia Union College
7600 Flower Avenue
Takoma Park, MD 20912
Phone: (301) 891-4000
http://www.cuc.edu

MASSACHUSETTS

Northeastern University
360 Huntington Avenue
Boston, MA 02115-9959
Phone: (617) 373-2000
http://www.northeastern.edu

Quincy College
34 Coddington Street
Quincy, MA 02169
Phone: (617) 984-1700
http://www.quincycollege.com

University of Massachusetts–Lowell
One University Avenue
Lowell, MA 01854-5104
Phone: (978) 934-4000
http://www.uml.edu

Westfield State College
577 Western Avenue
Westfield, MA 01086-1630
Phone: (413) 572-5300
http://www.wsc.ma.edu

MICHIGAN

Adrian College
110 South Madison Street
Adrian, MI 49221-2575
Phone: (517) 265-5161
http://www.adrian.edu

Madonna College
36600 Schoolcraft Road
Livonia, MI 48150
Phone: (734) 432-5300
http://www.madonna.edu

Wayne State University
656 West Kirby Street
Detroit, MI 48202
Phone: (313) 577-2424
http://www.wayne.edu

MINNESOTA

College of St. Catherine
2004 Randolph Avenue
St. Paul, MN 55105
Phone: (651) 690-6000
http://www.stkate.edu

Mankato State University
122 Taylor Center
Mankato, MN 56001
Phone: (507) 389-1822
http://www.mnsu.edu

Winona State University
Winona, MN 55987
Phone: (507) 457-5000
http://www.winona.edu

MISSISSIPPI

Mississippi University for Women
P.O. Box W-160
Columbus, MS 39701
Phone: (662) 329-4750
http://www.muw.edu

MISSOURI

Fontbonne College
6800 Wydown Boulevard
St. Louis, MO 63105
Phone: (314) 862-3456
http://www.fontbonne.edu

Missouri Western State College
4525 Downs Drive
St. Joseph, MO 64507
Phone: (816) 271-4200
http://www.mwsc.edu

Northwest Missouri State University
800 University Drive
Maryville, MO 64468-6001
Phone: (660) 562-1212
http://www.nwmissouri.edu

University of Missouri–St. Louis
8001 Natural Bridge Road
St. Louis, MO 63121-4499
Phone: (314) 516-5000
http://www.umsl.edu

Webster University
470 East Lockwood Avenue
St. Louis, MO 63119
Phone: (314) 968-6900
http://www.websteruniv.edu

NEBRASKA

Peru State College
P.O. Box 10
Peru, NE 68421-0010
Phone: (402) 872-3815
http://www.peru.edu

NEW JERSEY

Monmouth University
West Long Branch, NJ 07764-189
Phone: (732) 571-3400
http://www.monmouth.edu

William Paterson College
300 Pompton Road
Wayne, NJ 07470
Phone: (973) 720-2000
http://www.wpunj.edu

NEW YORK

Conservatory of Music
CUNY–Brooklyn College
2900 Bedford Avenue
Brooklyn, NY 11210
Phone: (718) 951-5286
E-mail: nhager@brooklyn.cuny.edu
http://depthome.brooklyn.cuny.edu/music

Five Towns College
305 North Service Road
Dix Hills, NY 11746-6055
Phone: (631) 424-7000
http://www.fivetowns.edu

Hofstra University
Hempstead, NY 11549
Phone: (516) 463-6600
E-mail: admissions@hofstra.edu
http://www.hofstra.edu

Manhattanville College
2900 Purchase Street
Purchase, NY 10577
Phone: (914) 694-2200
http://www.manhattanville.edu

New York University
New York, NY 10011-9108
Phone: (212) 998-1212
http://www.nyu.edu

SUNY–College at Fredonia
138 Central Avenue
Fredonia, NY 14063-1136
Phone: (716) 673-3111
http://www.fredonia.edu

SUNY–College at Potsdam
44 Pierrepont Avenue
Potsdam, NY 13676
Phone: (315) 267-2000
http://www.potsdam.edu

Syracuse University
201 Tolley Administration Building
Syracuse, NY 13244-1100
Phone: (315) 443-1870
http://www.syr.edu

NORTH CAROLINA

Appalachian State University
Boone, NC 28608
Phone: (828) 262-2000
http://www.appstate.edu

Catawba College
2300 West Innes Street
Salisbury, NC 28144
Phone: (704) 637-4111
http://www.catawba.edu

Elizabeth City State University
1704 Weeksville Road
Elizabeth City, NC 27909
Phone: (252) 335-3400
http://www.ecsu.edu

Johnson C. Smith University
100 Beatties Ford Road
Charlotte, NC 28216-5398
Phone: (704) 378-1000
http://www.jcsu.edu

Methodist College
5400 Ramsey Street
Fayetteville, NC 28311-1420
Phone: (800) 488-7110
http://www.methodist.edu

Wingate College
P.O. Box 159
Wingate, NC 28174-0157
Phone: (704) 233-8000
http://www.wingate.edu

OHIO

Baldwin-Wallace College
275 Eastland Road
Berea, OH 44017-2088
Phone: (440) 826-2900
http://www.bw.edu

Capital University
2199 East Main Street
Columbus, OH 43209-2394
Phone: (614) 236-6011
http://www.capital.edu

Heidelberg College
310 East Market Street
Tiffin, OH 44883-2462
Phone: (419) 448-2000
http://www.heidelberg.edu

Oberlin College
173 West Lorain Street
Oberlin, OH 44074
Phone: (440) 775-8121
http://www.oberlin.edu

Otterbein College
One Otterbein College
Westerville, OH 43081
Phone: (614) 890-3000
http://www.otterbein.edu

OKLAHOMA

Oklahoma City University
2501 North Blackwelder
Oklahoma City, OK 73106
Phone: (405) 521-5000
http://www.okcu.edu

Southern Nazarene University
6729 Northwest 39th Expressway
Bethany, OK 73008
Phone: (405) 789-6400
http://www.snu.edu

**Southwestern Oklahoma State
University**
100 Campus Drive
Weatherford, OK 73096
Phone: (580) 774-6611
http://www.swosu.edu

PENNSYLVANIA

Clarion University of Pennsylvania
Clarion, PA 16214
Phone: (814) 393-2000
E-mail: admissions@clarion.edu
http://www.clarion.edu

Geneva College
3200 College Avenue
Beaver Falls, PA 15010
Phone: (724) 846-5100
http://www.geneva.edu

Grove City College
100 Campus Drive
Grove City, PA 16127-2104
Phone: (724) 458-2000
E-mail: admissions@gcc.edu
http://www.gcc.edu

Mansfield University of Pennsylvania
Academy Street
Mansfield, PA 16933
Phone: (570) 662-4000
E-mail: admissns@mnsfld.edu
http://www.mnsfld.edu

Millersville University of Pennsylvania
P.O. Box 1002
Millersville, PA 17551-0302
Phone: (717) 872-3011
E-mail: admissions@millersville.edu
http://www.millersville.edu

Susquehanna University
514 University Avenue
Selinsgrove, PA 17870-1040
Phone: (570) 374-0101
http://www.susqu.edu

SOUTH CAROLINA

Coker College
300 East College Avenue
Hartsville, SC 29550
Phone: (843) 383-8000
http://www.coker.edu

South Carolina State University
P.O. Box 1020
Central, SC 29630-1020
Phone: (864) 644-5000
http://www.swu.edu

SOUTH DAKOTA

South Dakota State University
P.O. Box 2201
Brookings, SD 57007-0649
Phone: (800) 952-3541
http://www.sdstate.edu

TENNESSEE

Belmont College
1900 Belmont Boulevard
Nashville, TN 37212-3757
Phone: (615) 460-6000
http://www.belmont.edu

Bryan College
P.O. Box 7000
Dayton, TN 37321-7000
Phone: (423) 775-2041
http://www.bryan.edu

Middle Tennessee State University
1301 East Main Street
Murfreesboro, TN 37132
Phone: (615) 898-2300
http://www.mtsu.edu

Trevecca Nazarene College
333 Murfreesboro Road
Nashville, TN 37210
Phone: (615) 248-1200
http://www.trevecca.edu

Vanderbilt University
2201 West End Avenue
Nashville, TN 37235
Phone: (615) 322-7311
http://www.vanderbilt.edu

TEXAS

Hardin-Simmons University
P.O. Box 16050
Abilene, TX 79698
Phone: (915) 670-1000
http://www.hsutx.edu

VIRGINIA

Radford University
P.O. Box 6890, RU Station
Radford, VA 24142-6903
Phone: (540) 831-5000
http://www.radford.edu

Shenandoah University
1460 University Drive
Winchester, VA 22601-5195

Phone: (540) 665-4500
E-mail: admit@su.edu
http://www.su.edu

WASHINGTON

Central Washington University
400 East 8th Avenue
Ellensburg, WA 98926-7463
Phone: (509) 963-1111
http://www.cwu.edu

Eastern Washington University
526 Fifth Street
Cheney, WA 99004-2447
Phone: (509) 359-6200
E-mail: admissions@mail.ewu.edu
http://www.ewu.edu

University of Puget Sound
1500 North Warner Street
Tacoma, WA 98416-0003
Phone: (253) 879-3100
http://www.ups.edu

WEST VIRGINIA

Glenville State College
200 High Street
Glenville, WV 26351-1292
Phone: (304) 462-7361
http://www.glenville.edu

University of Charleston
2300 MacCorkle Avenue SE
Charleston, WV 25304
Phone: (304) 357-4800
http://www.ucwv.edu

WISCONSIN

Carroll College
100 North East Avenue
Waukesha, WI 53186-9988
Phone: (262) 547-1211
http://www.cc.edu

B. TWO-YEAR COLLEGES THAT OFFER DEGREES IN MUSIC MANAGEMENT

The following is a list of two-year schools offering degrees in music management. They are grouped by state.

Use this list as a beginning. Check the newest copy of *Lovejoy's* (found in the reference section of libraries, in guidance counseling centers, and in bookstores) for additional schools.

CALIFORNIA

American River College
4700 College Oak Drive
Sacramento, CA 95841
Phone: (916) 484-8011
http://www.arc.losrios.cc.ca.us

Hartnell College
156 Homestead Avenue
Salinas, CA 93901
Phone: (831) 755-6700
http://www.hartnell.cc.ca.us

Los Medanos College
2700 East Leland Road
Pittsburg, CA 94565
Phone: (925) 439-2181
http://www.losmedanos.net

Orange Coast College
2701 Fairview Road
Costa Mesa, CA 92628-5005
Phone: (714) 432-0202
http://www.occ.cccd.edu

FLORIDA

Art Institute of Fort Lauderdale
1799 Southeast 17th Street
Fort Lauderdale, FL 33316
Phone: (954) 463-3000
http://www.artinstitute.edu

GEORGIA

Art Institute of Atlanta
6600 Peachtree Dunwoody Road
Atlanta, GA 30328
Phone: (770) 394-8300
E-mail: aiaadm@aii.edu
http://www.aia.artinstitute.edu

ILLINOIS

Lincoln College
300 Keokuk
Lincoln, IL 62656
Phone: (217) 732-3155
http://www.lincolncollege.com

KANSAS

Independence Community College
P.O. Box 708
Independence, KS 67301
Phone: (620) 331-4100
E-mail: admissions@indycc.net
http://www.indy.cc.ks.us

MASSACHUSETTS

New England Institute of Art and Communications
10 Brookline Place West
Brookline, MA 02445-7295
Phone: (617) 739-1700
http://www.aine.artinstitutes.edu

MINNESOTA

Century Community and Technical College
3300 Century Avenue North
White Bear Lake, MN 55110

Phone: (651) 779-3200
http://www.century.mnscu.edu

NEBRASKA

Northeast Community College
P.O. Box 469
Norfolk, NE 68702-0469
Phone: (402) 371-2020
http://www.northeastcollege.com

NEW YORK

**Schenectady County Community
   College**
78 Washington Avenue
Schenectady, NY 12305
Phone: (518) 381-1200
http://www.sunysccc.edu

Villa Maria College of Buffalo
240 Pine Ridge Road
Buffalo, NY 14225
Phone: (716) 896-0700
E-mail: admissions@villa.edu
http://www.villa.edu

NORTH CAROLINA

Brevard College
400 North Broad Street
Brevard, NC 28712
Phone: (828) 883-8292
E-mail: admissions@brevard.edu
http://www.brevard.edu

PENNSYLVANIA

The Art Institute of Philadelphia
1622 Chestnut Street
Philadelphia, PA 19103-5198
Phone: (215) 567-7080
http://www.aiph.artinstitutes.edu

TEXAS

Art Institute of Dallas
Two North Park
East 8080 Park Lane, Suite 100
Dallas, TX 75231
Phone: (214) 692-8080
http://www.aid.edu

Houston Community College System
P.O. Box 667517
Houston, TX 77266-7517
Phone: (713) 718-2000
http://www.hccs.cc.tx.us

San Jacinto College–Central Campus
P.O. Box 2007
8060 Spencer Highway
Pasadena, TX 77505
Phone: (281) 476-1501
http://www.sjcd.cc.tx.us

San Jacinto College–North Campus
5800 Uvalde Road
Houston, TX 77049
Phone: (281) 458-4050
http://www.sjcd.cc.tx.us

WASHINGTON

Art Institute of Seattle
2323 Elliott Avenue
Seattle, WA 98121
Phone: (206) 448-0900
http://www.ais.edu

C. COLLEGES AND UNIVERSITIES THAT OFFER DEGREES IN ARTS MANAGEMENT AND ADMINISTRATION

The following is a list of four-year schools offering degrees in arts management and administration in music and the performing arts. They are grouped by state.

Check the newest copy of *Lovejoy's* (found in the reference section of libraries, in guidance or counseling centers, and in bookstores) for additional schools.

ALABAMA

Spring Hill College
4000 Dauphin Street
Mobile, AL 36608
Phone: (334) 380-4000
E-mail: admit@shc.edu
http://www.shc.edu

ARIZONA

Northern Arizona University
P.O. Box 4084
Flagstaff, AZ 86011
Phone: (520) 523-9011
E-mail: undergraduate.admissions@
   nau.edu
http://www.nau.edu

ARKANSAS

University of the Ozarks
415 North College Avenue
Clarksville, AR 72830

Phone: (479) 979-1000
E-mail: admiss@ozarks.edu
http://www.ozarks.edu

CALIFORNIA

Point Loma Nazarene University
3900 Lomaland Drive
San Diego, CA 92106
Phone: (619) 849-2200
E-mail: admissions@ptloma.edu
http://www.ptloma.edu

University of the Pacific
Stockton, CA 95211
Phone: (209) 946-2211
E-mail: admissions@uop.edu
http://www.pacific.edu

CONNECTICUT

University of Hartford
200 Bloomfield Avenue
West Hartford, CT 06117

Phone: (860) 768-4296
Fax: (860) 768-4961
E-mail: admission@mail.hartford.edu
http://www.hartford.edu/admission

DELAWARE

Delaware State University
1200 North Dupont Highway
Dover, DE 19901
Phone: (302) 857-6060
E-mail: dadmiss@dsc.edu
http://www.dsc.edu

FLORIDA

Barry University
11300 Northeast Second Avenue
Miami Shores, FL 33161
Phone: (305) 899-3000
E-mail: admissions@mail.barry.edu
http://www.barry.edu

Florida Southern College
111 Lake Hollingsworth Drive
Lakeland, FL 33801-5698
Phone: (863) 680-4111
http://www.flsouthern.edu

Jacksonville University
2800 University Boulevard North
Jacksonville, FL 32211
Phone: (904) 744-3950
E-mail: admissions@ju.edu
http://www.ju.edu

GEORGIA

Georgia College
Milledgeville, GA 31061-0490
Phone: (478) 445-5004
E-mail: gcsu@mail.gcsu.edu
http://www.gcsu.edu

Shorter College
315 Shorter Avenue
Rome, GA 30165
Phone: (706) 291-2121
E-mail: admissions@shorter.edu
http://www.shorter.edu

Brenau University
One Centennial Circle
Gainesville, GA 30501
Phone: (770) 534-6299
E-mail: wcadmissions@lib.brenau.edu
http://www.brenau.edu

IDAHO

Boise State University
1910 University Drive
Boise, ID 83725
Phone: (208) 426-1101
E-mail: bsuinfo@boisestate.edu
http://www.boisestate.edu

ILLINOIS

Columbia College
600 South Michigan Avenue
Chicago, IL 60605-1996
Phone: (312) 344-1600
E-mail: admissions@popmail.colum.edu
http://www.colum.edu

Elmhurst College
190 Prospect Avenue
Elmhurst, IL 60126-3296
Phone: (630) 617-3500
E-mail: admit@elmhurst.edu.
http://www.elmhurst.edu

Lewis University
One University Parkway
Romeoville, IL 60446-2200
Phone: (815) 838-0500
E-mail: admissions@lewisu.edu
http://www.lewisu.edu

Roosevelt University
430 South Michigan Avenue
Chicago, IL 60605
Phone: (312) 341-3500
E-mail: applyRU@roosevelt.edu
http://www.roosevelt.edu

**Southern Illinois
   University–Edwardsville**
Edwardsville, IL 62026-1600
Phone: (618) 650-2000
E-mail: admis@siue.edu
http://www.siue.edu

St. Xavier University
3700 West 103rd Street
Chicago, IL 60655
Phone: (773) 298-3000
E-mail: admissions@sxu.edu
http://www.sxu.edu

Trinity Christian College
6601 West College Drive
Palos Heights, IL 60463
Phone: (708) 597-3000
E-mail: adm@trnty.edu
http://www.trnty.edu

INDIANA

Anderson University
1100 East Fifth
Anderson, IN 46012
Phone: (765) 649-9071
E-mail: info@anderson.edu
http://www.anderson.edu

Butler University
4600 Sunset Avenue
Indianapolis, IN 46208
Phone: (317) 940-8000
E-mail: admission@butler.edu
http://www.butler.edu

DePauw University
313 South Locust Street
Greencastle, IN 46135-1611
Phone: (765) 658-4800
E-mail: admission@depauw.edu
http://www.depauw.edu

University of Evansville
1800 Lincoln Avenue
Evansville, IN 47722
Phone: (812) 479-2000
E-mail: admissions@evansville.edu
http://www.evansville.edu

Valparaiso University
651 South College Avenue
Valparaiso, IN 46383-6493
Phone: (219) 464-5000
E-mail: undergrad.admissions@valpo.edu
http://www.valpo.edu

IOWA

Drake University
2507 University Avenue
Des Moines, IA 50311
Phone: (515) 271-2011
E-mail: admitinfo@acad.drake.edu
http://www.drake.edu

KANSAS

Friends University
2100 West University Street
Wichita, KS 67213
Phone: (316) 295-5000
E-mail: learn@friends.edu
http://www.friends.edu

Sterling College
Box 98
Sterling, KS 67579-0098
Phone: (620) 278-2173
E-mail: admissions@sterling.edu
http://www.sterling.edu

KENTUCKY

Eastern Kentucky University
521 Lancaster Avenue
Richmond, KY 40475
Phone: (859) 622-1000
E-mail: admissions@eku.edu
http://www.eku.edu

Union College
310 College Street
Barbourville, KY 40906
Phone: (606) 546-4151
E-mail: enroll@unionky.edu
http://www.unionky.edu

University of Kentucky
206 Administration Building
Lexington, KY 40506
E-mail: admissio@pop.uky.edu
http://www.uky.edu

LOUISIANA

Southeastern Louisiana University
SLU 10752
Hammond, LA 70402
Phone: (985) 549-2000
E-mail: jmercante@selu.edu
http://www.selu.edu

MARYLAND

Goucher College
1021 Dulaney Valley Road
Baltimore, MD 21204
Phone: (410) 337-6000
E-mail: admissions@goucher.edu
http://www.goucher.edu

MASSACHUSETTS

Anna Maria College
50 Sunset Lane
Paxton, MA 01612
Phone: (508) 849-3300
E-mail: admission@annamaria.edu
http://www.annamaria.edu

Simmons College
300 The Fenway
Boston, MA 02115
E-mail: ugadm@simmons.edu
http://www.simmons.edu

University of Massachusetts–Lowell
One University Avenue
Lowell, MA 01854-5104
Phone: (978) 934-4000
E-mail: admissions@uml.edu
http://www.uml.edu

Westfield State College
577 Western Avenue
Westfield, MA 01086
Phone: (413) 572-5300
E-mail: admission@wsc.ma.edu
http://www.wsc.ma.edu

MICHIGAN

Adrian College
110 South Madison Street
Adrian, MI 49221-2575
Phone: (517) 265-5161
E-mail: admissions@adrian.edu
http://www.adrian.edu

Madonna University
36600 Schoolcraft Road
Livonia, MI 48150

Phone: (800) 852-4951
http://www.munet.edu

Wayne State University
656 West Kirby Street
Detroit, MI 48202
Phone: (313) 577-2424
E-mail: admissions@wayne.edu
http://www.wayne.edu

MISSISSIPPI

William Carey College
498 Tuscan Avenue
Hattiesburg, MS 39401-5499
Phone: (601) 318-5051
E-mail: admissions@wmcarey.edu
http://www.wmcarey.edu

MISSOURI

Fontbonne College
6800 Wydown Boulevard
St. Louis, MO 63105
Phone: (314) 862-3456
E-mail: pmusen@fontbonne.edu
http://www.fontbonne.edu

NEBRASKA

Bellevue University
1000 Galvin Road, South
Bellevue, NE 68005
Phone: (402) 291-8100
E-mail: bellevue_u@scholars.bellevue.
  edu
http://www.bellevue.edu

NEW MEXICO

Eastern New Mexico University
Station Two
Portales, NM 88130
Phone: (505) 562-1011
http://www.enmu.edu

NEW YORK

CUNY–Baruch College
17 Lexington Avenue
New York, NY 10010
Phone: (646) 312-1000
E-mail: admissions@baruch.cuny.edu
http://www.baruch.cuny.edu

CUNY–Brooklyn College
2900 Bedford Avenue
Brooklyn, NY 11210
Phone: (718) 951-5000

E-mail: admissions@brooklyn.cuny.edu
http://www.brooklyn.cuny.edu

Ithaca College
100 Job Hall
Ithaca, NY 14850-7020
Phone: (607) 274-3124
E-mail: admission@ithaca.edu
http://www.ithaca.edu

Manhattanville College
2900 Purchase Street
Purchase, NY 10577
Phone: (914) 694-2200
E-mail: admissions@mville.edu
http://www.manhattanville.edu

Marymount Manhattan College
221 East 71st Street
New York, NY 10021-4597
Phone: (212) 517-0400
E-mail: admissions@mmm.edu
http://marymount.mmm.edu

Russell Sage College
45 Ferry Street
Troy, NY 12180-4115
Phone: (518) 244-2000
E-mail: rscadm@sage.edu
http://www.sage.edu/rsc

SUNY–College at Oneonta
Ravine Parkway
Oneonta, NY 13820-4016
Phone: (607) 436-3500
E-mail: admissions@oneonta.edu
http://www.oneonta.edu

Wagner College
One Campus Road
Staten Island, NY 10301-4495
Phone: (718) 390-3100
E-mail: admissions@wagner.edu
http://www.wagner.edu

NORTH CAROLINA

Bennett College
900 East Washington Street
Greensboro, NC 27401-3239
Phone: (336) 273-4431
http://www.bennett.edu

Catawba College
2300 West Innes Street
Salisbury, NC 28144
Phone: (704) 637-4111
E-mail: admission@catawba.edu
http://www.catawba.edu

Elizabeth City State University
1704 Weeksville Road
Elizabeth City, NC 27909
Phone: (252) 335-3400
E-mail: bngolman@mail.ecsu.edu
http://www.ecsu.edu

Methodist College
5400 Ramsey Street
Fayetteville, NC 28311-1420
Phone: (800) 488-7110
E-mail: admissions@methodist.edu
http://www.methodist.edu

Pfeiffer College
Highway 52
P.O. Box 960
Misenheimer, NC 28109
Phone: (704) 463-1360
E-mail: admiss@pfeiffer.edu
http://www.pfeiffer.edu

Salem College
P.O. Box 10548
Winston-Salem, NC 27108
Phone: (336) 721-2600
E-mail: admissions@salem.edu
http://www.salem.edu

Wilkes College
P.O. Box 120
Wilkesboro, NC 28697-0120
Phone: (336) 838-6100
E-mail: warrenm@wilkes.cc.nc.us
http://www.wilkes.cc.nc.us

Wingate College
P.O. Box 159
Wingate, NC 28174-0157
Phone: (704) 233-8000
E-mail: admit@wingate.edu
http://www.wingate.edu

NORTH DAKOTA

Jamestown College
6086 College Lane
Jamestown, ND 58405
Phone: (701) 252-3467
E-mail: admissions@acc.jc.edu
http://www.jc.edu

OHIO

Baldwin-Wallace College
275 Eastland Road
Berea, OH 44017-2088
Phone: (440) 826-2900
E-mail: admit@bw.edu
http://www.bw.edu

Capital University
2199 E. Main Street
Columbus, OH 43209
Phone: (614) 236-6011
E-mail: admissions@capital.edu
http://www.capital.edu

Heidelberg College
310 East Market Street
Tiffin, OH 44883
Phone: (800) 925-9250
E-mail: admission@heidelberg.edu
http://www.heidelberg.edu

Marietta College
215 Fifth Street
Marietta, OH 45750
Phone: (740) 376-4643
E-mail: admit@marietta.edu
http://www.marietta.edu

Ursuline College
2550 Lander Road
Pepper Pike, OH 44124
Phone: (440) 449-4200
E-mail: joakley@ursuline.edu
http://www.ursuline.edu

OKLAHOMA

Phillips University
P.O. Box 2127
Enid, OK 73702
Phone: (580) 237-4433
E-mail: admin@phillips.edu
http://www.phillips.edu

OREGON

Southern Oregon University
1250 Siskiyou Boulevard
Ashland, OR 97520-5032
Phone: (541) 552-6411
E-mail: ssions@sou.edu
http://www.sou.edu

PENNSYLVANIA

Cabrini College
610 King of Prussia Road
Radnor, PA 19087-3698
Phone: (610) 902-8100
E-mail: admit@cabrini.edu
http://www.cabrini.edu

Geneva College
3200 College Avenue
Beaver Falls, PA 15010
Phone: (724) 846-5100

E-mail: admissions@geneva.edu
http://www.geneva.edu

Mansfield University of Pennsylvania
Alumni Hall
Mansfield, PA 16933
Phone: (570) 662-4000
E-mail: admissns@mnsfld.edu
http://www.mansfield.edu

Mercyhurst College
501 East 38th Street
Erie, PA 16546-0001
Phone: (814) 824-2000
E-mail: admug@mercyhurst.edu
http://www.mercyhurst.edu

Seton Hill University
Seton Hill Drive
Greensburg, PA 15601
Phone: (724) 834-2200
E-mail: admit@setonhill.edu
http://www.setonhill.edu

Saint Vincent College
300 Fraser Purchase Road
Latrobe, PA 15650-2690
Phone: (724) 539-9761
E-mail: admission@stvincent.edu
http://www.stvincent.edu

SOUTH CAROLINA

Newberry College
2100 College Street
Newberry, SC 29108
Phone: (800) 845-4955
E-mail: admissions@newberry.edu
http://www.newberry.edu

TENNESSEE

Middle Tennessee State University
1301 E. Main Street
CAB Room 205
Murfreesboro, TN 37132
Phone: (615) 898-2300
E-mail: admissions@mtsu.edu
http://www.mtsu.edu

TEXAS

Abilene Christian University
ACU Box 29100
Abilene, TX 79699
Phone: (915) 674-2000
E-mail: info@admissions.acu.edu
http://www.acu.edu

University of the Incarnate Word
4301 Broadway Avenue
San Antonio, TX 78209-6397
Phone: (210) 829-6000
E-mail: admis@universe.uiwtx.edu
http://www.uiw.edu

West Texas A&M University
P.O. Box 60999
Canyon, TX 79016
Phone: (806) 651-2000
E-mail: apifer@mail.wtamu.edu
http://www.wtamu.edu

VIRGINIA

Radford University
P.O. Box 6890, RU Station
Radford, VA 24142-6903
Phone: (540) 831-5000
E-mail: ruadmiss@radford.edu
http://www.radford.edu

Randolph-Macon College
Box 5005
Ashland, VA 23005-5505
Phone: (804) 752-7305
E-mail: admissions@rmc.edu
http://www.rmc.edu

WASHINGTON

Eastern Washington University
526 Fifth Street
Cheney, WA 99004
Phone: (509) 359-6200
E-mail: admissions@mail.ewu.edu
http://www.ewu.edu

University of Puget Sound
1500 North Warner Street
Tacoma, WA 98416
Phone: (253) 879-3100
http://www.ups.edu

Whitworth College
300 West Hawthorne Road
Spokane, WA 99251
Phone: (509) 777-1000
http://www.whitworth.edu

WISCONSIN

Viterbo University
815 South Ninth Street
La Crosse, WI 54601
Phone: (608) 796-3000
E-mail: admission@viterbo.edu
http://www.viterbo.edu

D. COLLEGES AND UNIVERSITIES THAT OFFER DEGREES IN MUSIC THERAPY

The following is a list of colleges and universities granting degrees in music therapy. They are grouped by state. Asterisks (*) following college names indicate that graduate degrees are available.

More colleges are beginning to host programs in this area every year. Check the newest copy of *Lovejoy's* (found in the reference section of libraries, in guidance counseling centers, and in bookstores) for additional schools offering programs in this field.

Names, addresses, phone numbers, and websites have been included when available to make it easier to get information regarding a specific school.

ALABAMA

University of Alabama
Box 870366
Tuscaloosa, AL 35487
Phone: (205) 348-1432
http://www.ua.edu

ARIZONA

Arizona State University
School of Music
Box 87405
Tempe, AZ 85287
Phone: (480) 965-7413
http://www.asu.edu

CALIFORNIA

**California State
    University–Northridge**
18111 Nordhoff Street
Northridge, CA 91330
Phone: (818) 677-3174
http://www.csun.edu

Chapman University
School of Music
One University Drive
Orange, CA 92866
Phone: (714) 532-6032
http://www.chapman.edu

University of the Pacific*
Conservatory of Music
Department of Music Therapy
Stockton, CA 95211
Phone: (209) 946-3194
http://www.uop.edu

COLORADO

Colorado State University*
Department of Music, Theatre, and Dance
Fort Collins, CO 80523
Phone: (970) 491-5888
http://www.colostate.edu

Naropa University*
2130 Arapahoe Avenue
Boulder, CO 80301
Phone: (303) 546-3590

DISTRICT OF COLUMBIA

Howard University
2400 Sixth Street, NW
Washington, DC 20059
Phone: (202) 806-7136
http://www.howard.edu

FLORIDA

Florida State University*
School of Music
Tallahassee, FL 32306
Phone: (850) 644-4565
http://www.fsu.edu

University of Miami*
School of Music
Music Therapy Program
P.O. Box 248165
Coral Gables, FL 33124
Phone: (305) 284-3943
http://www.miami.edu

GEORGIA

Georgia College and State University*
Department of Music Therapy
CPO 67
Milledgeville, GA 31061
Phone: (478) 445-2645
http://www.gcsu.edu

University of Georgia*
School of Music
Athens, GA 30602
Phone: (706) 542-2801
http://www.uga.edu

ILLINOIS

Illinois State University*
Music Department 5660
Normal, IL 61790-2200
Phone: (309) 438-8198
http://www.ilstu.edu

Western Illinois University
Department of Music
One University Circle
Macomb, IL 61455
Phone: (309) 298-1187
http://www.wiu.edu

INDIANA

Indiana University–Purdue University–Fort Wayne
2101 Coliseum Boulevard East
Classroom Medical Building
Fort Wayne, IN 46805
Phone: (219) 481-6715
http://www.ipfw.edu

Saint Mary-of-the-Woods College*
SMWC Conservatory
Department of Music Therapy
Saint Mary-of-the-Woods, IN 47876
Phone: (812) 535-5154
http://www.smwc.edu

University of Evansville
Department of Music
1800 Lincoln Avenue
Evansville, IN 47722
Phone: (812) 479-2886
http://www.evansville.edu

IOWA

University of Iowa*
School of Music
1006 Voxman Music Building
Iowa City, IA 52242

Phone: (319) 335-1657
http://www.uiowa.edu

Wartburg College
School of Music
2229 9th Street
Waverly, IA 50677
Phone: (313) 352-8401
http://www.wartburg.edu

KANSAS

University of Kansas*
MEMT Division, Room 448
Murphy Hall
1530 Naismith Drive
Lawrence, KS 66045
Phone: (785) 864-4784
http://www.ku.edu

KENTUCKY

University of Louisville
School of Music
Louisville, KY 40292
Phone: (502) 852-2316
http://www.louisville.edu

LOUISIANA

Loyola University–New Orleans*
College of Music
6363 St. Charles Avenue
New Orleans, LA 70118
Phone: (504) 865-2142
http://www.loyno.edu

MASSACHUSETTS

Anna Maria College
Music Therapy Program
Box 45
50 Sunset Lane
Paxton, MA 01612
Phone: (508) 849-3454
http://www.annamaria.edu

Berklee College of Music
Chair Music Therapy
1140 Boylston Street
Boston, MA 02215
Phone: (617) 747-2639
http://www.berklee.edu

Lesley University*
Division of Expressive Therapies
29 Everett Street
Cambridge, MA 02138
Phone: (617) 349-8166
http://www.lesley.edu

MICHIGAN

Eastern Michigan University
Department of Music
Ypsilanti, MI 48197
Phone: (734) 487-0292
http://www.emich.edu

Michigan State University*
School of Music
East Lansing, MI 48824
Phone: (517) 355-9122
http://www.admis.msu.edu

Western Michigan University*
School of Music
1903 West Michigan Avenue
Kalamazoo, MI 49008
Phone: (269) 387-4679
http://www.wmich.edu

MINNESOTA

Augsburg College
2211 Riverside Avenue
Minneapolis, MN 55454
Phone: (612) 330-1273
http://www.augsburg.edu

University of Minnesota*
School of Music
2106 4th Street South
Minneapolis, MN 55455
Phone: (612) 624-5740
http://www.music.umn.edu

MISSISSIPPI

Mississippi University for Women
Fine & Performing Arts Division
Box W-70
Columbus, MS 39701
Phone: (662) 241-7897
http://www.muw.edu

William Carey College
498 Tuscan Avenue
Hattiesburg, MS 39401-5499
Phone: (601) 582-6416
http://www.wmcarey.edu

MISSOURI

Drury University
900 North Benton Avenue
Springfield, MO 65802
Phone: (417) 873-7370
http://www.drury.edu

Maryville University
Department of Music
13550 Conway Road
St Louis, MO 63141-7299
Phone: (314) 529-9617
http://www.maryville.edu

University of Missouri–Kansas City*
Conservatory of Music
4949 Cherry, 316 Grant Hall
Kansas City, MO 64110
Phone: (816) 235-2920
http://www.umkc.edu/conservatory

NEW JERSEY

Montclair State University*
Music Department
Upper Montclair, NJ 07043
Phone: (973) 655-5268
http://www.montclair.edu

NEW YORK

Molloy College
Music Department
1000 Hempstead Avenue
Rockville Centre, NY 11571
Phone: (516) 678-5000
http://www.molloy.edu

Nazareth College
4245 East Avenue
Rochester, NY 14618-3790
Phone: (585) 389-2702
http://www.naz.edu

New York University*
Music Therapy Program
777 Educational Building
35 West 4th Street
New York, NY 10012
Phone: (212) 998-5452
http://www.nyu.edu

SUNY College–Fredonia
School of Music
Mason Hall
Fredonia, NY 14063-1136
Phone: (716) 673-4648
http://www.fredonia.edu

SUNY-New Paltz
Music Department
75 South Manheim Boulevard
New Paltz, NY 12561
Phone: (845) 257-2709
http://www.newpaltz.edu

NORTH CAROLINA

Appalachian State University
School of Music
P.O. Box 32096
Boone, NC 28608
Phone: (828) 262-6444
http://www.appstate.edu

East Carolina University*
212 Fletcher Music Center
Greenville, NC 27858
Phone: (252) 328-6343
http://www.ecu.edu

Queens University of Charlotte
Music Department
1900 Selwyn Avenue
Charlotte, NC 28374
Phone: (704) 337-2301
http://www.queens.edu

NORTH DAKOTA

University of North Dakota
Department of Music
P.O. Box 7125
Grand Forks, ND 58202
Phone: (701) 777-2828
http://www.und.edu

OHIO

Baldwin-Wallace College
Cleveland Consortium
275 Eastland Road
Berea, OH 44017
Phone: (440) 826-2171
http://www.bw.edu

College of Wooster
Department of Music
Wooster, OH 44691
Phone: (800) 877-9905
http://www.wooster.edu/

Ohio University*
School of Music
440 Music Building
Athens, OH 45701
Phone: (740) 593-4249
http://www.ohiou.edu

University of Dayton
Department of Music
300 College Park
Dayton, OH 45469
Phone: (937) 229-3908
http://www.udayton.edu

OKLAHOMA

**Southwestern Oklahoma State
    University**
Department of Music
100 Campus Drive
Weatherford, OK 73096
Phone: (580) 774-3218
http://www.swosu.edu

OREGON

Marylhurst University
17600 Pacific Highway (Highway 43)
P.O. Box 261
Marylhurst, OR 97036
Phone: (800) 634-9982 (ext. 3361)
http://www.marylhurst.edu

PENNSYLVANIA

Drexel University*
Hahnemann Creative Arts in Therapy
    Program–Music Therapy
245 North 15th Street, MS 905
Philadelphia, PA 19102
Phone: (215) 762-6927
http://nursing.drexel.edu/music/index.html

Duquesne University
School of Music
600 Forbes Avenue
Pittsburgh, PA 15282
Phone: (412) 396-6086
http://www.duq.edu

Elizabethtown College
Department of Fine and Performing Arts
One Alpha Drive
Elizabethtown, PA 17022
Phone: (717) 361-11289
http://www.etown.edu

Immaculata College*
Department of Music
P.O. Box 697
Immaculata, PA 19345
Phone: (610) 647-4400
http://www.immaculata.edu

Mansfield University of Pennsylvania
Department of Music
Mansfield, PA 16933
Phone: (570) 662-4717
http://www.mnsfld.edu

Marywood University
2300 Adams Avenue
Scranton, PA 18509-1598

Phone: (570) 348-6211
http://www.marywood.edu

Seton Hill University
Seton Hill Drive
Greensburg, PA 15601
Phone: (724) 837-5070
http://www.setonhill.edu

**Slippery Rock University of
    Pennsylvania**
Department of Music
Swope Music Building
Slippery Rock, PA 16057
Phone: (724) 738-2447
http://www.sru.edu

Temple University*
Music Therapy, TU –012-00
Esther Boyer College of Music
Philadelphia, PA 19122
Phone: (215) 204-8340
http://www.temple.edu

SOUTH CAROLINA

Charleston Southern University
9200 University Boulevard
Charleston, SC 29423
Phone: (843) 863-7869
http://www.csuniv.edu

TENNESSEE

Tennessee Technological University
Department of Music and Art
Box 5045
Cookeville, TN 38505
Phone: (931) 372-3065
http://www.tntech.edu

TEXAS

Sam Houston State University
Department of Music/SHSU
P.O. Box 2208
Huntsville, TX 77341
Phone: (936) 294-1376
http://www.shsu.edu

Southern Methodist University*
Meadows School of the Arts
Department of Music Therapy/Division of
    Music
Dallas, TX 75275
Phone: (214) 768-3178
http://www.smu.edu

Texas Woman's University*
P.O. Box 425768 TWU
Denton, TX 76209
Phone: (940) 898-2514
http://www.twu.edu

University of the Incarnate Word
4301 Broadway Avenue
San Antonio, TX 78209
Phone: (210) 829-3856
E-mail: admis@universe.uiwtx.edu
http://www.uiw.edu

West Texas A&M University
Department of Music & Dance
WTAMU Box 60879
Canyon, TX 79016
Phone: (806) 651-2822
http://www.wtamu.edu

UTAH

Utah State University
Music Therapy Program
UMC 4015
Logan, UT 84322

Phone: (435) 797-3030
http://www.usu.edu

VIRGINIA

Radford University*
Department of Music
Radford, VA 24142
Phone: (540) 831-5024
http://www.radford.edu

Shenandoah University
1460 University Drive
Winchester, VA 22601
Phone: (540) 665-4560
http://www.su.edu

WISCONSIN

Alverno College
3401 South 43rd Street
Milwaukee, WI 53234
Phone: (414) 382-6135
http://www.alverno.edu

University of Wisconsin–Eau Claire
105 Garfield Avenue
Eau Claire, WI 54701
Phone: (715) 836-4109
http://www.uwec.edu

University of Wisconsin–Oshkosh
Department of Music
800 Algoma Boulevard
Oshkosh, WI 54901
Phone: (920) 424-4224
http://www.uwosh.edu

E. COLLEGES AND UNIVERSITIES THAT OFFER DEGREES IN MUSIC EDUCATION

The following list contains four-year schools that offer degrees in music education. They are grouped by state.

Check the newest copy of *Lovejoy's* (found in the reference section of libraries, in guidance counseling centers, and in bookstores) for additional schools offering majors in this field.

ALABAMA

**Alabama Agricultural and Mechanical
    University**
P.O. Box 908
Normal, AL 35762
Phone: (256) 372-5245 or (800) 553-0816
    (toll-free)

Fax: (256) 851-9747
E-mail: aboyle@asnaam.aamu.edu
http://www.aamu.edu/Education/Music/
    Home.html

Alabama State University
915 South Jackson Street
Montgomery, AL 36104

Phone: (334) 229-4291
http://www.alasu.edu

Auburn University
Auburn, AL 36849
Phone: (334) 844-4000
E-mail: admissions@auburn.edu
http://www.auburn.edu

Birmingham-Southern College
900 Arkadelphia Road
Birmingham, AL 35254
Phone: (205) 226-4696
E-mail: admission@bsc.edu
http://www.bsc.edu

Huntingdon College
1500 East Fairview Avenue
Montgomery, AL 36106
Phone: (334) 833-4497
Fax: (334) 833-4347
E-mail: admiss@huntingdon.edu
http://www.huntingdon.edu

Jacksonville State University
700 Pelham Road North
Jacksonville, AL 36265
Phone: (256) 782-5363 or (800) 231-5291
    (toll-free)
Fax: (256) 782-5291
E-mail: lbedford@jsucc.jsu.edu
http://www.jsu.edu

Judson College
P.O. Box 120
Marion, AL 36756
Phone: (334) 683-5110 or (800) 447-9472
    (toll-free)
Fax: (334) 683-5158
E-mail: admissions@future.judson.edu
http://home.judson.edu

Oakwood College
7000 Adventist Boulevard, NW
Huntsville, AL 35896
Phone: (256) 726-7354 or (800) 358-3978
    (toll-free)
Fax: (256) 726-7154
E-mail: admission@oakwood.edu
http://www.oakwood.edu

Samford University
Birmingham, AL 35229
Phone: (205) 726-3673
E-mail: admission@samford.edu
http://www.samford.edu

Talladega College
627 West Battle Street
Talladega, AL 35160
Phone: (256) 761-6235
http://www.talladega.edu

Troy State University
Troy, AL 36082
Phone: (334) 670-3179
http://www.troyst.edu

University of Alabama
Box 870132
Tuscaloosa, AL 35487-0132
Phone: (205) 348-5666 or
    (800) 933-BAMA (toll-free)
Fax: (205) 348-9046
E-mail: admissions@ua.edu
http:///www.ua.edu

University of Montevallo
Montevallo, AL 35115-6000
Phone: (205) 665-6030
E-mail: admissions@montevallo.edu
http://www.montevallo.edu

ALASKA

University of Alaska–Anchorage
P.O. Box 141629
Anchorage, AK 99514-1629
Phone: (907) 786-1480
http://www.uaa.alaska.edu

ARIZONA

Arizona State University
Box 870112
Tempe, AZ 85287
Phone: (480) 965-7788
Fax: (480) 965-3610
E-mail: ugradinq@asu.edu
http://www.asu.edu

Grand Canyon University
3300 West Camelback Road
P.O. Box 11097
Phoenix, AZ 85061
Phone: (602) 589-2855
E-mail: admissions@grand-canyon.edu
http://www.grand-canyon.edu

Northern Arizona University
Box 4084
Flagstaff, AZ 86011
Phone: (888) MORE-NAU (toll-free)
E-mail: undergraduate.admissions@
    nau.edu
http://www.nau.edu

Prescott College
220 Grove Avenue
Prescott, AZ 86301
Phone: (928) 776-5180
E-mail: admissions@prescott.edu
http://www.prescott.edu

University of Arizona
P.O. Box 210011
Tucson, AZ 85721

Phone: (520) 621-3237
Fax: (520) 621-9799
E-mail: appinfo@arizona.edu
http://www.arizona.edu

ARKANSAS

Arkansas State University
P.O. Box 1630
Jonesboro, AR 72467
Phone: (870) 972-3024
E-mail: admissions@chickasaw.astate.edu
http://www.astate.edu

Arkansas Tech University
Russellville, AR 72801-2222
Phone: (479) 968-0343 or (800) 582-6953
    (toll-free)
Fax: (479) 964-0522
E-mail: tech.enroll@mail.atu.edu
http://www.atu.edu

Harding University
Station A, Box 12255
Searcy, AR 72149
Phone: (501) 279-4407 or (800) 477-4407
    (toll-free)
Fax: (501) 279-4129
E-mail: admissions@harding.edu
http://www.harding.edu

Henderson State University
1100 Henderson Street
P.O. Box 7560
Arkadelphia, AR 71999
Phone: (870) 230-5028 or (800) 228-7333
    (toll-free)
Fax: (870) 230-5066
E-mail: hardwrv@hsu.edu
http://www.hsu.edu

John Brown University
200 West University Street
Siloam Springs, AR 72761
Phone: (501) 524-7454 or
    (877) JBU-INFO (toll-free)
Fax: (501) 524-4196
E-mail: jbuinfo@acc.jbu.edu
http://www.jbu.edu

Ouachita Baptist University
410 Ouachita Street
Arkadelphia, AR 71998
Phone: (870) 245-5110 or (800) 342-5628
    (toll-free)
Fax: (870) 245-5500
E-mail: jonesj@obu.edu
http://www.obu.edu

Southern Arkansas University–Magnolia
P.O. Box 9382
Magnolia, AR 71754-9382
Phone: (870) 235-4040
Fax: (870) 235-5005
E-mail: addanne@saumag.edu
http://www.saumag.edu

University of Arkansas–Monticello
P.O. Box 3600
Monticello, AR 71656
Phone: (870) 460-1026 or (800) 844-1826
    (toll-free)
Fax: (870) 460-1321
E-mail: admissions@uamont.edu
http://www.uamont.edu

University of Arkansas–Pine Bluff
UAPB Box 17
1200 University Drive
Pine Bluff, AR 71601
Phone: (870) 575-8487 or (800) 264-6585
    (toll-free)
Fax: (870) 543-2021
http://www.uapb.edu

University of Central Arkansas
201 Donaghey Avenue
Conway, AR 72035
Phone: (501) 450-5145 or (800) 243-8245
    (toll-free)
Fax: (501) 450-5228
E-mail: admissions@mail.uca.edu
http://www.uca.edu

University of the Ozarks
415 North College Avenue
Clarksville, AR 72830
Phone: (479) 979-1421 or (800) 264-8636
    (toll-free)
Fax: (479) 979-1355
E-mail: admiss@ozarks.edu
http://www.ozarks.edu

Williams Baptist College
P.O. Box 3665
Walnut Ridge, AR 72476
Phone: (870) 886-6741 (ext. 4117); or
    (800) 722-4434 (toll-free)
Fax: (870) 886-3924
E-mail: admissions@wbcoll.edu
http://www.wbcoll.edu

CALIFORNIA

California State University–Chico
400 West First Street
Chico, CA 95929-0720
Phone: (530) 898-6116
E-mail: info@csuchico.edu
http://www.csuchico.edu

**California State University–Dominguez
    Hills**
1000 East Victoria Street
Carson, CA 90747
Phone: (310) 243-3696
http://www.csudh.edu

California State University–Fresno
5150 North Maple Avenue
Fresno, CA 93740-8026
Phone: (559) 278-2261
Fax: (559) 278-4812
E-mail: donna_mills@csufresno.edu
http://www.csufresno.edu

California State University–Fullerton
P.O. Box 6900
Fullerton, CA 92834-6900
Phone: (714) 278-2011
http://www.fullerton.edu

**California State
    University–Northridge**
18111 Nordhoff Street
Northridge, CA 91328
Phone: (818) 677-1200
E-mail: admissions.records@csun.edu
http://www.csun.edu

Chapman University
One University Drive
Orange, CA 92866
Phone: (714) 997-6815
E-mail: admit@chapman.edu
http://www.chapman.edu

Christian Heritage College
2100 Greenfield Drive
El Cajon, CA 92019-1157
Phone: (619) 441-2200
E-mail: chcadm@adm.christianheritage.
    edu
http://www.christianheritage.edu

Fresno Pacific College
1717 South Chestnut Avenue
Fresno, CA 93702
Phone: (559) 453-2069
Fax: (559) 453-5501
E-mail: ipso@fresno.edu
http://www.fresno.edu/dept/ipso

Hope International University
2500 East Nutwood Avenue
Fullerton, CA 92831-3199
Phone: (714) 879-3901
E-mail: mfmadden@hiu.edu
http://www.hiu.edu

Pacific Union College
One Angwin Avenue
Angwin, CA 94508
Phone: (707) 965-6336
E-mail: enroll@puc.edu
http://www.puc.edu

Pepperdine University–Seaver College
Malibu, CA 90263
Phone: (310) 506-4392
Fax: (310) 506-4861
http://www.pepperdine.edu

San Jose State University
One Washington Square
San Jose, CA 95192-0009
Phone: (408) 924-1000
E-mail: contact@sjsu.edu
http://www.sjsu.edu

Simpson College
2211 College View Drive
Redding, CA 96003-8606
Phone: (530) 224-5600
E-mail: admissions@simpsonca.edu
http://www.simpsonca.edu

Sonoma State University
1801 East Cotati Avenue
Rohnert Park, CA 94928
Phone: (707) 664-2880
E-mail: csumentor@sonoma.edu
http://www.sonoma.edu

University of La Verne
1950 Third Street
La Verne, CA 91750
Phone: (909) 392-2800
Fax: (909) 392-2714
E-mail: admissions@ulv.edu
http://www.ulv.edu

University of Redlands
P.O. Box 3080
Redlands, CA 92373-0999
Phone: (909) 793-2121
E-mail: admissions@redlands.edu
http://www.redlands.edu

University of the Pacific
Stockton, CA 95211
Phone: (209) 946-2211
E-mail: admissions@uop.edu
http://www.pacific.edu

COLORADO

Adams State College
Alamosa, CO 81102

Phone: (719) 587-7712
Fax: (719) 587-7522
E-mail: ascadmit@adams.edu
http://www.adams.edu

Colorado State University
Administration Annex
Fort Collins, CO 80523
Phone: (970) 491-6909
http://www.colostate.edu

University of Colorado–Boulder
Campus Box B-7
Boulder, CO 90309
Phone: (303) 492-6301
http://www.colorado.edu

Western State College of Colorado
College Heights
Gunnison, CO 81230
Phone: (800) 876-5309 (toll-free)
E-mail: talbers@western.edu
http://www.western.edu

CONNECTICUT

Central Connecticut State University
1615 Stanley Street
New Britain, CT 06050
Phone: (860) 832-CCSU
E-mail: admissions@ccsu.edu
http://www.ccsu.edu

Connecticut College
270 Mohegan Avenue
New London, CT 06320
Phone: (860) 439-2200
Fax: (860) 439-4301
E-mail: admission@conncoll.edu
http://www.connecticutcollege.edu

St. Joseph College
Saint Joseph College
1678 Asylum Avenue
West Hartford, CT 06117
Phone: (860) 231-5216
Fax: (860) 231-5744
E-mail: admissions@sjc.edu
http://www.sjc.edu

University of Connecticut
2131 Hillside Road, Box Unit 3088
Storrs, CT 06269-3088
Phone: (860) 486-3137
E-mail: beahusky@uconnvm.uconn.edu
http://www.uconn.edu

University of Hartford
200 Bloomfield Avenue
West Hartford, CT 06117

Phone: (860) 768-4296
Fax: (860) 768-4961
E-mail: admission@mail.hartford.edu
http://www.hartford.edu

Western Connecticut State University
181 White Street
Danbury, CT 06810
E-mail: hawkinsw@wcsu.edu
http://www.wcsu.edu

DELAWARE

Delaware State University
1200 North DuPont Highway
Dover, DE 19901
Phone: (302) 857-6353
http://www.dsc.edu

University of Delaware
Newark, DE 19716
Phone: (302) 831-2000
http:..//www.udel.edu

DISTRICT OF COLUMBIA

American University
4400 Massachusetts Avenue, NW
Washington, DC 20016-8001
Phone: (202) 885-1000
http://www.american.edu

Catholic University of America
620 Michigan Avenue, NE
Washington, DC 20064
Phone: (202) 319-5000
E-mail: cua-admissions@cua.edu
http://www.cua.edu

Howard University
2400 Sixth Street, NW
Washington, DC 20059
Phone: (202) 806-6100
E-mail: admissions@howard.edu
http://www.howard.edu

University of the District of Columbia
4200 Connecticut Avenue, NW
Washington, DC 20008
Phone: (202) 274-5000
http://www.udc.edu

FLORIDA

Bethune-Cookman College
640 Dr. Mary McLeod Bethune
   Boulevard
Daytona Beach, FL 32114-3099
Phone: (386) 255-1401

E-mail: admissions@cookman.edu
http://www.bethune.cookman.edu

Clearwater Christian College
3400 Gulf-to-Bay Boulevard
Clearwater, FL 33759-4595
Phone: (727) 726-1153
http://www.clearwater.edu

**Florida Agriculture and Mechanical
   University**
Lee Hall, Suite 303
Tallahassee, FL 32307
Phone: (850) 599-3000
http://www.famu.edu

Florida Atlantic University
777 Glades Road
Boca Raton, FL 33431-0991
Phone: (561) 297-3760
Fax: (561) 338-3863
http://www.fau.edu

Florida International University
University Park
Miami, FL 33199
Phone: (305) 348-2000
E-mail: admiss@fiu.edu
http://www.fiu.edu

Florida Memorial College
15800 Northwest 42 Avenue
Miami, FL 33054
Phone: (305) 626-3600
http://www.fmc.edu

Florida Southern College
111 Lake Hollingsworth Drive
Lakeland, FL 33801-5698
Phone: (863) 680-4111
E-mail: fscadm@flsouthern.edu
http://www.flsouthern.edu

Florida State University
Tallahassee, FL 32306-2400
Phone: (850) 644-2525
E-mail: admissions@admin.fsu.edu
http://www.fsu.edu

Jacksonville University
2800 University Boulevard North
Jacksonville, FL 32211
Phone: (904) 744-3950
E-mail: admission@ju.edu
http://www.ju.edu

Palm Beach Atlantic College
P.O. Box 24708
West Palm Beach, FL 33416-4708

Phone: (561) 803-2000
E-mail: admit@pbac.edu
http://www.pbac.edu

Saint Leo College
P.O. Box 6665 MC2008
Saint Leo, FL 33574-6665
Phone: (352) 588-8200
E-mail: admission@saintleo.edu
http://www.saintleo.edu

Southeastern College of the Assemblies of God
1000 Longfellow Boulevard
Lakeland, FL 33801
Phone: (863) 667-5000
E-mail: sgraymond@secollege.edu
http://www.secollege.edu

Stetson University
421 North Woodland Boulevard
DeLand, FL 32723
Phone: (386) 822-7000
E-mail: admission@stetson.edu
http://www.stetson.edu

University of Central Florida
4000 Central Florida Boulevard
Orlando, FL 32816-0111
Phone: (407) 823-2000
E-mail: admission@mail.ucf.edu
http://www.ucf.edu

University of Florida
201 Criser Hall
Gainesville, FL 32611-4000
Phone: (352) 392-3261
http://www.ufl.edu

University of Miami
P.O. Box 248025
Coral Gables, FL 33124-4616
Phone: (305) 284-2211
E-mail: admission@miami.edu
http://www.miami.edu

University of North Florida
4567 St. Johns Bluff Road, South
Jacksonville, FL 32224-2645
Phone: (904) 620-1000
http://www.unf.edu

University of South Florida
4202 East Fowler Avenue
Tampa, FL 33620-9951
Phone: (813) 974-2011
http://usfweb.usf.edu

Warner Southern College
13895 Highway 27
Lake Wales, FL 33853
Phone: (863) 638-1426
E-mail: admission@warner.edu
http://www.warner.edu

GEORGIA

Armstrong State College
11935 Abercorn Street
Savannah, GA 31419-1997
Phone: (912) 927-5211
http://www.armstrong.edu

Berry College
2277 Martha Berry Highway, North
Mount Berry, GA 30149-0159
Phone: (706) 232-5374
E-mail: admissions@berry.edu
http://www.berry.edu

Brenau University
One Centennial Circle
Gainesville, GA 30501
Phone: (770) 534-6299
http://www.brenau.edu

Clark-Atlanta University
223 James P. Brawley Drive, SW
Atlanta, GA 30314
Phone: (404) 880-8000
E-mail: admissions@panthernet.cau.edu
http://www.cau.edu

Columbus State University
4225 University Avenue
Columbus, GA 31907-5645
Phone: (706) 568-2001
E-mail: admissions@colstate.edu
http://www.colstate.edu

Kennesaw College
1000 Chastain Road
Kennesaw, GA 30144-5591
Phone: (770) 423-6000
E-mail: ksuadmit@kennesaw.edu
http://www.kennesaw.edu

Mercer University
1400 Coleman Avenue
Macon, GA 31207-0001
Phone: (478) 301-2700
E-mail: admissions@mercer.edu
http://www.mercer.edu

Morris Brown College
643 Martin Luther King Jr. Drive
Atlanta, GA 30314

Phone: (404) 739-1000
http://www.morrisbrown.edu

North Georgia College
Dahlonega, GA 30597
Phone: (706) 864-1400
E-mail: admissions@ngcsu.edu
http://www.ngcsu.edu

Paine College
1235 15th Street
Augusta, GA 30901-3182
Phone: (706) 821-8200
http://www.paine.edu

Shorter College
315 Shorter Avenue
Rome, GA 30165
Phone: (706) 291-2121
E-mail: admissions@shorter.edu
http://www.shorter.edu

Toccoa Falls College
Office of Admissions
Toccoa Falls, GA 30598-0368
Phone: (706) 886-6831
E-mail: admissions@toccoafalls.edu
http://www.toccoafalls.edu

University of Georgia
Athens, GA 30602
Phone: (706) 542-3000
E-mail: undergrad@admissions.uga.edu
http://www.uga.edu

Valdosta State College
1500 North Patterson Street
Valdosta, GA 31698
Phone: (229) 333-5800
E-mail: admissions@valdosta.edu
http://www.valdosta.edu

HAWAII

Brigham Young University–Hawaii
55-220 Kulanui Street
Laie, HI 96762-1294
Phone: (808) 293-3211
E-mail: admissions@byuh.edu
http://www.byuh.edu

IDAHO

Boise State University
1910 University Drive
Boise, ID 83725
Phone: (208) 426-1101
E-mail: bsuinfo@boisestate.edu
http://www.boisestate.edu

Idaho State University
741 South Seventh Avenue
Pocatello, ID 83209
Phone: (208) 282-0211
E-mail: info@isu.edu
http://www.isu.edu

University of Idaho
P.O. Box 442282
Moscow, ID 83844-4264
Phone: (208) 885-6111
E-mail: admappl@uidaho.edu
http://www.uidaho.edu

ILLINOIS

Augustana College
639 38th Street
Rock Island, IL 61201-2296
Phone: (309) 794-7000
E-mail: admissions@augustana.edu
http://www.augustana.edu

Bradley University
1501 West Bradley Avenue
Peoria, IL 61625
Phone: (309) 677-7611
http://www.bradley.edu

Chicago State University
9501 South King Drive
Chicago, IL 60628
Phone: (773) 995-2000
http://www.csu.edu

Eastern Illinois University
600 Lincoln Avenue
Charleston, IL 61920-3099
Phone: (217) 581-5000
http://www.eiu.edu

Elmhurst College
190 Prospect Avenue
Elmhurst, IL 60126-3296
Phone: (630) 617-3500
http://www.elmhurst.edu

Eureka College
300 College Avenue
Eureka, IL 61530
Phone: (309) 467-6350
E-mail: admissions@eureka.edu
http://www.eureka.edu

Greenville College
315 East College Avenue
Greenville, IL 62246-0159
Phone: (618) 664-2800
http://www.greenville.edu

Illinois State University
Admissions, Campus Box 2200
Normal, IL 61790-2200
Phone: (309) 438-2111
http://www.ilstu.edu

Illinois Wesleyan University
1312 North Park
Bloomington, IL 61702-2900
Phone: (309) 556-1000
http://www.iwu.edu

Judson College
1151 North State Street
Elgin, IL 60123
Phone: (847) 695-2500
http://www.home.judson.edu

MacMurray College
447 East College Avenue
Jacksonville, IL 62650-2590
Phone: (217) 479-7000
http://www.mac.edu

Millikin University
1184 West Main Street
Decatur, IL 62522-2084
Phone: (217) 424-6211
E-mail: admis@mail.millikin.edu
http://www.millikin.edu

Northeastern Illinois University
5500 North St. Louis Avenue
Chicago, IL 60625
Phone: (773) 583-4050
http://www.neiu.edu

Northern Illinois University
DeKalb, IL 60115-2854
Phone: (815) 753-1000
E-mail: admission-info@niu.edu
http://www.niu.edu

North Park College
3225 West Foster Avenue
Chicago, IL 60625-4895
Phone: (773) 244-6200
http://www.northpark.edu

Northwestern University
633 Clark Street
Evanston, IL 60204-3060
Phone: (847) 491-3741
http://www.northwestern.edu

Roosevelt University
430 South Michigan Avenue
Chicago, IL 60605-1394

Phone: (312) 341-3500
http://www.roosevelt.edu

**Southern Illinois
    University–Carbondale**
Carbondale, IL 62901-4701
Phone: (618) 453-2121
http://www.siuc.edu

**Southern Illinois
    University–Edwardsville**
Edwardsville, IL 62026-1600
Phone: (618) 650-2000
http://www.siue.edu

Trinity Christian College
6601 West College Drive
Palos Heights, IL 60463
Phone: (708) 597-3000
E-mail: adm@trnty.edu
http://www.trnty.edu

Trinity International University
2065 Half Day Road
Deerfield, IL 60015
Phone: (847) 945-8800
E-mail: tcdadm@tiu.edu
http://www.tiu.edu

**University of Illinois at Urbana-
    Champaign**
901 West Illinois
Urbana, IL 61801
Phone: (217) 333-1000
E-mail: admissions@oar.uiuc.edu
http://www.uiuc.edu

Western Illinois University
900 West Adams Street
Macomb, IL 61455
Phone: (309) 295-1414
E-mail: wiuadm@wiu.edu
http://www.wiu.edu

Wheaton College
501 College Avenue
Wheaton, IL 60187-5593
Phone: (630) 752-5000
E-mail: admissions@wheaton.edu
http://www.wheaton.edu

INDIANA

Anderson University
1100 East Fifth Street
Anderson, IN 46012
Phone: (765) 649-9071
E-mail: info@anderson.edu
http://www.anderson.edu

Ball State University
2000 University Avenue
Muncie, IN 47306-0855
Phone: (765) 285-8300
E-mail: askus@ball.edu
http://www.bsu.edu

Butler University
4600 Sunset Avenue
Indianapolis, IN 46208
Phone: (317) 940-8000
E-mail: admission@butler.edu
http://www.butler.edu

DePauw University
313 South Locust Street
Greencastle, IN 46135-1611
Phone: (765) 658-4800
E-mail: admission@depauw.edu
http://www.depauw.edu

Goshen College
1700 South Main Street
Goshen, IN 46526
Phone: (574) 535-7000
E-mail: admissions@goshen.edu
http://www.goshen.edu

Grace College
200 Seminary Drive
Winona Lake, IN 46590
Phone: (219) 372-5100
E-mail: enroll@grace.edu
http://www.grace.edu

Huntington College
2303 College Avenue
Huntington, IN 46750
Phone: (260) 356-6000
http://www.huntington.edu

Indiana State University
210 North Seventh Street
Terre Haute, IN 47809
Phone: (812) 237-6311
http://www.indstate.edu

Indiana University–Bloomington
300 North Jordan Avenue
Bloomington, IN 47405
Phone: (812) 855-4848
http://www.indiana.edu

Indiana University–Purdue
　University–Fort Wayne
2101 East Coliseum Boulevard
Fort Wayne, IN 46805-1499
Phone: (260) 481-6100
http://www.ipfw.edu

Indiana University–South Bend
1700 Mishawaka Avenue
South Bend, IN 46634-7111
Phone: (574) 237-4872
E-mail: admissions@usb.edu
http://www.iusb.edu

Indiana Wesleyan University
4201 South Washington Street
Marion, IN 46953-4999
Phone: (765) 674-6901
http://www.indwes.edu

Manchester College
604 East College Avenue
North Manchester, IN 46962-0365
Phone: (260) 982-5000
http://www.manchester.edu

Marian College
3200 Cold Spring Road
Indianapolis, IN 46222
Phone: (317) 955-6000
E-mail: admit@marian.edu
http://www.marian.edu

Oakland City College
143 North Lucretia Street
Oakland City, IN 47660
Phone: (812) 749-4781
http://www.oak.edu

St. Mary's College
Notre Dame, IN 46556-5001
Phone: (574) 284-4000
http://www.saintmarys.edu

Saint Mary-of-the-Woods College
Saint Mary-of-the-Woods, IN 47876
Phone: (812) 535-5151
http://www.smwc.edu

Taylor University
236 West Reade Avenue
Upland, IN 46989
Phone: (765) 998-2751
E-mail: admissions_u@tayloru.edu
http://www.tayloru.edu

University of Evansville
1800 Lincoln Avenue
Evansville, IN 47722
Phone: (812) 479-2000
http://www.evansville.edu

University of Indianapolis
1400 East Hanna Avenue
Indianapolis, IN 46227-3697
Phone: (317) 788-3368

E-mail: admissions@uindy.edu
http://www.uindy.edu

Valparaiso University
651 South College Avenue
Valparaiso, IN 46383-6493
Phone: (219) 464-5000
http://www.valpo.edu

IOWA

Buena Vista College
610 West Fourth Street
Storm Lake, IA 50588
Phone: (712) 749-2400
http://www.bvu.edu

Central College
12 University Street
Pella, IA 50219-1999
Phone: (800) 458-5503
E-mail: admissions@central.edu
http://www.central.edu

Clarke College
1550 Clarke Drive
Dubuque, IA 52001-3198
Phone: (563) 588-6300
http://www.clarke.edu

Coe College
1220 First Avenue Northeast
Cedar Rapids, IA 52402-9983
Phone: (319) 399-8500
http://www.coe.edu

Cornell College
600 First Street West
Mount Vernon, IA 52314-1098
Phone: (319) 895-4000
E-mail: admissions@cornellcollege.edu
http://www.cornellcollege.edu

Dordt College
498 Fourth Avenue Northeast
Sioux Center, IA 51250
Phone: (712) 722-6000
E-mail: admission@dordt.edu
http://www.dordt.edu

Drake University
2507 University Avenue
Des Moines, IA 50311-4505
Phone: (515) 271-2011
http://www.drake.edu

Graceland College
1 University Place
Lamoni, IA 50140

Phone: (866) 472-2352
http://www.graceland.edu

Iowa State University
Ames, IA 50011-2011
Phone: (515) 294-4111
E-mail: admissions@iastate.edu
http://www.iastate.edu

Iowa Wesleyan College
601 North Main Street
Mount Pleasant, IA 52641-1398
Phone: (319) 385-8021
http://www.iwc.edu

Loras College
1450 Alta Vista Street
Dubuque, IA 52004-0178
Phone: (563) 588-7100
http://www.loras.edu

Luther College
700 College Drive
Decorah, IA 52101-1042
Phone: (563) 387-2000
http://www.luther.edu

Morningside College
1501 Morningside Avenue
Sioux City, IA 51106
Phone: (712) 274-5000
http://www.morningside.edu

Mount Mercy College
1330 Elmhurst Drive Northeast
Cedar Rapids, IA 52402-4797
Phone: (319) 363-1323
http://www.mtmercy.edu

Northwestern College
1441 North Cable Road
Lima, OH 45805
Phone: (419) 227-3141
http://www.unoh.edu

Simpson College
701 North C Street
Indianola, IA 50125
Phone: (515) 961-6251
http://www.simpson.edu

St. Ambrose University
518 West Locust Street
Davenport, IA 52803-2898
Phone: (563) 333-6000
http://www.sau.edu

University of Dubuque
2000 University Avenue
Dubuque, IA 52001-5099

Phone: (563) 589-3000
http://www.dbq.edu

University of Iowa
107 Calvin Hall
Iowa City, IA 52242
Phone: (319) 335-3500
http://www.uiowa.edu

University of Northern Iowa
1227 West 27th Street
Cedar Falls, IA 50614-0018
Phone: (319) 273-2311
http://www.uni.edu

Upper Iowa University
Parker Fox Hall, Box 1859
Fayette, IA 52142
Phone: (563) 425-5200
http://www.uiu.edu

Wartburg College
P.O. Box 1003
Waverly, IA 50677-0903
Phone: (319) 352-8200
http://www.wartburg.edu

William Penn College
201 Trueblood Avenue
Oskaloosa, IA 52577
Phone: (641) 673-1012
E-mail: admissions@wmpenn.edu
http://www.wmpenn.edu

KANSAS

Baker University
P.O. Box 65
Baldwin City, KS 66006
Phone: (785) 594-6451
E-mail: admission@bakeru.edu
http://www.bakeru.edu

Benedictine College
1020 North Second Street
Atchison, KS 66002-1499
Phone: (913) 367-5340
E-mail: bcadmiss@benedictine.edu
http://www.benedictine.edu

Bethany College
421 North First Street
Lindsborg, KS 67456-1897
Phone: (785) 227-3311
http://www.bethanylb.edu

Emporia State University
1200 Commercial Street
Emporia, KS 66801-5087

Phone: (620) 341-1200
http://www.emporia.edu

Fort Hays State University
600 Park Street
Hays, KS 67601
Phone: (785) 628-4000
http://www.fhsu.edu

Friends University
2100 West University Street
Wichita, KS 67213
Phone: (316) 295-5000
http://www.friends.edu

Kansas State University
119 Anderson Hall
Manhattan, KS 66506
Phone: (785) 532-6250
http://www.ksu.edu

McPherson College
P.O. Box 1402
McPherson, KS 67460-1402
Phone: (620) 241-0731
http://www.mcpherson.edu

MidAmerica Nazarene College
2030 East College Way
Olathe, KS 66062
Phone: (913) 782-3750
http://www.mnu.edu

Pittsburg State University
1701 South Broadway
Pittsburg, KS 66762
Phone: (620) 231-7000
http://www.pittstate.edu

Southwestern College
100 College Street
Winfield, KS 67156
Phone: (620) 229-6000
http://www.sckans.edu

Sterling College
Box 98
Sterling, KS 67579-0098
Phone: (620) 278-2173
http://www.sterling.edu

Tabor College
400 South Jefferson
Hillsboro, KS 67063
Phone: (620) 947-3121
http://www.tabor.edu

University of Kansas
1502 Iowa Street
Lawrence, KS 66045

Phone: (785) 864-2700
http://www.ku.edu

Washburn University
1700 Southwest College Avenue
Topeka, KS 66621
Phone: (785) 231-1010
http://www.washburn.edu

KENTUCKY

Bellarmine College
2001 Newburg Road
Louisville, KY 40205
Phone: (502) 452-8000
http://www.bellarmine.edu

Berea College
Berea, KY 40404
Phone: (859) 985-300
http://www.berea.edu

Campbellsville College
One University Drive
Campbellsville, KY 42718-2799
Phone: (270) 789-5000
http://www.campbellsvil.edu

Cumberland College
6178 College Station Drive
Williamsburg, KY 40769
Phone: (606) 549-2200
http://www.cumber.edu

Eastern Kentucky University
521 Lancaster Avenue
Richmond, KY 40475
Phone: (859) 622-1000
http://www.eku.edu

Georgetown College
400 East College Street
Georgetown, KY 40324
Phone: (502) 863-8000
http://www.georgetowncollege.edu

Kentucky State University
400 East Main Street
Frankfort, KY 40601
Phone: (502) 597-6000
http://www.kysu.edu

Kentucky Wesleyan College
3000 Frederica Street
Owensboro, KY 42302-1039
Phone: (270) 926-3111
http://www.kwc.edu

Morehead State University
150 University Boulevard
Morehead, KY 40351
Phone: (606) 783-2221
http://www.moreheadstate.edu

Murray State University
One Murray Street
Murray, KY 42071
Phone: (270) 762-3741
http://www.murraystate.edu

Transylvania University
300 North Broadway
Lexington, KY 40508-1797
Phone: (859) 233-8300
http://www.transy.edu

University of Kentucky
101 Gillis Building
Lexington, KY 40506-0054
Phone: (859) 257-9000
http://www.uky.edu

University of Louisville
2301 South Third Street
Louisville, KY 40292
Phone: (502) 852-5555
http://www.louisville.edu

Western Kentucky University
One Big Red Way
Bowling Green, KY 42101-3576
Phone: (270) 745-0111
http://www.wku.edu

LOUISIANA

Centenary College of Louisiana
P.O. Box 41188
Shreveport, LA 71134-1188
Phone: (318) 869-5011
http://www.centenary.edu

Dillard University
2601 Gentilly Boulevard
New Orleans, LA 70122-3097
Phone: (504) 816-8822
http://www.dillard.edu

Grambling State University
100 Main Street
Grambling, LA 71245
Phone: (318) 274-3811
http://www.gram.edu

Louisiana College
1140 College Drive
Pineville, LA 71359

Phone: (318) 487-7011
http://www.lacollege.edu

Louisiana State University
110 Thomas Boyd Hall
Baton Rouge, LA 70803-2750
Phone: (225) 388-3202
http://www.lsu.edu

Loyola University–New Orleans
6363 St. Charles Avenue
New Orleans, LA 70118-6195
Phone: (504) 865-2011
http://www.loyno.edu

McNeese State University
4100 Ryan Street
Lake Charles, LA 70609-2495
Phone: (337) 475-5000
http://www.mcneese.edu

Nicholls State University
P.O. Box 2009
Thibodaux, LA 70310
Phone: (985) 446-8111
http://www.nicholls.edu

Southeastern Louisiana University
SLU 10752
Hammond, LA 70402
Phone: (985) 549-2000
http://www.selu.edu

University of New Orleans
Lakefront
2000 Lakeshore Drive
New Orleans, LA 70148-2135
Phone: (504) 280-6000
http://www.uno.edu

Xavier University of Louisiana
1 Drexel Drive
New Orleans, LA 70125-1098
Phone: (504) 486-7411
http://www.xula.edu

MAINE

University of Southern Maine
37 College Avenue
Gorham, ME 04038
Phone: (207) 780-4141
http://www.usm.maine.edu

MARYLAND

Bowie State College
14000 Jericho Park Road
Bowie, MD 20715

Phone: (301) 860-4000
http://www.umsa.umd.edu

College of Notre Dame of Maryland
4701 North Charles Street
Baltimore, MD 21210
Phone: (410) 435-0100
http://www.ndm.edu

Johns Hopkins University
3400 North Charles Street
Baltimore, MD 21218
Phone: (410) 516-8000
http://www.jhu.edu

University of Maryland–College Park
College Park, MD 20742-5235
Phone: (301) 405-1000
http://www.maryland.edu

**University of Maryland–Eastern
  Shore**
1 Backbone Road
Princess Anne, MD 21853
Phone: (410) 651-2200
http://www.umes.edu

MASSACHUSETTS

Anna Maria College
50 Sunset Lane
Paxton, MA 01612
Phone: (508) 849-3300
http://www.annamaria.edu

Atlantic Union College
P.O. Box 1000
South Lancaster, MA 01561
Phone: (978) 368-2000
http://www.atlanticuc.edu

Boston Conservatory
8 The Fenway
Boston, MA 02215
Phone: (617) 536-6340
http://www.bostonconservatory.edu

Boston University
121 Bay State Road
Boston, MA 02215
Phone: (617) 353-2000
http://www.bu.edu

Eastern Nazarene College
23 East Elm Avenue
Quincy, MA 02170-2999
Phone: (617) 745-3000
http://www.enc.edu

Gordon College
255 Grapevine Road
Wenham, MA 01984-1899
Phone: (978) 927-2300
http://www.gordon.edu

New England Conservatory of Music
290 Huntington Avenue
Boston, MA 02115
Phone: (617) 585-1100
http://www.newenglandconservatory.edu

Quincy College
34 Coddington Street
Quincy, MA 02169
Phone: (617) 984-1700
http://www.quincycollege.com

University of Massachusetts–Lowell
One University Avenue
Lowell, MA 01854-5104
Phone: (978) 934-4000
http://www.uml.edu

Westfield State College
577 Western Avenue
Westfield, MA 01086-1630
Phone: (413) 572-5300
http://www.wsc.ma.edu

MICHIGAN

Adrian College
110 South Madison Street
Adrian, MI 49221-2575
Phone: (517) 265-5161
http://www.adrian.edu

Alma College
614 West Superior Street
Alma, MI 48801-1599
Phone: (989) 463-7111
http://www.alma.edu

Andrews University
Berrien Springs, MI 49104
Phone: (616) 471-7771
http://www.andrews.edu

Aquinas College
1607 Robinson Road Southeast
Grand Rapids, MI 49506-1799
Phone: (616) 459-8281
http://www.aquinas.edu

Calvin College
3201 Burton Street Southeast
Grand Rapids, MI 49546

Phone: (616) 957-6000
http://www.calvin.edu

Central Michigan University
Mount Pleasant, MI 48859
Phone: (989) 774-4000
http://www.cmich.edu

Eastern Michigan University
Ypsilanti, MI 48197
Phone: (734) 487-1849
http://www.emich.edu

Grand Valley State University
One Campus Drive
Allendale, MI 49401
Phone: (616) 895-6611
http://www.gvsu.edu

Hope College
P.O. Box 9000
Holland, MI 49422-9000
Phone: (616) 395-7000
http://www.hope.edu

Madonna College
36600 Schoolcraft Road
Livonia, MI 48150
Phone: (734) 432-5300
http://www.madonna.edu

Marygrove College
8425 West McNichols Road
Detroit, MI 48221
Phone: (313) 927-1200
http://www.marygrove.edu

Michigan State University
East Lansing, MI 48824-1046
Phone: (517) 355-1855
http://www.msu.edu

Northern Michigan University
1401 Presque Isle Avenue
Marquette, MI 49855
Phone: (906) 227-1000
http://www.nmu.edu

Oakland University
Rochester, MI 48309-4475
Phone: (248) 370-2100
http://www.oakland.edu

Saginaw Valley State University
7400 Bay Road
University Center, MI 48710
Phone: (989) 964-4000
http://www.svsu.edu

Siena Heights College
1247 East Siena Heights Drive
Adrian, MI 49221-1796
Phone: (517) 263-0731
http://www.sienahts.edu

University of Michigan–Ann Arbor
Ann Arbor, MI 48109-1316
Phone: (734) 764-1817
http://www.umich.edu

University of Michigan–Flint
303 East Kearsley Street
Flint, MI 48502-1950
Phone: (810) 762-3000
http://www.flint.umich.edu

Wayne State University
656 West Kirby Street
Detroit, MI 48202
Phone: (313) 577-2424
http://www.wayne.edu

Western Michigan University
1903 West Michigan Avenue
Kalamazoo, MI 49008
Phone: (616) 387-1000
http://www.wmich.edu

MINNESOTA

Augsburg College
2211 Riverside Avenue
Minneapolis, MN 55454
Phone: (612) 330-1000
http://www.augsburg.edu

Bemidji State University
1500 Birchmont Drive Northeast
Bemidji, MN 56601
Phone: (218) 755-3732
http://www.bemidji.state.edu

Bethel College
3900 Bethel Drive
St. Paul, MN 55112-6999
Phone: (651) 638-6400
http://www.bethel.edu

College of St. Benedict
37 South College Avenue
St. Joseph, MN 56374
Phone: (320) 363-5011
http://www.csbsju.edu

College of St. Catherine
2004 Randolph Avenue
St. Paul, MN 55105
Phone: (651) 690-6000
http://www.stkate.edu

College of St. Scholastica
1200 Kenwood Avenue
Duluth, MN 55811-4199
Phone: (218) 723-6000
http://www.css.edu

Concordia College
901 South Eighth Street
Moorhead, MN 56562-9981
Phone: (218) 299-4000
http://www.concordiacollege.edu

Crown College
6425 County Road 30
St. Bonifacius, MN 55375-9001
Phone: (952) 446-4100
http://www.crown.edu

Gustavus Adolphus College
800 West College Avenue
St. Peter, MN 56082
Phone: (507) 933-8000
http://www.gustavus.edu

Hamline University
1536 Hewitt Avenue
St. Paul, MN 55104-1284
Phone: (651) 523-2800
http://www.hamline.edu

Minnesota State University–Mankato
122 Taylor Center
Mankato, MN 56001
Phone: (507) 389-1822
http://www.mnsu.edu

Minnesota State University–Moorhead
1104 Seventh Avenue South
Moorhead, MN 56563
Phone: (218) 236-2011
http://www.moorhead.msus.edu

Northwestern College
3003 Snelling Avenue North
St. Paul, MN 55113
Phone: (651) 631-5100
http://www.nwc.edu

Southwest State University
1501 State Street
Marshall, MN 56258-1598
Phone: (507) 537-7021
http://www.southwest.msus.edu

St. Cloud State University
720 Fourth Avenue South
St. Cloud, MN 56301-4498
Phone: (320) 255-2244
http://www.stcloudstate.edu

St. John's University
P.O. Box 2000
Collegeville, MN 56321-7155
Phone: (320) 363-2011
http://www.csbsju.edu

University of Minnesota–Duluth
10 University Drive
Duluth, MN 55812-2496
Phone: (218) 726-8000
http://www.d.umn.edu

University of Minnesota–Twin Cities
100 Church Street Southeast
Minneapolis, MN 55455-0115
Phone: (612) 625-5000
http://www.umn.edu/tc

MISSISSIPPI

Alcorn State University
1000 ASU Drive #930
Alcorn State, MS 39096
Phone: (601) 877-6100
http://www.alcorn.edu

Blue Mountain College
P.O. Box 160
Blue Mountain, MS 38610-0160
Phone: (662) 685-4771
http://www.bmc.edu

Delta State University
Highway 8 West
Cleveland, MS 38733
Phone: (662) 846-3000
http://www.deltast.edu

Jackson State University
1400 John R. Lynch Street
Jackson, MS 39217
Phone: (601) 979-2121
http://www.jsums.edu

Millsaps College
1701 North State Street
Jackson, MS 39210
Phone: (601) 974-1000
http://www.millsaps.edu

Mississippi College
P.O. Box 4001
Clinton, MS 39058
Phone: (601) 925-3000
http://www.mc.edu

Mississippi State University
P.O. Box 6334
Mississippi State, MS 39762

Phone: (662) 325-2323
http://www.msstate.edu

Mississippi University for Women
P.O. Box W-160
Columbus, MS 39701
Phone: (662) 329-4750
http://www.muw.edu

Mississippi Valley State University
14000 Highway 82 West
Itta Bena, MS 38941-1400
Phone: (601) 254-9041
http://www.mvsu.edu

Rust College
150 Rust Avenue
Holly Springs, MS 38635-2328
Phone: (662) 252-8000
http://www.rustcollege.edu

University of Southern Mississippi
Southern Station 5011
Hattiesburg, MS 39406-5011
Phone: (601) 266-4111
http://www.usm.edu

William Carey College
498 Tuscan Avenue
Hattiesburg, MS 39401-5499
Phone: (601) 318-5051
http://www.wmcarey.edu

MISSOURI

Calvary Bible College
15800 Calvary Road
Kansas City, MO 64147
Phone: (816) 322-0110
E-mail: admissions@calvary.edu
http://www.calvary.edu

Central Methodist College
411 Central Methodist Square
Fayette, MO 65248-1198
Phone: (660) 248-3391
http://www.cmc.edu

Central Missouri State University
Warrensburg, MO 64093
Phone: (660) 543-4111
E-mail: admit@cmsuvmb.cmsu.edu
http://www.cmsu.edu

College of the Ozarks
P.O. Box 17
Point Lookout, MO 65726-0017
Phone: (417) 334-6411
E-mail: www.admiss4@cofo.edu
http://www.cofo.edu

Culver-Stockton College
One College Hill
Canton, MO 63435-1299
Phone: (217) 231-6000
E-mail: enrollment@culver.edu
http://www.culver.edu

Drury College
900 North Benton
Springfield, MO 65802-9977
Phone: (417) 873-7879
E-mail: drury@drury.edu
http://www.drury.edu

Lincoln University of Missouri
820 Chestnut Street
Jefferson City, MO 65102-0029
Phone: (573) 681-5000
http://www.lincolnu.edu

Missouri Baptist College
One College Park Drive
St. Louis, MO 63141
Phone: (314) 434-1115
http://www.mobap.edu

Missouri Southern State College
3950 East Newman Road
Joplin, MO 64801-1595
Phone: (417) 625-9300
http://www.mssc.edu

Missouri Western State College
4525 Downs Drive
St. Joseph, MO 64507
Phone: (816) 271-4200
http://www.mwsc.edu

Northwest Missouri State University
800 University Drive
Maryville, MO 64468-6001
Phone: (660) 562-1212
http://www.nwmissouri.edu

Southeast Missouri State University
One University Plaza
Cape Girardeau, MO 63701
Phone: (573) 651-2000
http://www.semo.edu

Southwest Baptist University
1600 University Avenue
Bolivar, MO 65613-2597
Phone: (417) 328-5281
http://www.sbuniv.edu

Southwest Missouri State University
901 South National Avenue
Springfield, MO 65804-0094

Phone: (417) 836-5000
http://www.smsu.edu

University of Missouri–Columbia
Columbia, MO 65211
Phone: (573) 882-2121
http://www.missouri.edu

University of Missouri–Kansas City
5100 Rockhill Road
Kansas City, MO 64110-2499
Phone: (816) 235-1000
http://www.umkc.edu

University of Missouri–St. Louis
8001 Natural Bridge Road
St. Louis, MO 63121-4499
Phone: (314) 516-5000
http://www.umsl.edu

Webster University
470 East Lockwood Avenue
St. Louis, MO 63119
Phone: (314) 968-6900
http://www.websteruniv.edu

William Jewell College
500 College Hill
Liberty, MO 64068
Phone: (816) 781-7700
http://www.jewell.edu

MONTANA

Montana State University–Billings
1500 University Drive
Billings, MT 59101-0298
Phone: (406) 657-2011
http://www.msubillings.edu

Montana State University–Bozeman
Bozeman, MT 59717-2190
Phone: (406) 994-0211
E-mail: admissions@montana.edu
http://www.montana.edu

Rocky Mountain College
1511 Poly Drive
Billings, MT 59102-1796
Phone: (406) 657-1000
http://www.rocky.edu

University of Montana
32 Campus Drive
Missoula, MT 59812
Phone: (406) 243-6266
http://www.umt.edu

University of Montana–Western
710 South Atlantic Street
Dillon, MT 59725-3598
Phone: (406) 683-7011
http://www.umwestern.edu

NEBRASKA

Dana College
2848 College Drive
Blair, NE 68008-1099
Phone: (402) 426-7222
http://www.dana.edu

Hastings College
800 North Turner Avenue
Hastings, NE 68901-7696
Phone: (402) 463-2402
http://www.hastings.edu

Midland Lutheran College
900 North Clarkson
Fremont, NE 68025
Phone: (402) 721-5480
http://www.mlc.edu

Nebraska Wesleyan University
5000 St. Paul Avenue
Lincoln, NE 68504
Phone: (402) 466-2371
http://www.nebrwesleyan.edu

Peru State College
P.O. Box 10
Peru, NE 68421-0010
Phone: (402) 872-3815
http://www.peru.edu

Union College
3800 South 48th Street
Lincoln, NE 68506-4300
Phone: (402) 488-2331
http://www.ucollege.edu

University of Nebraska–Kearney
905 West 25th Street
Kearney, NE 68849
Phone: (308) 865-8441
http://www.unk.edu

University of Nebraska–Lincoln
313 North 13th Street
Lincoln, NE 68588-0417
Phone: (402) 472-7211
http://www.unl.edu

University of Nebraska–Omaha
6001 Dodge Street
Omaha, NE 68182-0005

Phone: (402) 554-2800
http://www.unomaha.edu

Wayne State College
1111 Main Street
Wayne, NE 68787
Phone: (402) 375-7000
http://www.wsc.edu

NEVADA

University of Nevada–Las Vegas
4505 Maryland Parkway
Las Vegas, NV 89154-1021
Phone: (702) 895-3011
http://www.unlv.edu

University of Nevada–Reno
Reno, NV 89557-0002
Phone: (775) 784-1110
E-mail: asknevada@unr.edu
http://www.unr.edu

NEW HAMPSHIRE

Keene State College
229 Main Street
Keene, NH 03435-2604
Phone: (603) 352-1909
E-mail: admissions@keene.edu
http://www.keene.edu

Plymouth State College
17 High Street
Plymouth, NH 03264-1595
Phone: (603) 535-5000
http://www.plymouth.edu

University of New Hampshire
Thompson Hall
105 Main Street
Durham, NH 03824
Phone: (603) 862-1234
E-mail: admissions@unh.edu
http://www.unh.edu

NEW JERSEY

Kean College of New Jersey
1000 Morris Avenue
Union, NJ 07083
Phone: (908) 737-KEAN
http://www.kean.edu

Monmouth University
West Long Branch, NJ 07764-1898
Phone: (732) 571-3400
http://www.monmouth.edu

Montclair State University
One Normal Avenue
Upper Montclair, NJ 07043-1624
Phone: (973) 655-4000
http://www.montclair.edu

Rowan College of New Jersey
201 Mullica Hill Road
Glassboro, NJ 08028
Phone: (856) 256-4000
http://www.rowan.edu

Seton Hall University
400 South Orange Avenue
South Orange, NJ 07079-2680
Phone: (973) 761-9000
http://www.shu.edu

The College of New Jersey
P.O. Box 7718
Ewing, NJ 08628
Phone: (609) 771-1855
http://www.tcnj.edu

William Paterson College
300 Pompton Road
Wayne, NJ 07470
Phone: (973) 720-2000
http://www.wpunj.edu

NEW MEXICO

Eastern New Mexico University
Station Two
Portales, NM 88130
Phone: (505) 562-1011
http://www.enmu.edu

New Mexico Highlands University
P.O. Box 9000
Las Vegas, NM 87701
Phone: (505) 425-7511
http://www.nmhu.edu

New Mexico State University
Box 30001, MSC 3A
Las Cruces, NM 88003-8001
Phone: (505) 646-0111
http://www.nmsu.edu

University of New Mexico
Albuquerque, NM 87131-2046
Phone: (505) 277-0111
http://www.unm.edu

Western New Mexico University
P.O. Box 680
Silver City, NM 88062
Phone: (505) 538-6011
http://www.wnmu.edu

NEW YORK

Adelphi University
One South Avenue
Garden City, NY 11530
Phone: (516) 877-3000
http://www.adelphi.edu

CUNY–Brooklyn College
2900 Bedford Avenue
Brooklyn, NY 11210
Phone: (718) 951-5000
http://www.brooklyn.cuny.edu

CUNY–City College
Convent Avenue at 138th Street
New York, NY 10031
Phone: (212) 650-7000
http://www.ccny.cuny.edu

CUNY–Queens College
65-30 Kissena Boulevard
Flushing, NY 11367
Phone: (718) 997-5000
http://www.qc.edu

College of Saint Rose
432 Western Avenue
Albany, NY 12203
Phone: (518) 454-5111
http://www.strose.edu

Concordia College
171 White Plains Road
Bronxville, NY 10708
Phone: (914) 337-9300
http://www.concordia-ny.edu

Dowling College
Idle Hour Boulevard
Oakdale, NY 11769-1999
Phone: (631) 244-3000
http://www.dowling.edu

Five Towns College
305 North Service Road
Dix Hills, NY 11746-6055
Phone: (631) 424-7000
http://www.fivetowns.edu

Hartwick College
One Hartwick Drive
P.O. Box 402
Oneonta, NY 13820-4022
Phone: (607) 431-4200
http://www.hartwick.edu

Hofstra University
Hempstead, NY 11549

Phone: (516) 463-6600
E-mail: admissions@hofstra.edu
http://www.hofstra.edu

Houghton College
One Hartwick Drive
P.O. Box 402
Oneonta, NY 13820-4022
Phone: (607) 431-4200
http://www.hartwick.edu

Ithaca College
100 Job Hall
Ithaca, NY 14850-7020
Phone: (607) 274-3124
E-mail: admissions@ithaca.edu
http://www.ithaca.edu

Long Island University–C.W. Post Campus
720 Northern Boulevard
Brookville, NY 11548-1300
Phone: (516) 299-2000
http://www.cwpost.liu.edu

Manhattanville College
2900 Purchase Street
Purchase, NY 10577
Phone: (914) 694-2200
http://www.manhattanville.edu

Nazareth College
4245 East Avenue
Rochester, NY 14618-3790
Phone: (585) 586-2525
http://www.naz.edu

New York University
New York, NY 10011-9108
Phone: (212) 998-1212
http://www.nyu.edu

Nyack College
One South Boulevard
Nyack, NY 10960
Phone: (845) 358-1710
http://www.nyackcollege.edu

Roberts Wesleyan College
2301 Westside Drive
Rochester, NY 14624-1997
Phone: (585) 594-6000
http://www.roberts.edu

SUNY–Buffalo
Buffalo, NY 14260
Phone: (716) 645-2000
http://www.buffalo.edu

SUNY–College at Fredonia
138 Central Avenue
Fredonia, NY 14063-1136
Phone: (716) 673-3111
http://www.fredonia.edu

SUNY–College at Potsdam
44 Pierrepont Avenue
Potsdam, NY 13676
Phone: (315) 267-2000
http://www.potsdam.edu

Syracuse University
201 Tolley Administration Building
Syracuse, NY 13244-1100
Phone: (315) 443-1870
http://www.syr.edu

University of Rochester
4245 East Avenue
Rochester, NY 14618-3790
Phone: (585) 586-2525
http://www.rochester.edu

Wagner College
One Campus Road
Staten Island, NY 10301-4495
Phone: (718) 390-3100
E-mail: admissions@wagner.edu
http://www.wagner.edu

NORTH CAROLINA

Appalachian State University
Boone, NC 28608
Phone: (828) 262-2000
http://www.appstate.edu

Barton College
P.O. Box 5000
Wilson, NC 27893
Phone: (252) 399-6300
http://www.barton.edu

Bennett College
900 East Washington Street
Greensboro, NC 27401-3239
Phone: (336) 273-4431
http://www.bennett.edu

Campbell University
P.O. Box 546
Buies Creek, NC 27506
Phone: (910) 893-1200
http://www.campbell.edu

Catawba College
2300 West Innes Street
Salisbury, NC 28144

Phone: (704) 637-4111
http://www.catawba.edu

Chowan College
200 Jones Drive
Murfreesboro, NC 27855-9901
Phone: (252) 398-6500
http://www.chowan.edu

East Carolina University
East Fifth Street
Greenville, NC 27858-4353
Phone: (252) 328-6131
http://www.ecu.edu

Elizabeth City State University
1704 Weeksville Road
Elizabeth City, NC 27909
Phone: (252) 335-3400
http://www.ecsu.edu

Elon University
2700 Campus Box
Elon College, NC 27244-2010
Phone: (336) 278-2000
http://www.elon.edu

Gardner-Webb College
P.O. Box 817
Boiling Springs, NC 28017
Phone: (704) 406-4000
http://www.gardner-webb.edu

Johnson C. Smith University
100 Beatties Ford Road
Charlotte, NC 28216-5398
Phone: (704) 378-1000
http://www.jcsu.edu

Lenoir-Rhyne College
Hickory, NC 28603
Phone: (828) 328-1741
http://www.lrc.edu

Livingstone College
701 West Monroe Street
Salisbury, NC 28144-5213
Phone: (704) 216-6000
http://www.livingstone.edu

Mars Hill College
701 West Monroe Street
Salisbury, NC 28144-5213
Phone: (704) 216-6000
http://www.livingstone.edu

Meredith College
3800 Hillsborough Street
Raleigh, NC 27607-5298

Phone: (919) 760-8600
http://www.meredith.edu

Methodist College
5400 Ramsey Street
Fayetteville, NC 28311-1420
Phone: (800) 488-7110
http://www.methodist.edu

**North Carolina Agricultural and
   Technical State University**
1601 East Market Street
Greensboro, NC 27411
Phone: (336) 334-7500
http://www.ncat.edu

North Carolina Central University
1801 Fayetteville Street
Durham, NC 27707
Phone: (919) 560-6100
http://www.nccu.edu

Pfeiffer College
Highway 52
P.O. Box 960
Misenheimer, NC 28109
Phone: (704) 463-1360
http://www.pfeiffer.edu

St. Augustine's College
1315 Oakwood Avenue
Raleigh, NC 27610-2298
Phone: (919) 516-4000
http://www.st-aug.edu

**University of North Carolina–Chapel
   Hill**
Campus Box 9100, 103 South Building
Chapel Hill, NC 27599-2200
Phone: (919) 962-2211
http://www.unc.edu

University of North Carolina–Charlotte
9201 University City Boulevard
Charlotte, NC 28223-0001
Phone: (704) 687-2000
http://www.uncc.edu

**University of North
   Carolina–Greensboro**
1000 Spring Garden Street
Greensboro, NC 27402-6166
Phone: (336) 334-5000
http://www.uncg.edu

**University of North
   Carolina–Wilmington**
601 South College Road
Wilmington, NC 28403-3297

Phone: (910) 962-3000
http://www.uncwil.edu

Western Carolina University
Cullowhee, NC 28723
Phone: (828) 227-7211
http://www.wcu.edu

Wilkes College
P.O. Box 120
1328 Collegiate Drive
Wilkesboro, NC 28697-0120
Phone: (336) 838-6100
http://www.wilkes.cc.nc.us

Wingate College
P.O. Box 159
Wingate, NC 28174-0157
Phone: (704) 233-8000
http://www.wingate.edu

Winston-Salem State University
601 Martin Luther King Jr. Drive
Winston-Salem, NC 27110
Phone: (336) 750-2000
http://www.wssu.edu

NORTH DAKOTA

Dickinson State University
291 Campus Drive
Dickinson, ND 58601
Phone: (701) 483-2331
http://www.dsu.nodak.edu

Minot State University
500 University Avenue West
Minot, ND 58707-5002
Phone: (701) 858-3000
http://www.minotstateu.edu

North Dakota State University
Ceres 124
P.O. Box 5454
Fargo, ND 58105-5454
Phone: (701) 231-8011
http://www.ndsu.edu

University of North Dakota
P.O. Box 8135
Grand Forks, ND 58202
Phone: (701) 777-2011
http://www.und.edu

Valley City State University
101 College Street Southwest
Valley City, ND 58072-4098
Phone: (701) 845-7990
http://www.vcsu.edu

OHIO

Baldwin-Wallace College
275 Eastland Road
Berea, OH 44017-2088
Phone: (440) 826-2900
http://www.bw.edu

Bluffton College
280 West College Avenue
Bluffton, OH 45817-1196
Phone: (419) 358-3000
http://www.bluffton.edu

Bowling Green State University
Bowling Green, OH 43403-0085
Phone: (419) 372-2531
E-mail: admissions@bgnet.bgsu.edu
http://www.bgsu.edu

Capital University
2199 East Main Street
Columbus, OH 43209-2394
Phone: (614) 236-6011
http://www.capital.edu

Case Western Reserve University
10900 Euclid Avenue
Cleveland, OH 44106
Phone: (216) 368-2000
http://www.cwru.edu

Cedarville College
251 North Main Street
Cedarville, OH 45314
Phone: (937) 766-2211
http://www.cedarville.edu

Central State University
P.O. Box 1004
Wilberforce, OH 45384-1004
Phone: (937) 376-6011
http://www.centralstate.edu

College of Wooster
1189 Beall Avenue
Wooster, OH 44691-2363
Phone: (330) 263-2000
http://www.wooster.edu

Denison University
1 Main Street
Granville, OH 43023
Phone: (740) 587-0810
http://www.denison.edu

Heidelberg College
310 East Market Street
Tiffin, OH 44883-2462

Phone: (419) 448-2000
http://www.heidelberg.edu

Kent State University
P.O. Box 5190
Kent, OH 44242-0001
Phone: (330) 672-2444
http://www.kent.edu

Malone College
515 25th Street Northwest
Canton, OH 44709-3897
Phone: (330) 471-8100
http://www.malone.edu

Miami University
Roudebush Hall
Oxford, OH 45056-3434
Phone: (513) 529-1809
http://www.muohio.edu

Mount Union College
1972 Clark Avenue
Alliance, OH 44601-3993
Phone: (330) 821-5320
http://www.muc.edu

Mount Vernon Nazarene College
800 Martinsburg Road
Mount Vernon, OH 43050
Phone: (740) 397-9000
http://www.mvnu.edu

Muskingum College
163 Stormont Street
New Concord, OH 43762-1160
Phone: (740) 826-8211
http://www.muskingum.edu

Oberlin College
173 West Lorain Street
Oberlin, OH 44074
Phone: (440) 775-8121
http://www.oberlin.edu

Ohio Northern University
525 South Main Street
Ada, OH 45810-1599
Phone: (419) 772-2000
http://www.onu.edu

Ohio State University
190 North Oval Mall
Columbus, OH 43210-1390
Phone: (614) 292-6446
http://www.osu.edu

Ohio Wesleyan University
61 South Sandusky Street
Delaware, OH 43015-2398
Phone: (800) 922-8953
http://www.owu.edu

Otterbein College
One Otterbein College
Westerville, OH 43081
Phone: (614) 890-3000
http://www.otterbein.edu

University of Akron
302 Buchtel Common
Akron, OH 44325-2001
Phone: (330) 972-7100
http://www.uakron.edu

University of Cincinnati
P.O. Box 210091
Cincinnati, OH 45221-0091
Phone: (513) 556-6000
http://www.uc.edu

University of Dayton
300 College Park
Dayton, OH 45469-1300
Phone: (937) 229-1000
http://www.udayton.edu

University of Toledo
2801 West Bancroft Street
Toledo, OH 43606-3398
Phone: (419) 530-8888
http://www.utoledo.edu

Wittenberg University
P.O. Box 720
Springfield, OH 45501-0720
Phone: (800) 677-7558
http://www.wittenberg.edu

Wright State University
3640 Colonel Glenn Highway
Dayton, OH 45435
Phone: (937) 775-3333
http://www.wright.edu

Xavier University
3800 Victory Parkway
Cincinnati, OH 45207-5311
Phone: (513) 745-3000
http://www.xu.edu

Youngstown State University
One University Plaza
Youngstown, OH 44555-0001
Phone: (330) 742-3000
http://www.ysu.edu

OKLAHOMA

Cameron University
2800 West Gore Boulevard
Lawton, OK 73505
Phone: (580) 581-2230
http://www.cameron.edu

East Central University
Ada, OK 74820
Phone: (580) 332-8000
http://www.ecok.edu

Northeastern State University
601 North Grand Avenue
Tahlequah, OK 74464
Phone: (918) 456-5511
http://www.nsuok.edu

Northwestern Oklahoma State University
709 Oklahoma Boulevard
Alva, OK 73717-2799
Phone: (580) 327-1700
E-mail: cher@nwosu.edu
http://www.nwalva.edu

Oklahoma Baptist University
500 West University
Shawnee, OK 74804
Phone: (405) 275-2850
E-mail: admissions@mail.okbu.edu
http://www.okbu.edu

Oklahoma Christian University of Science and Arts
P.O. Box 11000
Oklahoma City, OK 73136-1100
Phone: (405) 425-5000
E-mail: info@oc.edu
http://www.oc.edu

Oklahoma City University
2501 North Blackwelder
Oklahoma City, OK 73106
Phone: (405) 521-5000
http://www.okcu.edu

Oklahoma Panhandle State University
P.O. Box 430
Goodwell, OK 73939-0430
Phone: (580) 349-2611
E-mail: opsu@opsu.edu
http://www.opsu.edu

Oklahoma State University
Stillwater, OK 74078
Phone: (405) 744-5000
E-mail: admit@okstate.edu
http://www.okstate.edu

Oral Roberts University
7777 South Lewis Avenue
Tulsa, OK 74171
Phone: (918) 495-6161
E-mail: admissions@oru.edu
http://www.oru.edu

Southeastern Oklahoma State University
P.O. Box 4137
Durant, OK 74701
Phone: (580) 745-2000
http://www.sosu.edu

Southern Nazarene University
6729 Northwest 39th Expressway
Bethany, OK 73008
Phone: (405) 789-6400
http://www.snu.edu

Southwestern Oklahoma State University
100 Campus Drive
Weatherford, OK 73096
Phone: (580) 774-6611
http://www.swosu.edu

University of Central Oklahoma
100 North University Drive
Edmond, OK 73034-0151
Phone: (405) 974-2000
http://www.ucok.edu

University of Oklahoma–Norman
660 Parrington Oval
Norman, OK 73019-4076
Phone: (405) 325-0311
E-mail: admrec@ou.edu
http://www.ou.edu

University of Science and Arts of Oklahoma
1727 West Alabama
Chickasha, OK 73018-0001
Phone: (405) 224-3140
http://www.usao.edu

University of Tulsa
600 South College Avenue
Tulsa, OK 74104-3189
Phone: (918) 631-2307
E-mail: admission@utulsa.edu
http://www.utulsa.edu

OREGON

Pacific University
2043 College Way
Forest Grove, OR 97116-1797
Phone: (503) 357-6151
E-mail: admissions@pacificu.edu
http://www.pacificu.edu

University of Oregon
Eugene, OR 97403-1217
Phone: (541) 346-3111
E-mail: uoadmit@oregon.uoregon.edu
http://www.uoregon.edu

University of Portland
5000 North Willamette Boulevar
Portland, OR 97203-5798
Phone: (503) 943-7911
E-mail: admissio@up.edu
http://www.up.edu

Warner Pacific College
2219 Southeast 68th Avenue
Portland, OR 97215-4026
Phone: (503) 517-1000
http://www.warnerpacific.edu

Western Baptist College
5000 Deer Park Drive Southeast
Salem, OR 97301-9392
Phone: (503) 581-8600
E-mail: admissions@wbc.edu
http://www.wbc.edu

Willamette University
900 State Street
Salem, OR 97301-3922
Phone: (503) 370-6303
http://www.willamette.edu

PENNSYLVANIA

Bucknell University
Moore Avenue
Lewisburg, PA 17837-9988
Phone: (570) 577-2000
E-mail: admissions@bucknell.edu
http://www.bucknell.edu

Carnegie Mellon University
5000 Forbes Avenue
Pittsburgh, PA 15213-3890
Phone: (412) 268-2000
http://www.cmu.edu

Chestnut Hill College
9601 Germantown Avenue
Philadelphia, PA 19118-2693
Phone: (215) 248-7000
E-mail: apply@chc.edu
http://www.chc.edu

Clarion University of Pennsylvania
Clarion, PA 16214
Phone: (814) 393-2000

E-mail: admissions@clarion.edu
http://www.clarion.edu

Duquesne University
600 Forbes Avenue
Pittsburgh, PA 15282-0201
Phone: (412) 396-6000
E-mail: admissions@duq.edu
http://www.duq.edu

Edinboro University of Pennsylvania
Edinboro, PA 16444
Phone: (814) 732-2000
http://www.edinboro.edu

Elizabethtown College
One Alpha Drive
Elizabethtown, PA 17022
Phone: (717) 361-1000
E-mail: admissions@etown.edu
http://www.etown.edu

Geneva College
3200 College Avenue
Beaver Falls, PA 15010
Phone: (724) 846-5100
http://www.geneva.edu

Gettysburg College
300 North Washington Street
Gettysburg, PA 17325-1484
Phone: (717) 337-6000
E-mail: admiss@gettysburg.edu
http://www.gettysburg.edu

Grove City College
100 Campus Drive
Grove City, PA 16127-2104
Phone: (724) 458-2000
E-mail: admissions@gcc.edu
http://www.gcc.edu

Immaculata College
1145 King Road
Immaculata, PA 19345
Phone: (610) 647-4400
E-mail: admiss@immaculata.edu
http://www.immaculata.edu

Indiana University of Pennsylvania
201 Sutton Hall
1011 South Drive
Indiana, PA 15705-1088
Phone: (724) 357-2100
E-mail: admissions_inquiry@grove.iup.
    edu
http://www.iup.edu

Lebanon Valley College
101 North College Avenue
Annville, PA 17003

Phone: (717) 867-6100
E-mail: admission@lvc.edu
http://www.lvc.edu

Lycoming College
700 College Place
Williamsport, PA 17701
Phone: (800) 345-3920
http://www.lycoming.edu

Mansfield University of Pennsylvania
Mansfield, PA 16933
Phone: (570) 662-4000
E-mail: admissns@mnsfld.edu
http://www.mnsfld.edu

Marywood College
2300 Adams Avenue
Scranton, PA 18509-1598
Phone: (570) 348-6211
E-mail: ugadm@ac.marywood.edu
http://www.marywood.edu

Mercyhurst College
501 East 38th Street
Erie, PA 16546-0001
Phone: (814) 824-2000
E-mail: admug@mercyhurst.edu
http://www.mercyhurst.edu

Messiah College
One College Avenue
Grantham, PA 17027-0800
Phone: (717) 766-2511
http://www.messiah.edu

Millersville University of Pennsylvania
P.O. Box 1002
Millersville, PA 17551-0302
Phone: (717) 872-3011
E-mail: admissions@millersville.edu
http://www.millersville.edu

Moravian College
1200 Main Street
Bethlehem, PA 18018
Phone: (610) 861-1300
E-mail: admissions@moravian.edu
http://www.moravian.edu

Saint Vincent College
300 Fraser Purchase Road
Latrobe, PA 15650-2690
Phone: (724) 539-9761
E-mail: admission@stvincent.edu
http://www.stvincent.edu

Seton Hill University
Seton Hill Drive
Greensburg, PA 15601

Phone: (724) 834-2200
E-mail: admit@setonhill.edu
http://www.setonhill.edu

**Slippery Rock University of
    Pennsylvania**
Slippery Rock, PA 16057
Phone: (724) 738-9000
http://www.sru.edu

Susquehanna University
514 University Avenue
Selinsgrove, PA 17870-1040
Phone: (570) 374-0101
http://www.susqu.edu

Temple University
1801 North Broad Street
Philadelphia, PA 19122-6096
Phone: (215) 204-7000
http://www.temple.edu

West Chester University of Pennsylvania
West Chester, PA 19383
Phone: (610) 436-1000
http://www.wcupa.edu

Westminster College
Market Street
New Wilmington, PA 16172-0001
Phone: (724) 946-8761
http://www.westminster.edu

York College of Pennsylvania
York, PA 17405-7199
Phone: (717) 846-7788
E-mail: admissions@ycp.edu
http://www.ycp.edu

RHODE ISLAND

Rhode Island College
600 Mount Pleasant Avenue
Providence, RI 02908
Phone: (401) 456-8000
http://www.ric.edu

University of Rhode Island
Kingston, RI 02881-2020
Phone: (401) 874-1000
http://www.uri.edu

SOUTH CAROLINA

Anderson College
316 Boulevard
Anderson, SC 29621
Phone: (864) 231-2000
http://www.ac.edu

Charleston Southern University
P.O. Box 118087
Charleston, SC 29423
Phone: (843) 863-7000
http://www.csuniv.edu

Claflin College
400 Magnolia Street
Orangeburg, SC 29115
Phone: (803) 535-5000
http://www.claflin.edu

Coker College
300 East College Avenue
Hartsville, SC 29550
Phone: (843) 383-8000
http://www.coker.edu

Converse College
580 East Main Street
Spartanburg, SC 29302-0006
Phone: (864) 596-9000
http://www.converse.edu

Erskine College
2 Washington Street
Due West, SC 29639-0176
Phone: (864) 379-2131
http://www.erskine.edu

Furman University
3300 Poinsett Highway
Greenville, SC 29613
Phone: (864) 294-2000
http://www.furman.edu

Lander University
320 Stanley Avenue
Greenwood, SC 29649-2099
Phone: (864) 388-8400
http://www.lander.edu

Limestone College
1115 College Drive
Gaffney, SC 29340-3799
Phone: (864) 489-7151
http://www.limestone.edu

Newberry College
2100 College Street
Newberry, SC 29108
Phone: (800) 845-4955
http://www.newberry.edu

Presbyterian College
P.O. Box 975
Clinton, SC 29325-9989
Phone: (864) 833-2820
http://www.presby.edu

South Carolina State University
P.O. Box 1020
Central, SC 29630-1020
Phone: (864) 644-5000
http://www.swu.edu

Southern Wesleyan University
P.O. Box 1020
Central, SC 29630-1020
Phone: (864) 644-5000
http://www.swu.edu

University of South Carolina
Columbia, SC 29208
Phone: (803) 777-7000
http://www.sc.edu

Winthrop University
701 Oakland Avenue
Rock Hill, SC 29733
Phone: (803) 323-2211
http://www.winthrop.edu

SOUTH DAKOTA

Augustana College
2001 South Summit Avenue
Sioux Falls, SD 57197-9990
Phone: (605) 274-0770
http://www.augie.edu

Black Hills State College
1200 University Street, Unit 9502
Spearfish, SD 57799-9502
Phone: (605) 642-6011
http://www.bhsu.edu

Mount Marty College
1105 West Eighth Street
Yankton, SD 57078
Phone: (800) 658-4552
http://www.mtmc.edu

Northern State College
1200 South Jay Street
Aberdeen, SD 57401-7198
Phone: (605) 626-3011
http://www.northern.edu

South Dakota State University
P.O. Box 2201
Brookings, SD 57007-0649
Phone: (800) 952-3541
http://www.sdstate.edu

University of South Dakota
P.O. Box 2201
Brookings, SD 57007-0649
Phone: (800) 952-3541
http://www.sdstate.edu

TENNESSEE

Austin Peay State University
601 College Street
Clarksville, TN 37044
Phone: (931) 221-7011
http://www.apsu.edu

Belmont College
1900 Belmont Boulevard
Nashville, TN 37212-3757
Phone: (615) 460-6000
http://www.belmont.edu

Bethel College
325 Cherry Avenue
McKenzie, TN 38201
Phone: (731) 352-4000
http://www.bethel-college.edu

Bryan College
P.O. Box 7000
Dayton, TN 37321-7000
Phone: (423) 775-2041
http://www.bryan.edu

Carson-Newman College
1646 Russell Avenue
Jefferson City, TN 37760
Phone: (865) 471-2000
http://www.cn.edu

Crichton College
255 North Highland
Memphis, TN 38111
Phone: (901) 320-9700
http://www.crichton.edu

David Lipscomb College
3901 Granny White Pike
Nashville, TN 37204-3951
Phone: (615) 269-1000
http://www.lipscomb.edu

East Tennessee State University
807 University Parkway
Johnson City, TN 37614-0731
Phone: (423) 439-1000
http://www.etsu.edu

Fisk University
1000 17th Avenue North
Nashville, TN 37208-3051
Phone: (615) 329-8500
http://www.fisk.edu

Lambuth College
705 Lambuth Boulevard
Jackson, TN 38301-5296

Phone: (731) 425-2500
http://www.lambuth.edu

Lee College
P.O. Box 3450
Cleveland, TN 37311
Phone: (423) 614-8000
http://www.leeuniversity.edu

Maryville College
502 East Lamar Alexander Parkway
Maryville, TN 37804-5907
Phone: (865) 981-8000
http://www.maryvillecollege.edu

Middle Tennessee State University
1301 East Main Street
Murfreesboro, TN 37132
Phone: (615) 898-2300
http://www.mtsu.edu

Milligan College
P.O. Box 500
Milligan College, TN 37682
Phone: (423) 461-8700
E-mail: admissions@milligan.edu
http://www.milligan.edu

Tennessee Wesleyan College
P.O. Box 40
Athens, TN 37371
Phone: (423) 745-7504
http://www.twcnet.edu

Trevecca Nazarene College
333 Murfreesboro Road
Nashville, TN 37210
Phone: (615) 248-1200
http://www.trevecca.edu

Union University
1050 Union University Drive
Jackson, TN 38305-3697
Phone: (731) 668-1818
http://www.uu.edu

University of Tennessee–Chattanooga
615 McCallie Avenue
Chattanooga, TN 37403
Phone: (423) 755-4111
http://www.utc.edu

University of Tennessee–Knoxville
800 Andy Holt Tower
Knoxville, TN 37996-0230
Phone: (865) 974-1000
http://www.tennessee.edu

University of Tennessee–Martin
University Street
Martin, TN 38238
Phone: (731) 587-7000
http://www.utm.edu

Vanderbilt University
2201 West End Avenue
Nashville, TN 37235
Phone: (615) 322-7311
http://www.vanderbilt.edu

TEXAS

Abilene Christian University
ACU Box 29100
Abilene, TX 79699
Phone: (915) 674-2000
http://www.acu.edu

Angelo State University
Box 11014 ASU Station
San Angelo, TX 76909
Phone: (915) 942-2555
http://www.angelo.edu

Arlington Baptist College
3001 West Division
Arlington, TX 76012
Phone: (817) 461-8741
http://www.abconline.edu

Baylor University
Waco, TX 76798-7056
Phone: (254) 710-1011
http://www.baylor.edu

Dallas Baptist University
3000 Mountain Creek Parkway
Dallas, TX 75211-9299
Phone: (214) 333-7100
http://www.dbu.edu

East Texas Baptist University
1209 North Grove
Marshall, TX 75670-1498
Phone: (903) 935-7963
http://www.etbu.edu

Hardin-Simmons University
P.O. Box 16050
Abilene, TX 79698
Phone: (915) 670-1000
http://www.hsutx.edu

Houston Baptist University
7502 Fondren Road
Houston, TX 77074-3298
Phone: (281) 649-3000
http://www.hbu.edu

Howard Payne University
1000 Fisk Avenue
Brownwood, TX 76801
Phone: (915) 646-2502
http://www.hputx.edu

Jarvis Christian College
P.O. Box 1470
Hawkins, TX 75765-1470
Phone: (903) 769-5700
http://www.jarvis.edu

Lamar University
4400 Martin Luther King Boulevard
P.O. Box 10009
Beaumont, TX 77705
Phone: (409) 880-8888
http://www.lamar.edu

Lubbock Christian University
5601 19th Street
Lubbock, TX 79407
Phone: (806) 796-8800
http://www.lcu.edu

McMurry College
South 14th and Sayles Boulevard
Abilene, TX 79697-0001
Phone: (915) 793-3800
http://www.mcm.edu

Midwestern State University
3410 Taft Boulevard
Wichita Falls, TX 76308
Phone: (940) 397-4000
http://www.mwsu.edu

Prairie View A & M University
P.O. Box 2777
Prairie View, TX 77446-0188
Phone: (936) 857-3311
http://www.pvamu.edu

Sam Houston State University
1700 Sam Houston Avenue
Huntsville, TX 77341-2418
Phone: (936) 294-1111
http://www.shsu.edu

Southern Methodist University
P.O. Box 750181
Dallas, TX 75275-0296
Phone: (214) 768-2000
http://www.smu.edu

Southwestern University
1001 East University Avenue
Georgetown, TX 78626
Phone: (512) 863-6511
http://www.southwestern.edu

Southwest Texas State University
601 University Drive
San Marcos, TX 78666-5709
Phone: (512) 245-2111
http://www.swt.edu

Tarleton State University
Box T-0001 Tarleton Station
Stephenville, TX 76402
Phone: (254) 968-9000
http://www.tarleton.edu

Texas A & M University–Kingsville
700 University Boulevard
MSC 105
Kingsville, TX 78363-8201
Phone: (361) 593-2111
http://www.tamuk.edu

Texas Christian University
2800 South University Drive
Fort Worth, TX 76129
Phone: (817) 257-7000
http://www.tcu.edu

Texas Southern University
3100 Cleburne Street
Houston, TX 77004
Phone: (713) 313-7011
http://www.tsu.edu

Texas Tech University
Box 45005
Lubbock, TX 79409-5005
Phone: (806) 742-2011
http://www.ttu.edu

Texas Wesleyan College
1201 Wesleyan Street
Fort Worth, TX 76105-1536
Phone: (817) 531-4444
http://www.txwesleyan.edu

University of Mary Hardin–Baylor
900 College Street
Belton, TX 76513
Phone: (254) 295-8642
http://www.umhb.edu

University of Texas–Austin
P.O. Box 8058
Austin, TX 78712-1111
Phone: (512) 471-3434
http://www.utexas.edu

University of Texas–San Antonio
6900 North Loop 1604 West
San Antonio, TX 78249
Phone: (210) 458-4530
http://www.utsa.edu

University of the Incarnate Word
4301 Broadway
San Antonio, TX 78209-6397
Phone: (210) 829-6000
http://www.uiw.edu

Wayland Baptist University
1900 West Seventh Street
Plainview, TX 79072
Phone: (806) 291-1000
http://www.wbu.edu

Southwest Texas State University
601 University Drive
San Marcos, TX 78666-5709
Phone: (512) 245-2111
http://www.swt.edu

Wiley College
711 Wiley Avenue
Marshall, TX 75670
Phone: (903) 927-3300
http://www.wileyc.edu

UTAH

Brigham Young University
Provo, UT 84602-1110
Phone: (801) 378-1211
http://www.byu.edu

Southern Utah State College
351 West Center Street
Cedar City, UT 84720
Phone: (435) 586-7700
http://www.suu.edu

University of Utah
200 South University Street
Salt Lake City, UT 84112
Phone: (801) 581-7200
http://www.utah.edu

Utah State University
160 Old Main Hill
Logan, UT 84322-1600
Phone: (435) 797-1000
http://www.usu.edu

Weber State College
1103 University Circle
Ogden, UT 84408-1103
Phone: (801) 626-6000
http://www.weber.edu

VERMONT

Castleton State College
Castleton, VT 05735

Phone: (002) 468 5611
http://www.castleton.edu

Johnson State College
337 College Hill
Johnson, VT 05656
Phone: (802) 635-2356
http://www.jsc.vsc.edu

University of Vermont
Burlington, VT 05401-3596
Phone: (802) 656-3131
http://www.uvm.edu

VIRGINIA

Bluefield College
3000 College Drive
Bluefield, VA 24605
Phone: (276) 326-3682
http://www.bluefield.edu

Bridgewater College
402 East College Street
Bridgewater, VA 22812-1599
Phone: (540) 828-8000
http://www.bridgewater.edu

Christopher Newport University
One University Place
Newport News, VA 23606
Phone: (757) 594-7100
http://www.cnu.edu

Eastern Mennonite College
1200 Park Road
Harrisonburg, VA 22802-2462
Phone: (540) 432-4000
http://www.emu.edu

Emory & Henry College
P.O. Box 947
Emory, VA 24327
Phone: (276) 944-4121
E-mail: ehadmiss@ehc.edu
http://www.ehc.edu

Hampton University
Hampton, VA 23668
Phone: (757) 727-5000
E-mail: admissions@hamptonu.edu
http://www.hamptonu.edu

Liberty University
1971 University Boulevard
Lynchburg, VA 24502
Phone: (434) 582-2000
http://www.liberty.edu

Longwood College
Farmville, VA 23909-1898
Phone: (434) 395-2000
http://www.longwood.edu

Lynchburg College
1501 Lakeside Drive
Lynchburg, VA 24501
Phone: (434) 544-8100
E-mail: admissions@llynchburg.edu
http://www.lynchburg.edu

Mary Washington College
1301 College Avenue
Fredericksburg, VA 22401-5358
Phone: (540) 654-1000
E-mail: admit@mwc.edu
http://www.mwc.edu

Old Dominion University
5215 Hampton Boulevard
Norfolk, VA 23529
Phone: (757) 683-3000
http://www.odu.edu

Radford University
P.O. Box 6890, RU Station
Radford, VA 24142-6903
Phone: (540) 831-5000
http://www.radford.edu

Shenandoah University
1460 University Drive
Winchester, VA 22601-5195
Phone: (540) 665-4500
E-mail: admit@su.edu
http://www.su.edu

University of Richmond
28 Westhampton Way
University of Richmond, VA 23173
Phone: (804) 289-8000
E-mail: admissions@richmond.edu
http://www.richmond.edu

Virginia Commonwealth University
Box 842527
Richmond, VA 23284-2526
Phone: (804) 828-0100
E-mail: vcuinfo@vcu.edu
http://www.vcu.edu

Virginia Intermont College
1013 Moore Street
Bristol, VA 24201
Phone: (540) 669-6101
http://www.vic.edu

Virginia Polytechnic Institute and State University
104 Burruss Hall
Blacksburg, VA 24061
Phone: (540) 231-6000
E-mail: vtadmiss@vt.edu
http://www.vt.edu

Virginia Wesleyan College
1584 Wesleyan Drive
Norfolk, VA 23502-5599
Phone: (757) 455-3200
E-mail: admissions@vwc.edu
http://www.vwc.edu

WASHINGTON

Central Washington University
400 East 8th Avenue
Ellensburg, WA 98926-7463
Phone: (509) 963-1111
http://www.cwu.edu

Eastern Washington University
526 Fifth Street
Cheney, WA 99004-2447
Phone: (509) 359-6200
http://www.ewu.edu

Gonzaga University
502 East Boone Avenue
Spokane, WA 99258-0001
Phone: (509) 328-4220
http://www.gonzaga.edu

Pacific Lutheran University
Tacoma, WA 98447-0003
Phone: (253) 531-6900
http://www.plu.edu

Seattle Pacific University
3307 Third Avenue West
Seattle, WA 98119-1997
Phone: (206) 281-2000
http://www.spu.edu

University of Puget Sound
1500 North Warner Street
Tacoma, WA 98416-0003
Phone: (253) 879-3100
http://www.ups.edu

University of Washington
Seattle, WA 98195-5840
Phone: (206) 543-2100
http://www.washington.edu

Walla Walla College
204 South College Avenue
College Place, WA 99324-3000

Phone: (800) 541-8900
http://www.wwc.edu

Washington State University
Lighty 370
Pullman, WA 99164-1067
Phone: (888) GO-TO-WSU
http://www.wsu.edu

Western Washington University
Old Main 200
516 High Street
Bellingham, WA 98225-9009
Phone: (360) 650-3000
http://www.wwu.edu

Whitworth College
300 West Hawthorne Road
Spokane, WA 99251-0002
Phone: (509) 777-1000
http://www.whitworth.edu

WEST VIRGINIA

Alderson-Broaddus College
College Hill Road
Philippi, WV 26416
Phone: (304) 457-1700
http://www.ab.edu

Concord College
1000 Vermillion Street
Athens, WV 24712-1000
Phone: (304) 384-3115
http://www.concord.edu

Fairmont State College
1201 Locust Avenue
Fairmont, WV 26554
Phone: (304) 367-4000
http://www.fscwv.edu

Glenville State College
200 High Street
Glenville, WV 26351-1292
Phone: (304) 462-7361
http://www.glenville.edu

Marshall University
400 Hal Greer Boulevard
Huntington, WV 25755-2020
Phone: (304) 696-3170
http://www.marshall.edu

Shepherd College
P.O. Box 3210
Shepherdstown, WV 25443-3210
Phone: (304) 876-5000
http://www.shepherd.edu

University of Charleston
2300 MacCorkle Avenue Southeast
Charleston, WV 25304
Phone: (304) 357-4800
http://www.ucwv.edu

West Liberty State College
P.O. Box 295
West Liberty, WV 26074-0295
Phone: (304) 336-5000
http://www.wlsc.edu

West Virginia State College
P.O. Box 1000
Institute, WV 25112-1000
Phone: (304) 766-3000
http://www.wvsc.edu

West Virginia Wesleyan College
59 College Avenue
Buckhannon, WV 26201-2998
Phone: (304) 473-8000
http://www.wvwc.edu

WISCONSIN

Alverno College
3400 South 43rd Street
Milwaukee, WI 53234-3922
Phone: (414) 382-6000
E-mail: admissions@alverno.edu
http://www.alverno.edu

Beloit College
700 College Street
Beloit, WI 53511-5595
Phone: (608) 363-2000
E-mail: admiss@beloit.edu
http://www.beloit.edu

Carroll College
100 North East Avenue
Waukesha, WI 53186-9988
Phone: (262) 547-1211
http://www.cc.edu

Carthage College
2001 Alford Park Drive
Kenosha, WI 53140-1994
Phone: (262) 551-8500
http://www.carthage.edu

Lakeland College
P.O. Box 359
Sheboygan, WI 53082
Phone: (920) 565-2111
http://www.lakeland.edu

Lawrence University
706 East College Avenue
Appleton, WI 54912-0599
Phone: (920) 832-7000
http://www.lawrence.edu

Marian College of Fond Du Lac
45 South National Avenue
Fond du Lac, WI 54935-4699
Phone: (800) 262-7426
http://www.mariancollege.edu

Mount Mary College
2900 North Menomonee River Parkway
Milwaukee, WI 53222
Phone: (414) 258-4810
http://www.mtmary.edu

Northland College
1411 Ellis Avenue
Ashland, WI 54806
Phone: (715) 682-1699
http://www.northland.edu

Ripon College
P.O. Box 248
Ripon, WI 54971
Phone: (920) 748-8115
http://www.ripon.edu

Silver Lake College
2406 South Alverno Road
Manitowoc, WI 54220
Phone: (920) 684-6691
http://www.sl.edu

St. Norbert College
100 Grant Street
De Pere, WI 54115-2099
Phone: (920) 337-3181
http://www.snc.edu

University of Wisconsin–Eau Claire
105 Garfield Avenue
Eau Claire, WI 54701
Phone: (715) 836-2637
http://www.uwec.edu

University of Wisconsin–La Crosse
1725 State Street
La Crosse, WI 54601
Phone: (608) 785-8000
http://www.uwlax.edu

University of Wisconsin–Madison
716 Langdon Street
Madison, WI 53706-1400
Phone: (608) 262-1234
http://www.wisc.edu

University of Wisconsin–Milwaukee
P.O. Box 413
Milwaukee, WI 53201
Phone: (414) 229-1122
http://www.uwm.edu

University of Wisconsin–Oshkosh
800 Algoma Boulevard
Oshkosh, WI 54901-8602
Phone: (920) 424-1234
http://www.uwosh.edu

University of Wisconsin–Parkside
P.O. Box 2000
Kenosha, WI 53141-2000
Phone: (262) 595-2345
http://www.uwp.edu

University of Wisconsin–River Falls
410 South Third Street
River Falls, WI 54022-5001
Phone: (715) 425-3911
http://www.uwrf.edu

University of Wisconsin–Stevens Point
2100 Main Street
Stevens Point, WI 54481
Phone: (715) 346-0123
http://www.uwsp.edu

University of Wisconsin–Superior
Belknap & Catlin
P.O. Box 2000
Superior, WI 54880
Phone: (715) 394-8101
http://www.uwsuper.edu

University of Wisconsin–Whitewater
800 West Main Street
Whitewater, WI 53190-1791
Phone: (262) 472-1440
http://www.uww.edu

Viterbo College
815 South Ninth Street
La Crosse, WI 54601
Phone: (608) 796-3000
E-mail: admission@viterbo.edu
http://www.viterbo.edu

WYOMING

University of Wyoming
P.O. Box 3434
Laramie, WY 82071
Phone: (307) 766-1121
http://www.uwyo.edu

F. COLLEGES AND UNIVERSITIES THAT OFFER DEGREES IN PUBLIC RELATIONS

The following is a list of four-year schools that grant degrees in public relations. They are grouped by state.

Use this list as a beginning. More colleges are beginning to grant degrees in this area every year. Check the newest copy of *Lovejoy's* (found in the reference section of libraries, in guidance counseling centers, and in bookstores) for additional schools offering degrees in this field.

ALASKA

University of Alaska–Anchorage
3211 Providence Drive
Anchorage, AK 99508
Phone: (907) 786-1800
E-mail: ayenrol@uaa.alaska.edu
http://www.uaa.alaska.edu

ALABAMA

Auburn University
202 Martin Hall
Auburn, AL 36849
Phone: (334) 844-4000
E-mail: admissions@auburn.edu
http://www.auburn.edu

Spring Hill College
4000 Dauphin Street
Mobile, AL 36608
Phone: (334) 380-4000
E-mail: admit@shc.edu
http://www.shc.edu

University of Alabama
Box 870132
Tuscaloosa, AL 35487
Phone: (205) 348-6010
E-mail: uaadmit@enroll.ua.edu
http://www.ua.edu

University of North Alabama
UNA–Box 5121
Florence, AL 35632
Phone: (256) 765-4100
E-mail: admis1@unanov.una.edu
http://www.una.edu

ARIZONA

Northern Arizona University
P.O. Box 4084
Flagstaff, AZ 86011
Phone: (520) 523-9011
E-mail: undergraduate.admissions@nau.edu
http://www.nau.edu

ARKANSAS

Harding University
900 East Center
Searcy, AR 72149
Phone: (501) 279-4407
E-mail: admissions@harding.edu
http://www.harding.edu

John Brown University
2000 West University Street
Siloam Springs, AR 72761
Phone: (501) 524-3131
E-mail: jbuinfo@acc.jbu.edu
http://www.jbu.edu

CALIFORNIA

California State University–Stanislaus
801 West Monte Vista Avenue
Turlock, CA 95382
Phone: (209) 667-3122
E-mail: Outreach_Help_Desk@stan.csustan.edu
http://www.csustan.edu

Pacific Union College
One Angwin Avenue
Angwin, CA 94508
Phone: (707) 965-6336
E-mail: enroll@puc.edu
http://www.puc.edu

Pepperdine University
24255 Pacific Coast Highway
Malibu, CA 90263
Phone: (310) 456-4000
E-mail: admission-seaver@pepperdine.edu
http://www.pepperdine.edu

Point Loma Nazarene University
3900 Lomaland Drive
San Diego, CA 92106
Phone: (619) 849-2200
E-mail: admissions@ptloma.edu
http://www.ptloma.edu

San Jose State University
One Washington Square
San Jose, CA 95192
Phone: (408) 924-1000
E-mail: info@soar.sjsu.edu
http://www.sjsu.edu

University of Southern California
University Park Campus
Los Angeles, CA 90089
Phone: (213) 740-2311
E-mail: admapp@enroll1.usc.edu
http://www.usc.edu/

COLORADO

Colorado State University
Fort Collins, CO 80523
Phone: (970) 491-1101
E-mail: admissions@colostate.edu
http://www.colostate.edu

CONNECTICUT

Quinnipiac University
Mount Carmel Avenue
Hamden, CT 06518
Phone: (203) 582-8200
E-mail: admissions@quinnipiac.edu
http://www.quinnipiac.edu

DELAWARE

Delaware State University
1200 North Dupont Highway
Dover, DE 19901
Phone: (302) 857-6060
E-mail: dadmiss@dsc.edu
http://www.dsc.edu

DISTRICT OF COLUMBIA

American University
4400 Massachusetts Avenue, NW
Washington, DC 20016
Phone: (202) 885-1000
E-mail: afa@american.edu
http://www.american.edu

FLORIDA

Barry University
11300 Northeast Second Avenue
Miami Shores, FL 33161
Phone: (305) 899-3000
E-mail: admissions@mail.barry.edu
http://www.barry.edu

Florida A&M University
Tallahassee, FL 32307
E-mail: bcox2@famu.edu
http://www.famu.edu

Florida State University
Tallahassee, FL 32306
Phone: (850) 644-2525
E-mail: admissions@admin.fsu.edu
http://www.fsu.edu

University of Central Florida
4000 Central Florida Boulevard
Orlando, FL 32816
Phone: (407) 823-2000
E-mail: admission@mail.ucf.edu
http://www.ucf.edu

University of Florida
201 Criser Hall
Gainesville, FL 32611
Phone: (352) 392-3261
E-mail: freshman@ufl.edu
http://www.ufl.edu

University of Miami
P.O. Box 248025
Coral Gables, FL 33124
Phone: (305) 284-2211
E-mail: admission@miami.edu
http://www.miami.edu

GEORGIA

Augusta State University
2500 Walton Way
Augusta, GA 30904-2200
Phone: (706) 737-1400
E-mail: admissio@aug.edu
http://www.aug.edu

Columbus State University
4225 University Avenue
Columbus, GA 31907
Phone: (706) 568-2001
E-mail: admissions@colstate.edu
http://www.colstate.edu

Georgia Southern University
P.O. Box 8033
Statesboro, GA 30460
Phone: (912) 681-5611
E-mail: admissions@gasou.edu
http://www.gasou.edu

Shorter College
315 Shorter Avenue
Rome, GA 30165
Phone: (706) 291-2121
E-mail: admissions@shorter.edu
http://www.shorter.edu

Toccoa Falls College
P.O. Box 800-899
Toccoa Falls, GA 30598

Phone: (706) 886-6831
E-mail: admissions@toccoafalls.edu
http://www.toccoafalls.edu

University of Georgia
212 Terrell Hall
Athens, GA 30602
Phone: (706) 542-3000
E-mail: undergrad@admissions.uga.edu
http://www.uga.edu

HAWAII

Hawaii Pacific University
1164 Bishop Street
Honolulu, HI 96813
Phone: (808) 544-0200
E-mail: admissions@hpu.edu
http://www.hpu.edu

IDAHO

Northwest Nazarene University
623 Holly Street
Nampa, ID 83686
Phone: (208) 467-8011
E-mail: Admissions@nnu.edu
http://www.nnu.edu

University of Idaho
P.O. Box 443151
Moscow, ID 83844-3151
Phone: (208) 885-6111
E-mail: admappl@uidaho.edu
http://www.uidaho.edu/index-ext.shtml

ILLINOIS

Bradley University
1501 West Bradley Avenue
Peoria, IL 61625
Phone: (309) 676-7611
E-mail: admissions@bradley.edu
http://www.bradley.edu

Columbia College
600 South Michigan Avenue
Chicago, IL 60605-1996
Phone: (312) 344-1600
E-mail: admissions@popmail.colum.edu
http://www.colum.edu

Illinois State University
Campus Box 2200
Normal, IL 61790-2200
Phone: (309) 438-2111
E-mail: ugradadm@ilstu.edu
http://www.ilstu.edu

McKendree College
701 College Road
Lebanon, IL 62254-1299
Phone: (618) 537-4481
E-mail: scordon@atlas.mckendree.edu
http://www.mckendree.edu

Monmouth College
700 East Broadway
Monmouth, IL 61462
Phone: (309) 457-2131
E-mail: admit@monm.edu
http://www.monm.edu

North Central College
30 North Brainard Street
P.O. Box 3063
Naperville, IL 60566
Phone: (630) 637-5100
E-mail: ncadm@noctrl.edu
http://www.noctrl.edu

Roosevelt University
430 South Michigan Avenue
Chicago, IL 60605
Phone: (312) 341-3500
E-mail: applyRU@roosevelt.edu
http://www.roosevelt.edu

INDIANA

Ball State University
2000 University Avenue
Muncie, IN 47306
E-mail: askus@wp.bsu.edu
http://www.bsu.edu

Indiana University–Purdue University–Fort Wayne
2101 East Coliseum Boulevard
Fort Wayne, IN 46805
Phone: (219) 481-6100
E-mail: ipfwadms@ipfw.edu
http://www.ipfw.edu

University of Southern Indiana
8600 University Boulevard
Evansville, IN 47712
Phone: (812) 464-8600
E-mail: enroll@usi.edu
http://www.usi.edu

IOWA

Drake University
2507 University Avenue
Des Moines, IA 50311
Phone: (515) 271-2011
E-mail: admitinfo@acad.drake.edu
http://www.drake.edu

Loras College
1450 Alta Vista
Dubuque, IA 52001
Phone: (319) 588-7100
E-mail: adms@loras.edu
http://www.loras.edu

Mount Mercy College
1330 Elmhurst Drive, Northeast
Cedar Rapids, IA 52402
Phone: (319) 363-8213
E-mail: admission@mmc.mtmercy.edu
http://www.mtmercy.edu

University of Northern Iowa
1227 West 27th Street
Cedar Falls, IA 50614
Phone: (319) 273-2311
E-mail: admissions@uni.edu
http://www.uni.edu/index.html

KENTUCKY

Eastern Kentucky University
521 Lancaster Avenue
Richmond, KY 40475
Phone: (859) 622-1000
E-mail: admissions@eku.edu
http://www.eku.edu

Murray State University
P.O. Box 9
Murray, KY 42071
Phone: (270) 762-3741 or (800) 272-4678
   (toll-free)
E-mail: phil.bryan@murraystate.edu
http://www.murraystate.edu

Western Kentucky University
One Big Red Way
Bowling Green, KY 42101
Phone: (270) 745-0111
E-mail: admission@wku.edu
http://www.wku.edu

LOUISIANA

Louisiana State
   University–Shreveport
One University Place
Shreveport, LA 71115
Phone: (318) 797-5000
E-mail: admissions@pilot.lsus.edu
http://www.lsus.edu

University of Louisiana–Lafayette
P.O. Drawer 41008
Lafayette, LA 70504
Phone: (337) 482-1000

E-mail: enroll@louisiana.edu
http://www.usl.edu

MASSACHUSETTS

Boston University
121 Bay State Road
Boston, MA 02215
Phone: (617) 353-2000
E-mail: admissions@bu.edu
http://www.bu.edu

Emerson College
120 Boylston Street
Boston, MA 02116
Phone: (617) 824-8500
E-mail: admission@emerson.edu
http://www.emerson.edu

Northeastern University
360 Huntington Avenue
Boston, MA 02115
Phone: (617) 373-2000
E-mail: admissions@neu.edu
http://www.neu.edu

Simmons College
300 The Fenway
Boston, MA 02115
Phone: (800) 345-8468
E-mail: ugadm@simmons.edu
http://www.simmons.edu

Suffolk University
Eight Ashburton Place
Beacon Hill, Boston, MA 02108
Phone: (617) 573-800
E-mail: admission@admin.suffolk.edu
http://www.suffolk.edu

MICHIGAN

Andrews University
Berrien Springs, MI 49104
Phone: (800) 253-2874
E-mail: enroll@andrews.edu
http://www.andrews.edu

Central Michigan University
Mount Pleasant, MI 48859
Phone: (517) 774-4000
E-mail: cmuadmit@cmich.edu
http://www.cmich.edu

Eastern Michigan University
Ypsilanti, MI 48197
Phone: (734) 487-1849
E-mail: undergraduate.admissions@
   emich.edu
http://www.emich.edu/

Ferris State University
901 State Street
Big Rapids, MI 49307
Phone: (231) 591-2000
E-mail: admissions@ferris.edu
http://www.ferris.edu

Grand Valley State University
One Campus Drive
Allendale, MI 49401
Phone: (616) 895-6611
E-mail: go2gvsu@gvsu.edu
http://www.gvsu.edu

Madonna University
36600 Schoolcraft Road
Livonia, MI 48150
http://www.munet.edu

Northern Michigan University
1401 Presque Isle Avenue
Marquette, MI 49855
Phone: (906) 227-1000
E-mail: admiss@nmu.edu
http://www.nmu.edu

Wayne State University
656 West Kirby Street
Detroit, MI 48202
Phone: (313) 577-2424
E-mail: admissions@wayne.edu
http://www.wayne.edu/

Western Michigan University
1201 Oliver Street
Kalamazoo, MI 49008
Phone: (616) 387-1000
E-mail: ask-wmu@wmich.edu
http://www.wmich.edu

MINNESOTA

Concordia College–Moorhead
901 South Eighth Street
Moorhead, MN 56562
Phone: (218) 299-4000
E-mail: admissions@cord.edu
http://www.cord.edu

Metropolitan State University
700 East Seventh Street
St. Paul, MN 55106
Phone: (651) 772-7779
E-mail: admission@metrostate.edu
http://www.metrostate.edu

St. Cloud State University
720 South Fourth Avenue
St. Cloud, MN 56301

Phone: (320) 255-2244
E-mail: scsu4u@stcloudstate.edu
http://www.stcloudstate.edu

St. Mary's University of Minnesota
700 Terrace Heights
Winona, MN 55987
Phone: (507) 452-4430
E-mail: admissions@smumn.edu
http://www.smumn.edu

Winona State University
P.O. Box 5838
Winona, MN 55987
Phone: (800) 342-5978
E-mail: admissions@vax2.winona.msus.
    edu
http://www.winona.msus.edu

MISSISSIPPI

Mississippi University for Women
1110 College Street
Columbus, MS 39701
Phone: (662) 329-4750
E-mail: admissions@muw.edu
http://www.muw.edu

MISSOURI

Central Missouri State University
P.O. Box 800
Warrensburg, MO 64093
Phone: (660) 543-4111
E-mail: admit@cmsu1.cmsu.edu
http://www.cmsu.edu

Fontbonne College
6800 Wydown Boulevard
St. Louis, MO 63105
Phone: (314) 862-3456
E-mail: pmusen@fontbonne.edu
http://www.fontbonne.edu

Northwest Missouri State University
800 University Drive
Maryville, MO 64468
Phone: (800) 633-1175
E-mail: admissions@mail.nwmissouri.edu
http://www.nwmissouri.edu

Rockhurst University
1100 Rockhurst Road
Kansas City, MO 64110-2561
Phone: (816) 501-4000
E-mail: admission@rockhurst.edu
http://www.rockhurst.edu

St. Louis University
221 North Grand Boulevard
St. Louis, MO 63103

Phone: (314) 977-2222
E-mail: admitme@slu.edu
http://www.slu.edu

Stephens College
1200 East Broadway
Box 2121
Columbia, MO 65215
Phone: (573) 442-2211
E-mail: apply@sc.stephens.edu
http://www.stephens.edu

Webster University
470 East Lockwood Avenue
St. Louis, MO 63119
Phone: (314) 968-6900
E-mail: admit@webster.edu
http://www.webster.edu

MONTANA

Carroll College
1601 North Benton Avenue
Helena, MT 59625
Phone: (800) 992-3648
E-mail: enroll@carroll.edu
http://www.carroll.edu

Montana State University–Billings
1500 North 30th Street
Billings, MT 59101
Phone: (406) 657-2011
E-mail: admissions@msubillings.edu
http://www.msubillings.edu

NEBRASKA

Bellevue University
1000 Galvin Road, South
Bellevue, NE 68005
Phone: (402) 291-8100
E-mail: bellevue_u@scholars.bellevue.edu
http://www.bellevue.edu

College of St. Mary
1901 South 72nd Street
Omaha, NE 68124
Phone: (402) 399-2400
E-mail: enroll@csm.edu
http://www.csm.edu

Creighton University
2500 California Plaza
Omaha, NE 68178
Phone: (402) 280-2700
E-mail: admissions@creighton.edu
http://www.creighton.edu

Doane College
1014 Boswell Avenue
Crete, NE 68333
Phone: (402) 826-2161
E-mail: admissions@doane.edu
http://www.doane.edu

University of Nebraska–Kearney
905 West 25th Street
Kearney, NE 68849
Phone: (308) 865-8441
E-mail: admissionsug@unk.edu
http://www.unk.edu

NEW HAMPSHIRE

Rivier College
420 Main Street
Nashua, NH 03060
Phone: (800) 44-RIVIER
E-mail: rivadmit@rivier.edu
http://www.rivier.edu

NEW YORK

Buffalo State College
1300 Elmwood Avenue
Buffalo, NY 14222
Phone: (716) 878-4000
E-mail: admissions@buffalostate.edu
http://www.buffalostate.edu

College of New Rochelle
Castle Place
New Rochelle, NY 10805
Phone: (914) 654-5000
E-mail: admission@cnr.edu
http://www.cnr.edu

College of St. Rose
432 Western Avenue
Albany, NY 12203
Phone: (800) 637-8556
E-mail: admit@rosnet.strose.edu
http://www.strose.edu

CUNY–Lehman College
250 Bedford Park Boulevard, West
Bronx, NY 10468
Phone: (718) 960-8000
E-mail: enroll@lehman.cuny.edu
http://www.lehman.cuny.edu

Ithaca College
100 Job Hall
Ithaca, NY 14850-7020
Phone: (607) 274-3124
E-mail: admission@ithaca.edu
http://www.ithaca.edu

Keuka College
Keuka Park, NY 14478
Phone: (315) 536-4411
E-mail: admissions@mail.keuka.edu
http://www.keuka.edu

Long Island University–C.W. Post Campus
720 Northern Boulevard
Brookville, NY 11548-1300
Phone: (516) 299-2000
E-mail: enroll@cwpost.liu.edu
http://www.cwpost.liu.edu

Mount St. Mary College
330 Powell Avenue
Newburgh, NY 12550
Phone: (914) 561-0800
E-mail: mtstmary@msmc.edu
http://www.msmc.edu

SUNY–Oswego
7060 State Route 104
Oswego, NY 13126
Phone: (315) 312-2500
E-mail: admiss@oswego.edu
http://www.oswego.edu

Syracuse University
201 Tolley Administration Building
Syracuse, NY 13244
Phone: (315) 443-1870
E-mail: orange@syr.edu
http://www.syr.edu

Utica College
1600 Burrstone Road
Utica, NY 13502
Phone: (800) 782-8884
E-mail: admiss@utica.ucsu.edu
http://www.utica.edu

NORTH CAROLINA

Appalachian State University
Boone, NC 28608
Phone: (828) 262-2000
E-mail: admissions@appstate.edu
http://www.appstate.edu

East Carolina University
East Fifth Street
Greenville, NC 27858
Phone: (252) 328-6131
E-mail: admis@mail.ecu.edu
http://www.ecu.edu

Elon College
2700 Campus Box
Elon College, NC 27244

Phone: (336) 584-9711
E-mail: admissions@elon.edu
http://www.elon.edu

Mars Hill College
100 Athletic Street
Mars Hill, NC 28754
Phone: (866) MHC-4-YOU
E-mail: admissions@mhc.edu
http://www.mhc.edu

North Carolina A&T State University
1601 East Market Street
Greensboro, NC 27411
Phone: (336) 334-7500
E-mail: uadmit@ncat.edu
http://www.ncat.edu

University of North Carolina–Greensboro
1000 Spring Garden Street
Greensboro, NC 27412
Phone: (336) 334-5243
E-mail: undergrad_admissions@uncg.edu
http://www.uncg.edu/adm

OHIO

Ashland University
401 College Avenue
Ashland, OH 44805
Phone: (419) 289-4142
E-mail: auadmsn@ashland.edu
http://www.ashland.edu

Bowling Green State University
110 McFall Center
Bowling Green, OH 43403
Phone: (419) 372-2531
E-mail: admissions@bgnet.bgsu.edu
http://www.bgsu.edu

Capital University
2199 East Main Street
Columbus, OH 43209
Phone: (614) 236-6011
E-mail: admissions@capital.edu
http://www.capital.edu

David N. Myers College
112 Prospect Avenue
Cleveland, OH 44115
Phone: (216) 696-9000
E-mail: admissions@dnmyers.edu
http://www.dnmyers.edu

Heidelberg College
310 East Market Street
Tiffin, OH 44883

Phone: (800) 925-9250
E-mail: admission@heidelberg.edu
http://www.heidelberg.edu

Kent State University
P.O. Box 5190
Kent, OH 44242
Phone: (330) 672-2121
E-mail: kentadm@admissions.kent.edu
http://www.kent.edu

Marietta College
215 Fifth Street
Marietta, OH 45750
Phone: (740) 376-4643
E-mail: admit@marietta.edu
http://www.marietta.edu

Ohio University
Athens, OH 45701
Phone: (740) 593-1000
E-mail: FRSHINFO@ohiou.edu
http://www.ohiou.edu

Otterbein College
One Otterbein College
Westerville, OH 43081
Phone: (614) 890-3000
E-mail: uotterb@otterbein.edu
http://www.otterbein.edu

Ursuline College
2550 Lander Road
Pepper Pike, OH 44124
Phone: (440) 449-4200
E-mail: joakley@ursuline.edu
http://www.ursuline.edu

Wright State University
3640 Colonel Glenn Highway
Dayton, OH 45435
Phone: (937) 775-3300
E-mail: admissions@wright.edu
http://www.wright.edu

Youngstown State University
One University Plaza
Youngstown, OH 44555
Phone: (330) 742-3000
E-mail: enroll@ysu.edu
http://www.ysu.edu

OKLAHOMA

Oklahoma Baptist University
500 West University
Shawnee, OK 74804
Phone: (405) 275-2850
E-mail: admissions@mail.okbu.edu
http://www.okbu.edu

Oklahoma Christian University
Box 11000
Oklahoma City, OK 73136
Phone: (405) 425-5000
E-mail: kyle.wray@oc.edu
http://www.oc.edu

Oral Roberts University
7777 South Lewis
Tulsa, OK 74171
Phone: (918) 495-6161
E-mail: admissions@oru.edu
http://www.oru.edu

University of Oklahoma
660 Parrington Oval
Norman, OK 73019
Phone: (405) 325-0311
E-mail: admrec@ouwww.ou.edu
http://www.ou.edu

OREGON

Marylhurst University
17600 Pacific Highway & Highway 43
P.O. Box 261
Marylhurst, OR 97036-0261
Phone: (800) 634-9982
E-mail: admissions@marylhurst.edu
http://www.marylhurst.edu

University of Oregon
Eugene, OR 97403
Phone: (541) 346-1000
E-mail: uoadmit@oregon.uoregon.edu
http://www.uoregon.edu

University of Portland
5000 North Willamette Boulevard
Portland, OR 97203
Phone: (503) 943-7911
E-mail: admissio@up.edu
http://www.up.edu

Western Baptist College
5000 Deer Park Drive, Southeast
Salem, OR 97301
Phone: (503) 581-8600
E-mail: admissions@wbc.edu
http://www.wbc.edu

PENNSYLVANIA

Duquesne University
600 Forbes Avenue
Pittsburgh, PA 15282
Phone: (412) 396-6000
E-mail: admissions@duq.edu
http://www.duq.edu

Mansfield University of Pennsylvania
Mansfield, PA 16933
Phone: (570) 662-4000
E-mail: admissns@mnsfld.edu
http://www.mnsfld.edu

**Pennsylvania State
    University–University Park**
201 Shields Building, Box 3000
University Park, PA 16804-3000
Phone: (814) 865-5471
E-mail: admissions@psu.edu
http://www.psu.edu

Marywood University
2300 Adams Avenue
Scranton, PA 18509
Phone: (570) 348-6211
E-mail: ugadm@ac.marywood.edu
http://www.marywood.edu

Point Park College
201 Wood Street
Pittsburgh, PA 15222
Phone: (800) 321-0129
E-mail: enroll@ppc.edu
http://www.ppc.edu

University of Pittsburgh–Bradford
300 Campus Drive
Bradford, PA 16701
Phone: (800) 872-1787
E-mail: admissions@www.upb.pitt.edu
http://www.upb.pitt.edu

Westminster College
Market Street
New Wilmington, PA 16172
Phone: (724) 946-8761
E-mail: admis@westminster.edu
http://www.westminster.edu

York College of Pennsylvania
York, PA 17405-7199
Phone: (717) 846-7788
E-mail: admissions@ycp.edu
http://www.ycp.edu

RHODE ISLAND

University of Rhode Island
Kingston, RI 02881
Phone: (401) 874-1000
E-mail: uriadmit@uri.edu
http://www.uri.edu

SOUTH CAROLINA

University of South Carolina
Columbia, SC 29208
Phone: (803) 777-7000

E-mail: admissions-ugrad@sc.edu
http://www.sc.edu

TENNESSEE

David Lipscomb University
3901 Granny White Pike
Nashville, TN 37204
Phone: (800) 333-4358
E-mail: admissions@lipscomb.edu
http://www.lipscomb.edu

Middle Tennessee State University
1301 East Main Street
Murfreesboro, TN 37132
Phone: (615) 898-2300
E-mail: admissions@mtsu.edu
http://www.mtsu.edu

Southern Adventist University
P.O. Box 370
Collegedale, TN 37315
Phone: (423) 238-2111
E-mail: admissions@southern.edu
http://www.southern.edu

TEXAS

Southern Methodist University
P.O. Box 750296
Dallas, TX 75275
Phone: (214) 768-2000
E-mail: ugadmission@smu.edu
http://www.smu.edu

Texas Christian University
2800 South University Drive
Fort Worth, TX 76129
Phone: (800) TCU-FROG
E-mail: frogmail@tcu.edu
http://www.tcu.edu

Texas Tech University
Box 42013
Lubbock, TX 79409
Phone: (806) 742-2011
E-mail: nsr@ttu.edu
http://www.texastech.edu

University of Houston
4800 Calhoun Road
Houston, TX 77004
Phone: (713) 743-1000
E-mail: admissions@uh.edu
http://www.uh.edu

West Texas A&M University
P.O. Box 60999
Canyon, TX 79016
Phone: (806) 651-2000

E-mail: apifer@mail.wtamu.edu
http://www.wtamu.edu

VIRGINIA

Hampton University
Hampton, VA 23668
Phone: (757) 727-5000
E-mail: admissions@hamptonu.edu
http://www.hamptonu.edu

Virginia Commonwealth University
821 West Franklin Street
Richmond, VA 23284
Phone: (804) 828-0100
E-mail: ugrad@vcu.edu
http://www.vcu.edu

WASHINGTON

Central Washington University
400 East Eighth Avenue
Ellensburg, WA 98926
Phone: (509) 963-1111
E-mail: cwuadmis@cwu.edu
http://www.cwu.edu

Eastern Washington University
526 Fifth Street
Cheney, WA 99004

Phone: (509) 359-6200
E-mail: admissions@mail.ewu.edu
http://www.ewu.edu

Gonzaga University
502 East Boone Avenue
Spokane, WA 99258
Phone: (509) 328-4220
E-mail: ballinger@gu.gonzaga.edu
http://www.gonzaga.edu

Washington State University
Lighty 370
Pullman, WA 99164-1067
Phone: (888) GO-TO-WSU
E-mail: admiss2@wsu.edu
http://www.wsu.edu

WISCONSIN

Cardinal Stritch University
6801 North Yates Road
Milwaukee, WI 53217
Phone: (414) 410-4000
E-mail: admityou@stritch.edu
http://www.stritch.edu

Concordia University Wisconsin
12800 North Lake Shore Drive
Mequon, WI 53097

Phone: (262) 243-5700
E-mail: admission@cuw.edu
http://www.cuw.edu

Marquette University
P.O. Box 1881
Milwaukee, WI 53201
Phone: (414) 288-7250
E-mail: admissions@marquette.edu
http://www.marquette.edu

Mount Mary College
2900 North Menomonee River Parkway
Milwaukee, WI 53222
Phone: (414) 258-4810
E-mail: admiss@mtmary.edu
http://www.mtmary.edu

WEST VIRGINIA

West Virginia Wesleyan College
59 College Avenue
Buckhannon, WV 26201
Phone: (304) 473-8000
E-mail: admissions@wvwc.edu
http://www.wvwc.edu

G. WORKSHOPS, SEMINARS, ETC.

The following is a list of workshops, seminars, courses, and symposiums and the subject areas that they cover. This is by no means a complete listing. Many associations, schools, and companies offer other workshops. As subject matter changes frequently, many workshops and seminars are not listed. You may want to contact associations dealing with the employment area in which you are interested to obtain more information on programs not listed. This listing is for your information. It is offered to help you locate programs of interest to you. The author does not endorse any one program over another and is not responsible for subject content.

American Society of Composers, Authors and Publishers (ASCAP)
1 Lincoln Plaza
New York, NY 10023
Phone: (212) 621-6000
Fax: (212) 724-9064
E-mail: info@ascap.com
http://www.ascap.com
ASCAP offers a variety of workshops for songwriters in New York City, Los Angeles, and Nashville.

American Symphony Orchestra League (ASOL)
33 W. 60th Street, 5th Floor
New York, NY 10023
Phone: (212) 262-5161
Fax: (212) 262-5198

E-mail: league@symphony.org
http://www.symphony.org
The American Symphony Orchestra League offers regional workshops, seminars, and symposiums in every aspect of the orchestra business and craft, including orchestra management, marketing, fundraising, and conduction. Their annual conferences present many informative programs.

Billboard Latin Music Conference and Awards
Billboard Special Events
770 Broadway
New York, NY 10003
Phone: (646) 654-4660

http://www.billboardevents.com
Billboard Latin Music Conference and Awards is held annually.

Billboard R & B Hip Hop Conference and Awards
Billboard Special Events
770 Broadway
New York, NY 10003
Phone: (646) 654-4660
http://www.billboardevents.com
Billboard R & B Hip Hop Conference and Awards is held annually.

Broadcast Music, Inc. (BMI)
320 West 57th Street
New York, NY 10019
Phone: (212) 586-2000

Fax: (212) 956-2059
E-mail: newyork@bmi.com
http://bmi.com
Broadcast Music, Inc. conducts a
multitude of workshops and seminars
throughout the country for songwriters.

Career Opp. Seminars & Speakers
P.O. Box 711
Monticello, NY 12701
Phone: (845) 794-7312
http://www.shellyfield.com
Career Opp Seminars and Speakers offers
programs throughout the country on a
variety of career-oriented subjects,
including how to enter and succeed in
the music industry.

Dallas Songwriters Association
2932 Dyer Street
Dallas, TX 75205
Phone: (214) 750-0916
Fax: (214) 692-1392
E-mail: barbe@texasmusicgroup.com
http://www.dallassongwriters.org
The Dallas Songwriters Association
offers seminars, workshops, and
courses for songwriters.

**Emerging Artists Technology in Music
Conference and Showcase**
121 Quail Run Road
Henderson, NV 901015
Phone: (702) 792-9430
http://www.eat-m.com
The EAT'M Conference showcases
emerging artists.

Glitter, Glamour & Gold Seminars
P.O. Box 711
Monticello, NY 12701
Phone: (845) 794-7312
http://www.shellyfield.com
Glitter, Glamour & Gold Seminars
provide helpful programs for those
aspiring to work in the music industry
as well as for those already in it.

**Gospel Music Workshop of America
(GMWA)**
3908 West Warren Avenue
Detroit, MI 48208
Phone: (313) 898-6900
Fax: (313) 898-4520
E-mail: slpuddie@worldnet.att.net
http://www.ghwa.org
The Gospel Music Workshop of America
offers musical instruction in a variety
of areas encompassing composition
and performance.

Independent Music Conference
P.O. Box 290664
Nashville, TN 37230
Phone: (615) 316-9715
http://www.nashvillemusicfest.com
A conference showcasing independent
music.

**Making It in Music Seminars &
Speakers**
P.O. Box 711
Monticello, NY 12701
Phone: (845) 794-7312
http://www.shellyfield.com
Making It in Music Seminars & Speakers
offers programs throughout the
country for individuals in the business
end of the music industry as well as
for those in the performance end.

Metropolitan Opera Association
Lincoln Center
New York, NY 10023
Phone: (212) 362-6000
Fax: (212) 874-2659
E-mail: metinfo@visionfoundry.com
http://www.metopera.org
The Metropolitan Opera Association
sponsors a number of seminars and
training programs.

Metropolitan Opera Guild (MOG)
70 Lincoln Center Plaza
New York, NY 10023
Phone: (212) 769-7000
Fax: (212) 769-7007
E-mail: metinfo@visionfoundry.com
http://www.metopera.org
The Metropolitan Opera Guild offers a
variety of educational programs and
lectures relating to opera.

**Nashville Songwriters Association
International (NSAI)**
1701 West End Avenue
Nashville, TN 37203
Phone: (615) 256-3354
Fax: (615) 256-0034
E-mail: nsai@nashvillesongwriters.com
http://www.nashvillesongwriters.com
The Nashville Songwriters Association
International holds weekly workshops
for songwriters.

**National Academy of Popular Music
(NAPM)**
330 West 58th Street
New York, NY 10019-1827
Phone: (212) 957-9230

Fax: (212) 957-9227
E-mail: info@songwritershalloffame.org
http://www.songwritershalloffame.org
The National Academy of Popular Music
holds seminars and workshops in a
variety of areas for those interested in
songwriting and music.

**National Association for Campus
Activities (NACA)**
13 Harbison Way
Columbia, SC 29212
Phone: (803) 732-6222 or (800) 845-2338
(toll-free)
Fax: (803) 749-1047
E-mail: webmaster@naca.org
http://www.naca.org
The National Association for Campus
Activities offers workshops and
educational sessions of interest to
those seeking careers in the music
business. The association also holds a
variety of workshops on concert
management and promotion in various
locations throughout the country.

**National Association of College Wind
and Percussion Instructors
(NACWPI)**
Division of Fine Arts
Truman State University
Kirksville, MO 63501
Phone: (816) 785-4442
Fax: (816) 785-7463
E-mail: fa24@truman.edu
The National Association of College
Wind and Percussion Instructors holds
programs, clinics, and workshops at
the annual Music Educators National
Conference.

**National Association of Music
Merchants (NAMM)**
5790 Armada Drive
Carlsbad, CA 92008
Phone: (760) 438-8001 or (800) 767-6266
(toll-free)
Fax: (760) 438-7327
E-mail: info@namm.com
http://www.namm.com
The National Association of Music
Merchants offers a variety of seminars
at their conventions and expositions.
Programs change every year but
always revolve around better business
methods, selling, and so on. NAMM
also hosts professional development
seminars throughout the country.

National Academy of Recording Arts and Sciences (NARAS)
3402 Pico Boulevard
Santa Monica, CA 90405
Phone: (310) 392-3777
Fax: (310) 399-3090
E-mail: info@grammyfoundation.org
http://www.grammy.com
The National Academy of Recording Arts and Sciences offers seminars and discussions on a variety of subjects of interest to those in the recording industry.

National Association of Recording Merchandisers (NARM)
9 Eves Drive, Suite 120
Marlton, NJ 08053
Phone: (856) 596-2221
Fax: (856) 596-3268
E-mail: rosum@narm.com
http://www.namm.com
The National Association of Recording Merchandisers holds an annual convention with seminars on various subjects of interest to those working in all areas of merchandise.

National Music Publishers' Association (NMPA)
475 Park Avenue South, 29th Floor
New York, NY 10016-6901
Phone: (646) 742-1651
Fax: (646) 742-1779
E-mail: pr@nmpa.org
http://www.nmpa.org
The National Music Publishers Association holds periodic forums for people involved in music publishing.

Forums are put together by the Los Angeles, Nashville, and New York chapters. There is also a forum held in conjunction with NARAS in Atlanta annually.

New England Music Industry Summit
DC Entertainment
60 State Street
Boston, MA 02109
Phone: (617) 864-8055
http://www.dcentertainmnet.com
Summit discussing music industry.

Piano Technicians Guild (PTG)
3930 Washington
Kansas City, MO 64111
Phone: (816) 753-7747
Fax: (816) 531-0070
E-mail: ptg@ptg.org
http://www.ptg.org
The Piano Technicians Guild holds an annual convention featuring technical sessions. Seminars for piano technicians are also offered at various times throughout the year.

Recording Industry Association of America (RIAA)
1330 Connecticut Avenue
Washington, DC 20036
Phone: (202) 775-0101
Fax: (202) 775-7253
E-mail: webmaster@riaa.com
http://www.riaa.com
The Recording Industry Association of America sponsors conferences on a variety of issues, including anti-piracy.

Songwriters Guild of America (SGA)
1500 Harbor Boulevard
Weehawken, NJ 07087-6732
Phone: (201) 867-7603
Fax: (201) 867-7535
E-mail: songnews@aol.com
http://songnews.org
The Songwriters Guild of America offers workshops in both the business and craft of songwriting. These are held throughout the year. The guild has an "Ask A Pro" workshop, song critique workshop, and courses in all phases of songwriting.

Special Libraries Association (SLA)
1700 18th Street, NW
Washington, DC 20009-2514
Phone: (202) 234-4700
Fax: (202) 265-9317
E-mail: sla@sla.org
http://www.sla.org
The Special Libraries Association conducts an array of continuing education courses of interest to those working in music libraries.

Volunteer Lawyers for the Arts (VLA)
1 East 53rd Street
New York, NY 10022
Phone: (212) 319-2787
Fax: (212) 752-6575
E-mail: vlany@bway.net
http://www.vlany.com
The Volunteer Lawyers for the Arts runs educational programs, seminars, and workshops throughout the year on a multitude of areas.

APPENDIX II
UNIONS AND ASSOCIATIONS

The following is a list of the unions and associations discussed in this book. There are numerous other associations listed here that may also be useful to you.

The names, addresses, phone numbers, fax numbers, websites, and e-mail addresses are included to help you get in touch with any of the unions and associations for information.

National offices and websites of unions and associations are often able to provide you with the phone number and/or address of the closest local office.

Use this list to help you find internships, explore job opportunities, and obtain other useful information.

Academy of Country Music (ACM)
4100 West Alemeda, Suite 208
Burbank, CA 91505
Phone: (818) 842-8400
Fax: (323) 462-3253
E-mail: acmoffice@value.net
http://www.acmcountry.com

Acoustical Society of America (ASA)
2 Huntington Quadrangle, Suite 101
Melville, NY 11747
Phone: (516) 576-2360
Fax: (516) 576-2377
E-mail: asa@aip.org
http://asa.aip.org

Actors' Equity Association (AEA)
165 West 46th Street
New York, NY 10036
Phone: (212) 869-8530
Fax: (212) 719-9815
E-mail: info@actorsequity.org
http://www.actorsequity.org

Alliance for Canadian New Music Project
Alliance pour des Projets de Musique Canadienne Nouvelle (APMCN)
20 St. Joseph Street
Toronto, ON, Canada M4Y 1J9
Phone: (416) 963-5937
Fax: (416) 961-7198
E-mail: acnmptor@ica.net

American Academy of Teachers of Singing (AATS)
c/o Robert C. White, Jr.
600 West 116th, No. 52A
New York, NY 10027
Phone: (212) 222-5154
Fax: (212) 280-6343

E-mail: webmaster@
   voiceteachersacademy. org
http://www.voiceteachersacademy.org

American Advertising Federation (AAF)
1101 Vermont Avenue, NW, Suite 500
Washington, DC 20005-6306
Phone: (202) 898-0089
Fax: (202) 898-0159
http://www.aaf.org

American Bandmasters Association (ABA)
2221 Morgan Drive
Norman, OK 73069-6528
Phone: (405) 321-3373
Fax: (405) 321-4117
E-mail: thurston3@juno.com
http://www.americanbandmasters.org

American Bar Association (ABA)
541 North Fairbanks Court
Chicago, IL 60611
Phone: (312) 988-5522 or (800) 285-2221 (toll-free)
Fax: (312) 988-5528
E-mail: service@abanet.org
http://www.abanet.org

American Choral Directors Association (ACDA)
502 Southwest 38th Street
Lawton, OK 73505
Phone: (580) 355-8161
Fax: (580) 248-1465
E-mail: acda@acdaonline.org
http://www.acdaonline.org

American College of Musicians (ACM)
808 Rio Grande Street
Austin, TX 78701
Phone: (512) 478-5775

Fax: (512) 478-5843
E-mail: ngpt@aol.com
http://www.pianoguild.com

American Composers Alliance (ACA)
73 Spring Street, Room 505
New York, NY 10012
Phone: (212) 362-8900
Fax: (212) 925-6798
E-mail: info@composers.com
http://www.composers.com

American Composers Forum (ACF)
332 Minnesota Street, Suite E145
St. Paul, MN 55101-1300
Phone: (651) 228-1407
Fax: (651) 291-7978
E-mail: mail@compsersforum.org
http://www.composersforum.org

American Conference of Cantors (ACC)
5591 Chamblee Dunwoody Road
Building 1360, Suite 200
Atlanta, GA 30338
Phone: (770) 390-0006 or (866) 711-0006 (toll-free)
Fax: (770) 390-0020
E-mail: accantors@aol.com
http://www.accantors.org

American Disc Jockey Association (ADJA)
1964 Wagner Street
Pasadena, CA 91107
Phone: (626) 844-3204
Fax: (801) 681-0668
E-mail: membershipsecy@adja.org
http://www.adja.org

American Federation of Jazz Societies (AFJS)
P.O. Box 84063
Phoenix, AZ 85071

Phone: (602) 942-8348
Fax: (916) 372-3479
E-mail: info@jazzfederation.com
http://www.jazzfederation.com

**American Federation of Musicians of the
    United States and Canada (AFM)**
1501 Broadway, Suite 600
New York, NY 10036
Phone: (212) 869-1330
Fax: (212) 764-6134
E-mail: info@afm.org
http://www.afm.org

American Federation of Teachers (AFT)
555 New Jersey Avenue, NW
Washington, DC 20001
Phone: (202) 879-4400 or (800) 238-
    1133 (toll-free)
Fax: (202) 879-4545
E-mail: online@aft.org
http://www.aft.org

**American Federation of Television and
    Radio Artists (AFTRA)**
260 Madison Avenue
New York, NY 10016-2402
Phone: (212) 532-0800
Fax: (212) 532-2242
E-mail: aftra@aftra.com
http://www.aftra.com

**American Federation of Violin and
    Bow Makers (AFVBM)**
c/o Arthur Toman
56 Helene Road
Newton, MA 02468
Phone: (617) 527-3969
E-mail: artoman@aol.com
http://www.afvbm.com

**American Guild of Authors and
    Composers (Now Songwriters Guild)**
Songwriters Guild of America (SGA)
1500 Harbor Boulevard
Weehawken, NJ 07086
Phone: (201) 867-7603
Fax: (201) 867-7535
E-mail: songwritersnj@aol.com
http://www.songwriters.org

**American Guild of Musical Artists
    (AGMA)**
1430 Broadway, 14th Floor
New York, NY 10019
Phone: (212) 265-3687
Fax: (212) 262-9088
E-mail: agma@musicalartists.org
http://www.musicalartists.org

American Guild of Organists (AGO)
475 Riverside Drive, Suite 1260
New York, NY 10115
Phone: (212) 870-2310 or
    (800) AGO-5115 (toll-free)
Fax: (212) 870-2163
E-mail: info@agohq.org
http://www.agohq.org

**American Guild of Variety Artists
    (AGVA)**
363 7th Avenue, 17th Floor
New York, NY 10001
Phone: (212) 675-1003
Fax: (212) 633-0097

**American Institute of Certified Public
    Accountants (AICPA)**
1211 Avenue of the Americas
New York, NY 10036-8775
Phone: (212) 596-6200 or (888) 777-7077
    (toll-free)
Fax: (212) 596-6213
E-mail: committee@aicpa.org
http://www.aicpa.org

**American Institute of Musical Studies
    (AIMS)**
6621 Snider Plaza
Dallas, TX 75205-1351
Phone: (214) 363-2683
Fax: (214) 363-6474
E-mail: aims@airmail.net
http://www.aimsgraz.org

American Library Association (ALA)
50 East Huron Street
Chicago, IL 60611
Phone: (312) 944-7298 or (800) 545-2433
    (toll-free)
Fax: (312) 440-9374
E-mail: ala@ala.org
http://www.ala.org

American Marketing Association (AMA)
311 South Wacker Drive, Suite 5800
Chicago, IL 60606
Phone: (312) 542-9000 or (800) 262-1150
    (toll-free)
Fax: (312) 542-9001
E-mail: info@ama.org
http://www.ama.org

**American Musical Instrument Society
    (AMIS)**
8551 Research Way, Suite 180
Middleton, WI 53562
Phone: (608) 836-9000
Fax: (608) 831-8200

E-mail: amis@areditions.com
http://www.amis.org

American Music Center (AMC)
30 West 26th Street, Suite 1001
New York, NY 10010-2011
Phone: (212) 366-5260
Fax: (212) 366-5265
E-mail: richard@amc.net
http://www.amc.net/index.html

American Music Conference (AMC)
5790 Armada Drive
Carlsbad, CA 92008-4391
Phone: (760) 431-9124 or (800) 767-6266
    (toll-free)
Fax: (760) 438-7327
http://www.amc-music.com

**American Music Festival Association
    (AMFA)**
P.O. Box 2987
Anaheim, CA 92814
Phone: (562) 948-2281
Fax: (562) 948-4575

American Musicological Society (AMS)
201 South 34th Street
Philadelphia, PA 19104-6313
Phone: (215) 898-8698 or (888) 611-4267
    (toll-free)
Fax: (215) 573-3673
E-mail: ams@sas.upenn.edu
http://www.ams-net.org

**American Music Scholarship
    Association (AMSA)**
441 Vine Street, Suite 1030
Cincinnati, OH 45202
Phone: (513) 421-5342
Fax: (513) 421-2672
E-mail: amsa@queencity.com
http://www.amsa-wpc.org

**American Music Therapy Association
    (AMTA)**
8455 Colesville Road, Suite 1000
Silver Spring, MD 20910
Phone: (301) 589-3300
Fax: (301) 589-5175
E-mail: info@musictherapy.org
http://www.musictherapy.org

American Pianists Association (APA)
4600 Sunset Avenue
Indianapolis, IN 46208
Phone: (317) 940-9945
Fax: (317) 940-9010
E-mail: helen@americanpianists.org
http://www.americanpianists.org

American Recorder Society (ARS)
P.O. Box 631
Littleton, CO 80160-0631
Phone: (303) 347-1120
Fax: (303) 347-1181
E-mail: recorder@compuserve.com
http://ourworld.compuserve.com/
    homepages/recorder

American School Band Directors'
    Association (ASBDA)
P.O. Box 696
Guttenberg, IA 52052-0696
Phone: (563) 252-2500
Fax: (563) 252-2500
E-mail: asbda@alpinecom.net
http://www.asbda.com

American Society for Jewish Music
    (ASJM)
15 West 16th Street, No. 5
New York, NY 10011-6301
Phone: (212) 294-8328
Fax: (212) 294-6161
E-mail: asjm@cjh.org
http://www.cjh.org

American Society of Composers,
    Authors and Publishers (ASCAP)
1 Lincoln Plaza
New York, NY 10023
Phone: (212) 621-6000
Fax: (212) 724-9064
E-mail: info@ascap.com
http://www.ascap.com

American Society of Music Arrangers
    and Composers (ASMAC)
P.O. Box 17840
Encino, CA 91416
Phone: (818) 994-4661
Fax: (818) 994-6181
E-mail: dellhake@earthlink.net
http://www.asmac.org

American String Teachers Association
    with National School Orchestra
    Association (ASTA with NSOA)
4153 Chain Bridge Road
Fairfax, VA 22030
Phone: (703) 279-2113
Fax: (703) 279-2114
E-mail: asta@astaweb.com
http://www.astaweb.com

American Symphony Orchestra League
33 West 60th Street, 5th Floor
New York, NY 10023
Phone: (212) 262-5161

Fax: (212) 262-5198
E-mail: league@symphony.org
http://www.symphony.org

American Theatre Organ Society
    (ATOS)
P.O. Box 551081
Indianapolis, IN 46205-5581
Phone: (317) 251-6441
Fax: (317) 251-6443
E-mail: fellenzer@atos.org
http://www.atos.org

American Women Composers (AWC)
c/o George Washington University
Department of Music
The Academic Center B144
Washington, DC 20052
E-mail: cpickar@gwis2.circ.gwv.edu

Amusement and Music Operators
    Association (AMOA)
1145 North Arlington Heights Road,
    No. 300
Itasca, IL 60143-3171
Phone: (847) 290-5320 or (800) 937-2662
    (toll-free)
Fax: (847) 290-0409
E-mail: amoa@amoa.com
http://www.amoa.com

Association for Technology in Music
    Instruction (ATMI)
c/o Dr. Timothy Kloth
2336 Donnington Lane
Cincinnati, OH 45224
E-mail: vankloth@excite.com
http://www.music.org/atmi

Association for the Advancement of
    Creative Musicians (AACM)
P.O. Box 5757
Chicago, IL 60680
Phone: (312) 752-2212
Fax: (312) 752-2226
E-mail: mailaccm@aol.com
http://aacmchicago.org/aacmgoals.html

Association for the Preservation and
    Presentation of the Arts (APPA)
2011 Benning Road, NE
Washington, DC 20002
Phone: (202) 529-3244
Fax: (202) 396-8012

Association of Concert Bands (ACB)
6613 Cheryl Ann Drive
Independence, OH 44131

Phone: (800) 726-8720
E-mail: contact@acbands.org
http://www.acbands.org

Association of Independent Music
    Publishers (AIMP)
P.O. Box 1561
Burbank, CA 91507-1561
Phone: (818) 842-6257
E-mail: info@aimp.org
http://www.aimp.org

Association of Professional Composers
34 Hanway Street
London W1P 9DE, United Kingdom
Phone: 44 207 4360919
Fax: 44 207 4361913
E-mail: apc@dial.pipex.com

Association of Teachers of Singing
Coral Gould, Weir House
108 Newton Road
Burton-On-Trent DE15 0TT, United
    Kingdom
Phone: 44 1283 542198
Fax: 44 1283 542198
E-mail: jgould1665@aol.com
http://www.aotos.co.uk

Association of Theatrical Press Agents
    and Managers
1560 Broadway, Suite 700
New York, NY 10036-2501
Phone: (212) 719-3666
Fax: (212) 302-1585
http://www.atpam.com

Black Rock Coalition (BRC)
P.O. Box 1054, Cooper Station
New York, NY 10276
Phone: (212) 713-5097
Fax: (212) 226-6707
E-mail: info@blackrockcoalition.org
http://www.blackrockcoalition.org

Bluegrass Music Association of Maine
P.O. Box 1010
Brunswick, ME 04011-1010
Phone: (207) 729-5631

The Blues Foundation (TBF)
49 Union Avenue
Memphis, TN 38103
Phone: (901) 527-BLUE or
    (800) 861-8795 (toll-free)
Fax: (901) 529-4030
E-mail: bluesinfo@blues.org
http://www.blues.org

Blues Heaven Foundation (BHF)
2120 Michigan Avenue
Chicago, IL 60616
Phone: (312) 808-1286
Fax: (312) 808-0273
E-mail: blueshvn@aol.com

Broadcast Music, Inc. (BMI)
320 West 57th Street
New York, NY 10019
Phone: (212) 586-2000
Fax: (212) 956-2059
E-mail: newyork@bmi.com
http://bmi.com

Certification Board for Music Therapists (CBMT)
506 East Lancaster Avenue, Suite 102
Downingtown, PA 19335
Phone: (610) 269-8900 or
    (800) 765-CBMT (toll-free)
Fax: (610) 269-9232
E-mail: info@cbmt.com
http://www.cbmt.com

Choreographers Guild (CG)
256 South Robertson
Beverly Hills, CA 90211
Phone: (310) 275-2533
Fax: (213) 653-5608

Choristers Guild (CG)
2834 West Kingsley Road
Garland, TX 75041-2498
Phone: (972) 271-1521
Fax: (972) 840-3113
E-mail: choristers@choristersguild.org
http://www.choristersguild.org

Chorus America
1156 15th Street, NW, Suite 310
Washington, DC 20005
Phone: (202) 331-7577
Fax: (202) 331-7599
E-mail: service@chorusamerica.org
http://www.chorusamerica.org

Church Music Association of America (CMAA)
134 Christendom Drive
Front Royal, VA 22630
Phone: (540) 636-2900 or (800) 877-5456
    (toll-free)
Fax: (540) 636-1655
http://www.christendom.edu

Church Music Publishers Association (CMPA)
P.O. Box 158992
Nashville, TN 37215

Phone: (615) 791-0273
Fax: (615) 790-8847
http://www.cmpamusic.org

Coalition for Disabled Musicians (CDM)
P.O. Box 1002M
Bay Shore, NY 11706
Phone: (631) 586-0366
Fax: (631) 586-0366
E-mail: cdmnews@aol.com
http://www.disabled-musicians.org

College Band Directors National Association (CBDNA)
c/o Richard L. Floyd
University of Texas
Box 8028
Austin, TX 78713
Phone: (512) 471-5883
Fax: (512) 471-6589
E-mail: rfloyd@mail.utexas.edu
http://www.cbdna.org

College Music Society (CMS)
202 West Spruce
Missoula, MT 59802
Phone: (406) 721-9616 or (800) 729-0235
    (toll-free)
Fax: (406) 721-9419
E-mail: cms@music.org
http://www.music.org

Conductors Guild
c/o North Lakeside Cultural Center
6219 North Sheridan Road
Chicago, IL 60660
Phone: (773) 764-7563
Fax: (773) 764-7564
E-mail: conguild@aol.com
http://www.conductorsguild.org

Contemporary A Cappella Society of America (CASA)
1850 Union Street, Suite 1449
San Francisco, CA 94123
Phone: (415) 563-5224
Fax: (415) 563-5523
E-mail: casa@casa.org
http://www.casa.org

Council for Music in Hospitals
74 Queens Road
Walton-On-Thames KT12 5LW, United
    Kingdom
Phone: 44 1932 252809
Fax: 44 1932 252966
http://www.music-in-hospitals.org.uk

Council for Research in Music Education (CRME)
School of Music
1114 West Nevada
Urbana, IL 61801
Phone: (217) 333-1027
Fax: (217) 244-8136
E-mail: crme@uiuc.edu

Country Dance and Song Society (CDSS)
132 Main Street
P.O. Box 338
Haydenville, MA 01039-0338
Phone: (413) 268-7426
Fax: (413) 268-7471
E-mail: office@cdss.org
http://www.cdss.org

Country Music Association (CMA)
1 Music Circle South
Nashville, TN 37203-4312
Phone: (615) 244-2840
Fax: (615) 726-0314
E-mail: info@cmaworld.com
http://www.cmaworld.com

Country Music Foundation (CMF)
222 Fifth Avenue, South
Nashville, TN 37203
Phone: (615) 416-2001
Fax: (615) 255-2245
http://www.halloffame.org

Country Music Showcase International (CMSI)
P.O. Box 368
Carlisle, IA 50047
Phone: (515) 989-3748
Fax: (515) 989-0235
E-mail: haroldl@cmshowcase.org
http://www.cmshowcase.org

Dollywood Foundation (DWF)
1020 Dollywood Lane
Pigeon Forge, TN 37863-4101
Phone: (865) 428-9606 or (800) 365-5996
    (toll-free)
Fax: (865) 428-9612
E-mail: dollyfound@aol.com
http://www.dollywood.com/Foundation.
    htm

Electronic Music Consortium (EMC)
c/o Dr. Thomas Wells
Ohio State University
School of Music
Columbus, OH 43210
Phone: (614) 292-7837

Fax: (614) 292-1102
E-mail: core@electronicmusic.com
http://www.electronicmusic.com

Electronic Music Foundation (EMF)
116 North Lake Avenue
Albany, NY 12206
Phone: (518) 434-4110
Fax: (518) 434-0308
E-mail: emf@emf.org
http://www.emf.org

Financial Planning Association (FPA)
5775 Glenridge Drive, Northeast,
    Suite B-300
Atlanta, GA 30328-5364
Phone: (404) 845-0011 or (800) 322-4237
    (toll-free)
Fax: (404) 845-3660
E-mail: membership@fpanet.org
http://www.fpanet.org

Gospel Music Association (GMA)
1205 Division Street
Nashville, TN 37203
Phone: (615) 242-0303 or (888) 242-0303
    (toll-free)
Fax: (615) 254-9755
http://www.gospelmusic.org

**Gospel Music Workshop of America
    (GMWA)**
3908 West Warren
Detroit, MI 48208
Phone: (313) 898-6900
Fax: (313) 898-4520
E-mail: slpuddie@worldnet.att.net
http://www.gmwa.org

GRAMMY Foundation
3402 Pico Boulevard
Santa Monica, CA 90405
Phone: (310) 392-3777
E-mail: info@grammyfoundation.org
http://www.grammy.com

Guild of Church Musicians
c/o Hillbrow
Godstone Road
Blechingley
Surrey RH1 4PJ, United Kingdom
Phone: 44 1883 741854
Fax: 44 1883 740570
E-mail: johnmusicsure@aol.com
http://www.churchmusicians.org

Guild of Temple Musicians (GTM)
Temple Beth El & Center
1435 West 7th Street
San Pedro, CA 90732

Phone: (310) 833-2467
Fax: (310) 833-6504

**Guitar and Accessories Marketing
    Association (GAMA)**
c/o J&D Music Services, Ltd.
262 West 38th Street, Room 1506
New York, NY 10018-5815
Phone: (212) 302-0801
Fax: (212) 302-0783
E-mail: assnhdqs@earthlink.net
http://www.discoverguitar.com

Guitar Foundation of America (GFA)
c/o Gunnar Eisel
P.O. Box 1240
Claremont, CA 91711
Phone: (909) 624-7730
Fax: (909) 624-1151
E-mail: gfainfo@yahoo.com
http://www.guitarfoundation.org

**The Institute of the American Musical
    (IAM)**
121 North Detroit Street
Los Angeles, CA 90036-2915
Phone: (323) 934-1221
Fax: (323) 934-1221

Institute of Internal Auditors (IIA)
247 Maitland Avenue
Altamonte Springs, FL 32701
Phone: (407) 937-1100
Fax: (407) 931-1101
E-mail: iia@theiia.org
http://www.theiia.org

**International Alliance of Theatrical
    Stage Employees, Moving Picture
    Technicians, Artists and Allied
    Crafts of the United States, Its
    Territories and Canada**
1430 Broadway, 20th Floor
New York, NY 10018
Phone: (212) 730-1770
Fax: (212) 730-7809
http://www.iatse.lm.com

**International Association of
    Administrative Professionals (IAAP)**
10502 Northwest Ambassador Drive
P.O. Box 20404
Kansas City, MO 64195-0404
Phone: (816) 891-6600
Fax: (816) 891-9118
E-mail: service@iaap-hq.org
http://www.iaap-hq.org

**International Association of Assembly
    Managers (IAAM)**
635 Fritz Drive, Suite 100
Coppell, TX 75019-4442
Phone: (972) 255-8020 or (800) 935-4226
    (toll-free)
Fax: (972) 255-9582
E-mail: dexter.king@iaam.org
http://www.iaam.org

**International Brotherhood of Electrical
    Workers (IBEW)**
1125 15th Street, NW
Washington, DC 20005
Phone: (202) 833-7000
Fax: (202) 467-6316
E-mail: web@isbew.org
http://www.ibew.org

Meet the Composer (MTC)
2112 Broadway, Suite 505
New York, NY 10023
Phone: (212) 787-3601
Fax: (212) 787-3745
E-mail: hhitchens@meetthecomposer.org
http://www.meetthecomposer.org

Metropolitan Opera Association
Lincoln Center
New York, NY 10023
Phone: (212) 362-6000
Fax: (212) 874-2659
E-mail: metinfo@visionfoundry.com
http://www.metopera.org

Metropolitan Opera Guild (MOG)
70 Lincoln Center Plaza, 6th Floor
New York, NY 10023
Phone: (212) 362-6000
Fax: (212) 769-7007
E-mail: metinfo@visionfoundry.com
http://www.metopera.org

Mid-State Music Teachers Association
c/o Rebecca Nance Barlar, NCTM,
    President
11406 West Queensway Drive
Temple Terrace, FL 33617
Phone: (813) 988-5891
E-mail: barlarb@flcoll.edu

**MIDI Manufacturers Association
    (MMA)**
P.O. Box 3173
La Habra, CA 90632-3173
E-mail: mma@midi.org
http://www.midi.org

Music and Entertainment Industry Educators Association (MEIEA)
Box 83
6363 St. Charles Avenue
Loyola University–New Orleans
New Orleans, LA 70118
E-mail: musicbiz@loyno.edu
http://musicbiz.loyno.edu/meiea

Music Critics Association of North America (MCA)
7 Pine Court
Westfield, NJ 07090
Phone: (908) 233-8468
Fax: (908) 233-8468
E-mail: musiccritics@aol.com
http://www.mcana.org

Music Distributors Association (MDA)
c/o J&D Music Services
262 West 38th Street, Room 1506
New York, NY 10018-5815
Phone: (212) 302-0801
Fax: (212) 302-0783
E-mail: assnhdqs@earthlink.net
http://www.musicdistributors.org

Music Industry Conference (MIC)
c/o MENC: The National Association for Music Education
1806 Robert Fulton Drive
Reston, VA 20191
Phone: (703) 860-4000 or (800) 336-3768 (toll-free)
Fax: (703) 860-1531
E-mail: info@menc.org
http://www.menc.org

Music Library Association (MLA)
8551 Research Way
Suite 180
Middleton, WI 53562-3567
Phone: (608) 836-5825
Fax: (608) 831-8200
E-mail: mla@areditions.com
http://www.musiclibraryassoc.org/

Music Network
The Coach House
Dublin Castle
Dublin 2, Ireland
Phone: 353 1 6719429
Fax: 353 1 6719430
E-mail: info@musicnetwork.ie
http://www.musicnetwork.ie

Music Publishers' Association of the United States (MPA)
PMB 246, 1562 First Avenue
New York, NY 10028

Phone: (212) 327-4044
Fax: (212) 327-4044
E-mail: mpa-admin@mpa.org
http://www.mpa.org

Music Teachers National Association (MTNA)
441 Vine Street, Suite 505
Cincinnati, OH 45202-2814
Phone: (513) 421-1420 or (888) 512-5278 (toll-free)
Fax: (513) 421-2503
E-mail: mtnanet@mtna.org
http://www.mtna.org

National Association of Music Merchants (NAMM), The International Music Products Association
5790 Armada Drive
Carlsbad, CA 92008
Phone: (760) 438-8001 or (800) 767-6266 (toll-free)
Fax: (760) 438-7327
E-mail: info@namm.com
http://www.namm.com

Nashville Songwriters Association International (NSAI)
1701 West End Avenue, 3rd Floor
Nashville, TN 37203-2601
Phone: (615) 256-3354 or (800) 321-6008 (toll-free)
Fax: (615) 256-0034
E-mail: nsai@nashvillesongwriters.com
http://www.nashvillesongwriters.com

National Academy of Popular Music (NAPM)
330 West 58th Street, Suite 411
New York, NY 10019-1827
Phone: (212) 957-9230
Fax: (212) 957-9227
E-mail: info@songwritershalloffame.org
http://www.songwritershalloffame.org

National Academy of Recording Arts and Sciences (NARAS)
3402 Pico Boulevard
Santa Monica, CA 90405
Phone: (310) 392-3777
Fax: (310) 392-9262
E-mail: info@grammyfoundation.org
http://www.grammy.com

National Academy of Television Arts and Sciences (NATAS)
111 West 57th Street, Suite 1020
New York, NY 10019

Phone: (212) 586-8424
Fax: (212) 246-8129
E-mail: natashq@aol.com
http://www.emmyonline.org

National Association for Campus Activities (NACA)
13 Harbison Way
Columbia, SC 29212-3401
Phone: (803) 732-6222 or (800) 845-2338 (toll-free)
Fax: (803) 749-1047
http://www.naca.org

National Association for Music Education (MENC)
1806 Robert Fulton Drive
Reston, VA 20191
Phone: (703) 860-4000 or (800) 336-3768 (toll-free)
Fax: (703) 860-1531
E-mail: maryjor@menc.org
http://www.menc.org

National Association for the Study and Performance of African-American Music (NASPAAM)
c/o Orville Wright
35 Blake Street
Mattapan, MA 02126-1003
Phone: (617) 361-7460
Fax: (617) 361-4465
E-mail: owright@bellatlantic.net
http://www.naspaam.org

National Association of Accompanists and Coaches (NAAC)
395 Riverside Drive, Apt. 13A
New York, NY 10025
Phone: (212) 316-6164
Fax: (212) 663-1900
E-mail: mircharney@aol.com

National Association Broadcast Employees and Technicians–Communications Workers of America (NABET-CWA)
501 3rd Street, NW, 8th Floor
Washington, DC 20001
Phone: (202) 434-1254
Fax: (202) 434-1426
E-mail: nabet@nabetcwa.org
http://www.nabetcwa.org

National Association of Broadcasters (NAB)
1771 N Street, NW
Washington, DC 20036
Phone: (202) 429-5300

Fax: (202) 429-5410
E-mail: sdelanghe@nab.org
http://www.nab.org

**National Association of College Wind
   and Percussion Instructors
   (NACWPI)**
c/o Richard Weerts
Division of Fine Arts
Truman State University
Kirksville, MO 63501
Phone: (816) 785-4442
Fax: (816) 785-7463
E-mail: fa24@truman.edu
http://nacwpi.org

**National Association of Composers,
   U.S.A. (NAC)**
Box 49256, Barrington Station
Los Angeles, CA 90049
Phone: (310) 541-8213
Fax: (310) 373-3244
E-mail: bia@flash.net
http://www.music-usa.org/nacusa

**National Association of Mobile
   Entertainers (NAME)**
P.O. Box 144
Willow Grove, PA 19090
Phone: (215) 658-1193 or (800) 434-8274
   (toll-free)
Fax: (215) 658-1194
E-mail: bruce@djkj.com
http://www.djkj.com

**National Association of Music
   Executives in State Universities
   (NAMESU)**
c/o Professor Gary Cook
School of Music
University of Arizona
P.O. Box 210004
Tucson, AZ 85721
Phone: (520) 621-7023
Fax: (520) 621-8118

**National Association of Orchestra
   Leaders (NAOL)**
34 Metropolitan Oval
Bronx, NY 10462
Phone: (718) 863-8997

**National Association of Pastoral
   Musicians (NPM)**
225 Sheridan Street, NW
Washington, DC 20011-1492
Phone: (202) 723-5800
Fax: (202) 723-2262
E-mail: npmsing@npm.org
http://www.npm.org

**National Association of Professional
   Band Instrument Repair
   Technicians (NAPBIRT)**
P.O. Box 51
Normal, IL 61761
Phone: (309) 452-4257
Fax: (309) 452-4825
E-mail: napbirt@napbirt.org
http://www.napbirt.org

**National Association of Recording
   Merchandisers (NARM)**
9 Eves Drive, Suite 120
Marlton, NJ 08053
Phone: (856) 596-2221
Fax: (856) 596-3268
E-mail: rosum@narm.com
http://www.narm.com

**National Association of School Music
   Dealers (NASMD)**
13140 Coit Road, No. 320
Dallas, TX 75240
Phone: (972) 233-9107
Fax: (972) 490-4219
http://www.nasmd.com

**National Association of Schools of
   Music (NASM)**
11250 Roger Bacon Drive, Suite 21
Reston, VA 20190
Phone: (703) 437-0700
Fax: (703) 437-6312
E-mail: info@arts-accredit.org
http://www.arts-accredit.org

**National Association of Teachers of
   Singing (NATS)**
6406 Merrill Road, Suite B
Jacksonville, FL 32277
Phone: (904) 744-9022
Fax: (904) 744-9033
E-mail: info@nats.org
http://www.nats.org

National Band Association (NBA)
P.O. Box 121292
Nashville, TN 37212
Fax: (615) 385-2650
E-mail: nbassoc@bellsouth.net
http://www.nationalbandassoc.org

**National Catholic Band Association
   (NCBA)**
c/o John Badsing
3334 North Normandy
Chicago, IL 60634-3716
Phone: (773) 282-9153
E-mail: ncbamail@aol.com
http://www.thencba.org

National Christian Choir
983-A Russell Avenue
Gaithersburg, MD 20879-3276
Phone: (301) 670-6331 or (800) 599-4710
   (toll-free)
Fax: (301) 330-7299
E-mail: office@nationalchristianchoir.org
http://nationalchristianchoir.org

**National Conference of Personal
   Managers (NCOPM)**
46-19 220 Place
Bayside, NY 11361
Phone: (718) 224-3616
http://www.ncopm.com

**National Council of Acoustical
   Consultants (NCAC)**
66 Morris Avenue, Suite 1A
Springfield, NJ 07081-1409
Phone: (973) 564-5859
Fax: (973) 564-7480
E-mail: info@ncac.com
http://www.ncac.com

**National Council of Music Importers
   and Exporters (NCMIE)**
c/o J&D Music Services, Inc.
262 West 38th Street, Room 1506
New York, NY 10018-5815
Phone: (212) 302-0801
Fax: (212) 302-0783
E-mail: assnhdqs@earthlink.net

**National Federation of Independent
   Unions–American Musicians Union
   Local No. 152**
c/o Benjamin J. Intorre, Sr.
8 Tobin Court
Dumont, NJ 07628-3329
Phone: (201) 384-5378

**National Federation of Music Clubs
   (NFMC)**
1336 North Delaware Street
Indianapolis, IN 46202
Phone: (317) 638-4003
Fax: (317) 638-0503
E-mail: nfmc@nfmc.org
http://www.nfmc-music.org

**National Federation of State High
   School Associations (NFSHSA)**
P.O. Box 690
Indianapolis, IN 46206
Phone: (317) 972-6900
Fax: (317) 822-5700
http://www.nfhs.org

National Foundation for Advancement in the Arts (NFAA)
800 Brickell Avenue, Suite 500
Miami, FL 33131
Phone: (305) 377-1140 or (800) 970-ARTS (toll-free)
Fax: (305) 377-1149
E-mail: info@nfaa.org
http://www.nfaa.org

National Guild of Piano Teachers (NGPT)
808 Rio Grande
P.O. Box 1807
Austin, TX 78701-1807
Phone: (512) 478-5775
Fax: (512) 478-5843
E-mail: ngptpat@aol.com
http://www.pianoguild.com

National Guild of Piano Teachers (NGPT)
808 Rio Grande
P.O. Box 1807
Austin, TX 78701-1807
Phone: (512) 478-5775
Fax: (512) 478-5843
E-mail: ngptpat@aol.com
http://www.pianoguild.com

National High School Band Directors Hall of Fame
519 North Halifax Avenue
Daytona Beach, FL 32118
Phone: (386) 252-0381
Fax: (386) 252-0381
E-mail: cudepickenspub@aol.com
http://www.banddirectorshalloffame.homestead.com

National Music Council (NMC)
425 Park Street
Upper Montclair, NJ 07043
Phone: (973) 655-7974
Fax: (973) 655-5432
E-mail: sandersd@mail.montclair.edu

National Music Publishers' Association (NMPA)
475 Park Avenue South, 29th Floor
New York, NY 10016-6901
Phone: (646) 742-1651
Fax: (646) 742-1779
E-mail: clientrelations@harryfox.com
http://www.nmpa.org

National Music Theater Network (NMTN)
1697 Broadway, Suite 902
New York, NY 10019

Phone: (212) 664-0979
Fax: (212) 664-0978
E-mail: info@broadwayusa.org
http://www.broadwayusa.org

National Opera Association (NOA)
c/o Robert Hansen
P.O. Box 60869
Canyon, TX 79016-0869
Phone: (806) 651-2857
Fax: (806) 651-2958
E-mail: rhansen@mail.wtamu.edu
http://www.noa.org

National Orchestral Association (NOA)
575 Lexington Avenue, 9th Floor
New York, NY 10022-6102
Phone: (212) 350-4676
Fax: (212) 350-1440

National Piano Foundation (NPF)
c/o Donald W. Dillon
13140 Coit Road, Suite 320
Dallas, TX 75240-5737
Phone: (972) 233-9107
Fax: (972) 490-4219
E-mail: don@dondillon.com
http://www.pianonet.com

National School Band Association
72 Broomfield Road
Churchdown
Gloucester GL3 2PC, United Kingdom
Phone: 44 1664 434379
Fax: 44 1452 714976
E-mail: thensba@hotmail.com
http://www.nsba.org.uk

National Sheet Music Society (NSMS)
1597 Fair Park Avenue
Los Angeles, CA 90041

National Society of Accountants (NSA)
1010 North Fairfax Street
Alexandria, VA 22314-1574
Phone: (703) 549-6400 or (800) 966-6679 (toll-free)
Fax: (703) 549-2984
E-mail: jfelski@nsacct.org
http://www.nsacct.org

National Symphony Orchestra Association (NSOA)
JFK Center for the Performing Arts
Washington, DC 20566
Phone: (202) 416-8000 or (800) 444-1324 (toll-free)
Fax: (202) 416-8105
http://www.nationalsymphony.org

National Traditional Country Music Association (NTCMA)
P.O. Box 492
Anita, IA 50020
Phone: (712) 762-4363
Fax: (712) 762-4363
E-mail: bobeverhart@yahoo.com
http://www.oldtimemusic.bigstep.com

National Youth Orchestra Association of Canada (NYOC)
1032 Bathurst Street
Toronto, ON, Canada M5R 3G7
Phone: (416) 532-4470
Fax: (416) 532-6879
E-mail: info@nyoc.org
http://www.nyoc.org

National Youth Orchestra Association of Canada (NYOC)
1032 Bathurst Street
Toronto, ON, Canada M5R 3G7
Phone: (416) 532-4470
Fax: (416) 532-6879
E-mail: info@nyoc.org
http://www.nyoc.org

OPERA America
1156 15th Street, NW, No. 810
Washington, DC 20005
Phone: (202) 293-4466
Fax: (202) 393-0735
E-mail: frontdesk@operaamerica.org
http://www.operaam.org

Piano Manufacturers Association International (PMAI)
c/o Donald W. Dillon
13140 Coit Road, Suite 320
Dallas, TX 75240-5737
Phone: (972) 233-9107
Fax: (972) 490-4219
E-mail: don@dondillon.com
http://www.pianonet.com

Piano Technicians Guild (PTG)
3930 Washington
Kansas City, MO 64111-2963
Phone: (816) 753-7747
Fax: (816) 531-0070
E-mail: ptg@ptg.org
http://www.ptg.org

Professional Women Singers Association (PWSA)
P.O. Box 884
New York, NY 10024
Phone: (212) 969-0590
Fax: (928) 395-2560

E-mail: info@womensingers.org
http://www.womensingers.org

**Public Relations Society of America
(PRSA)**
33 Irving Place, 3rd Floor
New York, NY 10003-2376
Phone: (212) 995-2230
E-mail: hq@prsa.org
http://www.prsa.org

**Public Relations Student Society of
America**
33 Irving Place, 3rd Floor
New York, NY 10003-2376
Phone: (212) 995-2230
E-mail: hq@prsa.org
http://www.prsa.org

Radio Advertising Bureau (RAB)
1320 Greenway Way Drive, No. 500
Irving, TX 75038
Phone: (212) 681-7200 or (800) 232-3131
(toll-free)
Fax: (212) 681-7223
E-mail: gfries@rab.com
http://www.rab.com

**Recording Industry Association of
America (RIAA)**
1330 Connecticut Avenue, Suite 300
Washington, DC 20036
Phone: (202) 775-0101
Fax: (202) 775-7253
E-mail: webmaster@riaa.com
http://www.riaa.com

**Rhythm and Blues Rock and Roll
Society (RBRRSI)**
P.O. Box 1949
New Haven, CT 06510
Phone: (203) 924-1079

Screen Actors Guild (SAG)
5757 Wilshire Boulevard
Los Angeles, CA 90036-3600
Phone: (323) 954-1600
Fax: (323) 549-6603
http://www.sag.org

SESAC, Inc.
55 Music Square East
Nashville, TN 37203
Phone: (615) 320-0055
Fax: (615) 329-9627
http://www.sesac.com

**Society for Music Teacher Education
(SMTE)**
c/o Music Educators National
Conference
1806 Robert Fulton Drive
Reston, VA 20191
Phone: (703) 860-4000 or (800) 828-0229
(toll-free)
Fax: (703) 860-1531
E-mail: maryjor@menc.org
http://www.menc.org

Society for Music Theory (SMT)
University of California Press
Journals Division
2000 Center Street, Suite 303
Berkeley, CA 94704

Songwriters Guild of America (SGA)
1500 Harbor Boulevard
Weehawken, NJ 07086
Phone: (201) 867-7603
Fax: (201) 867-7535
E-mail: songnewsj@aol.com
http://www.songwriters.org

Songwriters and Lyricists Club (SLC)
c/o Robert B. Makinson
P.O. Box 605
Times Plaza Station
542 Atlantic Avenue
Brooklyn, NY 11217-0605
Phone: (718) 832-5859

**Society of Professional Audio
Recording Services (SPARS)**
P.O. Box 770845
Memphis, TN 38117-0845
Phone: (901) 747-3111 or (800) 771-7727
(toll-free)
E-mail: spars@spars.com
http://www.spars.com

Special Libraries Association (SLA)
1700 18th Street, NW
Washington, DC 20009-2514
Phone: (202) 234-4700
Fax: (202) 265-9317
E-mail: sla@sla.org
http://www.sla.org

**Urban Music Association of Canada
(UMAC)**
675 King Street West, Suite 30
Toronto, ON Canada M5V 1 M9
Phone: (416) 916-2874
E-mail: info@umac.ca
http://www.umac.ca

Volunteer Lawyers for the Arts (VLA)
1 East 53rd Street, 6th Floor
New York, NY 10022
Phone: (212) 319-2787
Fax: (212) 752-6575
E-mail: askvla@vlany.org
http://www.vlany.org

APPENDIX III
RECORD COMPANIES

The following is a list of major and independent record companies. As you will see, most of the major companies are located in the music capitals of the country. Whenever possible, branch offices have been included. Many independent labels are currently beginning to experience a great deal of success in the music industry. They are, therefore, valuable resources for intern and job possibilities as well as for record deals. Due to space limitations, all record companies and labels have not been included. Inclusion or exclusion on this list does not indicate the recommendation or endorsement of one company over another.

A&M Records
2220 Colorado Avenue
Santa Monica, CA 90404
Phone: (310) 865-1000
http://www.amrecords.com

Allied Artists
273 West Alien Avenue
San Dimas, CA 90028
Phone: (626) 330-0600
Fax: (626) 961-0411
E-mail: info@alliedartists.net
http://www.alliedartists.net

Alligator Records
1441 West Devon
Chicago, IL 60660
Phone: (773) 973-7736
Fax: (773) 973-2088
E-mail: info@alligator.com
http://www.alligator.com

Alula Records
P.O. Box 62043
Durham, NC 27715
Phone: (919) 416-9454
Fax: (919) 286-1788
E-mail: info@alula.com
http://www.alula.com

Angel Records
150 Fifth Avenue
New York, NY 10011
Phone: (212) 786-8600
Fax: (212) 786-8649
http://www.angelrecords.com

Arista Records
6 West 57th Street
New York, NY 10019
Phone: (212) 489-7400

Fax: (212) 830-2222
E-mail: info@arista.com
http://www.arista.com

Arista Records, Inc.
8750 Wilshire Boulevard
Beverly Hills, CA 90211
Phone: (310) 358-4600
Fax: (310) 358-4325
http://www.arista.com

Arista Records
2210 Park Lake Drive Northeast
Atlanta, GA, 30345
Phone: (770) 414-6250
Fax: (770) 414-6256
http://www.arista.com

Arista Records Nashville
1400 18th Avenue South
Nashville, TN 37212
Phone: (615) 301-4300
Fax: (615) 846-9195
E-mail: arista@twangthis.com
http://www.aristanashville.com

Arula Records
P.O. Box 332
Southbridge, MA 01550
Phone: (508) 248-1799
Fax: (508) 248-1799
E-mail: arularec@aol.com
http://www.arularecords.com

Asinni 2000 Records, Inc.
14601 BeMaire, Suite 308
Houston, TX 77083
Phone: (281) 564-4111
Fax: (281) 561-9200
E-mail: asini@swbell.net
http://www.asinni2000records.com

Astralwerks Records
104 West 29th Street, 4th Floor
New York, NY 10001
E-mail: feedback@astralwerks.net
http://www.astralwerks.com

The Atlantic Group
1290 Avenue of the Americas
New York, NY 10104
Phone: (212) 707-2000
Fax: (212) 405-5507
http://www.atlantic-records.com

Atlantic Records
9229 Sunset Boulevard
Los Angeles, CA, 90069
Phone: (310) 205-7450
Fax: (310) 205-5721
http://www.atlantic-records.com

Atlantic Records (Classical Division)
1290 Avenue of the Americas
New York, NY, 10104
Phone: (212) 707-2648
Fax: (212) 405-5470
http://www.atlantic-records.com

Baby Pea Records
320 North Hollywood Way
Burbank, CA 91505
Phone: (818) 238-9472
Fax: (818) 238-9938
http://www.babypearecords.com

Bad Boy Entertainment
1540 Broadway
New York, NY 10036
Phone: (212) 381-1540
Fax: (212) 381-1599
E-mail: badboy@badboyonline.com
http://www.badboyonline.com

Bam Records
183552 Dallas Parkway
Dallas, TX 75287
Phone: (214) 485-0001
http://www.bamrecordsmusic.com

Banner Records
P.O. Box 10440
Hamilton Square, NJ 08650
Phone: (609) 588-8808
Fax: (609) 588-8836
E-mail: jlello@optonline.net
http://www.bannerrecords.com

Bar/None Records
P.O. Box 1704
Hoboken, NJ 07030
Phone: (201) 770-9090
Fax: (201) 770-9920
E-mail: info@bar-none.com
http://www.bar-none.com

Basin Street Records
4151 Canal Street
New Orleans, LA 70119
Phone: (504) 483-0002 or (888) 452-2746
Fax: (504) 483-7877
E-mail: info@basinstreetrecords.com
http://www.basinstreetrecords.com

The Beggars Group
625 Broadway
New York, NY 10012
Phone: (212) 995-5582
Fax: (212) 995-5583
E-mail: banquet@beggars.com
http://www.beggars.com/us

Bettygirl Records
2305 Elliston Place
Nashville, TN 37203
Phone: (615) 480-3387
Fax: (615) 320-5983
E-mail: info@bettygirlrecords.com
http://www.bettygirlrecords.com

Big Heavy World
P.O. Box 428
Burlington, VT 05402
Phone: (802) 865-1140
E-mail: groundzero@bigheavyworld.com
http://www.bigheavyworld.com

Blackbird Recording Co.
185 Franklin Street
New York, NY 10013
Phone: (212) 226-5379
Fax: (212) 226-3913
E-mail: info@blackbirdusa.com
http://www.blackbirdusa.com

Blue Dog Publishing & Records
P.O. Box 3438
St. Louis, MO 63143
Phone: (314) 646-0191
Fax: (314) 646-8005
http://www.bluedogpublishing.com

Blue Note Records
150 Fifth Avenue
New York, NY 10011
Phone: (212) 786-8600
Fax: (212) 786-8649
http://www.bluenote.com

BMG Entertainment North America
1540 Broadway
New York, NY 10036
Phone: (212) 930-4000
Fax: (212) 930-4015
http://www.bmg.com

BNA Records
1400 18th Avenue South
Nashville, TN 37212
Phone: (615) 301-4400
Fax: (615) 301-4475
http://www.bnarecords.com

Boyd Records & Publishing
P.O. Box 226
Cincinnati, OH 45201
Phone: (877) 345-9257
Fax: (513) 729-0269
E-mail: boydrec@cholce.net
http://www.boydrec.com

Brainticket Records
P.O. Box 122048
Arlington, TX 76012
Phone: (817) 274-2332
Fax: (817) 274-2119
E-mail: john@brainticket.net
http://www.brainticket.com

Brandywine Productions
P.O. Box 413
Durham, NH 03824
Phone: (603) 749-2811

Bravo Records, Inc. / TJS Productions
2711 Broad Street
Houston, TX 77087
Phone: (713) 644-3795
Fax: (713) 644-3893
E-mail: charlie@tjsbravo.com
http://www.tjsbravo.com

Breeze Hill Records
P.O. Box 239
Hurley, NY 12443

Phone: (845) 339-1574
E-mail: info@breezehill.net
http://www.breezehill.net

Brentwood Records
741 Cool Springs Boulevard
Franklin, TN 37067
Phone: (615) 261-6500
Fax: (615) 261-5910
E-mail: bgentry@providentmusicgroup.
   com
http://www.brentwoodrecords.com

Brick Records
P.O. Box 281
Boston, MA 02117
Phone: (888) 513-3998
http://www.brickrecords.com

Broadbeach Records
3465 Encinal Canyon Road
Malibu, CA 90265
Phone: (310) 457-4405
E-mail: randy@nauert.com
http://www.nauert.com

Broken Bow Records
209 10th Avenue South
Nashville, TN 37203
Phone: (615) 244-8600
Fax: (615) 244-3700
E-mail: brokenbowrecords@aol.com
http://www.brokenbowrecords.com

Buddha Records / BMG Heritage
1540 Broadway
New York, NY 10036
Phone: (212) 930-4518
Fax: (212) 930-7098
http://www.buddharecords.com

Bullseye Blues Records
1 Camp Street
Cambridge, MA 02140
Phone: (617) 354-0700
Fax: (617) 491-1970
E-mail: info@rounder.com
http://www.rounder.com

Cadence Jazz Records Ltd.
Cadence Building
Redwood, NY 13679
Phone: (315) 287-2852
Fax: (315) 287-2860
E-mail: cjr@cadencebuilding.com
http://www.cadencebuilding.com

Cake Records
2339 Fawcett Avenue South
Tacoma, WA 98402

E-mail: contact@cakerecords.com
http://www.indicgrrlrecords.com

Canyon Records
3131 West Clarendon Avenue
Phoenix, AZ 85017
Fax: (602) 279-9233
E-mail: canyon@canyonrecords.
http://www.canyonrecords.com

Campesino Entertainment Group, Inc.
1990 Third Avenue
New York, NY 10029
Phone: (212) 289-6639
Fax: (212) 348-7558
E-mail: campesinomusic@aol.com
http://www.campesinomusid.dom

Capitol Records
1750 North Vine Street
Hollywood, CA 90028
Phone: (323) 462-6252,
Fax: (323) 871-5214
http://www.hollywoodandvine.com

Capitol Records
304 Park Avenue South
New York, NY 10010
Phone: (212) 253-3000
Fax: (212) 253-3150
http://www.hollywoodandvine.com

Capitol Nashville
3322 West End Avenue
Nashville, TN 37203
Phone: (615) 269-2000
Fax: (615) 269-2045
E-mail: capitol-nashville.com
http://www.capitol-nashville.com

**Caprice International/Canadian
    American Records**
39 Forney Avenue
Lititz, PA 17543
Phone: (717) 627-4800
Fax: (717) 627-4800
E-mail: capricerecords@webtv.net
http://www.songtek.com

Cardinal Records
7118 Peach Court
Brentwood, TN 37027
Phone: (615) 373-5223
Fax: (615) 661-4538
E-mail: chuck@chelseamusic.com
http://www.chelseamusic.com

Cargo Music, Inc
4901 Morena Boulevard
San Diego, CA 92117

Phone: (858) 483-9292
Fax: (858) 483-7414
E-mail: info@cargomusic.com
http://www.cargomusic.com

Casino Records
881 Ponce De Leon Avenue
Atlanta, GA 30306
Phone: (404) 876-1201
Fax: (404) 876-1408
E-mail: casinomusic@mindspring.com
http://www.casinomusic.com

Castle Records
United Artists Tower
50 Music Square West, Suite 201
Nashville, TN 37203
Phone: (615) 320-7003 or (615) 320-9501
Fax: (615) 320-7006
E-mail: castlerecords@castlerecords.com
http://www.castlerecords.com

CDX
2603 Westwood Drive
Nashville, TN 37204
Phone: (615) 292-0123
Fax: (615) 292-8750
E-mail: cdx@comcast.net

Ceill Music
329 Rockland Road
Hendersonville, TN 37075
Phone: (615) 264-8877
Fax: (615) 264-8899
info@skaggsfamilyrecords.com
http://www.ceilimusic.com

Century Media Records
2323 West El Segundo Boulevard
Hawthorne, CA 90520
Phone: (323) 418-1400
Fax: (323) 418-0118
E-mail: mail@centurymedia.com
http://www.centurymedia.com

Cinema Records, Inc.
812 West Darby Road
Havertown, PA 19083
Phone: (610) 446-7100
Fax: (610) 446-7721
E-mail: cinemarecords@comcast.net

CMI Records
P.O. Box 2127
Clifton, NJ 07015
Phone: (973) 473-0986
Fax: (973) 473-3211
E-mail: cmirecords@aol.com
http://www.mattgarbo.com

Coldhouse Records, Inc.
205 Alpine Drive
Danville, VA 14540
Phone: (434) 797-4501
Fax: (434) 797-4501
E-mail: coldhouse@gamewood.net
http://www.coldhouserecords.com

Columbia Records
550 Madison Avenue
New York, NY 10022
Phone: (212) 833-8000
Fax: (212) 833-5401
http://www.columbiarecords.com

Columbia Records
2100 Colorado Avenue
Santa Monica, CA, 90404
Phone: (310) 449-2100
Fax: (310) 552-1350
http://www.columbiarecords.com

Columbia Records
34 Music Square East
Nashville, TN 37203-4397
Phone: (615) 742-4321
Fax: (615) 742-5741
http://www.sonynashville.com

Compass Records
117 30th Avenue South
Nashville, TN 37212
Phone: (615) 320-7672
Fax: (615) 320-7378
E-mail: info@compassrecords.com
http://www.compassrecords.com

Crescent Moon Records
420 Jefferson Avenue
Miami Beach, FL 33139
Phone: (305) 695-7000
Fax: (305) 695-7120

Cropduster Records
78 Trask Avenue
Bayonne, NJ 07002
Phone: (201) 243-0100
Fax: (201) 437-1069
E-mail: info@cropduster.com
http://www.cropduster.com

Crossfield Music
3003 Blakemore Avenue
Nashville, TN 37212
Phone: (615) 269-8661 or (800) 485-0723
Fax: (615) 269-8661
E-mail: crossfield@crossfield.com
http://www.crossfield.com

C-Side Entertainment LLC
440 West 47th Street
New York, NY 10036
Phone: (212) 247-3370
Fax: (703) 370-2662
E-mail: tgobena@email.com
http://www.csideentertainment.com

Curb Records
47 Music Square East
Nashville, TN 37203
Phone: (615) 321-5080
Fax: (615) 327-3003
http://www.curb.com

Deep Shag Records
P.O. Box 889126
Atlanta, GA 30356
Phone: (678) 547-0272
Fax: (678) 547-0598
E-mail: info@deepshag.com
http://www.deepshag.com

Deep South Entertainment
188 Wind Chime Court, Suite 104
Raleigh, NC 27615
Phone: (919) 844-1515
Fax: (919) 847-5922
E-mail: info@deepsouthentertainment.
    com
http://www.deepsouthentertainment.com

Def Jam
825 Eighth Avenue, 28th Floor
New York, NY 10019
Phone: (212) 333-8000
Fax: (212) 603-7931
http://www.defjam.com

Dionysus Records
P.O. Box 1975
Burbank, CA 91507
Phone: (818) 848-2698
Fax: (818) 848-2699
E-mail: dionysus@dionysusrecords.com
http://www.dionysusrecords.com

Domo Records, Inc.
11340 West Olympic Boulevard
Los Angeles, CA 90064
Phone: (310) 966-4414
Fax: (310) 966-4420
E-mail: domo@domo.com
http://www.domo.com

Drag City Records
P.O. Box 476867
Chicago, IL 60647
Phone: (312) 455-1015

Fax: (312) 455-1057
E-mail: info@dragcity.com
http://www.dragcity.com

Dreamcatcher Entertainment
2910 Poston Avenue
Nashville, TN 37203
Phone: (615) 329-2303
Fax: (615) 329-2350
http://www.dreamcatcherenter.com

DreamWorks
9268 West Third Street
Beverly Hills, CA 90210
Phone: (310) 288-7700
Fax: (310) 288-7768
http://www.dreamworksrecords.com

Earthquake Sound Records
6 Nottingham Street
Dorchester, MA 02121
Phone: (617) 825-3440
E-mail: earthquakesound@aol.com

EastWest
75 Rockefeller Plaza
New York, NY 10019
Phone: (212) 275-2500
Fax: (212) 974-9314
http://www.elektra.com

Elektra
75 Rockefeller Plaza
New York, NY 10019-6907
Phone: (212) 275-4000
Fax: (212) 956-7284
http://www.elektra.com

Elektra
345 North Maple Drive, Suite 123
Beverly Hills, CA, 90210
Phone: (310) 288-3800
Fax: (310) 274-9491
http://www.elektra.com

Elektra Epic/Monument Nashville
34 Music Square East
Nashville, TN 37203
Phone: (615) 742-4379
Fax: (615) 742-4338
http://www.sonynashville.com

EMI Christian Music Group
101 Winners Circle
Brentwood, TN 37027
Phone: (615) 371-4300
Fax: (615) 371-6915
http://www.emicmg.com

EMI Latin Music Group
404 Washington Avenue
Miami Beach, FL 33139
Phone: (305) 674-7529
Fax: (305) 674-7546
http://www.emilatin.com

EMI Recorded Music
150 Fifth Avenue
New York, NY 10011
Phone: (212) 786-8000
http://www.emigroup.com

EMI Recorded Music
1750 North Vine Street
Hollywood, CA, 90028
Phone: (323) 871-5000
http://www.hollywoodandvine.com

Eminent Records
2807 Bransford Avenue
Nashville, TN 37204
Phone: (615) 386-8373
E-mail: mail@eminentrecords.com
http://www.eminentrecords.com

Epic Records Group
550 Madison Avenue
New York, NY 10022-3211
Phone: (212) 833-7442
Fax: (212) 833-4583
http://www.epicrecords.com

Epitaph Records
2798 Sunset Boulevard
Los Angeles, CA 90026
Phone: (213) 413-7353
Fax: (213) 413-9678
E-mail: christina@epitaph.com
http://www.epitaph.com

Essential Records
741 Cool Springs Boulevard
Franklin, TN 37067
Phone: (615) 261-6500
E-mail: essential@providentmusicgroup.
    com
http://www.essentialrecords.com

Fambam Records
P.O. Box 29846
Oakland, CA 94604-9846
Phone: (510) 819-3418
Fax: (510) 217-3861
http://www.fambamrecords.com

Flia Recordings, Inc.
4318 Kennedy Boulevard
Union City, NJ 07087

Phone: (201) 553-1899
Fax: (201) 553-0335
http://www.flia.net

Flip Records
8733 Sunset Boulevard
West Hollywood, CA 90069
E-mail: flip@flip-records.com
http://www.flip-records.com

Forefront Records
230 Franklin Road
Franklin, TN 37064
Phone: (615) 771-2900
Fax: (615) 771-2901
http://www.forefrontrecords.com

Fountainbleu Records
91-38 114th Street
Richmond Hill, NY 11418
Phone: (718) 847-3281
Fax: (718) 805-8502

Frontier Records
P.O. Box 22
Sun Valley, CA 91353
Phone: (818) 759-8279
E-mail: frontier@briefcase.com
http://www.frontierrecords.com

Gammon Records
111 East 14th Street
New York, NY 10003
Phone: (212) 219-0700
Fax: (212) 219-0122
E-mail: jordy@gammonrecords.com
http://www.gammonrecords.com

Geffen Records
2220 Colorado Avenue
Santa Monica, CA 90404
Phone: (310) 865-1000
Fax: (310) 865-7096
http://www.geffen.com

Gig Records
520 Butler Avenue
Point Pleasant, NJ 08742
Phone: (732) 701-9044 or (732) 701-9045
Fax: (732) 701-9777
E-mail: indian@gigrecords.com
http://www.gigrecords.com

Griffin Music
P.O. Box 1952
Lombard, IL 60148
Phone: (630) 424-0801
Fax: (630) 424-0806
E-mail: grifmus@aol.com
http://www.griffinmusic.com

Handpicked Records
P.O. Box 5656
Columbia, SC 29250
Phone: (803) 779-3505
Fax: (803) 779-7121
E-mail: info@handpickedrecords.com
http://www.handpickedrecords.com

Higher Octave Music, Inc.
23852 Pacific Coast Highway
Malibu, CA 90265
Phone: (310) 589-1515
Fax: (310) 589-1525
E-mail: info@higheroctave.com
http://www.higheroctave.com

Hightone Records
220 Fourth Street
Oakland, CA 94607
Phone: (510) 763-8500
Fax: (510) 763-8558
E-mail: hightone@hightone.com
http://www.hightone.com

Hip-O Records
2220 Colorado Avenue
Santa Monica, CA 90404
Phone: (310) 865-7298
Fax: (310) 865-6336
E-mail: hip-o@umusic.com
http://www.hip-o.com

Idol Records
P.O. Box 720043
Dallas, TX 75372
Phone: (214) 826-4365
Fax: (214) 370-5417
E-mail: info@idol-records.com
http://www.idol-records.com

Immortal Entertainment
1650 21st Street
Santa Monica, CA 90404
Phone: (310) 582-8300
Fax: (310) 582-8301
http://www.immortalrecords.com

Interscope
1790 Broadway
New York, NY, 10019
Phone: (212) 445-3200
http://www.interscope.com

Interscope
2220 Colorado Avenue
Santa Monica, CA 90404
Phone: (310) 865-4562
Fax: (310) 865-7083
E-mail: brenda.romano@umusic.com
http://www.interscope.com

Island Def Jam Music Group
825 Eighth Avenue
New York, NY 10019
Phone: (212) 333-8000
Fax: (212) 603-7931
http://www.islanddefjam.com

Island Def Jam Music Group
8920 Sunset Boulevard
Los Angeles, CA 90069
Phone: (310) 276-4500
http://www.islanddefjam.com

Island Def Jam South
1349 West Peachtree Street, Suite 1960
Atlanta, GA 30309
Phone: (404) 875-6695
Fax: (404) 876-1173
E-mail: india.fendrick@umusic.com
http://www.islanddefjam.com

J Records
745 Fifth Avenue
New York, NY 10151
Phone: (646) 840-5600 or (212) 830-2262
Fax: (212) 930-5959
http://www.j-records.com

Jive/Silvertone/Verity/Volcano Records
137-139 West 25th Street
New York, NY 10001
Phone: (212) 727-0016
Fax: (212) 645-3783
http://www.jiverecords.com

Jive/Silvertone/Verity/Volcano Records
9000 Sunset Boulevard
West Hollywood, CA 90069
Phone: (310) 247-8300
Fax: (310) 247-8366
http://www.jiverecords.com

Just Us Records
P.O. Box 6822
Alexandria, VA 22306
Phone: (703) 765-3166
Fax: (703) 765-4882
http://www.justusrecords.com

KMG Records, Inc.
33 Music Square West
Nashville, TN 37203
Phone: (615) 269-7000
Fax: (615) 269-9525
http://www.kmgrecords.com

Lamon Records
P.O. Box 25371
Charlotte, NC 28229

Phone: (704) 882-6134
Fax: (704) 882-2063
E-mail: mailbox@lamonrecords.com
http://www.lamonrecords.com

Lava Records
1290 Avenue of the Americas
New York, NY 10104
Phone: (212) 707-2550
Fax: (212) 405-5561
http://www.lavarecords.com

Lanor Records
406 West Jefferson Street
Jennings, LA 70546
Phone: (337) 824-6063
Fax: (337) 824-6064

Lazy Bones Recordings, Inc.
9594 First Avenue, Northeast
Seattle, WA 98115
Phone: (206) 447-0712
Fax: (425) 821-5720
E-mail: lbrinc@earthlink.net
http://www.lazybones.com

Legacy Recordings
550 Madison Avenue
New York, NY 10022
Phone: (212) 833-8000
Fax: (212) 833-6894
E-mail: sonymusiconline@sonymusic.com
http://www.legacyrecordings.com

John H. Lennon Music Ltd.
P.O. Box 526
3415 Dixie Road
Mlssissauga, ON L4Y 4J6, Canada
Phone: (800) 951-0044
E-mail: lennonmusic@
    johnhlennonmusic.com
http://www.johnhlennonmusic.com

Lens Records
3023 North Clark Street
Chicago, IL 60657
Phone: (773) 404-2692
Fax: (773) 404-2976
E-mail: lens@lensrecords.com
http://www.lensrecords.com

Little Dog Records
2219 West Olive Avenue
Burbank, CA 91506
Phone: (818) 557-1595
Fax: (818) 557-0524
E-mail: info@littledogrecords.com
http://www.littledogrecords.com

Logic Records
1540 Broadway
New York, NY 10036
Phone: (212) 930-4000
Fax: (212) 930-1366
E-mail: logicus1@aol.com
http://www.logicrecords.com

Logic Records
8750 Wilshire Boulevard
Beverly Hills, CA 90211
Phone: (310) 358-4160
Fax: (310) 358-4373
E-mail: logicrecordswest@aol.com
http://www.logicrecords.com

Lost Highway Records
c/o Mercury Nashville
54 Music Square East, Suite 300
Nashville, TN 37203
Phone: (615) 524-7500
http://www.losthighwayrecords.com

Lucky Dog Records
34 Music Square East
Nashville, TN 37203
Phone: (615) 742-4321
Fax: (615) 742-5741
http://www.sonynashville.com

Madjack Records
1519 Union Avenue, Suite 230
Memphis, TN 38104
E-mail: info@madjackrecords.com
http://www.madjackrecords.com

Malaco Records
3023 West Northside Drive
Jackson, MS 39213
Phone: (601) 982-4522
Fax: (601) 982-4528
http://www.malaco.com

Mars Records
5300 North Powerline Road
Fort Lauderdale, FL 33309
Phone: (954) 938-0526
Fax: (954) 938-0541
E-mail: marsrecords@marsmusic.com
http://www.marsmusic.com

Matador Records
625 Broadway
New York, NY 10012
Phone: (212) 995-5882
Fax: (212) 995-5883
E-mail: info@matadorrecords.com
http://www.matadorrecords.com

Maximum Velocity Records
960 Belmont Avenue, Suite C
North Haledon, NJ 07508
Phone: (973) 304-0505
Fax: (973) 304-0129
E-mail: scott@maximumvelocityrecords.
    com
http://www.maximumvelocityrecords.com

Manhattan Records
304 Park Avenue South
New York, NY 10010
Phone: (212) 253-3000
Fax: (212) 253-3150
http://www.manhattanrecords.com

Maverick Musica
420 Lincoln Road, Suite 500
Miami Beach, FL 33139
Phone: (305) 538-7932
Fax: (305) 538-8160
http://www.maverick.com

Maverick Recording
9348 Civic Center Drive
Beverly Hills, CA 90210-3606
Phone: (310) 385-7800
Fax: (310) 385-7711
http://www.maverick.com

MCA Nashville
60 Music Square East
Nashville, TN 37203
Phone: (615) 244-8944
http://www.mcanashville.com

MCA Records
2220 Colorado Avenue
Santa Monica, CA 90404
Phone: (310) 865-4500
http://www.mcarecords.com

MCA Records
1755 Broadway
New York, NY, 10019
Phone: (212) 841-8000
Fax: (212) 489-9096
http://www.umusic.com

Mercury Nashville
54 Music Square East, Suite 300
Nashville, TN 37203
Phone: (615) 524-7500
Fax: (615) 524-7600
http://www.mercurynashville.com

Merge Records
104 South Christopher Road
Chapel Hill, NC 27514
Phone: (919) 688-9969

Fax: (919) 688-9970
E-mail: merge@mergerecords.com
http://www.mergerecords.com

Metro Blue
304 Park Avenue South
New York, NY 10010
Phone: (212) 253-3000
Fax: (212) 253-3237
http://www.metroblue.com

Mojo Records
153 114th Street
Santa Monica, CA 90404
Phone: (310) 260-3181
Fax: (310) 260-3180
E-mail: info@mojorecords.com

Motel Records
210 East 49th Street
New York, NY 10017
Phone: (212) 755-4328
Fax: (212) 755-6092
E-mail: info@motelrecords.com
http://www.motelrecords.com

Motown Records
1755 Broadway
New York, NY 10010
Phone: (212) 841-8000
Fax: (212) 489-9096
http://www.motown.com

Music Mill Entertainment
809 18th Avenue South
Nashville, TN 37203
Phone: (615) 254-5925
Fax: (615) 244-5928
E-mail: daphene@musicmill.com
http://www.musicmill.com

Music World Entertainment
1505 Hadley Street
Houston, TX 77002
Phone: (713) 772-5175
Fax: (713) 772-3034
E-mail: kburse@
    musicworldentertainment.com
http://www.musicworldmusic.net

Muxxic Latina
1680 Michigan Avenue
730 Miami Beach, FL 33139
Phone: (305) 531-1355
Fax: (305) 531-1354
http://www.muxxiclatina.com

Nashville Sound Records
P.O. Box 11
Pleasant View, TN 37146

Phone: (615) 746-4444
Fax: (615) 746-2229
E-mail: info@nashvillesoundrecords.com
http://www.nashvillesoundrecords.com

Nashville Underground
P.O. Box 120086
Nashville, TN 37212
Phone: (615) 646-8301
Fax: (615) 646-8135
E-mail: themole@artistsunderground.com
http://www.nashville-underground.com

Neurodisc Records, Inc.
3801 North University Drive
Fort Lauderdale, FL 33351
Phone: (954) 572-0289
Fax: (954) 572-2874
E-mail: info@neurodisc.com
http://www.neurodisc.com

New West Records
8888 Olympic Boulevard, Suite 203
Beverly Hills, CA 90211
Phone: (310) 246-5766
Fax: (310) 246-5767
E-mail: Newest@newwestrecords.com
http://www.newwestrecords.com

Nighthawk Records
12643 Redcoat
St. Louis, MO 63043
Phone: (314) 576-1569
Fax: (314) 579-2407
E-mail: robert@nghthwk.com
http://www.nghthwk.com

Nonesuch Records
1290 Avenue of the Americas
New York, NY 10104
Phone: (212) 707-2912
Fax: (212) 707-3205
http://www.nonesuch.com

Octone Records
560 Broadway
New York, NY 10012
Phone: (646) 613-0200
Fax: (646) 613-9096
E-mail: info@octonerecords.com
http://www.octonerecords.com

Outback Records
7 Westwood Drive
Mount Vernon, IL 62864
Phone: (618) 244-9410
Fax: (618) 244-9411
E-mail: savmusic@juno.com
http://www.outbackrecords.com

Palmetto Records
9 Debrosses Street, Suite 101
New York, NY 10013
Phone: (800) 725-6237 or (212) 274-1500
Fax: (212) 334-4630
E-mail: info@palmetto-records.com
http://www.palmetto-records.com

Park Lane Productions, Inc.
11700 Northwest 35th Street
Sunrise, FL 33323
Phone: (954) 748-3082
Fax: (954) 384-3350
E-mail: geojerry@aol.com
http://www.parklaneprod.com

Peppermint Records
287 East Sixth Street
St. Paul, MN 55101
Phone: (651) 293-1010
Fax: (651) 293-4421
http://www.peppermintcds.com

Pinecastle Records
5108 South Orange Avenue
Orlando, FL 32809
Phone: (407) 856-0245
Fax: (407) 858-0007
E-mail: info@pinecastle.com
http://www.pinecastle.com

Pure Pain Records
703 West 37th Street
Savannah, GA 31401
Phone: (912) 447-8323
Fax: (912) 447-8324
E-mail: purepain@bellsouth.net
http://www.pure-pain.com

Portrait Records
2100 Colorado Avenue
Santa Monica, CA 90404
Phone: (310) 449-2100
Fax: (310) 449-2272
E-mail: portrait_records@sonymusic.com
http://www.portraitrecords.com

Priority Records
6430 Sunset Boulevard
Hollywood, CA 90028
Phone: (323) 462-6252
Fax: (323) 856-8796
http://www.priorityrecords.com

Provident Music Group
741 Cool Springs Boulevard
Franklin, TN 37067
Phone: (615) 261-6500
Fax: (615) 261-5910

E-mail: info@providentmusicgroup.com
http://www.providentmusic.com

Real Music
85 Libertyship Way
Sausalito, CA 94965
Phone: (415) 331-8273
Fax: (415) 331-8278
E-mail: realmusic@realmusic.com
http://www.realmusic.com

RCA Records
1540 Broadway
New York, NY 10036
Phone: (212) 930-4000
Fax: (212) 930-4479
http://www.rcarecords.com

RCA Records
8750 Wilshire Boulevard
Beverly Hills, CA 90211
Phone: (310) 358-4000
Fax: (310) 358-4040
http://www.rcarecords.com

RCA Records Nashville
1400 18th Avenue South
Nashville, TN 37212
Phone: (615) 301-4300
Fax: (615) 301-4347
http://www.rcarecordslabel.com

Red Ink
79 Fifth Avenue
New York, NY 10003
Phone: (212) 404-0600
Fax: (212) 404-0640
E-mail: redmusic@redmusic.com
http://www.redmusic.com/redink

Refuge/MCA
2220 Colorado Avenue
Santa Monica, CA 90404
Phone: (310) 865-0579
Fax: (310) 865-0301

Reprise Records
75 Rockefeller Plaza
New York, NY 10019
Phone: (212) 275-4500
Fax: (212) 275-4595
http://www.repriserec.com

Reprise Records
3300 Warner Boulevard
Burbank, CA 91505-4694
Phone: (818) 846-9090
Fax: (818) 846-8474
http://www.repriserec.com

Republic Records
1755 Broadway
New York, NY 10019-3743
Phone: (212) 841-5100
Fax: (212) 841-8012
http://www.republicrecords.com

Reunion Records
741 Cool Springs Boulevard
Franklin, TN 37067
Phone: (615) 261-6500
Fax: (615) 261-5910
http://www.reunionrecords.com

Rhodium Records
207 East Ohio Street
Chicago, IL 60611
Phone: (312) 274-0185
E-mail: info@rhodiumrecords.com
http://www.rhodiumrecords.com

Rhino Entertainment Co.
10635 Santa Monica Boulevard
Los Angeles, CA 90025
Phone: (310) 474-4778
Fax: (310) 441-6578
http://www.rhino.com

R&R Entertainment, Inc.
126 Winding Rose Drive
Rockville, MD 20850
Phone: (301) 294-4540
Fax: (301) 294-4541
E-mail: entertainment@rr-music.com
http://www.rr-music.com

Rock City Records
7030 Delongpre Avenue
Los Angeles, CA 90028
Phone: (323) 461-6600
Fax: (323) 461-6622
E-mail: webmaster@rockcitynews.com
http://www.rockcitynews.com

Rocketown Records
2035 Mallory Lane
Franklin, TN 37067
Phone: (615) 503-9994
Fax: (615) 503-9995
E-mail: info@rocketownrecords.com
http://www.rocketownrecords.com

Savoy Records
1123 Broadway
New York, NY 10010
Phone: (212) 675-3375
Fax: (212) 675-7703
http://www.malaco.com

Scarab Records
803 South Meridian Street
Indianapolis, IN 46225
Phone: (317) 822-0909
Fax: (317) 822-0939
E-mail: info@scarabrecords.com
http://www.scarabrecords.com

Select Records
19 West 21st Street
New York, NY 10010
Phone: (212) 691-1200
Fax: (212) 691-3375
E-mail: selectrec@aol.com

So So Def Recordings, Inc.
685 Lambert Drive, Northeast
Atlanta, GA 30324
Phone: (404) 888-9900
Fax: (404) 888-9901
http://www.sosodef.com

Sony Discos, Inc.
605 Lincoln Road
Miami Beach, FL 33139
Phone: (305) 535-0800
Fax: (305) 695-3664
http://www.sonydiscos.com

Sony Wonder/SMV
550 Madison Avenue
New York, NY 10022
Phone: (212) 833-8374
Fax: (212) 833-4238
http://www.sonywonder.com

Sparrow Label Group
101 Winner's Circle
Brentwood, TN 37027
Phone: (615) 371-6800,
Fax: (615) 371-6994
http://www.sparrowrecords.com

Standard Recording Co.
3717 South Reed Road
Kokomo, IN 46902
Phone: (765) 453-2460
Fax: (765) 453-2659
E-mail: info@standardrecording.com
http://www.standardrecording.com

Star Trak Entertainment
P.O. Box 5017
New York, NY 10185-5017
http://www.startrakmusic.con

StreetSmart Records
P.O. Box 32108
Oakland, CA 94604

Phone: (510) 763-4028
http://www.streetsmartrecords.com

Time Life Music & Video
2000 Duke Street
Alexandria, VA 22314
Phone: (703) 838-7000
Fax: (703) 838-7192
http://www.timeinc.com

Universal Classics
825 Eighth Avenue
New York, NY 10019

Universal Music Enterprises
2220 Colorado Avenue
Santa Monica, CA 90404
Phone: (310) 865-5000
Fax: (310) 865-1138
http://www.umusic.com

Universal Records
1755 Broadway
New York, NY 10019
Phone: (212) 373-0600
Fax: (212) 247-3954
http://www.umusic.com

Verify Records
741 Cool Springs Boulevard
Franklin, TN 37067
Phone: (615) 261-6500
Fax: (615) 261-5910
http://www.verityrecords.com

Virgin Records
304 Park Avenue South
New York, NY 10010
Phone: (212) 253-3100
Fax: (212) 253-3099
http://www.virginrecords.com

Virgin Records
338 North Foothill Road
Beverly Hills, CA 90210
Phone: (310) 278-1181
Fax: (310) 278-6231
http://www.virginrecords.com

Virgin Records Urban
338 North Foothill Road
Beverly Hills, CA 90210
Phone: (310) 288-2748
Fax: (310) 288-2466
http://www.virginrecords.com

Walt Disney Records
350 South Buena Vista Street
Burbank, CA 91521
Phone: (818) 973-4370
Fax: (818) 973-4322
http://www.disney.com/disneyrecords

Warner Bros. Records, Inc.
75 Rockefeller Plaza
New York, NY 10019
Phone: (212) 275-4500
Fax: (212) 275-4677
http://www.wbr.com

Warner Bros. Records, Inc.
3300 Warner Boulevard
Burbank, CA 91505
Phone: (818) 846-9090 or
       (818) 953-3223
Fax: (818) 846-8474
http://www.wbr.com

Warner Bros. Records, Inc.
20 Music Square East
Nashville, TN 37203
Phone: (615) 748-8000
Fax: (615) 214-1567
http://www.wbr.com

APPENDIX IV
RECORD DISTRIBUTORS

This is a list of record distributors, useful if you are looking for a job working with a distributor or are seeking to have an independent record distributed. Use this list as a beginning. Due to space limitations, all distributors have not been included. Inclusion or exclusion on this list does not indicate that any one company is recommended or endorsed over another.

A & A Music Enterprises, Inc.
2137 East 37th Street
Vernon, CA 90058
Phone: (323) 846-1722
Fax: (323) 846-6487

Action Music Sales, Inc.
6541 Eastland Road
Cleveland, OH 44142
Phone: (440) 243-0300
Fax: (440) 243-4063

The Agency
Seven Park Avenue
Kings Park, NY 11754
Phone: (631) 544-0703
Fax: (631) 544-0705
E-mail: agents@optonline.com

The Agency Group Ltd.
1775 Broadway
New York, NY 10019
Phone: (212) 581-3100
Fax: (212) 581-0015
http://www.theagencygroup.com

The Agency Group Ltd.
8490 Sunset Boulevard
Los Angeles, CA 90069
Phone: (310) 360-0771
Fax: (310) 360-0721
http://www.theagencygroup.com

Alternative Distribution Alliance
72 Spring Street
New York, NY 10012
Phone: (212) 343-2485
Fax: (212) 343-2504
E-mail: info@ada-music.com
http://www.ada-music.com

Arrow Distributing Co.
11012 Aurora Hudson Road
Streetsboro, OH 44241
Phone: (330) 528-0410
Fax: (330) 528-0423

E-mail: info@arrids.com
http://www.arrdis.com

Associated Distributors, Inc.
3803 North 36th Avenue
Phoenix, AZ 85019
Phone: (602) 278-5584
Fax: (602) 269-6356
E-mail: adimusic@aol.com

Baker & Taylor
501 South Gladiolus Street
Momence, IL 60954
Phone: (815) 472-2444
Fax: (815) 329-8989
http://www.btol.com

BMG Distribution
1540 Broadway
New York, NY 10036
Phone: (212) 930-4000
Fax: (212) 930-4794
http://www.bmg.com

The Breen Agency
110 30th Avenue North
Nashville, TN 37203
Phone: (615) 777-2227
Fax: (615) 321-4656
E-mail: tbatalent@aol.com
http://www.thebreenagency.com

Campus Records
76 Exchange Street
Albany, NY 12205
Phone: (518) 453-0960
Fax: (518) 453-0961
E-mail: campus@albany.net
http://www.campusrecords.com

Caroline Records Distribution
104 West 29th Street
New York, NY 10001
Phone: (212) 886-7500
Fax: (212) 643-5563

E-mail: sales@caroline.com
http://www.carolinedist.com

Caroline Records Distribution
6161 Santa Monica Boulevard
Los Angeles, CA 90038
Phone: (323) 468-8626
Fax: (323) 468-8627
E-mail: sales@caroline.com
http://www.carolinedist.com

Chordant Distribution Group
500 Capitol Way
Jacksonville, IL 62650
Phone: (217) 243-8661
Fax: (217) 243-1207
http://www.chordant.com

Cisco Music New York
386 Park Avenue South
New York, NY 10016
Phone: (212) 213-8197
Fax: (212) 213-8559
E-mail: cisco@ciscomusic.com
http://www.ciscomusic.com

City Hall Records
101 Glacier Point Road
Ben Rafael, CA 94901
Phone: (415) 457-9080
Fax: (415) 457-0780
E-mail: info@cityhallrecords.com
http://www.cityhallrecords.com

Denver Music Distributors
2626 West 32nd
Denver, CO 80211
Phone: (303) 433-6420

Disgruntled Music Distribution
4470 Sunset Boulevard
Los Angeles, CA 90027
Phone: (323) 224-3012
Fax: (323) 224-0412
E-mail: info@disgruntledmusic.com
http://www.disgruntledmusic.com

DLN Distribution, Inc.
P.O. Box 370038
Miami, FL 33137
Phone: (305) 576-2765
Fax: (305) 576-7788
E-mail: delanusa@aol.com

Disco Hit Productions–USA
6940 Southwest 12th Street
Miami, FL 33144
Phone: (786) 388-1513
Fax: (786) 388-1913
E-mail: discohit@earthlink.net

EMI Music Distribution
5750 Wilshire Boulevard
Los Angeles, CA 90046
Phone: (323) 563-6300
Fax: (323) 563-2410
http://www.emigroup.com

EMI Music Distribution
1134 Atlantic Avenue
Alameda, CA 94501
Phone: (510) 865-8441
Fax: (510) 865-8469
http://www.emigroup.com

Empire Music Group LLC
170 West 74th Street
New York, NY 10023
Phone: (212) 560-5969
Fax: (212) 874-8605
http://www.empiremusic.com

Europac Warehouse Sales
2042 Main Street
Chula Vista, CA 91911
Phone: (619) 423-3409
Fax: (619) 423-8167
http://www.europac.com

Frankies One Stop
1533 Corporate Drive
Freeport, LA 71107
Phone: (318) 424 9441
Fax: (318) 424-8223
E-mail: fosinc@aol.com

Gonzales Music
1012 South Orice Road
Gonzales, CA 70734
Phone: (225) 647-2133
Fax: (225) 647-2234

Galgano Records
3615 Grand Avenue
Guenee, IL 60031
Phone: (847) 599-9900

Fax: (847) 599-0001
http://www.galganorecords.com

Impact Music
1303 West 21st Street
Tempe, AZ 85282
Phone: (480) 894-8550
Fax: (480) 894-6640
http://www.ziarecords.com

Kino International
333 West 39th Street
New York, NY 10018
Phone: (212) 629-6880
Fax: (212) 714-0871
E-mail: contact@kino.com
http://www.kino.com

Koch International
1803 Westridge Drive
Austin, TX 78704
Phone: (512) 442-5570
Fax: (512) 442-5730
http://www.kochint.com

Koch International
740 Broadway
New York, NY 10003
Phone: (212) 979-2856
Fax: (212) 363-3797
http://www.kochint.com

Koch International
2 Tri Harbor Court
Port Washington, NY 11050
Phone: (516) 484-1000
Fax: (516) 484-4746
http://www.kochint.com

Koch International
420 North Fifth Street
Minneapolis, MN 55404
Phone: (612) 376-0466
Fax: (612) 376-0433
http://www.kochint.com

Koch International
One Center Street
Gloucester, MA 01930
Phone: (978) 282-5622
Fax: (978) 282-5634
http://www.kochint.com

Midnight International Records
263 West 23rd Street
New York, NY 10011
Phone: (212) 675-2768
Fax: (212) 741-7230
http://www.midnightrecords.com

**MK Music & Videos International
Distribution**
43 Sycamore Avenue
Hempstead, NY 11550
Phone: (516) 292-9470
Fax: (516) 481-6191

Music City Records
25 Lincoln Street
Nashville, TN 37210
Phone: (615) 255-7315
Fax: (615) 255-7329
http://www.mcrd.com

Music Video Distributors
422 Business Center
Oaks, PA 19456
Phone: (610) 650-8200
Fax: (610) 650-9102
http://www.musicvideodistributors.com

Navarre Corporation
3500 West Olive Avenue
Burbank, CA 91505
Phone: (805) 338-4094
Fax: (805) 435-3680
http://www.navarre.com

Navarre Corporation
204 South Wayside
Anaheim, CA 92805
Phone: (714) 774-3878
http://www.navarre.com

Navarre Corporation
114 North Doheny Drive
Los Angeles, CA 90048
Phone: (310) 273-2986
Fax: (310) 388-5573
http://www.navarre.com

Navarre Corporation
2832 North Linder Avenue
Chicago, IL 60641
Phone: (773) 725-7619
Fax: (773) 442-0781
http://www.navvarre.com

Navarre Corporation
2401 Capitol Avenue
Sacramento, CA 95816
Phone: (916) 498-0641
Fax: (916) 498-0642
http://www.navarre.com

Navarre Corporation
7400 49th Street
New Hope, MN 55428
Phone: (763) 535-8333

Fax: (763) 533-2156
http://www.navarre.com

Norwalk Distributors, Inc.
1193 Knollwood Circle
Anaheim, CA 92801
Phone: (714) 995-8111
Fax: (714) 995-8038
E-mail: sales@norwalkdist.com
http://www.norwalkdist.com

Off-Beat Records
165 Front Street
Chicopee, MA 01013
Phone: (413) 594-5105
Fax: (413) 594-5299
E-mail: sales@offbeatrec.com
http://www.offbeatrec.com

Oarfin/Boxof Records
216 Third Avenue North
Minneapolis, MN 55401
Phone: (612) 673-0508

Fax: (612) 673-0776
E-mail: oarfin@usinternet.com
http://www.oarfinrecords.com

Reyes Records, Inc.
140 Northwest 22nd Street
Miami, FL 33125
Phone: (305) 541-6686
Fax: (305) 642-2785
E-mail: reyesrecords@reysrecords.com
http://www.reyesrecords.com

Sony Music Distribution
7230 Metro Boulevard
Edina, MN 55439
Phone: (952) 832-5210
Fax: (952) 832-0088
http://www.sonymusic.com

Southwest Wholesale Records & Tapes
6775 Bingle Road
Houston, TX 77092
Phone: (713) 460-4300

Fax: (713) 460-6300
http://www.southwestwholesale.com

Unique
110 Denton Avenue
New Hyde Park, NY 11040
Phone: (516) 294-5900
Fax: (516) 294-1624
E-mail: general@uniquedist.com
http://www.uniquedist.com

Wax Works/Video Works
2606 Corporate Avenue
Memphis, TN 38132
Phone: (901) 345-4942
Fax: (901) 345-4952
E-mail: memphis@wwvw.com
http://www.waxworksonline.com

APPENDIX V
BOOKING AGENCIES

The following is a list of booking agencies located through-out the country. Although many of the agencies listed are major companies, we have also included some of the smaller regional agencies that may be of value to you.

Due to space limitations all booking agents could not be included. Inclusion or exclusion in this list does not indicate that any one agent is endorsed or recommended over another.

ACA Music
7095 Hollywood Boulevard
Hollywood, CA 90028
Phone: (323) 812-4320
Fax: (323) 702-0900
E-mail: messages@acamusic.com
http://www.acamusic.com

A Cappella Central
1450 Southgate Avenue
Daly City, CA 94015
Phone: (650) 550-0005
Fax: (650) 550-0006
E-mail: info@princesf.com
http://www.princesf.com

Access Talent
P.O. Box 24372
Nashville, TN 37202
Phone: (615) 226-3054
Fax: (615) 226-6419
E-mail: acesstalentnow.com
http://www.accesstalentnow.com

Adams & Green Entertainment Agency
2011 Masters Lane
Missouri City, TX 77459
Phone: (281) 835-6400
Fax: (281) 835-6004
E-mail: info@entertainmenthouston.com
http://www.entertainmenthouston.com

Admire Entertainment, Inc.
5 Chipman Road
Palisades, NY 10964
Phone: (845) 365-3436
Fax: (845) 365-3485
E-mail: admire1@optonline.net
http://www.admireentertainment.com

Agent 0007, Inc.
P.O. Box 117
Hopkinton, MA 01748
Phone: (781) 259-0007

Fax: (508) 544-1407
http://www.agent0007.com

AIF Music Productions
P.O. Box 691
Mamaroneck, NY 10543
Phone: (914) 381-3559
Fax: (914) 698-8615
E-mail: aifrecords@erols.com

Alkahest Agency, Inc.
P.O. Box 49571
Atlanta, GA 30359
Phone: (404) 315-0709
Fax: (404) 636-0844
E-mail: alkagency@aol.com
http://www.alkahest.net

Ambassador Artist Agency
P.O. Box 50358
Nashville, TN 37205
Phone: (615) 370-4700
Fax: (615) 661-4344
E-mail: info@ambassadoragency.com
http://www.ambassadoreagency.com

AM Only
622 Broadway
New York, NY 10012
Phone: (212) 253-5552
Fax: (212) 254-0101
E-mail: info@amonly.com
http://www.amonly.com

American Artists Corp.
315 South Beverly Drive
Beverly Hills, CA 90212
Phone: (310) 277-7877
Fax: (310) 277-9677
E-mail: philhacheaa@aol.com

American Artist, Entertainment Group
21 Chews Landing Road
Clementon, NJ 08021

Phone: (856) 566-1232
Fax: (856) 435-7453
http://www.aaeg.com

APA
9200 West Sunset Boulevard
Los Angeles, CA 90069
Phone: (310) 273-0744
Fax: (310) 888-4242

APA
3017 Poston Avenue
Nashville, TN 37203
Phone: (615) 297-0200
Fax: (615) 297-5434

Artist Direction Agency
P.O. Box 40
Bremen, GA 30110
Phone: (770) 537-9387
Fax: (770) 537-0104
E-mail: artistdir@aol.com
http://www.artistdirectionagency.ccom

Associated Booking Corp.
1995 Broadway
New York, NY 10023
Phone: (212) 874-2400
Fax: (212) 769-3649
E-mail: info@abcbooking.com
http://www.abcbooking.com

Associated Concert & Touring Services, Inc.
1103 Bell Grimes Lane
Nashville, TN 37207
Phone: (615) 254-8600
Fax: (615) 254-8867
http://www.actsnashville.com

Ballistic Booking Agency
17397 Ventura Boulevard
Encino, CA 91316
Phone: (818) 906-0517

E-mail: ballisticbooking@aol.com
http://www.ballisticbooking.com

Barra Cuda Enterprises
P.O. Box 121
Anaheim, CA 92815
Phone: (714) 991-5065
Fax: (714) 991-9781
E-mail: cuda@barracude-ent.com
http://www.barracudea-ent.com

Bender Cashman Talent Agency
3460 Crews Lake Drive
Lakeland, FL 33813
Phone: (863) 646-2431
Fax: (863) 644-1541
http://www.cale.com/bender

Berkeley Agency
2608 Ninth Street
Berkeley, CA 94710
Phone: (510) 843-4902
Fax: (510) 843-7271
E-mail: webmail@bekeleyagency.com
http://www.berkeleyagency.com

Black Pearl Artists
P.O. Box 839
Hillard, FL 32046
Phone: (904) 845-7012
Fax: (904) 845-3927
E-mail: blackprearlartists@worldnet.att.net

Sal Bonafeda, Inc.
9255 Sunset Boulevard
Los Angeles, CA 90069
Phone: (310) 271-4435
Fax: (310) 271-4173
E-mail: sbonafeda@aol.com

BSA Agency
55543 Edmondson Pike
Nashville, TN 37211
Phone: (615) 595-7500
Fax: (615) 595-7501
E-mail: postoffice@bsaworld.com
http://www.bsaworld.com

Capitol International Productions
44 Fox Trail
Lincolnshire, IL 60069
Phone: (947) 940-0030
Fax: (947) 940-0986
E-mail: info@capitolint.com
http://www.capitolint.com

Nancy Carlin Associates
1920 Cameron Court

Concord, CA 93518
Phone: (925) 686-5800
Fax: (925) 680-2582
http://www.nancycarlinassociates.com

Carmel Music & Entertainment
701 Main Street
Evanston, IL 60202
Phone: (847) 864-5969
Fax: (847) 864-6149
E-mail: info@carmelentertainment.com
http://www.carmelentertainmnet.com

Thomas Cassidy, Inc.
11761 East Speedway Boulevard
Tucson, AZ 85748
Phone: (520) 751-4751
Fax: (520) 298-8029
E-mail: americasmusic@att.net
http://www.americasmusicagency.com

Castle Hill Enterprises
1101 South Orlando Avenue
Los Angeles, CA 90035
Phone: (323) 653-3535
Fax: (323) 653-1511
http://www.castlehill.net

Cavaricci & White Ltd.
120 East 56th Street
New York, NY 10022
Phone: (212) 582-9700
Fax: (212) 212-758-9402

Tony CEE Associates
P.O. Box 410
Utica, NY 13503
Phone: (315) 735-9959
Fax: (315) 735-0368
http://www.tonyceeassociates.com

Celebrity Direct Inc.
730 5th Avenue
New York, NY 10019
Phone: (212) 541-3770
Fax: (212) 541-3799
http://www.celebrity-direct.com

Central Entertainment Group
485 Madison Avenue
New York, NY 10022
Phone: (212) 921-2190
Fax: (212) 921-8761
http://www.cegtalent.com

Chaotica
225 Lafayette Street
New York, NY 10012
Phone: (212) 965-0699

Fax: (212) 965-0728
E-mail: chaotica@att.net

Chaotica
6290 Sunset Boulevard
Hollywood, CA 90028
Phone: (323) 469-3796
Fax: (323) 469-3798
E-mail: chaotica@att.net

Creative Artists Agency, Inc.
9830 Wilshire Boulevard
Beverly Hills, CA 90212
Phone: (310) 288-4545
Fax: (310) 288-4795
http://www.caa.com

Creative Artists Agency, Inc.
3310 West End Avenue
Nashville, TN 37203
Phone: (615) 383-8787
Fax: (615) 383-4937
http://www.caa.com

Creative Entertainment Associates, Inc.
2201 South 21st Street
Philadelphia, PA 19145
Phone: (215) 271-1492
Fax: (215) 271-1493
E-mail: ceadano@aol.com

Creative Entertainment Group
505 8th Avenue
New York, NY 10018
Phone: (212) 634-0427
Fax: (212) 634-0432
E-mail: info@cegmusic.com
http://www.cegmusic.com

Creative Soundz, Inc.
P.O. Box 275
Mount Prospect, IL 60056
Phone: (847) 299-5522
Fax: (847) 299-5034
http://www.creativesoundz.com

DMR Booking Agency
The Galleria of Syracuse
Syracuse, NY 13202
Phone: (315) 475-2500
Fax: (315) 375-0753
E-mail: david@dmrbooking.com
http://www.dmrbooking.com

Disco Tech Productions
3232 West 18th Street
Los Angeles, CA 90019
Phone: (213) 804-7387

Do It Booking
P.O. Box 711966
Salt Lake City, UT 84171
Phone: (801) 566-1221
Fax: (801) 566-1222
E-mail: info@doitbooking.com
http://www.doitbooking.com

Donaleshen & Associates Inc.
1223 Wilshire Boulevard
Santa Monica, CA 90403
Phone: (310) 453-8999
Fax: (310) 454-4585
E-mail: rickd@zis.com

EastCoast Entertainment
296 14th Street NW
Atlanta, GA 30318
Phone: (404) 351-2263
Fax: (404) 351-1558
http://www.eastcoastentertainment.com

Eastern Star Productions
2905 Ellis Street
Berkeley, CA 94703
Phone: (415) 752-0635
Fax: (415) 276-5760

Ellicott Talent Group
2503 Marilyn Circle
Petaluma, CA 94952
Phone: (707) 773-3170
Fax: (707) 773-3173

Tom Elliott Productions
14 Russell Street
Waltham, MA 02154
Phone: (781) 647-2825

Entertainment Alliance
P.O. Box 5734
Santa Rosa, CA 95042
Phone: (707) 526-1471
http://www.entertainmentalliance.com

Entertainment Artists Nashville
2409 Hillsboro Road
Nashville, TN 37212
Phone: (615) 320-7041
Fax: (615) 320-0856
http://www.entertainmentartists.com

Evolution Talent Agency
1776 Broadway
New York, NY 10019
Phone: (212) 554-0300
Fax: (212) 554-0399
http://www.evolutiontalent.com

Exceptional Talent
P.O. Box 65948
Omaha, NE 68108
Phone: (402) 341-0444
Fax: (402) 341-0333
http://www.exceptionalartists.com

Famous Artists Agency, Inc.
250 West 57th Street
New York, NY 10107
Phone: (212) 245-3939
Fax: (212) 459-9065
http://www.famousartistsagency.com

Fast Lane International
4856 Haygood Road
Virginia Beach, VA 23455
Phone: (757) 497-2669
Fax: (757) 497-5159

Fat City Artists
1906 Chet Atkins Plaza, Suite 502
Nashville, TN 37212
Phone: (615) 320-7678
Fax: (615) 321-5382
http://www.fatcityartist.com

Five Star Talent
P.O. Box 233
San Clemente, CA 92672
Phone: (949) 366-1854
Fax: (949) 366-9220
http://www.fivestartalent.com

Frontier Booking International
1560 Broadway
New York, NY 10034
Phone: (212) 221-1919
Fax: (212) 221-0821

Front Page Publicity
1142 Cahal Avenue
Nashville, TN 37206
Phone: (615) 383-0412
Fax: (615) 383-0866

Full House Entertainment Agency
3268 Belmont Street
Bellaire, OH 43906
Phone: (740) 676-5259
Fax: (740) 676-5921
E-mail: agent@fullhouseentertainment.
   com
http://www.fullhouseentertainment.com

Gersh Agency
130 West 32nd Street
New York, NY 10036

Phone: (212) 997-1818
Fax: (212) 997-1978

Great American Talent
1010 17th Avenue South
Nashville, TN 37212
Phone: (615) 320-3009
Fax: (615) 321-3090
http://www.gatalent.com

Greater Talent Network
437 Fifth Avenue
New York, NY 10016
Phone: (212) 645-4200
Fax: (212) 627-1471
http://www.gtnspeakers.com

Green Light Talent
Box 3172
Beverly Hills, CA 90212
Phone: (323) 655-4407
Fax: (323) 655-8078
http://www.greenlighttalentagency.com

Hallmark Direction Company
15 Music Square West
Nashville, TN 37203
Phone: (615) 320-7714
Fax: (615) 320-5799

Harmony Artists, Inc.
8455 Beverly Boulevard
Los Angeles, CA 90048
Phone: (323) 655-5007
Fax: (323) 655-5154
http://www.harmonyartists.com

Innovative Entertainment
888 Brannan Street
San Francisco, CA 94103
Phone: (415) 552-4276
Fax: (415) 552-3545
http://www.inn-entertainment.com

**International Creative Management
   (ICM)**
40 West 57th Street
New York, NY 10019
Phone: (212) 556-5758
Fax: (212) 556-6847
http://www.icmartists.com

**International Creative Management
   (ICM)**
8942 Wilshire Boulevard
Beverly Hills, CA 90211
Phone: (310) 560-4000
Fax: (310) 550-4314
http://www.icmartists.com

International Entertainment Bureau
3612 North Washington Boulevard
Indianapolis, IN 46205
Phone: (317) 926-7566
http://www.leonardscorp.com

JP Productions
57 18th Avenue
Ronkonkoma, NY 11779
Phone: (631) 471-2181
Fax: (631) 471-2199

Las Vegas Entertainment Productions
251 East Pyle
Las Vegas, NV 89123
Phone: (702) 897-7293
Fax: (702) 897-8600
http://www.lasvegasparties.com

Buddy Lee Attractions, Inc.
38 Music Square East
Nashville, TN 37203
Phone: (615) 244-4336
Fax: (615) 726-0429
E-mail: info@blanash.com
http://www.buddyleeattractions.com

Long Distance Entertainment
568 East Woodbright Road
Boynton Beach, FL 33435
Phone: (561) 369-0755
E-mail: idepr@aol.com

Mainstage Management International
8144A Big Bend Boulevard
Saint Louis, MO 63119
Phone: (314) 962-4478
Fax: (314) 962-4478
http://www.mainstagemgmt.com

Management Associates, Inc.
1920 Benson Avenue
Saint Paul, MN 55116
Phone: (651) 699-1155
Fax: (651) 699-1536

Monterey Artists, Inc.
509 Hartnell Street
Monterey, CA 93940
Phone: (831) 375-4889
Fax: (831) 375-2623

Monterey Peninsula Artists
24 East 21st Street
New York, NY 10010
Phone: (212) 653-9500
Fax: (212) 653-9515

Monterey Peninsula Artists
124 12th Street
Nashville, TN 37203
Phone: (615) 251-4400
Fax: (615) 251-4401

Monterey Peninsula Artists
200 West Superior
Chicago, IL 60610
Phone: (312) 640-7500
Fax: (312) 640-7514

William Morris Agency, Inc.
1325 Avenue of the Americas
New York, NY 20029
Phone: (212) 586-5100
Fax: (212) 246-3583
http://www.wma.com

William Morris Agency, Inc.
151 El Camino Drive
Beverly Hills, CA 90212
Phone: (310) 859-4277
Fax: (310) 859-4440
http://www.wma.com

William Morris Agency, Inc.
2100 West End Avenue
Nashville, TN 37203
Phone: (615) 963-3000
Fax: (615) 963-3090
http://www.wma.com

Nationwide Entertainment Services
2756 North Green Valley Parkway
Las Vegas, NV 89014
Phone: (702) 451-8090
http://www.entertainmentservices.com

New Orleans Entertainment Agency
3530 Rue Delphine
New Orleans, LA 70131
Phone: (504) 391-9866
Fax: (504) 392-2695
http://www.neworleanstalent.com

Pegasus Productions
424 Pershing Drive
Silver Spring, MD 20910
Phone: (301) 587-1135
Fax: (301) 588-1952

John Penny Entertainment
484 Lexington Street
Waltham, MA 02154
Phone: (781) 891-7800
Fax: (781) 893-1771

Pretty Polly Productions
397 Moody Street
Waltham, MA 02453
Phone: (781) 894-9600
Fax: (781) 894-9696
E-mail: info@prettypolly.com
http://www.prettypolly.com

Pyramid Entertainment
89 Fifth Avenue
New York, NY 10003
Phone: (212) 242-7274
Fax: (212) 242-6932

Bobby Roberts Company, Inc.
P.O. Box 1547
Goodlettsville, TN 37070
Phone: (615) 859-8899
Fax: (615) 859-2200
http://www.bobbyroberts.com

Howard Rose Talent Agency
9460 Wilshire Boulevard
Beverly Hills, CA 90212
Phone: (310) 858-3838
Fax: (310) 858-1995

Rosebud Agency
P.O. Box 170429
San Francisco, CA 94117
Phone: (415) 386-3456
Fax: (415) 386-0599
E-mail: info@roebudus.com
http://www.rosebudus.com

Top Billing International
P.O. Box 121089
Nashville, TN 37212
Phone: (615) 297-2711
Fax: (615) 321-0384

Traditional Arts Services
16045 36th Avenue Northeast
Seattle, WA 98155
Phone: (206) 367-9144
Fax: (206) 267-2390
http://www.tradarts.com

Universal Attractions
225 West 57th Street
New York, NY 10019
Phone: (212) 582-7575
Fax: (212) 333-4508
http://www.universalattractions.com

Variety Artists International
1924 Spring Street
Paso Robles, CA 93446
Phone: (805) 237-4275

Fax: (805) 237-4283
E-mail: varietyart@aol.com

Variety Attractions, Inc.
505 Fulkerson Road
Zanesville, OH 43701
Phone: (740) 453-0394
Fax: (740) 453-4087
http://www.varietyattractions.com

Washington Talent Agency
14670 Rothgeb Drive
Rockville, MD 20850

Phone: (301) 762-1800
Fax: (301) 251-1118
E-mail: info@washingtontalent.com
http://www.washingtontalent.com

Wolfman Jack Entertainment, Inc.
105 Rivershore Drive
Harttord, NC 27944
Phone: (252) 264-4000
Fax: (252) 264-3746
E-mail: tod@wolfmanjack.com
http://www.wolfmanjack.com

World Entertainment Associates
7380 Sand Lake Road
Orlando, FL 32819
Phone: (321) 281-2890

APPENDIX VI
MUSIC PUBLISHERS

This list contains many of the larger music publishers as well as some of the smaller ones. Larger music publishers may take longer to get back to you because of the high volume of songs they work with. Smaller music publishers may work harder with the songs they have. Try sending your material to both.

Some music publishers may also hire staff songwriters. Call or write to inquire about possibilities.

Due to space limitations all music publishers could not be included. Inclusion or exclusion in this list does not indicate any one publisher is recommended or endorsed over another.

ABKCO Music & Records, Inc.
1700 Broadway
New York, NY 10019
Phone: (212) 399-0300
Fax: (212) 582-5090
http://www.abkco.com

ADRA Music
19 West 21nd Street
New York, NY 10010
Phone: (212) 691-1200
Fax: (212) 691-3375
E-mail: selectrec@aol.com

Affiliated Publishers, Inc.
1009 16th Avenue South
Nashville, TN 37212
Phone: (615) 256-9850
Fax: (615) 327-9035

Ahab Music
1707 Grand Avenue
Nashville, TN 37212
Phone: (615) 327-4629
Fax: (615) 321-5455

AIM High Music Group
1300 Division Street
Nashville, TN 37203
Phone: (615) 244-2440
Fax: (615) 242-1177
http://www.aimhighmusic.com

Alfred Publishing Co., Inc.
16380 Roscoe Boulevard
Van Nuys, Ca 91406
Phone: (818) 891-5999
Fax: (818) 891-2181
E-mail: customerservice@alfred.com
http://www.alfred.com

Alkatraz Corner Music
P.O. Box 193316
San Francisco, CA 94110

Phone: (510) 486-2156
Fax: (510) 486-2015
http://www.ragbaby.com

Almo Music Corp./Irving Music, Inc.
1904 Adelicia Avenue
Nashville, TN 37212
Phone: (615) 321-0820
Fax: (615) 329-1018

Alpha Music, Inc.
747 Chestnut Ridge Road
Chestnut Ridge, NY 10977
Phone: (845) 356-0800
Fax: (845) 356-0895
http://www.alphamusicva.com

Americana Entertainment
903 18th Avenue South
Nashville, TN 37212
Phone: (615) 341-0060
Fax: (615) 341-0072
http://www.americanamusic.com

Americatone International USA
1817 Loch Lomond Way
Las Vegas, NV 89102
Phone: (702) 384-0030
Fax: (702) 382-1926
http://www.americatone.com

BMG Music Publishing Worldwide
1540 Broadway
New York, NY 10036
Phone: (212) 930-4000
Fax: (212) 930-4263
http://www.bmgmusicsearch.com

BMG Music Publishing
8750 Wilshire Boulevard
Beverly Hills, CA 90211
Phone: (310) 358-4700

Fax: (310) 358-4727
http://www.bmgmusicsearch.com

BMG Song Nashville
1400 18th Avenue South
Nashville, TN 37212
Phone: (615) 858-1300
Fax: (615) 858-1330
http://www.bmgmusicsearch.com

Burt Bacharach Music Group
10585 Santa Monica Boulevard
Los Angeles, CA 90025
Phone: (310) 441-8600
Fax: (310) 470-3232
http://www.warnerchappell.com

Bellamy Bros. Music
13917 Restless Lane
Dade City, FL 33525
Phone: (352) 588-3628
Fax: (352) 588-3322
http://www.bellamybrothers.com

Belmont Music Publishers
1221 Bienveneda Avenue
Pacific Palisades, CA 90272
Phone: (310) 454-1867
Fax: (310) 573-1925
http://www.geocities.com/
    belmontmusic90272

Leonard Bernstein Music Publishing Co.
25 Central Park West
New York, NY 10023
Phone: (212) 315-0640
Fax: (212) 315-0643
http://www.leonardbernstein.com

Best Built Songs
1317 17th Street South
Nashville, TN 37212

Phone: (615) 385-4466
Fax: (615) 383-4216
http://www.bestbuiltsongs.com

Better Times Publishing
P.O. Box 35005
Greensboro, NC 27425
Phone: (336) 882-9990

Big Blue Dolphin Music, Inc.
760 West Sample Road
Pompano Beach, FL 33064
Phone: (954) 943-9865
Fax: (954) 943-9865

Brentwood/Benson Music Publishing, Inc.
741 Cool Springs Boulevard
Franklin, TN 37067
Phone: (615) 261-3300
Fax: (615) 261-3386
http://www.brentwood-bensonmusic.com

Bright Tune Music Corp.
157 East 32nd Street
New York, NY 10016
Phone: (212) 679-1092
Fax: (212) 683-8420
http://www.thetokens.com

Bug Music, Inc.
6777 Hollywood
Los Angeles, CA 90028
Phone: (332) 466-4352
Fax: (332) 466-2366
http://www.bugmusic.com

Bill Butler Music
2006 Avenue E
Nashville, TN 78861
Phone: (830) 426-2112
Fax: (830) 426-2112
E-mail: billmusic@aol.com

Glen Campbell Music
10351 Santa Monica Boulevard
Los Angeles, CA 90025
Phone: (310) 552-0960
Fax: (310) 557-3468

Campesino Entertainment Group, Inc.
1990 Third Avenue
New York, NY 10029
Phone: (212) 289-6639
Fax: (212) 348-7558
http://www.campesinomusic.com

Carlin America, Inc.
126 East 38th Street
New York, NY 10016

Phone: (212) 779-7977
Fax: (212) 779-7920
http://www.carlinamerica.com

Carwin Music, Inc.
810 Seventh Avenue
New York, NY 10019
Phone: (212) 830-2000
Fax: (212) 830-5196
http://www.emimusicpub.com

Don Casale Music, Inc.
377 Plainfield Street
Westbury, NY 11590
Phone: (516) 333-7898
Fax: (516) 997-8606
http://www.studiopro.50megs.com

Cherry Lane Music Publishing Co., Inc.
Six East 32nd Street
New York, NY 10016
Phone: (212) 561-3000
Fax: (212) 683-2040
E-mail: publishing@cherrylane.com
http://www.cherrylane.com

Chrysalis Music Group, Inc.
8500 Melrose Avenue, Suite 207
Los Angeles, CA 90069
Phone: (310) 550-0785
Fax: (310) 550-0785

Compendia Music Group
210 25th Avenue North
Nashville, TN 37203
Phone: (615) 277-1800
Fax: (615) 277-1801
E-mail: info@compendiamusic.com
http://www.compendiamusic.com

Compendia Music Group
1034 Windward Ridge Parkway
Alpharetta, GA 30005
Phone: (770) 664-7316
Fax: (770) 664-7316
E-mail: info@compendiamusic.com
http://www.compendiamusic.com

Condominium Publishing Group
P.O. Box 32
New York, NY 10163

Corlew Music Group
50 Music Square West
Nashville, TN 37203
Phone: (615) 321-5767
Fax: (615) 321-5519
http://www.winsweptpacific.com

Cotton Row Recording, Inc.
1502 Madison Avenue
Memphis, TN 38104
Phone: (901) 276-8520
Fax: (901) 726-5939

Countdown Entertainment
110 West 26th Street
New York, NY 10001
Phone: (212) 645-3058
Fax: (212) 562-3291
http://www.countdownentertainment.com

Countdown Media
1707 Division Street
Nashville, TN 37203
Phone: (615) 252-4125
Fax: (615) 252-4130
http://www.countdownmedia.com

Country Music Group
P.O. Box 121626
Nashville, TN 37212
Phone: (615) 726-3556

Crowe Enterprises
1010 16th Avenue South
Nashville, TN 37212
Phone: (615) 255-7900
Fax: (615) 255-4411
http://www.croweentertainment.com

Crutchfield Music Group
1106 17th Avenue
Nashville, TN 37212
Phone: (615) 321-5558
Fax: (615) 321-5598
E-mail: crutchfieldmusic@aol.com

Dalto Music Publishing
600 Columbus Avenue
New York, NY 10024
Phone: (212) 352-6412
Fax: (212) 769-0259

David/Sarah Music Inc.
1560 Broadway
Suite 706
New York, NY 10036
Phone: (212) 302-5360
Fax: (212) 302-5364

Disney Music Company
3800 West Alameda Avenue
Burbank, CA 91505
Phone: (818) 569-3223
Fax: (818) 845-9705

Drake Music Group
1300 Division Street
Nashville, TN 37203
Phone: (615) 297-4355
Fax: (615) 297-1584
http://www.countryrecords.com

DreamWorks Music Publishing
9268 West Third Street
Beverly Hills, CA 90210
Phone: (310) 288-7700
Fax: (310) 288-7415
http://www.dreamworksrecords.com

DreamWorks Music Publishing
1516 16th Avenue South
Nashville, TN 37212
Phone: (615) 463-4600
Fax: (615) 463-4601
http://www.dreamworksrecords.com

DRG Music
740 Broadway
New York, NY 10003
Phone: (212) 614-2800
Fax: (212) 614-2153
http://www.drgrecords.com

EMI Music Publishing
810 Seventh Avenue
New York, NY 10019
Phone: (212) 830-2000
Fax: (212) 830-5196
http://www.emimusicpub.com

Famous Music Companies
1633 Broadway
New York, NY 10019
Phone: (212) 654-7433
Fax: (212) 654-4748
http://www.syncsite.com

Famous Music Publishing Companies
10635 Santa Monica Boulevard
Los Angeles, CA 90025
Phone: (310) 441-1300
Fax: (310) 441-4722
http://www.syncsite.com

Famous Music Publishing Companies
65 Music Square East
Nashville, TN 37203
Phone: (615) 329-0500
Fax: (615) 321-4121

Fantasy, Inc.
2600 Tenth Street
Berkeley, CA 94710
Phone: (510) 592-2500

Fax: (510) 486-2015
http://www.fantasyzazz.com

Fox Music Publishing
10201 West Pico Boulevard
Los Angeles, CA 90035
Phone: (310) 369-2541
Fax: (310) 369-1137

Glenwood Music Corp/Beachwood Music Corp.
c/o EMI Music Publishing
810 Seventh Avenue
New York, NY 10019
Phone: (212) 830-2000
Fax: (212) 830-5196
http://www.emimusicpub.com

Goodland Group, Inc.
1620 16th Avenue South
Nashville, TN 37212
Phone: (615) 269-7074
Fax: (615) 269-7074
http://www.artistomedia.com

Gospel Publishing House
1445 Boonville Avenue
Springfield, MO 65802
Phone: (417) 831-8000
http://www.gospelpublishing.com

Hacate Entertainment Group
161 West 54th Street
New York, NY 10019
Phone: (212) 586-4229
Fax: (212) 586-4239
http://www.hacate.com

Hall of Fame Music Company
P.O. Box 921
Beverly Hills, CA 90213
Phone: (310) 276-2726
Fax: (310) 557-0534

Handy Brothers Music Company
1697 Broadway
New York, NY 10019
Phone: (212) 247-0362
Fax: (212) 247-6179
http://www.wchandymusicpublishers.com

Hanover Music Corp.
P.O. Box 6296
Beverly Hills, CA 90212
Phone: (310) 455-4034
Fax: (310) 455-2649
http://www.corinthianrecords.com

Harlem Music, Inc.
1762 Main Street
Buffalo, NY 14208
Phone: (716) 883-9250
Fax: (716) 884-1432
http://www.amherstrecords.com

Harrison Music Corp.
3808 Riverside Drive
Burbank, CA 91505
Phone: (818) 238-9343
Fax: (818) 238-0749

Doc Holiday's Power Plan Studios
2706 Build America Drive
Hampton, VA 23669
Phone: (757) 827-8733
Fax: (757) 827-0385

House of Fame, Inc.
P.O. Box 2527
Muscle Shoals, AL 35662
Phone: (256) 381-0801
Fax: (256) 381-6337
http://www.fame2.com

IDM Publishing
438 West 37th Street
New York, NY 10018
Phone: (212) 695-3911
Fax: (212) 967-6284
http://www.idmmusic.com

Island Bound Music
1204 17th Avenue South
Nashville, TN 37212
Phone: (615) 320-5440
Fax: (615) 320-0849
http://www.islandboundmusic.com

Jamie Music Publishing Company
2055 Richmond Street
Philadelphia, PA 19125
Phone: (215) 426-4384
Fax: (215) 426-4385
http://www.jamguy.com

Jay Jay Publishing
35 NE 62nd Street
Miami, FL 33138
Phone: (305) 758-0000
Fax: (305) 758-0000

JB Music Publishing
235 Park Avenue South
New York, NY 10003
Phone: (212) 777-5678
Fax: (212) 777-7788
http://www.jellybeanrecording.com

Waylon Jennings Music
1117 17th Avenue South
Nashville, TN 37212
Phone: (615) 329-9180
Fax: (615) 321-5747
http://www.waylon.com

Quincy Jones Music Publishing
3800 Barham Boulevard
Los Angeles, CA 90068
Phone: (323) 882-1340
Fax: (323) 874-0143
http://www.quincyjonesmusic.com

Koch Entertainment
740 Broadway
New York, NY 10003
Phone: (212) 353-8800
http://www.kochentertainment.com

K-tel International, Inc.
2655 Cheshire Lane North
Plymouth, MN 55447
Phone: (763) 559-5566
Fax: (763) 559-5505
http://www.ktel.com

La Louisianne Music
711 Stevenson Street
Lafayette, LA 70501
Phone: (337) 234-5577
Fax: (337) 233-2595
http://www.lalouisiannerecords.com

Latin American Music Co., Inc.
425 East 148th Street
Bronx, NY 10455
Phone: (718) 993-5551
Fax: (718) 993-5553
http://www.acemla.com

Leiber-Stolleer Music Publishing
9000 Sunset Boulevard
Los Angeles, CA 90045
Phone: (310) 273-6401
Fax: (310) 273-1591

Hal Leonard Corp.
777 West Bluemound Road
Milwaukee, WI 52313
Phone: (414) 774-3630
Fax: (414) 774-3259

Lowery Group
3051 Clairmont Road, NE
Atlanta, GA 30329
Phone: (404) 325-0832
Fax: (404) 325-1075
http://www.lowerymusic.com

Makin' Music, Inc.
1230 17th Avenue South
Nashville, TN 37212
Phone: (615) 269-6770
Fax: (615) 385-9310

Melody House Music Publishers
603 Seagaze Drive
Oceanside, CA 92054
Phone: (760) 757-7446
Fax: (760) 918-6967

Metro-Goldwyn-Mayer, Inc.
2500 Broadway Street
Santa Monica, CA 90404
Phone: (310) 449-3000
Fax: (310) 586-8799

Mighty 3 Music Group
309 South Broad Street
Philadelphia, PA 19107
Phone: (215) 985-0900
Fax: (215) 985-1195
http://www.gamble-huffmusic.com

MPL Communications, Inc.
41 West 54th Street
New York, NY 10019
Phone: (212) 246-5881
Fax: (212) 977-8408
http://www.mplcommunications.com

Peermusic
1207 16th Avenue South
Nashville, TN 37212
Phone: (615) 329-0603
Fax: (615) 320-0490
http://www.peermusic.com

Peermusic
5258 Melorose Avenue
Los Angeles, CA 90038
Phone: (323) 960-3400
Fax: (323) 960-3410
http://www.peermusic.com

Peermusic
810 Seventh Avenue
New York, NY 10019
Phone: (212) 265-3910
Fax: (212) 489-2465
http://www.peermusic.com

Polybyrd Publications Ltd.
10 Universal City Plaza
Universal City, CA 91618
Phone: (818) 506-8533
Fax: (818) 506-8534

Theodore Presser Company
588 North Gulph Road
King of Prussia, PA 19406
Phone: (610) 525-3636
Fax: (610) 527-7841
http://www.presser.com

Rhino Entertainment Company
10635 Santa Monica Boulevard
Los Angeles, CA 90025
Phone: (310) 474-4778
Fax: (310) 441-6578
http://www.rhino.com

Rondor Music International
2440 Sepulveda Boulevard
Los Angeles, CA 90064
Phone: (310) 235-4800
Fax: (310) 235-4801
http://www.music.com

Screen Gems–EMI Music Inc.
810 Seventh Avenue
New York, NY 10019
Phone: (212) 830-2000
Fax: (212) 830-5196
http://www.emimusicpub.com

Song Source Music Publishing Group
P.O. Box 120603
Nashville, TN 37212
Phone: (615) 385-4058

Sony/ATV Tree Music Publishing
550 Madison Avenue
New York, NY 10022
Phone: (212) 833-4729
Fax: (212) 833-8659
http://www.sonyatv.com

Sony/ATV Tree Music Publishing
8 Music Square West
Nashville, TN 37203
Phone: (615) 726-8300
Fax: (615) 726-8329
http://www.sonyatv.com

Soul Street Music Publishing Inc.
265 Main Street
East Rutherford, NJ 07073
Phone: (201) 933-0676
Fax: (201) 951-2332

Ray Stevens Music
1707 Grand Avenue
Nashville, TN 37212
Phone: (615) 327-4629
Fax: (615) 321-5455
http://www.raystevens.com

Tex Ritter Music Publishing
6124 Selma Avenue
Hollywood, CA 90028
Phone: (323) 469-2296
Fax: (323) 962-5751

Third Story Music, Inc.
740 North La Brea Avenue
Los Angeles, CA 90038
Phone: (323) 938-5000
Fax: (323) 936-6354

Top 40 Hits Music Publishing Company
P.O. Box 12239
Las Vegas, NV 89112
Phone: (702) 456-2632
Fax: (702) 456-6189

Ernest Tubb Partners
P.O. Box 599
Nashville, TN 37222
Phone: (615) 256-7593
Fax: (615) 255-2256
http://www.ernesttubb.com

Warner/Chappell Music, Inc.
75 Rockefeller Plaza
New York, NY 10019
Phone: (212) 275-1200
Fax: (212) 275-3306
http://www.warnerchappell.com

Warner/Chappell Music, Inc.
10585 Santa Monica Boulevard
Los Angeles, CA 90025
Phone: (310) 441-8600
Fax: (310) 470-3232
http://www.warnerchappell.com

Warner/Chappell Music, Inc.
20 Music Square East
Nashville, TN 37203
Phone: (615) 733-1880
Fax: (615) 733-1885
http://www.warnerchappell.com

Worldwide Entertainment Group
411 Lafayette Street
New York, NY 10003

Phone: (212) 420-0893
Fax: (212) 420-0752
http://www.wweg.com

Zamalama Music
1100 18th Avenue South
Nashville, TN 37212
Phone: (615) 321-0033
Fax: (615) 321-2244

Zomba Music Publishing
138 West 25th Street
New York, NY 10001
Phone: (212) 824-1899
Fax: (212) 242-7462
http://www.zomba.com

APPENDIX VII
RIGHTS SOCIETIES

A. RECORDING RIGHTS SOCIETIES

The following is a list of societies that secure recording rights to music. Addresses, phone and fax numbers, e-mail addresses, and websites have been included when available to make it easier to get information.

American Mechanical Rights Associations (AMRA)
150 South Barrington Avenue
Los Angeles, CA 90049
Phone: (310) 440-8778
Fax: (310) 440-0059
E-mail: amaracalif@aol.com
http://www.amermerchrights.com

Harry Fox Agency, Inc.
711 Third Avenue
New York, NY 10017
Phone: (212) 370-5330
Fax: (212) 953-2384
E-mail: soundcheck@harryfox.com
http://www.harryfox.com

SESAC, Inc.
55 Music Square East
Nashville, TN 37203
Phone: (615) 320-0055
Fax: (615) 329-9627
http://www.sesac.com

SESAC, Inc.
1633 Broadway
New York, NY 10019
Phone: (646) 756-2890
Fax: (646) 756-2529
http://www.sesac.com

B. PERFORMING RIGHTS SOCIETIES

The following is a list of societies that secure performance rights for music.

American Society of Composers–Atlanta
541 Tenth Street Northwest
Atlanta, GA 30318
Phone: (404) 351-1224
Fax: (404) 351-1252
E-mail: info@ascap.com
http://www.ascap.com

American Society of Composers–Chicago
1608 North Milwaukee, Suite 1007
Chicago, IL 60647
Phone: (773) 394-4286
Fax: (773) 394-5639
E-mail: info@ascap.com
http://www.ascap.com

American Society of Composers–London
8 Cork Street
London W1X1PB
Phone: 011-44-207-439-0909
Fax: 011-44-207-434-0073
E-mail: info@ascap.com
http://www.ascap.com

American Society of Composers–Los Angeles
7920 West Sunset Boulevard
Los Angeles, CA 90046
Phone: (323) 883-1000
Fax: (323) 883-1049
E-mail: info@ascap.com
http://www.ascap.com

American Society of Composers–Miami
420 Lincoln Road, Suite 385
Miami Beach, FL 33139
Phone: (305) 673-3446
Fax: (305) 673-2446
E-mail: info@ascap.com
http://www.ascap.com

American Society of Composers–Nashville
Two Music Square West
Nashville, TN 37203
Phone: (615) 742-5000
Fax: (615) 742-5020
E-mail: info@ascap.com
http://www.ascap.com

American Society of Composers–New York
1 Lincoln Plaza
New York, NY 10023
Phone: (212) 621-6000
Fax: (212) 724-9064
E-mail: info@ascap.com
http://www.ascap.com

American Society of Composers–Puerto Rico
654 Avenue Muñoz Rivera
IBM Plaza Suite 1101 B
Hato Rey, PR 00918
Phone: (787) 281-0782
Fax: (787) 767-2805
E-mail: info@ascap.com
http://www.ascap.com

Broadcast Music Inc. (BMI)–Atlanta
P.O. Box 19199
Atlanta, GA 31126
Phone: (404) 261-5151
Fax: (404) 261-5151
http://www.bmi.com

**Broadcast Music Inc. (BMI)–
    Los Angeles**
8730 Sunset Boulevard
West Hollywood, CA 90069-2211
Phone: (310) 659-9109
Fax: (310) 657-6947
E-mail: losangeles@bmi.com
http://www.bmi.com

Broadcast Music Inc. (BMI)–Miami
5201 Blue Lagoon Drive
Miami, FL 33126
Phone: (305) 266-3636
Fax: (305) 266-2442
E-mail: latin@bmi.com
http://www.bmi.com

**Broadcast Music Inc.
    (BMI)–Nashville**
10 Music Square East
Nashville, TN 37203
Phone: (615) 401-2000
Fax: (615) 401-2812
http://www.bmi.com

**Broadcast Music Inc.
    (BMI)–New York**
320 West 57th Street
New York, NY 10019
Phone: (212) 586-2000
Fax: (212) 245-8986
E-mail: newyork@bmi.com
http://www.bmi.com

SESAC, Inc.
55 Music Square East
Nashville, TN 37203
Phone: (615) 320-0055
Fax: (615) 329-9627
http://www.sesac.com

SESAC, Inc.
1633 Broadway
New York, NY 10019
Phone: (646) 756-2890
Fax: (646) 756-2529
http://www.sesac.com

APPENDIX VIII
PUBLIC RELATIONS AND PUBLICITY FIRMS

The following is a list of public relations and publicity firms handling music and/or entertainment clients. This list is just a beginning. There are many other public relations companies and independent publicists located throughout the country. For additional names check the Yellow Pages of your local phone book under "Public Relations" or "Publicists." Inclusion on or exclusion from this list does not indicate recommendation or endorsement.

Allison Auerbach Pubic Relations
2607 Westwood Drive
Nashville, TN 37204
Phone: (615) 297-1033
Fax: (615) 297-5030
E-mail: alisonapr@aol.com

Aristo Media
1620 16th Avenue South
Nashville, TN 37212
Phone: (615) 269-7071
Fax: (615) 269-0131
E-mail: jwalker@aristomedia.com
http://www.aristomedia.com

Be-Bop Communications, Inc.
22 East 21st Street
New York, NY 10100
Phone: (212) 358-9092
Fax: (212) 358-9068
E-mail: info@be-boppr.com
http://www.be-boppr.com

Bender, Goldman & Helper, Inc.
1150 West Olympic Boulevard, Suite 665
Los Angeles, CA 90064
Phone: (310) 473-4147
Fax: (310) 478-4727
http://www.bhimpact.com

Bender, Goldman & Helper, Inc.
220 Fifth Avenue
New York, NY 10001
Phone: (212) 689-6360
Fax: (212) 689-6601
http://www.bhimpact.com

The Brokaw Company
9255 Sunset Boulevard
Los Angeles, CA 90069
Phone: (310) 273-2060
Fax: (310) 276-4037
E-mail: brokaw@aol.com
http://www.brokawcompany.com

Catalano Public Relations
One Central Street
Stoneham, MA 02180
Phone: (781) 438-4643
E-mail: catalanopr@aol.com
http://www.catalanopr.com

D. Baron Media Relations, Inc.
1112 Hartzell Street
Pacific Palisades, CA 90272
Phone: (310) 573-1984
Fax: (310) 573-4224
E-mail: diana@dbaronmedia.com
http://www.dbaronmedia.com

Dan Kiores Associates
386 Park Avenue South
New York, NY 10016
Phone: (212) 685-4300
Fax: (212) 212-685-9024
E-mail: dan_kiores@dkcnews.com
http://www.dkcnews.com

Dassinger Creative
32 Ardsely Road
Montclair, NJ 07042
Phone: (973) 746-6474
Fax: (973) 746-5082
E-mail: dassingercreative@hotmail.com

DMG Public Relations
10 Universal City Plaza
Universal City, CA 91618
Phone: (818) 506-8533
Fax: (818) 506-8534
E-mail: dmgusa@aol.com

Front Page Publicity
112 Canal Avenue
Nashville, TN 37206
Phone: (615) 383-0412
Fax: (615) 383-0866
E-mail: kathyallmand@
    frontpagepublicity.com

Glammedia
311 North Robertson Boulevard, Suite 286
Beverly Hills, CA 90211
Phone: (310) 248-4802
E-mail: debzilla@aol.com
http://www.glammedia.com

Glodow & Nead Publicity Services
1700 Montgomery Street, Suite 2003
San Francisco, CA 94111
Phone: (415) 394-6500
Fax: (415) 403-9060
E-mail: info@glodownead.com
http://www.glodownead.com

Gurley & Company
2015 Overmill Drive
Nashville, TN 37215
Phone: (615) 269-0474
Fax: (615) 385-2052
E-mail: megsullivan@comcast.com
http://www.gurleybiz.com

Henri Bollinger Public Relations
P.O. Box 57227
Sherman Oaks, CA 91413
Phone: (818) 784-0534
Fax: (818) 789-8862
E-mail: henri@bollingerpr.com
http://www.bollingerpr.com

Hill & Knowlton Worldwide
600 New Hampshire Avenue, NW
Suite 601
Washington, DC 20037
Phone: (202) 333-7400
Fax: (202) 944-1960
E-mail: alb@hillandknowlton.com
http://www.hillandknowlton.com

Hoopla Media & Public Relations
8455 Beverly Boulevard, Suite 402
Los Angeles, CA 90048
Phone: (323) 852-9444

Fax: (310) 852-1958
E-mail: info@hooplapr.com
http://www.hooplapr.com

Hot Schatz Public Relations
1024 16th Avenue South
Nashville, TN 37212
Phone: (615) 782-0078
Fax: (615) 782-0088
E-mail: hotchatzpr@csi.com

Howard Rubenstein Associates, Inc.
1345 Avenue of the Americas
New York, NY 10105
Phone: (212) 843-8000
Fax: (212) 843-9200
http://www.rubenstein.com

Jensen Communications
709 East Colorado Boulevard
Pasadena, CA 91101
Phone: (626) 585-9575
Fax: (626) 564-8920
E-mail: jensencomm@aol.com
http://www.jensencom.com

Little Richie Johnson Agency
318 Horizon Vista Boulevard
Belen, NM 87002
Phone: (505) 864-7441
Fax: (505) 864-7442

Levine Communications
10333 Ashton Avenue
Los Angeles, CA 90024
Phone: (310) 248-6222
Fax: (310) 248-6227
E-mail: levinepr@earthlink.net
http://www.levinepr.com

Levinson Associates
1440 Veteran Avenue, Suite 650
Los Angeles, CA 90024
Phone: (323) 663-6940
Fax: (323) 663-2820
E-mail: levinec@aol.com

The Lippin Group
6100 Wilshire Boulevard
Los Angeles, CA 90048
Phone: (323) 965-1990
Fax: (323) 525-1929
E-mail: losangeles@lippingroup.com
http://www.lippingroup.com

McCain & Company Public Relations
1318 Riverwood Drive
Nashville, TN 37216
Phone: (615) 262-1727
Fax: (615) 262-0058
E-mail: morgan@mccainpr.com
http://www.mccainpr.com

Middleberg & Associates
102 Madison Avenue
New York, NY 10016
Phone: (212) 888-6610
Fax: (212) 6909-2599
http://www.middleberg.com

Mixed Media
20 Lockmere Road
Cranston, RI 02910
Phone: (401) 942-8025
Fax: (401) 942-5487
E-mail: ginny@mixed-media.org
http://www.mixed-media.org

Norman Winter & Associates
6255 Sunset Boulevard
Suite 705
Los Angeles, CA 90028
Phone: (323) 469-3434
Fax: (323) 469-6422
E-mail: normwinpr@earthlink.net

Porter/Novelli Public Relations
10960 Wilshire Boulevard
Los Angeles, CA 90024
Phone: (310) 444-7000
Fax: (310) 444-7004
http://www.porternovelli.com

The Press Office
P.O. Box 90528
Nashville, TN 37209
Phone: (615) 469-9730
Fax: (615) 469-3669
E-mail: publicity@thepressoffice.net
http://www.thepressoffice.com

PRP
12702 Landale Street
Studio City, CA 91604
Phone: (818) 766-0443
Fax: (818) 766-1644

Ren Grevatt Associates, Ltd.
209 Cooper Avenue, Suite 9 A-B
Upper Montclair, NJ 07043

Phone: (973) 509-2801
Fax: (973) 509-2804
E-mail: rgravatt@aol.com

Richard Gersh Associates, Inc.
Radio City Station
New York, NY 10019
Phone: (212) 757-1101
Fax: (212) 245-6746
E-mail: gershpr@rgapr.com

Rogers & Cowan
1888 Century Park East, Suite 500
Los Angeles, CA 90067
Phone: (310) 201-8849
Fax: (310) 788-6611
http://www.rogerandcowan.com

Serge Entertainment Group
2600 Bentley Road
Marietta, GA 30067
Phone: (770) 850-9560
Fax: (770) 850-9646
E-mail: musikmanag@aol.com
http://www.serge.org

Shelly Field Organization
P.O. Box 711
Monticello, NY 12701
Phone: (845) 794-7312
http://www.shellyfield.com

Shirine Coburn Communications
89 Greene Street
New York, NY 10012
Phone: (212) 680-3101
Fax: (212) 680-3102
E-mail: shirine@sccommunication.com

Slick Norris Artists & Associates
145 Kilgore Avenue
Baytown, TX 77520
Phone: (281) 424-4235

Workhouse Publicity
32 Thompson Street
New York, NY 10013
Phone: (212) 334-8006
Fax: (212) 334-1919
E-mail: workhousepr.com
http://www.workhousepr.com

APPENDIX IX
ENTERTAINMENT INDUSTRY ATTORNEYS AND LAW FIRMS

The following is a list of attorneys and law firms that handle music and/or entertainment clients. There are many other law firms and attorneys who specialize in music and/or entertainment clients throughout the country. Check out the Yellow Pages of the phone book or contact your local or state bar association for other names.

This listing is provided for informational purposes only. The author does not endorse or recommend any one attorney or law firm over another.

Abrams, Garfinkel, & Rosen
237 West 35th Street
New York, NY 10001
Phone: (212) 201-1170
Fax: (212) 201-1171

Ira Abrams
56938 Fox Hollow Drive
Boca Raton, FL 33486
Phone: (561) 362-2512
Fax: (561) 362-0345

Akin, Gump, Strauss, Hauer & Feld, LLP
2029 Century Park East
Los Angeles, CA 09957
Phone: (310) 229-1000
Fax: (310) 229-1001

Charles D. Andrews
1611 Horton Avenue
Nashville, TN 37212
Phone: (615) 292-3753
Fax: (615) 297-1404

Dennis Angel
1075 Central Park Avenue
Scarsdale, NY 10587
Phone: (914) 472-0820
Fax: (914) 472-0826

Stephen Baerwitz
10940 Wilshire Boulevard
Los Angeles, CA 90024
Phone: (310) 443-4243
Fax: (310) 443-4263

Baker & Hostetler LLP
333 South Grand Avenue
Los Angeles, CA 90071
Phone: (213) 975-1600

Fax: (212) 975-1740
http://www.bakerlaw.com

Ralph A. Barballo, Jr.
231 Sutton Street
North Andover, MA 01845
Phone: (978) 686-9811
Fax: (978) 683-8510
http://www.ralphbarballo.com

Bartley, Goldstein, Bollato and Lange, L.L.C.
4399 Lacledo Avenue
St. Louis, MO 63108
Phone: (314) 531-1054
Fax: (314) 531-1131

Bass Berry & Sims PLC
29 Music Square East
Nashville, TN 37203
Phone: (615) 255-6161
Fax: (615) 254-4490
http://www.bassberry.com

Bass Berry & Sims PLC
1700 Riverview Tower
Knoxville, TN 37902
Phone: (865) 521-6200
Fax: (865) 521-6234
http://www.bassberry.com

Bass Berry & Sims PLC
The Tower at Peabody Place
100 Peabody Place
Memphis, TN 38103
Phone: (901) 543-5900
Fax: (901) 543-5999

Beinstock & Michael, P.C.
250 West 57th Street
New York, NY 10107

Phone: (212) 399-0099
http://www.musicesg.com

Beitchman & Hudson
215 14th Street NW
Atlanta, GA 30318
Phone: (404) 897-5252
Fax: (404) 897-5677
http://www.arts-entertainment.com

Craig Benson & Associates
1207 17th Avenue South
Nashville, TN 37212
Phone: (615) 320-0660
Fax: (615) 320-0909

Berger, Kahn, Moss, Figler, Simon & Gladstone
4215 Glencoe Avenue
Marina Del Rey, CA 90292
Phone: (310) 821-9000
Fax: (310) 578-6178

Boelter & Perry
330 Washington Boulevard
Marina Del Ray, CA 90292
Phone: (310) 822-5037
Fax: (310) 823-4325

Steven Ames Brown
69 Grand View Avenue
San Francisco, CA 94114
Phone: (415) 647-7700
Fax: (415) 285-3048

Cynthia M. Cleves, Esq.
27 East Fourth Street
Covington, KY 41011
Phone: (859) 331-2050
Fax: (859) 331-5848

Codikow, Carroll, Guido & Groffman, L.L.P.
9111 Sunset Boulevard
Los Angeles, CA 90069
Phone: (310) 271-0241
Fax: (310) 271-0775
http://www.ccgglaw.com

Coudert Bros. LLP
1114 Avenue of the Americas
New York, NY 10036
Phone: (212) 626-4400
Fax: (212) 626-4120
http://www.coudert.com

Coudert Bros. LLP
333 South Hope Street
Los Angeles, CA 90071
Phone: (213) 229-2900
Fax: (213) 229-2999
http://www.coudert.com

Cowan, Liebowitz & Latman, P.C.
1133 Avenue of the Americas
New York, NY 10036
Phone: (212) 790-9200
Fax: (212) 575-0671
http://www.cll.com

Eastman & Eastman
39 West 54th Street
New York, NY 10019
Phone: (212) 246-5757
Fax: (212) 977-8408

Edwin M. Cramer
110 East 59th Street
New York, NY 10022
Phone: (212) 421-3350
Fax: (212) 826-9315

Thomas L. Ferro
31 East Ridgewood Avenue
Ridgewood, NJ 07450
Phone: (201) 444-3000
Fax: (201) 666-4844

Franklin, Weirib, Rudell, & Vassallo, P.C.
488 Madison Avenue
New York, NY 10022
Phone: (212) 935-5500
Fax: (212) 308-0642
http://www.fwrv.com

George, Donaldson & Ford, L.L.P.
114 North Seventh Street, Suite 1000
Austin, TX 78701
Phone: (512) 495-1400

Fax: (512) 499-0094
http://www.gdf.com

Glenn A. Goldstein
One Liberty Place
Philadelphia, PA 19103
Phone: (215) 851-6536
Fax: (215) 981-5959

Golland & Alperin
11355 West Olympic Boulevard
Los Angeles, CA 90064
Phone: (310) 444-7505
Fax: (310) 444-7885

Gordon, Martin, Jones & Harris, Shrum & Benson P.A.
49 Music Square West
Suite 600
Nashville, TN 37203
Phone: (615) 321-5400
Fax: (615) 321-5469
http://www.rowlaw.com

Peter D. Gordon, Esq.
8052 Melrose Avenue
Los Angels, CA 90046
Phone: (323) 651-5111
Fax: (323) 651-3726

Grubman, Indursky, & Schindler, P.C.
152 West 52nd Street
New York, NY 10019
Phone: (212) 554-0400
Fax: (212) 554-0444

Hall, Booth, Smith & Slover, P.C.
The Tower, 611
Nashville, TN 37203
Phone: (615) 313-9913
Fax: (615) 313-8008

Hertz, Schram & Saretsky, P.C.
1760 East Telegraph
Bloomfield Hills, MI 48302
Phone: (248) 335-5000
Fax: (248) 335-3346
http://www.hsspc.com

Marcy E. Holloway
13424 Saddle Back Pass
Austin, TX 78736
Phone: (512) 263-2246
Fax: (512) 263-7846

Paul W. Insinna, Esq.
286 Hall Avenue
White Plains, NY 10604
Phone: (914) 686-3414
Fax: (914) 287-6487

Jacobson & Colfin, P.C.
19 West 21st Street
New York, NY 10010
Phone: (212) 691-5630
Fax: (212) 645-5038
http://www.thefirm.com

Johnson & Rishwain, LLP
12121 Wilshire Boulevard
Las Angeles, CA 90025
Phone: (310) 826-2410
Fax: (310) 826-5450
http://www.jrlip.com

Kauff, McClain & McGuire
950 Third Avenue
New York, NY 10022
Phone: (212) 644-1010
Fax: (212) 644-1936
http://www.kmm.com

Edward Kelman
521 Fifth Avenue
New York, NY 10175
Phone: (212) 371-9490
Fax: (212) 750-1356

Law Office of M. William Krasilovsky & John M. Gross
51 East 42nd Street
Suite 1601
New York, NY 10017
Phone: (212) 682-8552
Fax: (212) 971-0422
http://www.thisbusinessofmusic.org

Lawrence Lighter
488 Madison Avenue
New York, NY 10022
Phone: (212) 371-8730
Fax: (212) 753-3630

Loeb & Loeb
10100 Santa Monica Boulevard
Los Angeles, CA 99067
Phone: (310) 282-2192
Fax: (310) 282-2192
http://www.loeb.com

Loeb & Loeb
345 Park Avenue
New York, NY 10154
Phone: (212) 407-4000
Fax: (212) 407-4880
http://www.loeb.com

Loeb & Loeb
1906 Acklen Avenue
Nashville, TN 37212

Phone: (615) 749-8300
Fax: (615) 749-83308
http://www.loeb.com

Mayer, Glassman & Gaines
11726 San Vincente Boulevard
Los Angeles, CA 90049
Phone: (310) 207-0007
Fax: (310) 297-3578
http://www.mggla.com

McGovern & Associates
One Lafayette Place
Greenwich, CT 06830
Phone: (203) 622-1101
Fax: (203) 622-9192
http://www.mcgovernlaw.com

Ober, Kaler, Grimes & Shriver
120 East Baltimore Street
Baltimore, MD 21202
Phone: (410) 347-7388
Fax: (410) 547-0699
http://www.ober.com

O'Melveny & Meyers LLP
1999 Avenue of the Stars
Century City, CA 90067
Phone: (310) 553-6700
Fax: (310) 246-6779
http://www.omm.com

Palmer & Dodge, LLP
111 Huntington Avenue
Boston, MA 02198
Phone: (617) 239-0484
Fax: (617) 227-4420
http://www.palmerdodge.com

Perkins, Smith & Cohen
One Beacon Street
Boston, MA 02108
Phone: (617) 854-4000
Fax: (617) 854-4040
http://www.pscboston.com

Phillips, Nizer, Benamin, Krim & Ballon
666 Fifth Avenue
New York, NY 10103
Phone: (212) 977-9700
Fax: (212) 262-5152
http://www.phillipsnizer.com

Probstein & Weiner
1875 Century Park East
Los Angeles, CA 90067
Phone: (310) 556-1956
Fax: (310) 203-8334
http://www.pwandh.com

Probstein & Weiner
488 Madison Avenue
New York, NY 10022
Phone: (212) 972-3250
Fax: (212) 202-6495
http://www.pwandh.com

Stewart I. Rosenblum
308 Penn Estates
East Stroudsburg, PA 18301
Phone: (570) 424-9599
Fax: (570) 424-0452
http://www.stewrose.com

Rubin, Ballin, Ortoll, Mayer & Baker, LLP
405 Park Avenue
New York, NY 10022
Phone: (212) 935-0900
Fax: (212) 826-9307

Sachnoff & Weaver, Ltd.
30 South Wacker Drive
Chicago, IL 60606
Phone: (312) 207-1000
Fax: (312) 207-6400
http://www.sachnoff.com

Schiffman & Frank
380 Lexington Avenue
Suite 1117
New York, NY 10168

Phone: (212) 682-2373
Fax: (212) 682-8974

Solomon & Associates
209 Tenth Avenue South
Nashville, TN 37203
Phone: (615) 726-0400
Fax: (615) 256-3366

Steele & Utz
2300 M Street, NW
Washington, DC 20037
Phone: (202) 785-2130
Fax: (202) 261-3508

Stollman & Grubman, PA
2424 North Federal Highway
Boca Raton, FL 33431
Phone: (561) 393-9733
Fax: (561) 393-8770

White, Feischner & Fine
140 Broadway
New York, NY 10005
Phone: (212) 487-9700
Fax: (212) 487-9777

Wolf, Block, Schorr & Solis-Cohen
250 Park Avenue
New York, NY 10177
Phone: (212) 986-1116
Fax: (212) 986-0604

Zimmerman, Rosenfeld, Gersh & Leeds, LLP
9107 Wilshire Boulevard
Beverly Hills, CA 90210
Phone: (310) 278-7560
Fax: (310) 273-5602
http://www.beverlyhillslaw.com

GLOSSARY

The following is a list of abbreviations, acronyms, and music business lingo that should prove helpful to individu-als interested in the music industry. Entries are listed alphabetically.

AAF   American Advertising Federation

AAMT   American Association for Music Therapy

A & R   Artist & Repertoire (the department in a record company that finds new songs, signs new artists, etc.)

ABA   American Bar Association

A/C   Adult contemporary music

ACC   American Conference of Cantors

ACDA   American Choral Directors Association

ACM   Academy of Country Music

advance   A prepayment of monies against future royalties or fees

affiliate   A broadcast station that belongs to a network. For example, WABC in New York and KABC in Los Angeles are both affiliates of the ABC network.

AFM   American Federation of Musicians of the United States and Canada (the union that most musicians belong to)

AFT   American Federation of Teachers

AFTRA   American Federation of Television and Radio Artists

AGAC   American Guild of Authors and Composers (now known as The Songwriters Guild)

agent   The person who obtains work for an act or artist

AGM   American Guild of Music

AGMA   American Guild of Musical Artists

AGO   American Guild of Organists

AGVA   American Guild of Variety Artists

AICPA   American Institute of Certified Public Accountants

airplay   The broadcasting of records by radio stations

ALA   American Library Association

AMA   American Marketing Association

AMC   American Music Conference

AOR   Album-oriented rock (a type of music played by radio stations)

arbitron ratings   A television and radio rating service that indicates what percentage of the people are viewing or listening to a particular show or station. They may be referred to as the "arbitrons." Rates for commercial air time are often based on these ratings.

arrangement   The adaptation of a song for a performance or recording

ASCAP   American Society of Composers, Authors & Publishers

A-side   The side of a single record that is promoted more actively

ASMA   American Society of Music Arrangers

ASMC   American Society of Music Copyists

ASOL   American Symphony Orchestra League

assignment   The transfer of rights from a songwriter to publisher

ATPAM   Association of Theatrical Press Agents & managers

bar code   The black stripes that encode product informa-tion. Bar codes are assigned according to the Universal Product Code (UPC).

bio   Biography of artist or act, most commonly used in press kits and for other publicity

BMA   Black Music Association

BMI   Broadcast Music Incorporated

B-side   The flip side of a single

booking agent   Individual responsible for seeking and soliciting work for entertainers

bootlegging   The unauthorized selling of records, tapes, CDs, videos, etc.

bullet   A printed mark designating songs that have poten-tial on the charts; used in trade magazines, they may look like a bullet, a rocket, or a star

B & W glossy   Black and white glossy photograph, also known as an 8 × 10 glossy

B/W   Backed with. The opposite of the A-side of a record.

catalog   The collection of songs to which a publisher owns the rights

C & W   Country and Western

CBDNA   College Band Directors National Association

CD   Compact Disc

CDG   Compact disc with graphics

chart action   The movement of a specific record on the charts

charts   Lists of the current hits, found in the trade magazines

CMA   Country Music Association

commission   A percentage of money paid to an agent, manager, etc. for services

compact disc   Disc containing encoded music read by laser beam in CD or compact disc player

contractor   The person who hires session members for a recording session

co-publish   Agreement whereby two individuals or com-panies open the publishing rights to a song

copyright   A legal protection granted to an author or com-poser for the exclusive rights to his or her works

cover record   Another version of a tune that has already been recorded

CPA   Certified public accountant

CPM   Conference of Personal Managers

crossover record   A record that is popular in one type of music and then becomes popular in one or more other markets of music (e.g., a song that becomes a Top 40 hit and then becomes a hit on the country and/or R & B charts)

cut   A specific selection on an album or CD; to record a song

day job   The job many individuals work to pay the bills while waiting for their "big break" in the music business.

demo   Demonstration record used for selling a record, tune, or act

demographics   Information—such as age, gender, sex, marital status, education level, etc.—used to target buyers; radio stations also use this information to target listeners and advertisers.

distributor   Individual or company who moves records, CDs, etc. from the manufacturer to retail outlets

D.J.   Disc jockey

EIA   Electronic Industry Association

E.P.   Extended play record

Equity   Actors Equity Association, the actors' union

exploit   The process of finding legitimate uses of songs or acts for income

fan club   A club made up of people devoted to a specific artist or act

FCC   Federal Communications Commission

format   The style of programming that a radio station uses (e.g., all talk, country, Top 40, etc.)

GAMMA   Guitar and Accessories Music Marketing Association

gig   A job for musicians

GMA   Gospel Music Association

gold album   An LP that has sold 500,000 units as certified by the R.I.A.A.

gold single   A single record or CD single that has sold 500,000 units as certified by the R.I.A.A.

Grammy   One of the most prestigious awards in the music business; given by the NARAS

headliner   The main act people come to see in a concert

hip-hop   Musical style combining rap, R&B, and disco music

hit   A record that is popular and sells a lot of copies

hook   The repetitive part of a song that is most remembered when people think about that tune

hype   Extensive publicity used to promote acts, new records, etc. (Incidentally, hype is not always true.)

IAAM   International Association of Auditorium Managers

IAFP   International Association of Financial Planning

IATSE   International Alliance of Theatrical Stage Employees

ICFP   Institute of Certified Financial Planners

IIA   Institute of Internal Auditors

independent record label   Record label not owned by major company

indie   Independent record label

IRC   International reply coupon. These are used when requesting the return of materials from other countries.

jingle   A musical tune in a commercial

K.J.   Karaoke Jockey

label   Record company

LD   Laser disc

lead sheet   Written version of a song containing the melody, lyrics, and chords, etc.

local   The local in a union is the local affiliation in a particular geographic area of a national or international union.

log   The list of music played by radio stations used to determine performance royalties; logs also contain additional programming information

LP   Long-playing record, commonly known as an album

lyrics   The words of a song

Major   A major record label, such as EMI, Sony, BMG, Universal Music, or Warner Music

market   Can refer to geographical location, such as the East Coast market, the West Coast market, etc., or may refer to a type of musical market, such as Top 40, R&B, country, etc.

master   The finished tape that is turned into a record

MCA   Music Critics Association

MD   Mini disc; these are used for recording and playing digitally encoded music

mechanical license   A license obtained from a song publisher, needed to record the song

MENC   Music Educators National Conference

MIEA   Music Industry Educators Association

mix   Putting all the different tracts for a record together electronically

MLA   Music Library Association

MOR   Middle of the road music, also called easy listening music

music video   A video used by musical acts and singers to promote their songs on television

Muzak   Canned music such as that heard in dentist's offices, department stores, elevators, etc.

NAA   National Association of Accountants

NAB   National Association of Broadcasters

NABET   National Association of Broadcast Employees and Technicians

NACA   National Association for Campus Activities

NACWPI   National Association of College Wind and Percussion Instructors

NAMM   National Association of Music Merchants

NAMT   National Association for Music Therapy, Inc.

NARAS   National Academy of Recording Arts & Sciences

NARM   National Association of Record Merchandisers

NASM   National Association of Schools of Music

NASSM   National Association of State Supervisors of Music

Net   The Internet

network   A group of television or radio stations affiliated and interconnected for simultaneous broadcast of the same programming

NFMC   National Federation of Music Clubs

NMPA   National Music Publishers Association

NOA   National Orchestra Association

NPMA   National Piano Manufacturers Association

NSPA   National Society of Public Accountants

oldies   Songs that were hits some years ago

one-stop   Wholesale distributor of records and video products and accessories

on-line   Connecting to the Internet

overdub   Adding another part (vocal or instrument) to a basic multi-track recording

payola   Money or other "gratuities" given to D.J.'s or program directors in order to have certain records played more often (this is illegal)

P.D.   Public domain; program director

performing rights   The right to license music and collect monies for use by anyone playing that music

personal manager   Person who directs the career of a performer

platinum single or album   A single record, album, cassette, CD, etc. that has sold 1,000,000 units

playlist   A list of songs that a radio station compiles designating which songs it will play

portfolio   A collection of sample pieces done by someone in the creative field (either a writer or artist), which is put together into a book so that prospective employers can get an idea of a person's potential

P.R.   Public relations

press kit   A promo kit containing publicity, photos, and other promotional materials on an act

print rights   Permission granted to reproduce the printed sheet music of a copyrighted song or other work

promo   Promotion

PRSA   Public Relations Society of America

PSA   Public service announcements on radio or television given to not-for-profit organizations

public domain   Songs or other works that have no copyright or whose copyright has expired

R & B   Rhythm and blues

R & R   Rock 'n' roll

release date   The actual date a manufacturer releases a product

repertoire   A list of songs that an act performs or records, etc.

RIA   Recording Institute of America

RIAA   Recording Industry Association of America, Inc.

royalties   Monies paid periodically for the sales of records, sheet music, etc.

royalty statement   An itemized accounting of earnings for songwriters or recording artists

SAG   Screen Actors Guild

scale   The minimum union wages

search the Net   Look for information on the Internet

self-contained act   A group that has all members included and needs no outside augmentation

SESAC   Society of European Songwriters, Authors and Composers

ship date   The actual date a manufacturer physically ships a product

short form   A music video with only one song

Short Form Albums   Short form albums have a minimum of three songs and a maximum of five. They run approximately 30 minutes.

single   A record with one tune on each side

site   Website

SLA   Special Libraries Association

SPARS   Society of Professional Audio Recording Studios

S.R.O.   Standing room only—all seats for a concert or show are sold out

standard   A song that becomes popular in all markets and then becomes timeless, it may also be known as a classic.

street date   The actual date a CD, cassette, record, etc. arrives in retail stores (or other markets for sale).

superstar   Act that is famous, talented, rich, and well known

supporting act   Act that opens the show before the main event

surf the net   Going on-line, visiting various sites on the Internet

TEIA   Touring Entertainment Industry Association

tip sheet   A newspaper, newsletter, or magazine that lists new records and fast-moving tunes (Tip sheets are used by program directors and/or music directors at radio stations to help make up the station's playlists.)

Top 40   The forty songs in the country that are selling the best and/or requested the most on radio stations (The Top 40 may be found in the trades. Often there is a Top 40 for different categories of music, such as Country, R & B, Albums, etc.)

Top Ten   The top ten songs on the charts

tour   A series of concerts, usually in different geographic areas

tour support   Monies paid to acts to offset the high cost of tours (Tour support is most often paid by the act's label. However, many companies are now underwriting concert tours, including soft drink companies, beer companies, perfume companies, etc.)

trades   Magazines and newspapers that deal with the music/record/entertainment industry

12″ single   A 12-inch recording of one or more mixes of a tune, usually played in dance clubs

U/C   Urban contemporary music

UPC   Universal Product Code

union card A card that is used to identify members of specific unions

V.J. Video Jockey

VeeJay Video Jockey

venue A hall, auditorium, or club where an act performs

Web The World Wide Web

Website A place on the World Wide Web

Work for Hire A work (song, press release, book, etc.) done by an employee as part of his or her job. The work is owned and copyrightable by the employer, not the employee.

WWW World Wide Web

YCA Young Concert Artists

BIBLIOGRAPHY

A. BOOKS

Thousands of books explore all aspects of music. The books listed below are separated into general categories. The subject matter in many of the books overlaps.

These books can be found in bookstores or libraries. If your local library does not have the books you want, you might ask your librarian to order them for you through the interlibrary loan system.

This list is meant as a beginning. For other books that might interest you, look in the music section of bookstores. You can also check Books in Print (found in the reference section of libraries).

Recording and the Record Business

Artistpro Publishing. *2003 Recording Industry Sourcebook.* Vallejo, Calif.: Artistpro Publishing, 2003.

Clark, William, Jim Cogan, and Quincy Jones. *Temples of Sound: Inside the Great Recording Studios.* San Francisco: Chronicle Books, 2002.

Cleveland, Barry, ed. *Recording Industry Sourcebook, 1999: The Complete Source for Music Business and Production Services.* Overland Park, Kans.: Primedia Business Magazines & Media, 1999.

Fara, Frank, and Patty Parker. *How to Open Doors in the Music Industry: The Independent Way.* Scottsdale, Ariz.: Starfield Press, 1987.

Gracyk, Tim. *Popular American Recording Pioneers: 1895–1925.* Binghamton, N.Y.: Haworth Press, Inc., 2000.

Hustwit, Gary. *Releasing an Independent Record: How to Successfully Start and Run Your Own Record Label.* San Diego: Rockpress Publishing, 1998.

Muench, Teri, and Susan Pomerantz. *Attention: A & R: A Step-By-Step Guide into the Recording Industry: For Artists and Songwriters.* Van Nuys, Calif.: Alfred Pub Co., 1988.

Passman, Donald. *All You Need to Know about the Music Business: Revised and Updated for the 21st Century.* New York: Simon & Schuster, 2000.

Schafer, A.R. *Making a First Recording.* Mankato, Minn.: Capstone Press, Inc., 2003.

Schwartz, Daylle Deanna. *Start and Run Your Own Record Label.* New York: Watson-Guptill Publishers, 1998.

Stanfield, Jane. *The Musician's Guide to Making & Selling Your Own CDs & Cassettes.* Cincinnati, Ohio: Writers Digest Books, 1997.

Sweeny, Tim, and Mark Geller. *Guide to Releasing Independent Records.* Torrance, Calif.: TSA Books, 1996.

Record Production

Avalon, Moses. *Confessions of a Record Producer: How to Survive the Scams and Shams of the Music Business.* Gilroy, Calif.: Miller Backbeat Books, 2001.

Burgess, Richard, James. *The Art of Record Production.* London: Omnibus Press, 1997.

Cunningham, Mark E. *Good Vibrations: A History of Record Production.* London: Sanctuary Publishing, Ltd., 1999.

Katz, David. *People People Funny Boy.* Edinborough, Scotland: Canongate Books, 2000.

Massey, Howard. *Behind the Glass: Top Record Producers Tell How They Craft the Hits.* San Francisco: Miller Freeman, 2000.

Poe, Randy. *Music Publishing: A Songwriters Guide.* Cincinnati, Ohio: Writer's Digest Books, 1997.

Music Business

Bakersville, David. *Music Business Handbook and Career Guide.* Thousand Oaks, Calif.: Sage Publications, 2002.

Halloran, Mark. *The Musician's Business and Legal Guide.* Englewood Cliffs, N.J.: Prentice-Hall, 2001.

Krasilovsky, M. William, and Sidney, Shemel. *This Business of Music.* New York: Billboard Books, 2000.

Levine, Mike. *How to Be a Working Musician: A Practical Guide to Earning Money in the Music Business.* New York: Watson-Guptill Publications, 1997.

Passman, Donald S. *All You Need to Know about the Music Business.* New York: Simon and Schuster, 2000.

Stim, Richard. *Music Law: How to Run Your Band's Business.* Berkeley, Calif.: Nola Press, 2001.

Artist Management

Davison, Marc. *All Area Access: Personal Management for Unsigned Musicians.* Milwaukee, Wisc.: Hal Leonard Publishing, 1997.

Frascogna, Zavier, and H. Lee Hertherington. *This Business of Artist Management.* New York: Billboard Books, 1997.

Marcone, Stephen. *Managing Your Band: Artist Management: The Ultimate Responsibility.* Wayne, N.J.: HiMarks Publishing Company, 2003.

Schwartz, Daylle Deanna. *The Real Deal: How to Get Signed to a Record Label from A to Z.* New York: Watson-Guptill Publications, 1997.

Radio
Apple, Terri, and Gary Owens. *Making Money in Voice-Overs: Winning Strategies to a Successful Career in TV, Commercials, Radio and Animation.* Hollywood: Lone Eagle Publishing Company, 1999.

Brewster, Bill. *Last Night a DJ Saved My Life: The History of the Disc Jockey.* New York: Grove Press, 2000.

Clark, Elaine A. *There's Money Where Your Mouth Is: An Insider's Guide to a Career in Voice-Overs.* New York: Watson-Guptill Publications, 2000.

Field, Shelly. *Career Opportunities in Radio.* New York: Facts On File, 2004.

Music and the Internet
Simpson, Ron. *The Professional Musician's Internet Guide.* Milwaukee, Wisc.: Hal Leonard Publishing, 2000.

Sweeney, Tim, and John Dawes. *The Complete Guide to Internet Promotion for Musicians, Artists, & Songwriters.* Temecula, Calif.: Tim Sweeney and Associates, 2000.

Music Marketing and Promotion
Baker, Bob. *Guerrilla Music Marketing Handbook: 201 Self-Promotion Ideas for Songwriters, Musicians & Bands.* Saint Louis, Mo.: Spotlight Publications, 2001.

Fisher, Jeffrey P. *Ruthless Self Promotion in the Music Industry.* Milwaukee, Wisc.: Hal Leonard Publishing, 1999.

Hall, Charles. *Marketing in the Music Industry.* New York: Pearson, 2000.

Hollan, James F. *The Concert Book.* Chicago: Bonus Books, 1999.

Lathrop, Tad, and Jim Pettigrew. *This Business of Music Marketing and Promotion.* New York: Billboard Books, 1999.

Letts, Richard. *Successful Promotion by Musicians: The Art of Self Promotion.* Newton, Australia: Allen & Unwin Pty., Limited, 1997.

Summers, Jodi. *Making and Marketing Music: The Musician's Guide to Financing, Distributing and Promoting Albums.* New York: Allworth Press, 1999.

Publicity and Promotion
Field, Shelly. *Career Opportunities in Advertising and Public Relations.* New York: Facts On File, 2002.

Goldstein, Norm. *The Associated Press Stylebook and Briefing on Media Law.* Boulder, Colo.: Perseus Publishing, 2002.

Yudkin, Marcia. *6 Steps to Free Publicity: For Corporate Publicists or Solo Professionals, Including . . . Publish-ers, Consultants, Conference Planners, Politicians, Inventors.* Franklin Lakes, N.J.: Career Press, 2003.

Music Publishing
Collingwood, Donna, ed. *The Songwriter's Market Guide to Song & Demo Submission Formats.* Cincinnati, Ohio: Writers Digest, 1994.

Koller, Fred. *How to Pitch and Promote Your Songs.* New York: Allworth Press, 1996.

Poe, Randy. *Music Publishing: A Songwriter's Guide.* Cincinnati, Ohio: Writers Digest Books, 1997.

Whitsett, Tim. *Music Publishing: The Real Road to Music Business Success.* Vallejo, Calif.: Mix Books, 2001.

Talent and Songwriting
Aschmann, Lisa. *750 Songwriting Ideas: For Brave and Passionate People.* Vallejo, Calif.: Artistpro.com, 2003.

Blume, Jason. *Inside Songwriting: Getting to the Heart of Creativity.* New York: Watson-Guptill Publications, 2003.

———. *6 steps to Songwriting Success: The Comprehensive Guide to Writing and Marketing Hit Songs.* New York: Billboard Books, 1999.

Cox, Terry. *You Can Write Song Lyrics.* Cincinnati, Ohio: Writers Digest Books, 2002.

Davis, Sheila. *The Craft of Lyric Writing.* Cincinnati, Ohio: Writers Digest Books, 1985.

———. *The Songwriter's Idea Book: 400 Strategies to Excite Your Imagination, Help You Design Distinctive Songs, and Keep Your Creative Flow.* Cincinnati, Ohio: Writers Digest Books, 1996.

———. *Successful Lyric Writing: A Step-By-Step Course and Workbook.* Cincinnati, Ohio: Writers Digest Books, 1988.

Hall, Tom T. *The Songwriter's Handbook.* Nashville, Tenn.: Rutledge Hill Press, 2001.

Leiken, Molly-Ann. *How to Make a Good Song a Hit Song: Rewriting and Marketing Your Lyrics and Music.* Milwaukee, Wisc.: Hal Leonard Publishing, 1996.

———. *How to Write a Hit Song: The Complete Guide to Writing and Marketing Chart Topping Lyrics & Music.* Milwaukee, Wisc.: Hal Leonard Publishing, 2001.

Peterik, Jim, Dave Austin, and Mary Ellen Bickford. *Songwriting for Dummies.* New York: Dummies, 2002.

Songwriter's Market. Cincinnati, Ohio: Writers Digest Books, published annually.

Weismann, Dick. *Songwriting: The Words, the Music and the Money.* Milwaukee, Wisc.: Hal Leonard, 2001.

Talent and Music
Joefs, Jai. *Writing Music for Hit Songs: Including New Songs from the '90s.* New York: Music Sales Corp., 2000.

Music Videos & Music Television

Jackson, John A. *American Bandstand: Dick Clark and the Making of a Rock 'n' Roll Empire.* New York: Oxford University Press, 1999.

Music—General

Barnett, Richard D. *Controversies of the Music Industry.* Westport, Conn.: Greenwood Publishing Group, 2001.

Fara, Frank. *How to Open Doors In the Music Industry: The Independent Way.* Fountain Hills, Ariz.: Starfield Press, 1986.

Forest, Greg. *The Complete Music Business Office: Survival Skills for a Rough Trade.* Milwaukee, Wisc.: Hal Leonard Publishing, 1999.

Fong-Torres, Ben. *The Hits Just Keep on Coming: The History of Top 40.* New York: Backbeat Books, 2001.

Justin Goldberg. *The Ultimate Survival Guide for the New Music Industry: A Handbook for Hell.* Hollywood, Calif.: Lone Eagle Publishing Co., 2003.

Hatschek, Keith. *How to Get a Job in the Music and Recording Industry.* Boston: Berklee Press, 2001.

Kingsbury, Paul, and Chet Flippo. *The Country Reader: Twenty-Five Years of the Journal of Country Music.* Nashville, Tenn.: Vanderbilt University Press, 2000.

McNutt, Randy, and Rick Kennedy. *Little Labels–Big Sound: Small Record Companies and the Rise of American Music.* Bloomington, Ind.: Indiana University Press, 1999.

Stamm, K. Brad. *Music Industry Economics: A Global Demand Model for Pre-Recorded Music.* Lewiston, N.Y.: Edwin Mellon Press, 2000.

The Music Industry

Brabec, Jeffrey and Todd Brabec. *Music, Money, and Success: The Insider's Guide to the Music Industry.* New York: Gale Group, 2000.

Eliot, Marc. *Rockonomics: The Money behind the Music.* Secaucus, N.J.: Citadel Press, 1993.

Goodman, Fred. *The Mansion on the Hill: Dylan, Young, Geffen, Springsteen, and the Head-On Collision of Rock and Commerce.* New York: Vintage Books, 1998.

Halloran, Mark. *The Musician's Business & Legal Guide.* Upper Saddle River, N.J.: Prentice-Hall, 2001.

Kimpel, Dan. *Networking in the Music Business.* Milwaukee, Wisc.: Hal Leonard Publishing, 1999.

Naggar, David, and Jeffrey D. Brandstetter. *The Music Business (Explained in Plain English): What Every Artist & Songwriter Should Know to Avoid Getting Ripped Off!* San Francisco, Calif.: DaJe Publishing, 2000.

Instrument Repair and Design

Karp, Cary, ed. *The Conservation and Technology of Musical Instruments: A Supplemental Bibliography to Art and Archaeology Technical Abstracts.* Santa Monica, Calif.: Getty Trust Publications, 1992.

Cumpiano, William R., and Jonathan D. Natelson. *Guitarmaking: Tradition and Technology: A Complete Reference for the Design & Construction of the Steel-String Folk Guitar & the Classical Guitar.* New York: Music Sales Corp., 1994.

Erlewine, Dan. *Guitar Player Repair Guide: How to Set-Up, Maintain, and Repair Electrics and Acoustics.* San Francisco, Calif.: Miller Freeman Books, 1994.

Kamimoto, Hideo. *Electric Guitar Setups.* New York: Music Sales Corp., 1996.

Sandberg, Larry. *The Acoustic Guitar Guide: Everything You Need to Know to Buy and Maintain a New or Used Guitar.* Chicago: Chicago Review Books, 2000.

Siminoff, Roger H. *Constructing a Solid Body Guitar: A Complete Technical Guide.* Milwaukee, Wisc.: Hal Leonard Publishing, 1986.

Siminoff, Roger H. *How to Set up the Best Sounding Banjo.* Milwaukee, Wisc.: Hal Leonard Publishing, 1999.

Teeter, Don T. *The Acoustic Guitar: Adjustment, Care, Maintenance and Repair.* Norman, Okla.: Univ. of Oklahoma Press, 1998.

Williams, Jim. *The Guitar Maker's Manual.* Milwaukee, Wisc.: Hal Leonard Publishing, 1988.

Symphony Orchestras

American Symphony Orchestra League. *The Gold Book.* Washington, DC: The American Symphony Orchestra League, published annually.

Berkowitz, David. *Behind the Gold Curtain: Fifty Years in the Metropolitan Opera.* Delhi, N.Y.: Birch Brook Press, 1995.

Hopkins, Karen Brooks, and Carolyn Stolper Friedman. *Successful Fundraising For Arts and Cultural Organizations.* Westport, Conn.: Greenwood Publishing Group, 1996.

Kotler, Philip. *Standing Room Only: Strategies for Marketing the Performing Arts.* Allston, Mass.: Harvard Business School Press, 1997.

Reiss, Alvin H. *Don't Just Applaud—Send Money!: The Most Successful Strategies for Funding and Marketing the Arts.* New York: Theatre Communications Group, 1995.

Education: Music Therapy

Andrews, Ted. *Music Therapy for Non-Musicians.* Jackson, Tenn.: Dragonhawk Publishing, 1997.

Bruscia, Kenneth E. *Defining Music Therapy.* Gilsum, N.H.: Barcelona Pub., 1998.

Kirkland, Kevin H., and Howard McIlveen. *Full Circle: Spiritual Therapy for the Elderly.* Binghamton, N.Y.: Haworth Press, 2000.

Lingerman, Hal A. *The Healing Energies of Music.* Wheaton, Ill.: Quest Books, 1995.

Education: Music Librarian

Careers in Music Librarianship: Perspectives from the Field. MLA Technical Report. Canton, Mass.: Music Library Assn., 1991.

Bradley, Carol June. *American Music Librarianship.* Westport, Conn.: Greenwood Publishing Group, 1990.

Education: Music

Bennett Reimer. *A Philosophy of Music Education: Advancing the Vision.* Englewood Cliffs, N.J.: Prentice Hall, 2002.

Boonshaft, Peter Loel. *Teaching Music with Passion: Conducting, Rehearsing and Inspiring.* Galesville Md.: Meredith Music, 2002.

Colwell, Richard. *The New Handbook of Research on Music Teaching and Learning: A Project of the Music Educators National Conference.* Cary, N.C.: Oxford University Press, 2002.

Ericksen, Connie M. *Band Director's Curriculum Resource: Ready-To-Use Lessons & Worksheets for Teaching Music Theory.* Upper Saddle River, N.J.: Prentice-Hall, 1999.

Uszler, Marienne, Stewart Gordon, and Scott McBride Smith. *The Well-Tempered Keyboard Teacher.* New York: Schirmer Books, 2000.

Church Music

Revinney, Richard. *The Wednesday Workout: Practical Techniques for Rehearsing the Church Choir.* Nashville, Tenn.: Abingdon Press, 1993.

Turner, Steve. *Amazing Grace: The Story of America's Most Beloved Song.* New York: Ecco, 2002.

Westermeyer, Paul. *The Church Musician.* Minneapolis, Minn.: Augsburg Fortress Publications, 1997.

———. *Parish Educational Series: Study Guides Relating to Music and Worship.* Minneapolis, Minn.: Fortress Publications, 1992.

B. PERIODICALS

Magazines, newspapers, membership bulletins, and newsletters may be helpful for finding information about a specific job category or finding a job in a specific field.

As with the books in the previous section, this list should serve only as a beginning. Many periodicals are not listed because of space limitations. Periodicals also tend to come and go. Look in your local library or in newspaper/magazine shops for other periodicals that might interest you. Also check for on-line versions of periodicals on the Internet.

The periodicals in this section are listed in general categories. Subject matter may overlap. Check all categories relevant to the type of career you seek.

The Trades

Amusement Business
P.O. Box 24970
Nashville, TN 37202
Phone: (615) 321-4250
Fax: (615) 327-1575
E-mail: maze@cahners.com
http://www.amusementbusiness.com

Billboard
770 Broadway, 5th Floor
New York, NY 10036
Phone: (646) 654-5600
Fax: (646) 654-5514
E-mail: crosen@billboardgroup.com
http://www.billboard.com

The Hollywood Reporter
5055 Wilshire Boulevard, 6th Floor
Los Angeles, CA 90036
Phone: (323) 525-2000
Fax: (323) 525-2091
http://www.hollywoodreporter.com

Variety
5700 Wilshire Boulevard, Suite 120
Los Angeles, CA 90036
Phone: (213) 965-4476
Fax: (213) 857-0742
http://variety.com

Concert Industry

Pollstar
4697 West Jacquelyn Avenue
Fresno, CA 93722-6413
Phone: (559) 271-7900
Fax: (559) 271-7979
E-mail: info@pollstar.com
http://www.pollstar.com

Facility Management

Facility Manager
International Association of Assembly Managers
635 Fritz Drive
Coppell, TX 75019

Phone: (972) 255-8020 or (800) 935-4226 (toll-free)
Fax: (972) 255-9582
E-mail: info@iaam.org
http://www.iaam.org

Recording and the Recording Industry

Mix
6400 Hollis Street, Suite 12
Emeryville, CA 94608
Phone: (510) 653-3307 or (800) 541-7706 (toll-free)
Fax: (510) 653-5142
E-mail: mixeditorial@intertec.com
http//www.mixonline.com

Pro Sound News
460 Park Avenue South, 9th Floor
New York, NY 10016
Phone: (212) 378-0400
Fax: (212) 378-2160

E-mail: pro@psn.com
http://www.psn.com

Recording
5412 Idylwild Trail, Suite 100
Boulder, CO 80301
Phone: (303) 516-9118
Fax: (303) 516-9119
E-mail: info@recordingmag.com
http://www.recordingmag.com

Radio

Airplay Monitor
505 Wilshire Boulevard
Los Angeles, CA 90036
Phone: (323) 525-2000

Broadcasting and Cable
Entertainment Division
1705 DeSales Street, NW
Washington, DC 20036
Phone: (202) 659-2340
Fax: (202) 429-0651
http://www.broadcastingcable.com

R and R Directory
10100 Santa Monica Boulevard, 5th Floor
Los Angeles, CA 90067-4004
Phone: (310) 553-4330
Fax: (310) 203-8727
http://www.rronline.com

Radio & Records
10100 Santa Monica Boulevard, 5th Floor
Los Angeles, CA 90067
Phone: (310) 553-4330
Fax: (310) 203-8727
http://www.rronline.com

Retailing and Wholesaling

Musical Merchandise Review
50 Brook Road
Needham, MA 02494
Phone: (781) 453-9310 or (800) 964-5150
Fax: (781) 453-9389
http://www.mmrmagazine.com

Musical Merchandise Review—
   Directory of Musical Instrument
   Dealers
6200 Canoga Avenue, Suite 303
Woodland Hills, CA 91367-3431 USA
E-mail: mmr@tiac.com
http://www.mmrmagazine.com

NAPRA Review
Networking Alternatives for Publishers,
   Retailers, & Artists, Inc.
109 North Beach Road
P.O. Box 9
Eastsound, WA 98245-0009
Phone: (360) 376-2702 or (800) 367-1907
   (toll-free)
Fax: (360) 376-2704
E-mail: napra@napra.com
http://www.napra.com

Up Beat Daily
102 North Haven Road
Elmhurst, IL 60126
Phone: (630) 941-2030 or (800) 535-7496
   (toll-free)
Fax: (630) 941-3210
E-mail: musicincupbeat@woldnet.att.net

Repair and Restoration

Piano Technicians Journal
3930 Washington
Kansas City, MO 64111
Phone: (816) 753-7747
Fax: (816) 531-0070
E-mail: ptg@ptg.org

Public Relations and Publicity

Bulldog Reporter, Eastern Edition
5900 Hollis Street, Suite R2
Emeryville, CA 94608
Phone: (510) 596-9300 or (800) 959-1059
   (toll-free)
Fax: (510) 596-9331

Bulldog Reporter, Western Edition
5900 Hollis St., Ste. R2
Emeryville, CA 94608
Phone: (510) 596-9300 or (800) 959-1059
   (toll-free)
Fax: (510) 596-9331
http://www.infocomgroup.com

Expert PR
311 Arsenal Street
Watertown, MA 02472
Phone: (617) 393-3200
Fax: (617) 393-3254
E-mail: info@mediamap.com
http://www.mediamap.com/expertpr

PR News
1201 Seven Locks Road
Potomac, MD 20854
Phone: (301) 340-7788

Fax: (301) 340-0542
E-mail: pbi@phillips.com

PR Reporter
PR Publishing Company, Inc.
Dudley House
P.O. Box 600
Exeter, NH 03833-0600
Phone: (603) 778-0514
Fax: (603) 778-1741
E-mail: prr@prpublishing.com

Public Relations Quarterly
P.O. Box 311
Rhinebeck, NY 12572
Phone: (845) 876-2081 or (800) 572-3451
   (toll-free)
Fax: (845) 876-2561
E-mail: hudsonsdir@aol.com

Public Relations Review
38091 Beach Road
P.O. Box 180
Coltons Point, MD 20626-0180
Phone: (301) 769-3899
E-mail: 102062-2525@compuserve.com

Orchestras/Operas

Harmony
Symphony Orchestra Institute
1618 Orrington Avenue, Suite 318
Evanston, IL 60201
Phone: (847) 475-5001
Fax: (847) 475-2460
E-mail: soi@soi.org
http://www.soi.org

National Opera Association Newsletter
c/o Robert Thieme
3 Briar Parch Lane
Morgantown, WV 26505-3610
Phone: (304) 599-4945
Fax: (304) 293-7491

OPERA America Newsline
1156 15th Street, NW, Suite 810
Washington, DC 20005-1704
Phone: (202) 293-4466
Fax: (202) 393-0735
E-mail: frontdesk@operaamerica.org

Opera News
Metropolitan Opera Guild, Inc.
70 Lincoln Center Plaza
New York, NY 10023
Phone: (212) 769-7080
Fax: (212) 769-8500

E-mail: info@metguild.org;
info@operanews.com
http://www.operanews.com

Symphony
American Symphony Orchestra League
33 W. 60th Street, Fifth Floor
New York, NY 10023-7905
Phone: (212) 262-5161
Fax: (212) 262-5198
E-mail: league@symphony.org

Symphony Magazine—Annual Orchestra
and Business Directory Issue
American Symphony Orchestra League
33 West 60th Street, 5th Floor
New York, NY 10023 USA
Phone: (212) 262-5161
Fax: (212) 262-5198
E-mail: league@symphony.org

Symphony Magazine—Directory of
Summer Music Festivals
American Symphony Orchestra League
33 West 60th Street, 5th Floor
New York, NY 10023 USA
Phone: (212) 262-5161
Fax: (212) 262-5198
E-mail: league@symphony.org

The Woman Conductor
Women Band Directors National
Association
345 Overlook Drive
West Lafayette, IN 47906
Phone: (765) 463-1738
Fax: (765) 463-1738
E-mail: agwright@gte.net

Education

American Music Teacher
Music Teachers National Association
The Carew Tower
441 Vine Street, Suite 505
Cincinnati, OH 45202
Phone: (513) 421-1420
Fax: (513) 421-2503
http://www.mtna.org

Bulletin of the Council for Research in
Music Education
School of Music
University of Illinois
1114 West Nevada
Urbana, IL 61801
Phone: (217) 333-1027
Fax: (217) 244-4585
E-mail: crme@uiuc.edu

Journal for Research in Music Education
Louisiana State University
School of Music
Baton Rouge, LA 70803-2504
Phone: (225) 388-2481
Fax: (225) 388-3333
E-mail: mbrserv@menc.org;
hprice@bana.ua.edu

Music Educators Journal
MENC: The National Association for
Music Education
1806 Robert Fulton Drive
Reston, VA 20191
Phone: (703) 860-4000 or (800) 336-
3768 (toll-free)
Fax: (703) 860-4826
E-mail: mbrserv@menc.org

Music Reference Services Quarterly
The Haworth Press Inc.
NIU Libraries
DeKalb, IL 60115-2868
Phone: (815) 753-9856
Fax: (815) 753-2003
E-mail: getinfo@haworthpress.com

Teaching Music
MENC: The National Association for
Music Education
1806 Robert Fulton Drive
Reston, VA 20191
Phone: (703) 860-4000 or (800) 336-3768
(toll-free)
Fax: (703) 860-4826
E-mail: mbrserv@menc.org

Talent and Writing

Acoustic Guitar
P.O. Box 767
San Anselmo, CA 94979-0767
Phone: (415) 485-6946 or (800) 827-6837
(toll-free)
Fax: (415) 485-0831
E-mail: ag@stringletter.com
http://www.acguitar.com

Aiding & Abetting
1308 Shawnee
Durham, NC 27701
Phone: (919) 682-0045

American Federation of Musicians
Music Association of San Diego County
1717 Morena Boulevard
San Diego, CA 92110
Phone: (619) 276-4324
Fax: (619) 276-4876

American Songwriter Magazine
1009 17th Avenue South
Nashville, TN 37212-2201
Phone: (615) 321-6096 or (800) 739-8712
(toll-free)
Fax: (615) 321-6097
E-mail: info@americansongwriter.com
http://www.americansongwriter.com

Bandmagazine.com
P.O. Box 840
Northampton, MA 01061
http://www.bandmagazine.com

Bass Player
2800 Campus Drive
San Mateo, CA 94403
Phone: (650) 513-4300
Fax: (650) 513-4642
E-mail: bassplayer@musicplayer.com
http://www.bassplayer.com

Big Takeover Magazine
249 Eldridge Street
New York, NY 10002
Phone: (212) 533-6057
http://www.bigtakeover.com

BMI Music World
Broadcast Music, Inc. (BMI)
320 West 57th Street
New York, NY 10019
Phone: (212) 586-2000
Fax: (212) 956-2059

Composer/USA
National Association of Composers/USA
P.O. Box 49256, Barrington Station
Los Angeles, CA 90049
Phone: (310) 541-8213
Fax: (310) 544-1413
E-mail: dbryce@gete.net

Country Dance and Song Society
Newsletter
P.O. Box 338
132 Main Street
Haydenville, MA 01039-0338
Phone: (413) 268-7426
Fax: (413) 268-7471
E-mail: office@cdss.org

Down Beat
Maher Publications, Inc.
102 North Haven Road
Elmhurst, IL 60126
Phone: (630) 941-2030 or (800) 535-7496
(toll-free)
Fax: (630) 941-3210

Electronic Musician
6400 Hollis Street, Suite 12
Emeryville, CA 94608
Phone: (510) 653-3307 or (800) 541-7706
   (toll-free)
Fax: (510) 653-5142
http://www.emusician.com

Guitar
10 Midland Avenue
Port Chester, NY 10573
Phone: (914) 935-5200
Fax: (914) 937-0614

Guitar Player
411 Borel Avenue, Suite 100
San Mateo, CA 94402
Phone: (650) 358-9500
Fax: (650) 358-9966
E-mail: guitplyr@mfi.com
http://www.guitarplayer.com

Guitar World
Harris Publications, Inc.
1115 Broadway, 8th Floor
New York, NY 10010-2803
Phone: (212) 807-7100
Fax: (212) 627-4678
E-mail: gwedit@aol.com

Hit Parader
Hit Parader Publications, Inc.
210 Route 4 East, Suite 211
Paramus, NJ 07652
Phone: (201) 843-4004
Fax: (201) 843-8636

International Musician
American Federation of Musicians
1501 Broadway, Suite 600
New York, NY 10036
Phone: (212) 869-1330
Fax: (212) 302-4374
E-mail: info@afm.org

Keyboard
2800 Campus Drive
San Mateo, CA 94403
Phone: (650) 513-4300
http://www.keyboardonline.com

Music Connection
4215 Coldwater Canyon
Studio City, CA 91604
Phone: (818) 755-0101
http://www.musicconnection.com

Musicians Hotline
1003 Central Avenue
P.O. Box 1052
Fort Dodge, IA 50501

Phone: (515) 955-1600 or (800) 247-2000
   (toll-free)
Fax: (515) 574-2199
E-mail: ahlsales@aviatorshotline.com
http://www.musicianshotline.com

Music Monitor
107 East Aycock Street
Raleigh, NC 27608
Phone: (919) 821-9343
http://www.trexonline.com

Music Product Directory–Piano and
   Electronic Keyboard Editions
Box 46532D
Cincinnati, OH 45246 USA
Phone: (513) 772-2282

Music Trades—Purchaser's Guide to the
   Music Industry Issue
80 West Street
Englewood, NJ 07631
Phone: (201) 871-1965 or (800) 423-6530
Fax: (201) 871-0455
E-mail: music@musictrades.com

National Sheet Music Society Newsletter
c/o Marilyn Brees
1597 Fair Park Avenue
Los Angeles, CA 90041 USA
http://www.ourworld.compuserve.com/ho
   mepages/bobcourt

Orion Blue Book: Vintage Guitar
Orion Research Corp.
14555 North Scottsdale Road, No. 330
Scottsdale, AZ 85254-3457
Phone: (480) 951-1114 or (800) 844-0759
   (toll-free)
Fax: (480) 951-1117
E-mail: orion@bluebook.com
http://www.bluebook.com

Piano and Keyboard
P.O. Box 2626
San Anselmo, CA 94979
Phone: (415) 458-8672 or (800) 233-3690
Fax: (415) 458-2955
E-mail: pianokeybd@aol.com

Sing Out!
The Sing Out Corp.
512 East 4th Street
P.O. Box 5253
Bethlehem, PA 18015-0253
Phone: (610) 865-5366 or
   (888) SING-OUT (toll-free)
Fax: (610) 865-5129
E-mail: info@singout.org

Song Manh Magazine
Song Sao Cho Manh, Inc.
P.O. Box 21245
San Jose, CA 95151-1245
Phone: (408) 605-0605
Fax: (408) 729-5595
E-mail: webmaster@songmanh.org
http://www.songmanh.org

Song Plugger
P.O. Box 4638
North Hollywood, CA 91617
Phone: (818) 761-5859
Fax: (818) 761-7099

Songwriter's Market
Writer's Digest Books
4700 East Galbraith Road
Cincinnati, OH 45236
Phone: (513) 531-2690 or (800) 289-0963
   (toll-free)
E-mail: songmarket@fwpubs.com

STRINGS
P.O. Box 767
San Anselmo, CA 94979
Phone: (415) 485-6946
Fax: (415) 485-0831
E-mail: editors.st@stringletter.com

Vintage Guitar
P.O. Box 7301
Bismarck, ND 58507
Phone: (701) 255-1197 or (800) 844-1197
   (toll-free)
Fax: (701) 255-0250
E-mail: vguitar@vguitar.com
http://www.vintageguitar.com

Music Business

Entertainment Law Reporter
Entertainment Law Reporter
   Publishing Co.
2118 Wilshire Boulevard, No. 311
Santa Monica, CA 90403-5784
Phone: (310) 829-9335
Fax: (310) 829-9335
E-mail: editor@
   entertainmentlawreporter.com

Church Music

The American Organist
American Guild of Organists
475 Riverside Drive, No. 1260
New York, NY 10115
Phone: (212) 870-2310
Fax: (212) 870-2163
E-mail: info@agohq.org

The Church Music Report
William H. Rayborn
P.O. Box 1179
Grapevine, TX 76099-1179
Phone: (817) 488-0141
Fax: (817) 481-4191
E-mail: tcmrtalk@airmail.net
http://www.tcmr.com

The Gospel Voice
50 Music Square West, Suite 601
P.O. Box 22975
Nashville, TN 37202
Phone: (615) 329-2200
Fax: (615) 327-2726

Hymn
Hymn Society in the U.S. & Canada
c/o Carol A. Pemberton, Editor
Normandale Community College
9700 France Avenue South
Bloomington, MN 55431
Phone: (612) 832-6571

Pastoral Music
National Association of Pastoral
    Musicians
225 Sheridan Street, NW
Washington, DC 20011
Phone: (202) 723-5800
Fax: (202) 723-2262
E-mail: npmsing@aol.com

Singing News Magazine
330 University Hall Drive
P.O. Box 2810
Boone, NC 28607-2810
Phone: (704) 264-3700
Fax: (704) 264-4621

Worship
Lifeway Christian Resources of the
    Southern Baptist Convention
Nashville, TN 37234-0160
Phone: (615) 507-1944
Fax: (615) 309-0158
E-mail: worshipmusic@lifeway.com

Miscellaneous Music Magazines

Academy of Country Music Newsletter
6255 Sunset Boulevard, Suite 923
P.O. Box 508
Hollywood, CA 90028
Phone: (323) 462-2351
Fax: (323) 462-3253
E-mail: academyoffice@aol.com
http://www.acmcountry.com

BAM Magazine
1351 Apple Drive
Concord, CA 94518-3700
Phone: (925) 934-3700
Fax: (925) 946-2985
E-mail: sales@bammedia.com
http://www.musicuniverse.com

BBC Music Magazine
Warner Enterprises
P.O. Box 61099
Tampa, FL 33661

Blender
1040 Avenue of the Americas
New York, NY 10017
Phone: (212) 302-2525
Fax: (212) 302-9671
http://www.blender.com

Blue Suede Shoes
P.O. Box 25
Duvall, WA 98019
Phone: (425) 788-2776
http://www.bluesuedenews.com

Buzzline
P.O. Box 18857
Encino, CA 91418
Phone: (818) 995-6133
http://www.buzzline.com

Circus
6 West 18th Street, 2nd Floor
New York, NY 10011
Phone: (212) 242-4902
Fax: (212) 242-5734

Country Music
Silver Eagle Publishers
1 Turkey Hill Road South
Westport, Conn. 06880
Phone: (203) 221-4950
Fax: (203) 221-4948

Country Music News
P.O. Box 7323, Vanier Terminal
Ottawa, ON, Canada K1L 8E4
Phone: (613) 745-6006
Fax: (613) 745-0576

Country Music Showcase, International,
    Inc. Members Action-Gram Newsletter
P.O. Box 368
Carlisle, IA 50047
Phone: (515) 989-3748
Fax: (515) 989-0235
http://www.cmshowcase.org

Country Weekly
118 16th Avenue South
Nashville, TN 37304
Phone: (615) 259-1111
http://www.countryweekly.com

Entertainment Today
2325 West Victory Boulevard
Burbank, CA 91506
Phone: (818) 566-4030
Fax: (818) 566-4295
E-mail: enttoday@artnet.net
http://www.ent-today.com

Entertainment Weekly
Time-Life Building, Rockefeller Center
1271 Avenue of the Americas
New York, NY 10020
Phone: (212) 522-1212
http://www.PathFinder.com/ew

Exclaim! Magazine
78 Pleasant Boulevard
Toronto, ON M4T 1K2
Canada
Phone: (416) 535-9735
http://www.exclaim.ca

Gig Magazine
2800 Campus Drive
San Mateo, CA 94403
Phone: (650) 513-4300
http://www.gigmag.com

Jazziz Magazine
2650 North Military Trail
Fountain Square II Building
Boca Raton, FL 33431
Phone: (561) 893-6868
http://www.jaziz.com

Journal of Country Music
Country Music Foundation Press
4 Music Square East
Nashville, TN 37203
Phone: (615) 256-1639
Fax: (615) 255-2245
E-mail: countrymusichalloffame@aol.com

Katrillion Media
2050 Center Avenue
Fort Lee, NJ 07024
Phone: (201) 947-1100
http://www.katrillion.com

Music City News
50 Music Square West
P.O. Box 22975
Nashville, TN 37203-3212

Phone: (615) 329-2200 or (877) 626-1500
   (toll-free)
Fax: (615) 327-2726
http://www.mcnonline.com

Music Connection Magazine
4731 Laurel Canyon Boulevard
North Hollywood, CA 91607
Phone: (818) 755-0101

Fax: (818) 755-0102
E-mail: muscon@earthlink.net
http://www.musicconnection.com

Rolling Stone
1290 Avenue of the Americas
New York, NY 10104
Phone: (212) 484-1616
Fax: (212) 767-8209

Vox
P.O. Box 712412
Los Angeles, CA 90071
http://www.voxonline.com

INDEX

ABOUT THE AUTHOR

Shelly Field is a nationally recognized motivational speaker, career expert, stress specialist, and author of more than 25 best-selling books in the business and career fields.

Her books instruct people on the techniques of choosing the best careers and how to obtain jobs in a wide variety of areas, including the hospitality, retail, wholesale, music, sports, and communications industries; casinos and casino hotels; advertising; public relations; theater and the performing arts; entertainment; animal rights; health care; writing; and art.

She is a frequent guest on local, regional, and national radio, as well as on cable, television talk, information, and news shows, and she also does numerous print interviews and makes personal appearances.

Field is a featured speaker at conventions, expos, corporate functions, employee training and development sessions, casinos, career fairs, spouse programs, and events nationwide. She speaks on empowerment, motivation, careers, gaming, and human resources; attracting, retaining, and motivating employees; customer service; and stress man-

agement. Her popular seminars, "STRESS BUSTERS: Beating the Stress in Your Work and Your Life," "The De-Stress Express," and "Lighten up, Loosen up, and Make Life More Fun" are favorites around the country.

Field is a career consultant as well as a personal life and career coach to celebrities, executives, businesses, educational institutions, employment agencies, women's groups, and individuals. She is a corporate consultant to businesses throughout the country, appearing at job fairs and providing assistance with human-resources issues, such as attracting, retaining, and motivating employees, customer-service training and stress management in the workplace.

President and CEO of the Shelly Field Organization, a public relations and management firm handling national clients, she also does corporate consulting and has represented celebrities in the sports, music, and entertainment industries as well as authors, businesses, and corporations.

For information about personal appearances or seminars, contact The Shelly Field Organization at P.O. Box 711, Monticello, NY 12701, or log on to www.shellyfield.com.